CRYPTOMANIA

CRYPTOMANIA

HYPE, HOPE, AND THE FALL OF FTX'S
BILLION-DOLLAR FINTECH EMPIRE

Andrew R. Chow

Simon Acumen
New York London Toronto Sydney New Delhi

SIMON
ACUMEN

An Imprint of Simon & Schuster, LLC
1230 Avenue of the Americas
New York, NY 10020

Copyright © 2024 by Andrew R. Chow

First Simon Acumen hardcover edition August 2024

SIMON ACUMEN and colophon is a trademark of Simon & Schuster, LLC

Simon & Schuster: Celebrating 100 Years of Publishing in 2024

For information about special discounts for bulk purchases,
please contact Simon & Schuster Special Sales at 1-866-506-1949
or business@simonandschuster.com.

The Simon & Schuster Speakers Bureau can bring authors to your live event.
For more information or to book an event, contact the Simon & Schuster Speakers
Bureau at 1-866-248-3049 or visit our website at www.simonspeakers.com.

Interior design by Davina Mock-Maniscalco

Manufactured in the United States of America

1   3   5   7   9   10   8   6   4   2

Library of Congress Cataloging-in-Publication Data has been applied for.

ISBN 978-1-6680-3816-1
ISBN 978-1-6680-3818-5 (ebook)

What's lighter than the mind? A thought. Than thought?
This bubble world. What, than this bubble? Nought.
—*Francis Quarles,* Emblemes, *1635,*
in the midst of Tulip mania

———————

"Crypto forever," screams your stupid boyfriend
Fuck you, Kevin
—*Lana del Rey, "Sweet Carolina," 2021*

CONTENTS

CRYPTOMANIA

PROLOGUE

On November 15, 2022, Sam Bankman-Fried was sitting alone in his $30 million, twelve-thousand-square-foot penthouse in The Bahamas when he received a message from someone he thought of as an old friend. Sam had received a lot of messages that week: from livid investors, anguished employees, harried lawyers, all begging him to call them back. It was after midnight, and he hadn't gotten a full night's sleep in ages. His eyes were strained from staring at spreadsheets that, no matter how many times he refreshed them, showed he was sinking into an $8 billion hole.

But Sam liked and trusted Kelsey Piper, especially because they were part of the same philosophical community called effective altruism. So he stayed up with her, chatting for over an hour via direct messages on X, the platform then known as Twitter, before returning to the spreadsheets and then eventually passing out.

The next day, Sam was scrolling Twitter when he came across their conversation posted on the news site *Vox*. Piper, he had somehow forgotten, was a journalist. She claimed that they weren't really friends at all but had merely met at professional conferences. And now the offhand answers Sam had sent her were going viral on Twitter, because they debunked the entire persona that he had cultivated for years.

While Sam had long waxed poetic about devoting his life toward the betterment of humanity, he told Piper that his philosophizing was part of a "dumb game we woke westerners play . . . so everyone likes us." He had spent hundreds of hours and at least $93 million in Washington cozying up to politicians and regulators, but now crassly dismissed them:

"Fuck regulators. . . . They can't actually distinguish between good and bad." And the messianic image he and others had cultivated promising a crypto-induced utopia? "Some of [this decade's] most beloved people are basically shams."

The interview pulled back the curtain, revealing the sociopath behind the curly haired saint. It not only threatened to crush his reputation but also that of cryptocurrency writ large. Sam Bankman-Fried had played an instrumental role in convincing millions of people across the world that crypto was a beacon of transparency, democracy, and financial uplift. World leaders, tech gurus, and famous quarterbacks had supported him and shared in his optimism. Now, in the cruel light of Sam's honesty, crypto looked a lot more like a con, a phantom, a giant Ponzi scheme.

Sam scrolled through torrents of loathing on his social media accounts, from people who accused him of losing hundreds of thousands of dollars' worth of their investments. "My childrens future is forever changed. We trusted in you and your site and we were robbed," messaged one FTX customer to him. "Please give me back my $20,000. I have a new baby now 4 months old and all my money was there," wrote another. All told, Sam had somehow lost more than $8 billion of customers' deposits. It wasn't so long ago that he was running a $32 billion crypto empire and receiving messages telling him how many lives he and crypto had improved across the world. Where did it all go so wrong?

INTRODUCTION

This is the story of how a cutting-edge technology—designed to create a fairer, more rational global financial system—was corrupted by greed, opportunism, and the whims of a very few powerful individuals, replicating the same predatory dynamics that its advocates promised to eliminate.

On March 11, 2021, a collection of digital artwork by an artist named Beeple sold for $69 million worth of cryptocurrency. Crypto fanatics hailed the sale as the harbinger of a new global order, in which crypto would usher in imminent revolutions across art, finance, politics, and gaming. Exactly twenty months later, on November 11, 2022, the powerhouse crypto exchange FTX—led by industry wunderkind and benevolent philanthropist Sam Bankman-Fried—filed for bankruptcy in a humiliating $8 billion collapse, marking the end of a boom-and-bust cycle that had played out like a fever dream.

Sam was the poster child of this internet money uprising. While crypto had made him the world's richest person under thirty, he preferred to talk about how crypto was benefiting those most in need, "banking the unbanked" and leading to "financial inclusion" and "equitable access." His ardent supporters went even further, claiming that crypto would lead to universal wealth and become the bedrock of a new era of the internet that would be fairer, friendlier, more empowering.

In the midst of a suffocating pandemic, this rose-gold vision soon captured the hearts of artists, investors, and gamers across the world, many

3

of them risk-seeking idealists who thought they had finally discovered an oasis outside the traditional strictures of analog society where they could pursue their passions—and make untold riches in the process. They included the Nigerian artist Owo Anietie, who became an overnight NFT millionaire, and the Hong Kong–based financial analyst Christine Chew, who followed Sam to The Bahamas to join FTX.

But while Sam monologued about leading people like Owo and Christine toward new horizons, he was actually building a Jenga tower of insanely risky financial instruments on a foundation of mistakes borrowed from the 2008 financial crisis—and replicating many manias that had swept up societies throughout history. As Bankman-Fried built out his own centralized, speculative vision of cryptocurrency, crypto builders like Ethereum founder Vitalik Buterin watched in dismay as a tool initially created with the goal of narrowing power imbalances warped toward unfettered gambling.

When FTX crashed, many crypto enthusiasts loudly argued that its demise had nothing to do with crypto itself. But the same set of values that had expanded the bubble caused it to burst. Sam's colossal failure crushed crypto's momentum and much of the goodwill that it had collected from mainstream investors during its magical expansion. "FTX was one in a string of failures, but it was the most significant," one former crypto executive who had a front-row view of FTX's rise and fall—and who I'll call Mark—tells me. "If the exchange you deemed the most trustworthy is going through that, what does it say about everyone else?"

In the wake of FTX, American regulators slammed down hard on crypto with lawsuits and criminal charges. One crypto exec after another has been slapped with steep fines or the threat of jail time. A digital art movement that was supposed to spur a creative renaissance found itself mostly defined by digitally rendered monkeys that once sold for millions, now worth a fraction of that. And some of the people crypto was supposed to uplift were chewed up and left to fend for themselves.

In 2024, however, a funny thing happened: Crypto's prices once again lurched upward, recovering many investors' losses and emboldening crypto fanatics anew. Many enthusiasts now argue that the saga of Sam Bankman-Fried is an irrelevant story of the past and beg the world to move on. But the industry's continued obsession with price increases, and its embrace of shady projects, suggest the most vocal crypto backers have learned very little from the crash at all. Given their repetition of past mistakes, it's entirely possible that we'll look back at the SBF-induced pandemic-era crash as not the big one, but the one preceding it.

There will always be another bubble and another burst. This book is the story of crypto's craziest sequence yet—and, I hope, offers some warnings for the future of the industry, which is hell-bent on exposing many more investors to its risks and volatilities. The book traces how a new technology with legitimately good ideas turned into something far worse than what it sought to replace, thanks to modern capitalist dynamics and age-old human flaws of ego and arrogance.

PART I

THE IDEALISTS

CHAPTER 1

Gas Money

O n the morning of February 11, 2021, the twenty-five-year-old artist Owo Anietie sheepishly climbed into the passenger seat of his neighbor's Toyota Camry and hitched a ride to work.

Owo normally took an Uber or the bus into his job at an ad agency in Lagos, Nigeria, but he was a bit strapped for cash these days. He had just taken out a loan to cover a full year's rent for a new apartment, because in Lagos there was no option to pay month-to-month. He spent a chunk more to fill out his new space with some cheap furniture, including a chair and a rickety plastic table. His older brother and roommate Nsikak was in between jobs and had just borrowed money from a friend to buy a mattress, which rested on the floor.

And on top of his current debt, Owo had one more big expense looming. He was about to cough up $100—a hefty portion of his $650 monthly paycheck—to upload a piece of artwork onto a website.

The website was called KnownOrigin, and the $100 was the price of creating something called an NFT. When Owo initially heard about the fee, he thought it was a scam. It seemed absurd to pay for an image upload when everyone else posted their artwork on Instagram for free.

But Owo had recently learned that artists from around the world were making hundreds, thousands, or even millions of dollars from selling NFTs. A new market for digital art had somehow sprung to life during the pandemic. Owo had always considered himself a risk-taker—and he wanted in on this new and inexplicable action.

"We might struggle for a minute," he told a skeptical Nsikak.

(Technically, both brothers went by Owo, as it was their shared family name.) Two days later, they were sitting around in their mostly bare living room when the younger Owo got a notification. His artwork, which depicted an ancient African mask wearing a COVID-19 mask, had just sold on KnownOrigin for $669 worth of the cryptocurrency ether, to a collector in Australia. After fees, .425 ether, or about $568, materialized in Owo's crypto account, which he then withdrew and converted into the Nigerian currency, naira. Owo and Nsikak jumped around their house, ecstatic and in disbelief.

"My brother and I went out, bought a cheap bottle of Captain Morgan, drank our asses off, and slept," Owo recalls. He bought some food and groceries, then stowed away the several hundred dollars that remained. "I thought this might be the only money I make from this thing," he says.

———

Several days after his first sale, Owo called his mom and told her he had just sold artwork on the internet thanks to a new technology. His mother, an administrator in the civil service, didn't really know what he was talking about, but wished him luck. After all, this was just the latest impulse decision that Owo had made in his twenty-five years in the world. And most of them, however improbable, seemed to work out.

Owo was born in Akwa Ibom, one of the southernmost states in Nigeria, in 1995 and raised with his brother and sister in a one-bedroom apartment with no indoor kitchen. Every night, all four of them, plus a cousin or four depending on who was around, would clear the furniture out of the living room, lay out mattresses, and sleep side-to-side.

Owo's upbringing wasn't rich, but it was happy: filled with love and art and dreams. Owo's mother made a steady living working for the state government. But electricity in their town was spotty, and outages were frequent. These blackouts forced Owo and his friends out of the house, where they would entertain each other with tales tall and long. "In the evening, everybody comes out and you just tell stories," Owo says.

Owo sports tidy dreadlocks, a clean fashion sense, and a wide smile—and his storytelling prowess is obvious from the moment you meet him. He's a garrulous conversationalist who modulates his deep voice with inflections to punch home the dramatic parts of a story. One of those stories he heard in his youth was about a man who was challenged to outdrink the rest of the village, did so, and then hopped on his motorcycle and drove home. When the man's friend, concerned about his safety, hurried after him, he found the bike lying in the dust outside his friend's home—and his friend, unharmed and oblivious, chugging another bottle.

Such stories were entertaining, but reinforced the bounds of Owo's provincial world. In contrast, Owo was awed by movies—especially because opportunities to watch them were so rare. If he was lucky enough to catch a full film at his neighbor's house on a night when the power never flickered, he would then be tasked with conveying it in full to his friends on the playground the very next day.

"You had to be able to narrate the story in such a way that you could do all the reactions, all the movements: the way Rambo jumped off the cliff, bounced through the branches, and had to land," he recalls, his eyes widening dramatically. "You had to narrate it in such a way that they can see the movie through you."

As Owo honed his narrative instincts, he also learned how to create visual art. His family was full of artists who encouraged him to take lessons. He was soon copying entire *X-Men* comic books, borrowed from his neighbor's father, onto printer paper, which he would distribute to his friends. Later, he created and sold his own comics based on the movies he would watch, like *Rambo* and *Drunken Master*, starring Jackie Chan.

When Owo was eight, he thought of another use for his artistic skills. If he could trace paper bills to look exactly like real ones, why couldn't he use them to buy things? One of his friends from school loved the idea, and paid him to draw bills worth 10 and 20 naira, with the intention of taking them to the market at night, when it might be too dark for vendors to tell the difference. Before they could embark, however, a family friend got wind of the scheme and shut it down. While the experiment ended prematurely, Owo had made 10 naira off his friend. It would not be the last time he turned his art directly into currency.

As a teenager, Owo excelled in painting portraits in bold, expressive strokes. But his heart's desire was to become a creator of cinematic universes like Marvel's Stan Lee. Lee's work had started out as comic books and then transcended the medium into international blockbuster films. Stan Lee set a high bar—but Owo felt he had all the composite skills to pursue a similar path. He could draw comics, craft suspenseful plotlines, birth charismatic protagonists, and wield his considerable powers of persuasion to convince people to buy into his vision. He had seen *Black Panther* galvanize interest in African culture all over the world. But *Black Panther* had been written by Americans. Owo wanted to further that franchise's mission, seen from his own authentic point of view.

But coming out of Akwa Ibom to become an international artist, much less a cultural juggernaut, was an improbable if not impossible dream. The region had a rich tradition of artisanal masks and fabrics, but Owo wanted to create in Photoshop and 3D modeling software. And he was completely lost when it came to forging connections that might get him closer to Hollywood—or even art galleries in Lagos.

So Owo went to work in advertising, first creating simple church fliers, then brand logos and television campaigns. All the while, he made more personal digital art on the side. But doing so in Lagos was an unpredictable and painstaking experience. Internet outages could halt projects while they were being rendered, erasing hours of work. "Lagos is like you're living in the devil's armpit: It's smelly, stinky, and everybody's trying to drag you down," Owo says. "But in a way, the energy helps you be creative." From his apartment, Owo created intricate digital works of glaring neon colors with hulking architectural structures or shiny, metallic humanoids walking through washed-out landscapes. These vivid images earned him praise and a small following of supporters on Instagram.

In late 2020, as Owo continued to hone his craft and digital fan base, he saw lots of people on Twitter talking about a new app called Clubhouse, which allowed groups of all sizes to join virtual audio rooms and chat with each other for hours. There were rooms for politics, sports, gardening, film trivia, and much more. Its audio-only nature made it particularly conducive for artists, as it allowed them to doodle and create visual art while their phones sat next to them, voices blaring away. When Owo downloaded the app, he quickly found that people were "talking day and night about NFTs, every day."

CHAPTER 2

A Chance to Be Free

Five thousand miles away, across the Atlantic, I was listening to the same conversations. As a culture reporter for *Time* magazine, I was always on the lookout for strange new trends at the intersection of art and technology. In March 2019, I had been the very first reporter to interview a nineteen-year-old Atlantan named Lil Nas X, whose tinny song "Old Town Road" was blowing up on a newly ascendant app called TikTok. A year later, I wrote a feature on the musicians experimenting with artificial intelligence, well before the generative AI boom.

In late 2021, most of the people I knew were spending most of their time at home. England had just entered a national lockdown due to a new coronavirus wave. The U.S. had just passed 10 million infections and 250,000 deaths. To cope with stress, isolation, and Zoom fatigue, people sought novel forms of entertainment and social connection. That included Clubhouse, a decidedly lo-fi bit of technology similar to the AIM chat rooms of my adolescent years. In January 2021, Clubhouse's weekly active user base doubled to 2 million within weeks. It was as if Twitter's unruly communal energy had popped off the screen.

After downloading the app, I found it was full of audio rooms where artists were raving about NFTs, which were allowing them to get funded for their artwork like never before. I was bewildered—and transfixed. I could go for minutes without understanding a single sentence. But I kept listening because of their passion and conviction. It seemed clear to me that a new kind of global culture was unfolding in real time.

NFTs, I soon learned, were essentially a file type, like PDFs or JPEGs. Unlike those mediums, each NFT contained a bit of code that established its origin, recorded its transaction history, and ensured it was unique. NFT stood for "non-fungible token." Unlike JPEG files of memes that were copied and circulated around the internet countless thousands of times, the code of two distinct NFTs was never the same.

The unique data that each NFT possessed allowed, for example, a photographer to prove that they had snapped a historic photo. When a photographer "minted" an NFT on a digital database called a blockchain— usually by uploading it onto a platform like SuperRare or OpenSea, which triggered a "smart contract"—they generated a digital paper trail that proved they had created the image. They would then be able to challenge forgeries or duplicates and to hard-code royalties into the image every time it was disseminated digitally.

In the social media age, artists and other content creators essentially worked for free for the benefit of large corporations like Meta, which hid the algorithms that determined what got promoted and what didn't. Artists tossed their labors of love into an infinite digital ocean—and then were expected to relentlessly hype themselves on platforms that paid them crumbs, if anything, for their content. Now NFTs presented a fundamentally new way to protect and monetize digital intellectual property.

Owo already knew most of this. He was generally familiar with NFTs because he had done some motion design work for crypto firms to earn some cash in 2020. As he listened to Clubhouse, he became convinced that NFTs could solve many of the problems he faced as a Nigerian artist. For the very first time, he might be able to make money from his artwork from international collectors, build a lasting digital porfolio, and conjure a self-sustaining career path. Owo's main goal was to get to Hollywood: to create movies just like the ones he had turned into comics as a kid. In Clubhouse rooms, he was now in the same spaces as people who were living his dream. The distance from Lagos to Los Angeles, which had seemed nearly insurmountable as a child, now felt insignificant. He felt like he was on the barricades of a technological and cultural revolution.

"That period was really wild," recalls his brother Nsikak. "We barely slept, and he was always on Clubhouse, drinking energy drinks to stay up all night. He would get really excited: 'I just met this guy! I met *this* guy!'" During one stretch, Owo let Clubhouse play for seventy-two hours straight. Nsikak could hear the voices murmuring from the other side of the bedroom wall well into the small hours of the morning.

Owo's mind was in the metaverse, but his body was still in Nigeria—and his obsession came with a tangible cost. Because the electricity grid cut out so often in Lagos, Owo relied on a generator, which cost some $40 in fuel a week—especially if he was constantly charging his phone and creating art on his computer. When fuel was especially scarce, Owo hunted for oil going from filling station to filling station, eventually carrying it home in a yellow twenty-five-liter jerry can.

One of the artists on Clubhouse that Owo particularly admired was the thirty-nine-year-old Wisconsinite Mike Winklemann, who went by the pseudonym Beeple. While Beeple wasn't especially famous to most people, he was something of a cult idol to digital artists, who closely followed his quest to release a new piece of art every single day. He had now achieved an unbroken streak of thirteen years, which he had begun when he was twenty-five. Beeple started with simple pencil sketches of cartoonish faces with bulging eyes and bulbous noses. His technique and craftsmanship gradually improved, but his subject matter mostly remained childish and intentionally repulsive. He made a crea-ture with Mark Zuckerberg's face, metallic spider legs, and robot breasts (October 8, 2019); Donald Trump and Hillary Clinton French-kissing with wet tongues (October 31, 2019); Joe Biden with giant breasts coming out of a birthday cake (June 20, 2020). Some people dismissed his artwork as an insipid exercise in pure shock value. Others argued it offered perceptive commentary on authoritarianism, abuse of power, and the omnipresence of mass media.

Beeple didn't think all too hard about the art's deeper meanings. He strove first and foremost to improve every day, and to create from a place free of restraint or shame. "People take their work way too seriously sometimes," he would later explain. "We've lost the sense of just creating to create, like you did when you were a kid."

Beeple released a new entry in his *Everydays* series for more than a decade, including on his wedding day and the day on which each of his two sons was born. His perseverance paid off. His shocking subject matter and bold execution cut through the noise of social media. By 2020, he was racking up tens of thousands of likes every day on Instagram from his million-plus followers.

In late 2020, Beeple's friends and fans kept telling him that he needed to start turning his work into NFTs. Beeple thought that NFTs seemed a bit like magic beans, and he didn't understand crypto at all. But his friends were making money from these beans: thousands and thousands of dollars. And when they explained it to him more, he was gradually persuaded. Beeple was the textbook example of an artist who had grown immensely popular on Instagram but wasn't directly profiting off those posts. He liked the idea of finally assigning a value to the work he created every day and the assurance that this art would permanently exist on a deeper layer of the internet called the blockchain. New NFT platforms were serving as both marketplaces and quasi-galleries, allowing digital artists to display their work in unprecedented ways. And when Beeple considered NFTs in the context of an earlier epoch-changing technology, everything clicked. "I realized, 'Wait a second. This isn't new. This is exactly like when photography was not considered art, and then it became art,'" he said.

Thanks to his renown on social media, the demand for Beeple NFTs was immediate and voracious. One of his first NFTs—an image that changed depending on who won the November presidential election—sold for $66,666.66. A few weeks later, he closed a $3.5 million sale of a collection of puerile artwork: of Jabba the Hutt placentas, Shrek nudes, hulking 3D toadstools from Mario. Friends and family gathered in his backyard in Charleston, South Carolina, to shower him with champagne. Beeple was now the top dog of a new, high-flying art scene, and his success was forcing juggernaut institutions like Christie's and Sotheby's to re-evaluate their entire mindsets about what deserved their attention.

Beeple's success invigorated Owo, because he had been a fan of Beeple way before Clubhouse. Owo long had admired the VJ art loops (repeating visual sequences) that Beeple created for concert backdrops, as well as the radical persistence of the *Everydays* series. In 2020, Owo started his own *Everydays* series, too, believing that its structure would be artistically motivating as well as a good personal brand strategy in a digital age that rewarded saturation. Now Beeple's sales seemed proof that he, too, was on the right path.

"It felt like a win for every visual artist," Owo says. "Because we've seen athletes win. We've seen musicians and actors win. But visual artists were struggling. To see someone like Beeple win, it was a win for all of us, because people started to take us seriously."

There were more success stories every day. In February 2021, Owo listened as the Seattle-based teenage artist Victor Langlois, who went by FEWOCiOUS, narrated as he raked in more than $1 million in NFT sales. Langlois grew up as a transgender male in an abusive household. Social-service authorities sent him to live with his grandparents when he was twelve. Painting colorful, Picasso-esque abstracted faces served both as an escape and unbound expression. Now his NFT art was making him rich and renowned.

"This technology is really giving this person a chance to be free," Owo told his brother as they listened to Langlois celebrate.

In February, the monthly sales volume of the NFT marketplace Open-Sea catapulted to $86 million, compared to $8 million the month before. An artwork of a flying Nyan Cat meme sold for $580,000. The bull run—stock market slang for a period of rising prices—was on.

That month, Owo nearly went broke minting his first NFT. He wasn't sure if he was ever going to sell another one, but he sure as hell was going to try to milk this craze for all it was worth. A new chapter of his art and his life had begun.

CHAPTER 3

Down the Rabbit Hole

To Beeple and Owo, the calculus was simple. Before NFTs, they were uploading art on social media for free. Now they were uploading art and raking in hundreds (for Owo) or millions (for Beeple), and serving as beacons for other artists to make the same leap.

But to really understand how their success was possible, you have to take several steps back into how crypto works. Wading into crypto often feels like an endless chain of jargon, each layer more convoluted than the next. Crypto aficionados, who sometimes call themselves "crypto natives," describe the learning curve as "going down the rabbit hole," as if financial technology education is just as mind-expanding as Alice's foray into Wonderland. It's decidedly not—but it's also unfortunately important to this story.

Understanding Beeple's success requires understanding another man named Vitalik Buterin. It's not an overstatement to say that he made the NFT frenzy possible. Vitalik, who was twenty-seven when the 2021 crypto bull run kicked off, can be considered the godfather of all modern mainstream crypto activity and one of its most important philosophers and builders. But although his ideas would underpin the NFT craze, it caught him completely off guard.

In 2011, Vitalik was a nerdy, withdrawn teenager in Toronto when his father told him about bitcoin. Bitcoin was the first cryptocurrency, born in the ashes of the 2008 financial crash. In the mid-00s, New York financial institutions had packaged risky subprime mortgages into financial products, which they then sold to investors with the promise of high returns. But when homeowners were unable to repay their mortgages, the value of these financial products plummeted, sending banks and financial institutions into tailspins. The Dow Jones more than halved, while unemployment in the United States more than doubled.

After the U.S. government bailed out the banks to the tune of $700 billion, public trust in institutions cratered. Established financial players had been caught using dirty tactics to accumulate and hoard wealth, but were largely shielded from the consequences. For everyone else, traditional pathways to success were seemingly being whittled away. Thousands of protesters flooded downtown Manhattan in the Occupy Wall Street movement, railing against the besuited executives above.

Meanwhile, as the internet became increasingly central to work and play, a handful of tech corporations learned to exploit consumer data and identities for ad revenue. The internet was supposed to bring humankind together and democratize knowledge, but instead it had created a new fiefdom of billionaires with an outsize influence over public discourse.

Bitcoin emerged into the world as a protest against these consolidations of wealth and power. Up until that point, money was only issued and its supply controlled by the central banks of governments. Bitcoin, in contrast, would be an independent digital money system, operating outside of the whims of any government or corporation.

Similar ideas had been tested before. In 1994, the computer scientist David Chaum launched eCash, an anonymous digital currency that was used by several thousand customers in the U.S. for small online payments. But the system was plagued by slow transaction times and regulatory resistance, and still required banks to adopt it. ECash's issuing corporation DigiCash went bankrupt in 1998.

While eCash was independent from governments, it was still controlled by one corporation. In contrast, Bitcoin's founding document, known in the tech world as a white paper, laid out a vision in which the currency would be minted and supervised by its users. The paper was written in 2008 by someone (or someones) named Satoshi Nakamoto, whose real identity remains unknown. Satoshi wrote in the paper that Bitcoin would operate on a new technology that would later come to be known as a blockchain: a public, digital journal of all transactions.

The Bitcoin blockchain, Satoshi wrote, would start as a blank slate. Transactions would be added to the ledger when watchdogs approved them using cryptography, the art of securing information through code or mathematical puzzles. Cryptography has long been used to safeguard information—including by ancient Egyptian and Mesopotamian merchants—and has become increasingly important to protecting secrets in this digital era.

The watchdogs approving the transactions—known as miners—would be financially rewarded for their work in a safekeeping process known as proof of work. Each transaction would be added onto the next one in a constantly expanding, un-editable record, with all parties incentivized to monitor its activities. The collective infrastructure recalled other peer-to-peer networks that were popular (and legally questionable) at the time, including Napster, LimeWire, and BitTorrent.

Satoshi's vision for bitcoin was a currency that could be created without a central bank and sent across the world without middlemen like Visa and PayPal. Instead of having to trust the stability and veracity of the bookkeeping of the U.S. government or any of the banks that had screwed people over by selling subprime mortgages during the early 2000s, the blockchain would present a singular, unbiased, unyielding truth that anyone could verify. Sending money on the blockchain would also be anonymous—at least, until it was time to use a financial institution to turn cryptocurrency back into hard cash.

Two months after publishing the white paper, Satoshi created the Bitcoin blockchain network as open-source code, for anyone to interact with. On the very first Bitcoin block, they inserted a headline from that day's London *Times* (January 3, 2009): "Chancellor on brink of second bailout for banks." As governments and the moneyed elite seemingly conspired to once again bend the financial order in their favor, Satoshi offered a pointedly different financial vision of the future—one controlled by the people themselves.

But why did bitcoin hold any value? How could someone just spin up a new currency—and actually use it to pay for stuff?

Early adopters quickly pointed to the fact that most monetary systems are based on collective belief, anyway. Gold had inherent physical value as a metal, but was worth far more due to its scarcity and aura. The U.S. used to be on the gold standard, but for the last ninety years has been based only on faith in the U.S. financial system. So, too, bitcoin's success rested on social acceptance. Enough people had to believe that it had value; that this new decentralized monetary system was more efficient and fairer than the old ones it hoped to replace.

And bitcoin, just like gold, would be scarce, Satoshi declared. There will only ever be 21 million coins of bitcoin created. Bitcoin didn't start with any value, but if people bought into Satoshi's premise and then bought bitcoin for real money, value would be injected into the network, and the worth of each coin would increase, slowly but surely. This economic structure, Satoshi argued, would make it both inflation-resistant and potentially exponentially valuable over time.

Perhaps unsurprisingly, many of bitcoin's early adopters were libertarian: belonging to an ideology of maximum individual freedom and minimal government intervention. Bitcoin seemed like the Holy Grail to the Cypherpunks, a 1990s libertarian-leaning group who dreamed about using encryption technologies to take back power from governments and corporations. Many of those ideologues quickly flocked to the technology, believing it would rid society of its paternalistic ills.

Bitcoin also drew the interest of participants in the black market, who suddenly could pay for drugs and weapons in a seemingly secure and anonymous way. Drug enthusiasts could send money across international lines without having to put down a credit card or bank account number, or make any sort of declaration about their identity. Bitcoin became the main currency for dark web marketplaces like Silk Road, a digital warehouse for everything from fake IDs to stolen credit cards to opiates, illegal weapons, and child pornography.

Bitcoin served as a lifeline for WikiLeaks, Julian Assange's archive for classified documents that revealed state and corporate secrets. When faced with financial blockades, WikiLeaks raised money through bitcoin. It also sparked attention in countries with unstable currencies. In Argentina in the early 2010s, government mismanagement, fiscal deficits, and high public spending led to runaway inflation. When the population started to exchange their pesos for more stable U.S. dollars, the Argentinean government banned such conversions, as they weakened the peso even further. Bitcoin, suddenly, was an alternative, uncensorable currency that could safeguard people's savings while pesos lost value every day.

The demand for bitcoin from Argentina and other countries with volatile currencies led to the rise of consumer-friendly PayPal-like online platforms where you could trade in your pesos or dollars for bitcoin. Crypto exchanges, as they became known, were soon a key part of the ecosystem, allowing people to turn their money from crypto to fiat (government-issued currency like dollars or pesos) and back again.

In its first few years, bitcoin was far from mainstream and dismissed by many as magic internet money. Still, a curious mix of people across the world swapped their real dollars for these new digital ones: By 2012, there were over fifty thousand active Bitcoin addresses. And the more people adopted bitcoin, the more its price went up.

In Toronto, Vitalik Buterin became enthralled by bitcoin and its potential. "Bitcoin has legitimately revolutionary properties," he wrote in his own newly formed publication, *Bitcoin Magazine*, in 2013. "Bitcoin allows users to transfer money instantly around the world essentially for free, semi-anonymously and without restrictions."

Vitalik was a lonely teenager who understood math much better than he did humans. As a budding coder and mathematical savant, he was innately drawn to bitcoin's cryptographic ingenuity. But its decentralist goals also resonated given his family history. Vitalik was born outside Moscow in 1994, a few years after the fall of the Soviet Union. Monetary and social systems had collapsed; the parents of his mother, Natalie

Ameline, lost their life savings to rising inflation. She and Vitalik's father, Dmitry Buterin, were computer scientists who cared for baby Vitalik in a university dorm. There were no disposable diapers available, so his parents washed his cloth diapers by hand. Dmitry told me in 2021: "Growing up in the USSR, I didn't realize most of the stuff I'd been told in school that was good, like Communism, was all propaganda. So I wanted Vitalik to question conventions and beliefs."

Vitalik grew up with a turbulent, teeming mind. Dmitry says Vitalik learned how to read before he could sleep through the night, and was slow to form sentences compared with his peers. Instead, he gravitated to the clarity of numbers. At seven, he could recite more than a hundred digits of pi, and would shout out math equations to pass the time. In search of opportunity and stability, the family moved to Toronto in 2000, the same year Putin was first elected president.

When Dmitry learned about bitcoin in 2011, he became intrigued by the idea of an alternative global money source that was outside the control of authorities, and he shared articles with his precocious son. Vitalik was at first skeptical, but he was interested in learning more. In order to better understand bitcoin, he began to write about it for the magazine *Bitcoin Weekly*, for which he earned 5 bitcoin a pop (back then, worth about $4; in March 2024, about $300,000). To continue to test bitcoin's usefulness, Vitalik came up with a business model in which he would upload the first paragraph of an article online, and only publish the rest if the community sent over two and a half bitcoin to his digital wallet for his work.

There were lots of readers who were willing to pay, because information about this new technology was scarce and Vitalik was a pithy, articulate writer. In one tongue-in-cheek article titled "Five Reasons You Should Not Use the Internet," he penned an op-ed as if he were a scornful nineties web critic, whose dismissals of the soon-to-be dominant technology mapped neatly onto those of the crypto critics of Vitalik's own era. "People are starting to use the internet to stream video to each other, but the result is a horrendously inefficient use of bandwidth that is rapidly using up billions of dollars of infrastructural investment," he wrote mockingly. "If only users were willing to submit to the truly minor inconvenience of having to wait a few hours to watch."

By 2013, nineteen-year-old Vitalik was a full crypto convert, and dreamed of leveraging Bitcoin's underpinning blockchain technology for all sorts of uses beyond currency. If a digital dollar could be exchanged over a blockchain, why not a science paper, a work of art, a vote for a council member? What if everything that we did over the internet could instead be completed over a blockchain, thus cutting Big Tech and its invasive data and surveillance practices out of the equation?

So Vitalik created the blockchain Ethereum, an elegant, open-ended system that would become the basis of a huge swath of crypto activity. He proudly stated in his white paper for the new blockchain that it would host a "substantial array of applications that have nothing to do with money at all."

The shorthand for the new digital world Vitalik hoped to build would soon be known as "Web 3." Web 1.0 was the clunky 1990s internet in which users read information, but rarely interacted with each other. Web 2.0 was the 2000s internet driven by user-generated content on centralized platforms like Facebook. While Web 2.0 platforms propelled unprecedented social connection, they also became warped by ugly incentives: Facebook's auditors warned in 2020 that its algorithms might be "driving people toward self-reinforcing echo chambers of extremism."

Web 3, then, signified a new era of online activity, which would unshackle the world from Big Tech's dominance. In this new landscape, individuals might be able to cut out the middlemen, earn money by broadcasting their voices, making art, or writing new computer programs— all of which they actually owned. Maybe, Vitalik argued, Ethereum could provide the infrastructure for decentralized versions of Uber, Airbnb, and eBay, which would direct all profit back to individual suppliers while lowering prices for customers.

Vitalik hoped Ethereum would improve society for those on the margins. "We as cryptocurrency developers should be taking advantage of this perhaps brief period in which cryptocurrency is still an idealist-controlled industry to design institutions that maximize utilitarian social-welfare metrics, not profit," he wrote in 2014.

But as much as Vitalik wanted to shape Ethereum, he felt it was more important for it to not need him at all. If Vitalik became the chief coder or CEO of Ethereum, then it would be no different from the corporations he was trying to replace. He even fought bitterly with some of his Ethereum cofounders who wanted to retain major leadership roles and financial stakes in the blockchain. "I deeply believed in decentralization as this holistic vision, and was negotiating down the percentages that both myself and the other top level founders would get because I wanted to be more egalitarian," he told me in 2022. "And that made them upset."

Vitalik fired some of those founders, and thanks to Ethereum's flexibility and ease of construction, it soon became the first all-purpose blockchain to gain widespread usership. The programs written on it, called "smart contracts," were open-sourced, meaning that anyone could use or improve them. Developers loved Ethereum because it was a new programming frontier for them to explore: By 2018, sixty-six thousand developers were writing programs on it. Entrepreneurs loved it, too, because it proved an easy way to crowdfund ambitious technological projects. One technologist who became fascinated by Ethereum and crypto overall was Harper Reed, a Chicago-based fintech entrepreneur who had worked at PayPal and also served as Barack Obama's chief technology officer during his re-election campaign. Reed had navigated a labyrinth of headaches while creating fintech startups: dealing with banks, payment providers, card processors, and other middlemen. "But in crypto, it was like, 'Oh, we could build an e-commerce platform, but don't have to have any of the parts,'" he says. "It's fast and limber, and allows someone to offer their products and get paid directly instead of having to be behind Temu or Amazon."

Before long, entrepreneurs and developers were not only building on Ethereum but also building competing blockchains and cryptocurrencies, many of which emulated Vitalik's creations. Over the 2010s, thousands of cryptocurrencies were created, which rose and fell in bursts of activity. But generally, the top two cryptocurrencies remained constant: bitcoin, the standard-bearer, and ether, the currency of Vitalik's rapidly expanding digital universe.

As crypto prices rose upward, a brasher, younger set of traders smelled blood—and quickly made a fortune by completing all sorts of risky trades on Ethereum, Bitcoin, and other blockchains. One of those traders was a Hong Kong–based Californian named Sam Bankman-Fried. In June 2019, his trading firm Alameda Research bragged that it was trading $600 million to $1 billion a day in crypto. While these numbers were eye-popping, Sam was still just one in a crowd of rapidly rising hustlers, who were playing games with currencies created out of thin air and were hailed as geniuses for it.

Vitalik never measured the success of Ethereum through numbers. At the end of 2017, the cryptocurrency market cap hit half a trillion dollars— about the GDP of Sweden—which seemed proof of its widespread adoption. But Vitalik wasn't satisfied. "How many unbanked people have we banked?" he asked on Twitter. "How many Venezuelans have actually been protected by us from hyperinflation? How much actual usage of micropayment channels is there actually in reality?"

To each of those questions, he had a simple answer: "Not enough."

CHAPTER 4

Earn to Give

Vitalik Buterin's brainchild Ethereum went through several fits and starts until 2020, when COVID-19 emerged and rocked the world, hobbling countless institutions. The values of bitcoin and ethereum were slashed in half in March 2020, as investors pulled their money out of risky assets.

But as governments sent out stimulus checks and made it easier for people to obtain credit, one prominent investor, Paul Tudor Jones, predicted in May 2020 that their actions would lead to massive inflation. Bitcoin, in contrast, he argued, would serve as the ideal hedge—a counter bet against the rest of the market—because it was unconnected to any governmental whims and was hard-coded precisely to fight against inflation. Jones himself said he held more than 1 percent of his assets in bitcoin. Other power players like Elon Musk jumped in too, with Tesla announcing it would accept bitcoin as payment for its products.

Jones's statements, combined with Musk's decision, were demonstrative of how interested individuals can exert outsize influence over the value of crypto. When they persuade people to buy in, the demand increases, so the price goes up. Essentially, they can speak value into existence, which brings in even more cheerleaders who might have even more impact.

So between May 2020 and January 2021, the cost of buying one bitcoin jumped from $9,000 to $34,000, and then surged to $60,000 in March. The cost of buying one ether, the currency of Ethereum, ascended from $200 to $1,200 to $1,900 over the same time frame.

This leap in prices was turbocharged by the unprecedented circumstances of the pandemic. Some people had lost their in-person jobs and desperately sought shortcuts to stay afloat. Others worked remote jobs, but grew bored at home and dove into digital hobbies that could trigger much-needed hits of dopamine. Crucially, both subsets of people were boosted by stimulus checks, which essentially served as free money to play with. Investors were further emboldened by low interest rates, which allowed them to borrow money at little cost. Many put their money into real estate, stocks, and all kinds of speculative investments. "Speculation" happens when investors put money into a high-risk asset hoping it will increase. Speculation has long been a central part of capitalist markets, but it tends to accelerate when easy access to money meets a technology boom. Many bubbles have formed around legitimately transformative technologies, including railroads, the machine gun, and the fire engine.

Darker psychological undercurrents played a role, too. As the pandemic approached its one-year mark with seemingly no end in sight, a simmering, jagged resentment grew worldwide. In Washington, thousands of rioters who denied the results of the 2020 election stormed the Capitol on January 6, searching for politicians to intimidate or worse. Weeks later, day traders who congregated on the social network Reddit launched an unprecedented short squeeze on GameStop. Wealthy Wall Street hedge fund managers had bet the stock of the video game store would lose value, given that nobody bought video games from stores anymore. But the hedge funds' bet against the store left them vulnerable, because if the stock were somehow pushed upward, then they could stand to lose billions. Reddit users realized that if they all banded together and bought the stock, they could successfully wage war against an economic ruling class that seemed to be more powerful than ever. That year, Federal Reserve data showed that the wealthiest 10 percent of American households now owned 89 percent of all U.S. stocks. The Financial Stability Board found in 2021 that the shadow banking economy, which included hedge funds and private equity firms, had actually grown since the 2008 crisis, despite repeated regulatory attempts to reel it in.

People across the world felt powerless: physically, politically, economically. They felt that the current systems were broken and manipulated by those in power to retain their influence. So they hard-charged toward new systems that might bring freedom.

Owo Anietie, in Nigeria, was one of those rebels. Another was twenty-five-year-old Shin Yeu Chew, who also went by Christine. Christine had bright dyed hair; she loved yoga and reading and dance music; and she hated her job working at a private equity fund in Hong Kong. She had initially entered the finance world for a few reasons. The first was to follow in the footsteps of her parents, who both worked in finance and held high expectations for her. "I thought working in finance would make my parents love and appreciate me," she says.

The second reason was that during college, Christine had stumbled across the philosophy of effective altruism, which explored how individuals might best impact the world. Popular EA blogs like *80,000 Hours* made the case that one way that idealistic young people with fancy degrees could improve the world was not by working at nonprofits, but by earning as much money as possible through finance, and then donating it all to vetted causes. This idea made sense to Christine: the more money she could give, the more she might help the world.

So upon graduating—she had spent her childhood between Taiwan, Hong Kong, and the U.S.—Christine dutifully applied to finance jobs and got hired by a private equity fund.

But while the job was prestigious and paid well, Christine became disillusioned with the firm's seemingly singular purpose for existing. "If we raised another billion, the money is basically just going into making the founder even richer," she says. "It doesn't really go into changing the world for the better."

In January 2021, Christine's sister was working in crypto and suggested she learn more about the technology. Before long, Christine was spending hours on Twitter, reading articles and watching videos, and combing through white papers and NFT project mission statements. These crypto enthusiasts argued that they could build a fairer world—and benefit lots of smaller investors in the process. "I had never felt that kind of passion for my day job," she says. "I believed that we were about to create a financial world potentially equal to that of the central and federal banks—where people who didn't have access to banks in Latin America or in Turkey could become more financially empowered."

She started investing in various cryptocurrencies, startups, and, of course, NFTs, which she saw as the Trojan Horse to get everyday people onto the blockchain. As she invested her own money, she switched jobs and became an analyst for the Hong Kong crypto venture capital firm Genesis Block Ventures (GBV), where she analyzed which crypto startups to champion.

Many other people plunged with her down the crypto rabbit hole. A CNBC study in mid-2021 found that 11 percent of a polled group of 5,530 eighteen- to thirty-four-year-old Americans used their stimulus checks to buy crypto. And much of that crypto, in turn, was used to buy NFTs on Vitalik Buterin's blockchain, Ethereum. NFTs could only be bought and sold with crypto, entwining the two asset classes together: Anyone who wanted to participate in this new NFT cultural craze had to buy and hold crypto first.

On March 11, 2021, the NFT craze ascended to staggering heights when a collection of five thousand of Beeple's *Everydays* sold for $69 million at the venerable Christie's auction house. The auction's bidders were not traditional art collectors but crypto bros: Thirty of the thirty-three active bidders were new to Christie's, and twenty-four of them were under forty years old. In the minutes before the gavel came down, Beeple watched the price jump in increments of $10 million every few seconds.

With his oft-repulsive creations, Beeple was probably not the most worthy artist to lead the movement. Even Anand Venkateswaran, a core member of the crypto fund (Metapurse) that bought Beeple's $69 million *Everydays*, was more or less ambivalent about the artwork. "The artwork is almost irrelevant," Venkateswaran told me later. "Beeple is a conduit to what happens around him—that's all he is. The idea was to divert focus onto the NFT space." Essentially, he wanted to wield Beeple's hype—and Metapurse's deep pockets—to bring NFTs mainstream.

Beeple himself was exceedingly aware that this new set of collectors did not share the same priorities as his old ones. "It was a completely different group of people, to be quite honest, that had never really thought about art," he says. "But they also had a bunch of fascinating ideas for the technology in terms of its artistic possibilities. So I sort of tossed myself into this crypto world."

Whether or not he realized it, Beeple's values aligned deeply with those of crypto mavens like Venkateswaran. Beeple's *Everydays* were an act of furious self-belief that prized creation above all else: to wrangle something new into the world, no matter the consequences. Beeple, to his new fans, was an Ayn Rand-ian hero, working outside of gatekeepers and institutions, charting an untrod path and earning riches through diligence, growth, and social media showmanship. And the disdain he received from critics and old school collectors only strengthened his crypto bona fides: Who had given them the authority to make the rules? It was time to create new value systems. Their new world would not rely on subtlety or expertise but on memes, maximalism, middlebrow pop culture, shock value, and unashamed self-branding.

By the time the dust had settled, Beeple, who was still driving around in a Toyota Matrix assessed at $830 by insurance, was suddenly the third most valuable living artist behind Jeff Koons and David Hockney. Leaders across finance, art, and crypto quickly claimed the watershed moment for their own. CNBC journalist Robert Frank proclaimed NFTs a new financial asset class on *Squawk Box*. Guillaume Cerutti, the CEO of Christie's, compared Beeple's sale to that of Da Vinci's *Salvator Mundi* in 2017, gushing on CNN: "Yesterday, it was something of the same magnitude: this feeling to discover a new world and that clearly, there will be a before and an after."

And crypto leaders threw their weight behind a man who hadn't heard of NFTs just a few months prior. Beeple's lack of understanding of crypto barely mattered, as they had been waiting for a vessel of mainstream appeal for years. The underbidder on Beeple's *Everydays* was the crypto entrepreneur Justin Sun, who had created the blockchain TRON. And on the day of the Christie's launch, Changpeng Zhao, the CEO of Binance, the largest crypto exchange, eagerly joined a Clubhouse room with Beeple to encourage him and sing his praises. "I do believe very strongly that NFTs have crossed the tipping point—that there will be a solid user base around it," he said happily. "Crypto opens new doors, big doors, for creators around the world. . . . With this new level of interest and funding, we're gonna see better art."

CHAPTER 5

A Piece of History

M any artists were thrilled by this newfound attention. "A lot of critics describe it as being a gold rush or a big hype bubble," the experimental artist Andrew Benson told me in March 2021. "But I see it as being the solution we needed for a long time. It's going to enable me to keep doing the kind of work I want to do already."

"I do believe that it's going to be a net positive for everybody," Beeple told a documentary crew in early 2021. "It's like the internet. You can fight against it, but it's going to fucking happen. You can figure out how to use it for good, or you can bitch and moan and get run over by it."

But why did it make sense for the collectors? Why, exactly, were people suddenly spending hundreds, thousands, or millions of dollars on digital art? After all, anyone could navigate to Beeple's sale page and hit right-click "save" on his artwork. That person could then make it their phone background, print it out, or put it on their wall—for the price of nothing at all. Online skeptics mocked these poor rubes who had seemingly been conned into paying for things that could be downloaded for free.

But the rise of NFT sales in 2021 makes a whole lot more sense when viewed through two drastically different contexts: the newfound wealth sloshing around crypto and hundreds of years of art history.

Let's start with art history. Many art critics and historians viewed NFTs as a clean break from the modern art market. But in many ways, NFTs only confirmed a long-held truth: that the value of art has never truly been about aesthetics or how a piece might look on your wall.

In 2008, economics professor Don Thompson wrote a book on the subject: Its title was *The $12 Million Stuffed Shark: The Curious Economics of Contemporary Art,* which referenced a famous bit of taxidermy-sold-as-art by Damien Hirst. Thompson spent years studying the art world and concluded that lore, personal narrative, perceived scarcity, and the machinations of power players were much more important factors toward an artwork's price tag than sheer aesthetics. For instance, Thompson found that a work sold during a daytime art auction was worth on average 20 percent less than a work sold during more prestigious evening auctions, which served as fêtes for wealthy collectors to see and be seen. The stamp of approval from a magnate like Charles Saatchi could instantly double a work's price.

Provenance and personal lore, of course, played major roles in a work's value. In 2003, thirty-two drip paintings were discovered in a storage locker in East Hampton, New York. Some art historians who examined them asserted that they were created by Jackson Pollock, but others disagreed. Appraisers were flummoxed. If the canvases were indeed Pollock's, they would be worth as much as $275 million. If not, they would likely go for $100,000: a seismic price cut for an aesthetic difference indiscernible even to the trained eye.

So why would a collector pay so much more for a real Pollock? The answer lies in an intangible feeling: the assumption that they would own a piece of history created by a twentieth-century master in the midst of a legendary artistic journey. Owning a Pollock confers instant credibility and astonishment from visitors. It also serves as a strong economic investment, given the resale market for such a rare canvas. Some pieces of rare art only appreciate in value over time, as their legend grows.

Similar dynamics exist in fashion. People will pay far more for an authentic Louis Vuitton handbag than a knockoff, even if the most eagle-eyed designer can't distinguish the stitching. NFT enthusiasts argued that all of these factors remained true in NFT art. Just as it's understood that a Pollock or Louis Vuitton reproduction shouldn't be worth the same as the real thing, neither should a copy of Beeple's digital Trump painting. You could frame the Beeple on your wall, but if you didn't have the blockchain record of ownership, then anyone with an internet connection could discover that your "ownership" was a sham. You could enjoy the cartoon for its audacious aesthetics—but the value of fine art has never really been about that.

In fact, some artists started to argue that NFTs weren't just *as* valuable as their physical predecessors, but *more so*, because they solved the eternally vexing problem of artistic authenticity. The art market has long been flooded with scams, especially as contemporary art became more conceptual as opposed to technical. Anyone could re-create one of Duchamp's readymades, for example, by mounting a bicycle wheel onto a stool. The value of Duchamp's own work, then, lay in its rebellious ingenuity and the fact it was conceived by a brilliant iconoclast. There needed to be a new way to both price and verify these works.

In 1968, the conceptual artist Sol LeWitt created an analogue NFT of a sort while experimenting with artwork drawn not on canvas but walls: constellations of sharp geometric lines crisscrossing entire rooms. Because such patterns could be executed by anyone, it was theoretically difficult to tell whether a wall piece had been created by LeWitt himself.

So LeWitt started to sell certificates of authenticity, which contained instructions for executing the art and a signature certifying its uniqueness. LeWitt declared that the artworks were only complete with the accompanying certificate, and that if someone sold off the certificate but left the adorned room intact, those walls ceased to be LeWitt artwork.

More recently, the modern artist Felix Gonzalez-Torres received six-figure bids at Christie's in 2003 for installations in which he placed thousands of fortune cookies in large piles. In order to prevent fakes, Gonzalez-Torres also issued certificates. Another museum could have bought the same number of fortune cookies wholesale and piled them up themselves. But that work would not have been a Gonzalez-Torres creation, and therefore wouldn't have been worth nearly as much as the original conceit and execution.

So the idea of people paying a premium for art for indiscernible aesthetic reasons wasn't new at all. But in 2021, the value of NFTs exploded thanks to recent breakthroughs in crypto tech and economics. Four years earlier, Ethereum researchers had launched the technical standard for NFTs, differentiating them from the fungible cryptocurrencies that had existed before. (For example, one bitcoin—which is fungible—will always be exactly equal to another bitcoin.) In the following years, developers and project creators would gradually learn how to use NFTs—and then build new technology to streamline the process of creating and releasing them.

NFTs weren't going to be sold en masse until there was a market for them. And in 2021, that market materialized, thanks to a whole cadre of crypto investors who had suddenly become unfathomably rich thanks to widespread adoption and interest in cryptocurrencies. Ether had increased fifteenfold between March 2020 and March 2021, making it a far more successful asset than any significant company listed on the New York Stock Exchange.

This newfound wealth had strange and unexpected ripple effects. It allowed Frances Haugen to quit Facebook, move to Puerto Rico, and become a whistleblower against the company, disclosing internal documents that revealed the company's knowledge of the harms it perpetrated. But most other members of this new crypto elite wielded their magic internet money with less purpose. Many cashed out their crypto into houses, boats, cars, and jewelry. Buying a Lamborghini, especially, became a common boast among crypto millionaires on social media.

But while these investors upgraded their worldly possessions, they also faced intense pressure to keep their money inside cryptocurrency. Due to classic supply-and-demand dynamics, cryptocurrencies like bitcoin and ether gain in value when more people buy into them. If too many crypto investors take their money out of crypto, the price goes down, which hurts everyone's wallet.

So the growing community of crypto holders on social media, particularly Twitter, soon developed war cries demanding other investors keep their assets inside the crypto ecosystem. Their main refrains were

"HODL," a meme-ified misspelling of "HOLD"; "GM," for "good morning"; and "WAGMI," which stood for "We're all gonna make it." Those who "HODL"-ed and held on to their crypto investments were hailed for having "diamond hands." Conversely, those who pulled their money out of crypto were accused of having "paper hands" (the opposite of "diamond hands") and relentlessly mocked. Beeple himself was criticized for converting his ether earnings from the Christie's sale back into cash.

Before 2021, there simply wasn't much for normal consumers to do inside of the crypto ecosystem except buy other cryptocurrencies. (In addition to bitcoin and ethereum, a slew of other cryptocurrencies had been created on their own blockchains.) That all changed with the emergence of NFTs. These colorful images baked artistic invention and meme culture right into a crypto-native asset class. They enticed finance novices while re-energizing experienced traders sick of staring at the same boring spreadsheets. "Instead of looking at candlestick charts, I can look at beautiful artwork," the NFT investor Danny Maegaard, who had bought and sold millions of dollars' worth of NFTs by March 2021, told me that month.

In the midst of the pandemic, NFTs became a salve for sheer boredom: a hobby with moneymaking potential. Crypto enthusiasts also argued that NFTs were proof that crypto wasn't just penny stock gambling, but was already helping artists and would soon reshape every part of society. Maegaard told me NFTs would have a much broader appeal than cryptocurrencies because they could be integrated into insurance, art, events, and music.

In particular, NFTs resonated with the trading card community, which had long perceived massive value in flimsy bits of cardboard. A company called NBA Top Shot, which sold basketball highlights on the blockchain, was soon raking in hundreds of millions of dollars a month in 2021. Similarly, the VeVe marketplace made a killing off of digital collectibles licensed from film franchises like DC Comics. Before NFTs, collectors preferred to spend their money on physical cards or figurines. But during the pandemic, the opportunities to show off physical possessions was severely limited. A LeBron James GIF, in contrast, could garner praise and admiration across social media while its owner was stuck at home alone.

The concept of the metaverse—immersive visual worlds for gaming, shopping, and socializing—sparked the public imagination, especially as the pandemic dragged on. Teenagers already spent hours a day in games like Fortnite and Roblox, forming flourishing communities and shelling out for virtual goods that they didn't really own. Why couldn't they buy a virtual sword or a plot of land in a place where they spent so much time and then sell it later?

So metaverse real estate, with NFTs representing plots of land, boomed in metaverse worlds like Axie Infinity and Decentraland. In February 2021, Danny Maegaard sold a tract of virtual land in Axie Infinity—a game world in which cartoon monsters battled each other—to another investor for a record $1.5 million. For Maegaard, the sale served as an ironclad justification for the amount he was spending on JPEGs and virtual land. "In the beginning, everyone was like, 'Who is this poor Danny guy? He's completely overspending,'" Maegaard told me. "I kept saying, seriously, watch this space."

NFTs were also boosted by a new class of financial influencers, who used platforms like YouTube and TikTok to dole out investment advice. These influencers found rabid audiences in a younger generation who dismissed the idea of old-school financial advisers as quaint and unnecessary. A 2021 study from the investment firm TIAA found that one-third of those polled trusted social media content, influencers, and celebrities for financial advice. Some of the influencers who rushed to meet this demand for financial knowledge were well intentioned and well researched, and hoped to democratize financial knowledge for those who had previously been shut out. Others were just in it for the hustle, paid by financial projects for promotion and incentivized by search algorithms to promote the wildest and most controversial investments that might garner outrage clicks. Both archetypes contributed to a growing cottage industry of crypto and NFT influencers, who implored their followers to buy into the latest

NFT project before it was too late—while sometimes profiting directly off the hype they created.

All of this activity was extremely good for artists. Not only did the fundamentals of NFTs make sense to them, thanks to art history, but there was now a huge subset of new collectors who had boatloads of crypto to spend on a cause they believed in.

The spending intensified. Eleven days after Beeple's Christie's sale, Twitter cofounder Jack Dorsey sold an NFT of his first tweet for $2.9 million. A few days after that, Sam Bankman-Fried's FTX bought the naming rights to the Miami Heat arena in a $135 million, nineteen-year deal.

Vintage Mozart's *The Children With No Name: Eden* sold for $469 on July 16, 2021. LIAM VRIES, A.K.A. VINTAGE MOZART

CHAPTER 6

Losers' Club

In early 2021, Owo Anietie was the lone African NFT artist in many Clubhouse rooms. But this rapidly changed. Hundreds of other artists across the continent arrived over the coming months, forming a vibrant digital art scene that fought for attention and respect in a mostly lily-white space.

The first African NFT artist that Owo befriended was a Zimbabwean named Liam Vries, who went by Vintage Mozart. In his hometown of Harare, Liam worked at graphic design firms while, on the side, creating dreamy psychedelic collage art inspired by Afrofuturism, an artistic movement that combined African aesthetic traditions with sci-fi and technology. Liam hoped to sell prints of his work, but had no idea how to go about it or what market would accept him. Etsy didn't even allow Zimbabweans to set up digital shops.

Liam was long accustomed to the everyday restrictions that Zimbabweans faced. In order to make ends meet in a broken economy, both his parents had resorted to forms of cross-border trading arbitrage: His mother bought and sold food out of South Africa, while his father filled up oil drums at the Zambian border. It was precisely because their economy was so cobbled together and at times extralegal that crypto made sense to many Zimbabweans. In 2019, the World Economic Forum published an article by UN regional program adviser George Lwanda, who touted crypto as a potential solution to the country's hyperinflation, lack of banking access, and widespread distrust of the central bank.

In early 2021, Liam bought an old iPhone specifically to download

Clubhouse, as it was unavailable on Android devices, and was soon listen-ing for hours a day. Liam and Owo met on the app and quickly formed a close friendship. They admired each other's work and bonded over their love of Afrofuturism. They also shared frustrations over how few Africans they met in the space, and how no one seemed to be working to rec-tify this. Many of the most famous NFT artists were white men: Beeple, Tyler Hobbs, Trevor Jones, Justin Roiland. NFTs were supposed to be an equalizing global force—and while they were creating new pathways to digital stardom, the faces of this new world looked awfully like those of the old one.

Casual racism reared its head in crypto communities all the time. In February 2021, users of the cryptocurrency tracking app Blockfolio— which was owned by Sam Bankman-Fried—received notifications con-taining a racial slur against Black people. "We are sad to announce we closure of our services to all black people and N——, with immediate loss of all funds," a message read. Sam wrote on Twitter that the messages were the work of a "competitor" who had gained access to an employee's account in an act of sabotage. He apologized and vowed to lead a security review of the company. But a bad taste lingered for many Black NFT enthusiasts.

In response to these racial dynamics, artists created a handful of Club-house rooms tailored to people of color, most notably one called Black NFT Art. There, Black Americans, Caribbeans, Black British, Africans, and countless others from across the diaspora gathered to learn from each other, banter, flirt, and share their work.

In these conversations, artists talked about the resistance they had faced in traditional art settings: the challenges in staging gallery shows, affording art school, or convincing collectors that work showcasing subjects of color was valuable. In contrast, this new era of NFT art allowed them to create from anywhere in the world and find buyers online, many of whom were happily ignorant of the hyper-specific value systems and snobbery of the traditional art guard.

Crucially, most NFT platforms also allowed artists to earn royalties on every secondary sale. Artists traditionally profit only from the first sale, while collectors can later resell their works for ten or even a hundred times the original price if an artist becomes famous in the intervening years. But thanks to hard-coded smart contracts, artists could guarantee themselves a percentage of every single NFT resale—usually paid out in the cryptocurrency ether—for years to come.

In March, Liam minted his first NFT: a cosmic GIF of the mythological angel Azraelle, covered in serpentine body paint and surrounded by crashing lighting. It sold twenty-six hours after minting, following a bidding war, for $1,583. Liam was astounded, but also extremely frustrated by the process of putting his work on the blockchain. In Zimbabwe, where Liam lived, crypto was largely illegal: The country had banned financial institutions from trading in cryptocurrency in 2018, citing "risk of loss due to price volatility, theft or fraud, money laundering and other criminal activities." To sell his NFT, Liam had to go through a convoluted and covert process that included a cousin's PayPal account in the UK.

In May 2021, Owo and Liam talked about how there should be a space specifically for African NFT artists, who faced legal and social barriers to entering crypto. Liam ran with the idea, and together with Michael "Kwame" Brako—a Ghanaian-born forklift-driver-turned-animator living in California—launched a recurring Clubhouse room called the African NFT Community. It quickly gained traction, because there were so many African artists who had grown tired of mostly listening to white artists. "Imagine you have three hundred people that felt that they were ignored. So it was kind of like a loser's club," Liam says.

These rooms were wildly successful—and helped get African artists paid. "Someone would go up and say, 'I've got this piece available'—and then a collector would come up and say, 'I've just bought it,'" Liam recalls. "There was a rush, and people were excited not about the money, but the art."

As momentum built and more members joined, the room morphed into a more formalized collective, complete with a server on Discord—a social platform heavily utilized by crypto natives—a website, and a treasury that helped new NFT artists pay transaction fees known as gas fees. Newcomers volunteered to spearhead various efforts. Artists live-streamed themselves sculpting as other members DJed music sets, blaring Black diasporic music from Rema and Major Lazer. Members of the community promoted and bought each other's work, gave each other tips for navigating certain marketplaces, and collaborated on artwork. They also walked newcomers through the painstaking process of actually minting an NFT, which included creating a crypto account on an exchange like Binance or FTX, setting up a MetaMask wallet (a popular digital wallet for storing ether), moving ether from the exchange to the wallet, and then paying hundreds of dollars in gas fees.

In these post-Beeple months, artistic communities rapidly formed all over the world. There was Art Blocks, a movement of generative artists who created art through code; Friends with Benefits, a social club for creatives; and the Mint Fund, a global incubator for artists of color. "When it comes to crypto, we haven't been part of the initial folks that have created or perpetuated a lot of the growth," Ameer Carter, the creator of the Mint Fund, observed around that time. "We have to continually fight for exposure, visibility, and the right to participate in a very big way."

While there were many kinks to be ironed out and structures to dismantle, a euphoric optimism prevailed among many NFT artists of color who were not only making money for the first time but also forming close bonds with like-minded friends and collaborators over the internet. Owo and Liam were both working at ad agencies at the time, and would text all day long to commiserate about their jobs and the fragile state of their countries. Owo would give Liam tips about graphic design; Liam would give Owo suggestions about NFT marketing. They even started collaborating on NFTs, with Liam adding his signature psychedelic flair to Owo's muscular 3D creations. "We had the same vision," Liam says.

As Owo and Liam began to accumulate wealth in crypto and bring other Africans aboard, leaders like Vitalik Buterin and Sam

Bankman-Fried cheered them on. Both Vitalik and Sam directly benefited, economically and otherwise, from the increase in crypto activity
on the continent—and they also espoused the beneficial impacts that
crypto might have there. Sam's interest in Africa stemmed from his learn-
ings from the effective altruism community, which sought to devise a
system for how people could do the most good for the world. EA leaders often talked about how much cheaper it was to save lives in Africa
with basic medicine compared to more complicated problems elsewhere.
Sam began parroting that language: He told *Vox* in March 2021 that
Africa was "where the most underserved globally are and where there's a
whole lot of lowest-hanging fruit in terms of being able to make people's
lives better." He was particularly invested in the distribution of anti-
malarial pills, which he said could prevent deaths by donating "single-
digit thousands of dollars per life." As Sam grew in fame and stature, he
made a point of mentioning this statistic in many of his interviews. On
FTX's homepage, an animated video declared that thanks to crypto,
"people in developing countries with greater barriers to banking can
access new financial opportunities." The video showed a shaggy cartoon
version of Sam standing in front of a smiling crowd of mostly people
of color.

In March, Sam delivered a keynote speech by Zoom at the 2021 Blockchain Africa Conference. Sitting at his desk in Hong Kong, his eyes flit-
ting across his many screens, he talked about how crypto would facilitate
financial inclusion and allow migrants across the diaspora to send back
money to their families in Africa. In the following months, he poured
millions of real dollars into crypto marketing and ads on the continent,
which encouraged thousands of artists and investors to start minting NFTs
and open up FTX accounts.

Vitalik, for his part, traveled to South Africa, Zambia, and Kenya
for hackathons (feverish cram sessions in which programmers built computer programs together) and other Ethereum-related events, and tried to
promote blockchain uses that could circumvent broken colonial systems.

At a Zambian open market, he bought a purple cloth laptop bag speckled with white and green elephants, which became a part of his travel starter pack as he toured the globe.

Vitalik was surprised by the rise of NFTs, which dominated the blockchain that he had dreamed up eight years before. But as more and more newcomers flocked to his platform, he remained cautiously optimistic that this strange new asset with nebulous value would become a force for good in the world. "The NFT industry could be a significant boon to artists, charities, and other public-goods providers far beyond our own virtual corner of the world, but this outcome is not predetermined," he wrote on his blog two weeks after the $69 million Beeple sale. "It depends on active coordination and support."

Thanks to both top-down funding and organic growth, some African artists thrived. In the summer of 2021, Liam Vries, in Zimbabwe, and Michael Brako, in California, sat squarely in the center of the African NFT movement and raked in hundreds of dollars at a time from sales of their art. Liam was one of the first artists in Africa to sell multiple editions of his NFTs: batches of the same artwork to multiple buyers, as if he were selling limited prints of a photography collection. While the approach lessened the scarcity of each work, it also lowered the price point for buyers and allowed smaller collectors to enter the NFT market.

By June 2021, the price of ether—the main cryptocurrency used to buy and sell NFTs—was over $2,000, or roughly ten times what it was the year prior. Africa's cryptocurrency market had grown by 1,200 percent and by $105.6 billion over the same time frame, making the continent the third-fastest growing crypto economy in the world. The African NFT Community grew to over six hundred members. To many, it was a beacon of hope: a new community in which they could exercise their will, spearhead projects, and shape its direction as they saw fit.

Also in June 2021, El Salvador's president Nayib Bukele announced that his country would be the first to make bitcoin legal tender, saying in a statement that the decision would "bring financial inclusion, investment, tourism, innovation and economic development for our country." After years of lurking in the shadows of finance and culture, crypto had finally broken through on the global stage.

CHAPTER 7

Planet of the Apes

One day in May 2021, Owo Anietie and Liam Vries, aka Vintage Mozart, tuned into a Clubhouse room cohosted by Q, one of their favorite NFT influencers. Q was a huge champion of Black NFT artists and would soon become a major collector of both of their works. This time he was talking about a very different kind of NFT project, made up of ten thousand cartoon monkeys. These monkeys wore facial expressions that suggested an utter indifference to the world around them. Many could barely open their eyes. Some smirked, while others stuck their tongues out limply. The project was low-energy by name and nature.

The Bored Ape Yacht Club, its boosters argued, would be a new kind of crypto community: one part fan club and one part investment club. It would birth a series of characters that might become crypto's version of the Marvel Cinematic Universe. Q scooped one up for 0.2 ETH, or about $590.

Liam was immediately repulsed by the Bored Ape Yacht Club. He thought the art was bad and didn't connect with his vision of the NFT space as a haven for independent artists. Owo, on the other hand, was intrigued by the audacity of the artwork's commercial vision. But he didn't have hundreds of dollars to spare to buy one.

Within months, however, these Apes were improbably worth more than a million dollars apiece, and practically defined the NFT space to the mainstream observer. Apes were held aloft on *The Tonight Show Starring Jimmy Fallon* and served as avatars for Eminem and Snoop Dogg in a music video. Hollywood writers built stories around them; hour-long lines formed outside pop-up restaurants selling branded Ape smash burgers.

As the hype around the Bored Apes spiraled upward, the project reoriented the entire NFT medium. While early Bored Ape enthusiasts insisted that their simians were vehicles for the democratization of artistic creation, what they really set in motion was a shift away from artists and toward hyper-capitalist NFT investment-social clubs. Their rise ushered in a new set of core values for the crypto mainstream: hype, wealth-signaling, exclusivity, and sheer, proud idiocy.

The Bored Ape Yacht Club once had loftier ambitions. Creators Greg Solano and Wylie Aronow hoped to make a collective art project in which NFT buyers would be able to contribute to a digital quilt. They hoped it would look something like a Mondrian: a blank space filled with bold, colorful shapes. But a friend advised them against the idea, saying that the first thing that buyers would draw on the digital canvas would be penises. The democratization of art was a nice idea in the abstract—but often failed to live up to its ideals when applied to the untamed and juvenile internet jungle.

So Solana and Aronow turned away from art and toward building a collection that more closely emulated one of the most successful NFT projects of the moment, CryptoPunks. CryptoPunks were a series of eccentric pixelated characters, and were the prime example of an NFT genre known as profile picture projects, or PFP projects. PFPs are exactly as described: Each NFT is an image of a single character, usually an animal, framed in a way that resembles a profile picture on Facebook or Instagram. PFP projects could be minted quickly and cheaply by creating a set of visual layers—like background color, clothing, and mouth shape—then stacking them up on each other in different combinations using code to generate thousands of variations.

One of the first major NFT PFP projects in 2017 was CryptoPunks, algorithmically generated characters whose lo-fi, punk rock aesthetics hewed toward crypto's countercultural self-conception. A few months later came CryptoKitties, cartoon pets whose runaway success clogged the young and inefficient Ethereum blockchain with so much activity, they threatened to crash the entire network. In August 2021, Visa shelled out 50 ETH, or about $165,000, for a CryptoPunk, as a way to signal their newfound commitment to the trend. While CryptoPunks weren't exactly the pinnacle of artistic achievement, their founders and community still allied themselves with the art world. The Punks' creators, Matt Hall and John Watkinson, also created a project called *Autoglyphs*, a generative art experiment inspired directly by one of Sol LeWitt's illustrated walls (the creator of the 1960s NFT precursor). Most NFT artists felt that they and the Punks belonged to the same conceptual movement—and that as a whole, NFT culture genuinely centered on artists and increasing their autonomy.

But the Punks also soon gained steam as an investment tool. The more that crypto people thought the Punks were cool and likely to become a major piece of crypto history, the more their value went up. Solano and Aronow saw the Punks' upward price movement, and realized that most NFT buyers didn't want to simply buy art and hold it. Instead, they wanted to make money off their purchases like they had with meme stocks (e.g., GameStop).

Traditional art isn't particularly tradeable: its value is too subjective, and it takes too long for artists to create, distribute, and insure. Creating a PFP project of programmable characters instead would allow them to set up a trading card–like system, in which each character had different attributes that clearly delineated its rarity and thus its value. And because these characters would be algorithmically generated, they would be easily reproducible at scale. While Liam Vries might spend weeks on a single NFT artwork, mixing various mediums together, a whole collection of thousands of PFPs could be created in the same time frame—and be sold to thousands of eager collectors.

So at the end of April 2021, Solana and Aronow created the Bored Ape Yacht Club, a set of ten thousand generated cartoonish apes created through code. The Apes stooped to the tastes of a rebellious twelve-year-old, wearing brightly colored pieces of clothing and evoking the right amount of materialism and sleaze. Each Ape had a unique combination of attributes, including paisley shirts, smoking jackets, cigars, and halos. And unlike the art of Liam or Owo, these Bored Apes were designed specifically to serve as profile pictures, so that their marketing model would be built directly into their online usage.

Aronow and Solano's Yuga Labs served as the Bored Apes' production company. The company did not release the Apes and walk away but kept the community constantly engaged through a relatively new concept in the NFT space known as "utility." When newcomers were told about NFTs, they invariably asked what they were supposed to do with a piece of expensive art they couldn't hang on their wall. Aronow and Solano wanted to provide many answers to this question—and to turn NFT ownership from a single purchase into a rolling commitment and a source of shared identity.

The Apes, they decided, would carry many benefits for their buyers. First, the duo resurrected the initial "digital quilt" idea, rebranding it as a bathroom graffiti wall. Only those with an Ape were allowed to doodle on the digital canvas. Next, they decreed that whoever bought an Ape would acquire its IP rights. The buyer could then use the Ape's likeness in branded products, comic books, and TV shows. This dangled the hope in front of buyers that they, too, could create media empires of their own. Having an Ape was not the end goal but the starting point: an investment that encouraged even more investment.

The Apes started at around $200 a pop, and all 10,000 sold out in days. Their images quickly populated Twitter, replacing their owners' human profile pictures. The community then got to work covering the virtual bathroom wall with drawings of Charmander, Donkey Kong, and the "Cool S" found on countless grade-school notebooks. As predicted, the very first image drawn was an ejaculating dick. This raucous energy made the Bored Apes the it-brand of the moment, an exclusive club with a line out its digital door. Suddenly every Ape owner was a small-scale Paul

Tudor Jones—incentivized to make as much noise as possible, because their investment would appreciate with each new big Ape sale.

The hype around the Apes bewildered many of the NFT artists who had given birth to the movement. "It was very surprising to me," Beeple says. "At that point, I was like, 'Guys, this is just a complete copy of Crypto-Punks. What are we talking about here?'" (Beeple wasn't so far removed from facing disdain from a previous set of gatekeepers himself and would eventually come around on the project.)

Yuga Labs proceeded to augment the hype by releasing a whole universe of Ape-themed characters. To create a collection of secondary NFT creatures at first seemed risky, because a huge part of the allure of these PFP projects was their perceived scarcity. There are and will only ever be ten thousand CryptoPunks, just as there will only ever be 21 million bitcoin. As more and more people coveted one of these finite assets, each individual piece would be harder to obtain, and thus more valuable.

But Yuga Labs, in contrast, proceeded to send new Ape variations and companions to Ape holders: squashy cartoon dogs in the Bored Ape Kennel Collection, and Mutant Apes, whose skin melted off of their zombie-fied faces. These bonus NFTs indicated that Ape investors would not only own one static NFT but also receive a continuous stream of valuable digital assets. Suffice to say, it worked: the dogs themselves, which were ostensibly pets of the fictional Apes, were soon selling for more than 1 ETH, or $4,000, a pup.

Yuga Labs promised that Bored Ape holders would receive access to exclusive merch and in-person events. Meanwhile, Bored Ape holders took their IP licenses and created craft beers, animated YouTube series, and skateboard decks. One owner started writing stories on Twitter about his Ape, which he dubbed Jenkins the Valet. Jenkins, the owner wrote, was a lower-class striver who served as butler, confidant, and fixer for the Yacht Club's high rollers: He was the club's glue guy and witness to its many shenanigans. Other owners were ecstatic about the idea of building lore around their NFTs, so a fictional universe about the Yacht Club soon unfurled around Jenkins, tweet by tweet. Before long, Jenkins the Valet was Bored Ape's everyman, and a kind of metaphor for the entire NFT movement: With a little bit of shrewdness and self-promotion, you, too, could will your way from humble beginnings into riches and stardom.

But as the Bored Apes became the de facto brand of the NFT movement, criticism mounted. NFT artists realized that the formula for success had changed: that hand-creating art was no longer good enough. And with investors no longer even pretending to care about artistic aesthetics anymore, some corners of the Bored Ape Yacht Club looked awfully like a multilevel marketing scheme—in which the only way that an investor made their money back was to convince someone else to buy Ape spinoffs at a higher and higher price.

Vitalik Buterin, who was at first enthusiastic about NFT art, sensed that the Apes were different and watched their ascent nervously. In July 2021, he referred dismissively to the more gamble-y aspects of crypto as the "apes" and the "orangutans," and warned that the increasingly reckless games being played by crypto "degenerates"—a self-anointed label for the full-throttle traders who lived and breathed on crypto's bleeding edge— were "actually increasing the financial instability and the risk this whole thing is going to collapse."

Sam Bankman-Fried also initially cautioned against the NFT-as-clout trend, telling CNBC: "It could lead, frankly, to sort of a sour taste in people's mouth if there's a crash, and no one ever quite figured out what it was."

CHAPTER 8

Casino with a View

Christine Chew, in Hong Kong, was only a couple months into her new job as an analyst for the crypto VC fund Genesis Block (GBV) when she realized it wasn't all that different from her previous gig in private equity. Crypto was supposed to be about dismantling old systems and bringing new types of people into the financial system. But Christine found that while her new colleagues dressed and talked differently than their traditional finance counterparts, many were just as cutthroat and greedy. Crypto VCs, she now believed, cared mostly about extracting as much immediate money as possible from new crypto tokens, even if they were worthless in the long run. "The investors barely do any due diligence. Sometimes they don't care about the teams or the fundamentals," she says.

One day in August 2021, Christine was feeling disillusioned and adrift when she was invited to a party thrown by the company that shared an office with hers: Sam Bankman-Fried's FTX. GBV and FTX were connected entities in many ways. They shared executives and had loan agreements. Blockchain analysts would later discover that cryptocurrency ostensibly sent to GBV was actually processed and received by Sam Bankman-Fried's trading firm, Alameda Research.

The celebration was a farewell party for an FTX employee named Ryan Salame. Christine had never met him before, but Salame, Christine's boss told her, was headed to The Bahamas to start an FTX office there. Christine's boss then surprised her with another question: Would she consider going with Ryan? He was leaving the day after tomorrow.

Most people wouldn't be willing to uproot their lives to board a one-way, nine-thousand-mile flight across the world. Christine had never been to the Caribbean, and when she told her parents about the idea, they advised her against it. She had no idea what job she would do once she arrived.

But Christine had grown weary of her job at GBV, which she felt was predatory. And she had immense respect for FTX, which was one of the fastest-growing cogs in crypto's ecosystem. The prior month, the exchange had been valued at $18 billion in a $900 million funding tranche, the largest fundraising round in crypto history. Sam Bankman-Fried had wowed venture capital firms with talk of inevitable global domination: In pitches, he laid out his dream of FTX allowing the user to transform their dollar into anything—from bitcoin to a banana—and bragged that acquiring Goldman Sachs was "not out of the question at all."

FTX's investors included new and old tech money, including Soft-Bank, Sequoia Capital—which invested $213 million—and the hedge fund titan Paul Tudor Jones, whose Bitcoin thesis had helped kick off the whole run. Deven Parekh, managing director at Insight Partners, called FTX "the leading global crypto exchange" in a press release. (This assessment was a huge exaggeration: FTX was still logging single-digit percentages of the world's overall trading volume on centralized exchanges, trailing far behind Binance's 62 percent.)

Beyond the numbers, Christine was even more impressed with Sam himself. Like her, he subscribed to the philosophies of effective altruism and earn-to-give. Sam said his entire mission in crypto was to earn billions of dollars just so he could give it all away. And Sam, just like Christine, was a vegan who despised factory farming.

"Everything I saw about Sam was that he was doing good for the public," Christine says. "I thought it was a great opportunity."

So a week after Ryan Salame's party, Christine boarded a twenty-three-hour flight, paid for by GBV. When she arrived on the other side of the world, she was greeted with palm trees and endlessly blue skies, and was put up at the SLS Baha Mar, a four-star hotel. She loved the views from her room, the pools, and the beach. One detail she disliked, however, was having to walk through a casino every time she went downstairs. The pulsating music, smell of cigarettes, and air of desperation gave her a headache. But she also quickly grew fond of the handful of FTX employees who had arrived alongside her to build what they hoped would be a crypto idyll in the Caribbean. "It was a very tight-knit, positive community," Christine says. "They are almost like your friends and family and colleagues, all at the same time."

AfroDroid 3019, Owo Anietie, with screen artwork by Vintage Mozart.
OWO ANIETIE

CHAPTER 9

Million-Dollar Man

As Christine was flying to The Bahamas to join FTX in August 2021, the Nigerian artist Owo Anietie watched Bored Ape holders chatter bombastically on social media and made up his mind: He was going to create his own answer to the Bored Ape Yacht Club.

Owo had recently quit his day job in graphic design to plunge into NFTs full-time. He had grown tired of the relentless grind of juggling his job, freelance gigs, and NFTs. Besides, he was making some promising sales on his one-off NFT artworks. The pieces he minted were full of depth, moody colors, and history: In one of them, a Buddha-like stone figure sat in the middle of a whirl of hieroglyphics in the ancient Nsibidi language. It sold for $711: more than the monthly salary he had been earning a few months before.

But these works of art each took time and effort to make and had limited resale value. Profile picture projects like the Bored Apes, on the other hand, could all be created in one fell swoop, and were designed to generate consistent hype and be flipped over and over again by degen traders—short for "degenerates." At that time, Apes were pulling in over $1 million a day and dominating Twitter. Ape investors would storm into NFT conversations on Clubhouse and drown them out by making "ooh ooh" monkey noises.

Success begets copycats. The economist Edward Chancellor once posited that "as a mania progresses, the quality of the stocks that attract speculations declines." The comedian Groucho Marx wrote that in the

1920s before the stock market crash, he could close his eyes and choose a stock at random, and that it would start rising. Nearly a century later in the lead-up to the 2008 financial crisis, complex assets called CDOs, or collateralized debt obligations, proliferated despite being filled with risky debt, due to a widespread belief that the housing prices would continue to soar.

In 2021, the Apes' mammoth profits kick-started a frenzy of knockoffs, each one more shameless than the last: Pudgy Penguins, Lazy Lions, SupDucks. "It was every adjective-animal combination you could ever imagine," says Michael Keen, a former ticket broker who started the marketing company NFT Catcher in 2021. Some of these NFT projects greatly increased in price, while others tanked on launch day.

While NFT investors knew a lot of these Ape knockoffs were shoddy and redundant, they still bought in because of an overwhelming sense of FOMO—fear of missing out—in the crypto space. "Loss aversion" has long been studied by behavioral psychologists: the idea that the pain of losing is much more powerful than the pleasure of winning. James Block, a psychiatry resident and a blockchain analyst, says that loss aversion pushed people to spend irrationally on NFTs and new cryptocurrencies in order to both cover for their already-realized losses and avoid theoretical losses from not investing in winners.

Crypto Twitter, a crucial hub for investment advice and NFT advocacy, compounded these deep-seated psychological tendencies. With every trade or NFT purchase, investors were betting not only their money but also their clout in social circles. If you didn't buy in now, then maybe you would miss out on thousands of dollars and inclusion in what everyone was convinced would be a lasting, happy, and wealthy community.

Zeneca, a prominent NFT collector and influencer, expressed the idea of "infinite regret" on his podcast: that no matter how many successful trades degens had made, they always remembered the ones that didn't go their way. Crypto Twitter was always taunting them with alternate realities in which they would have been multimillionaires if they had just bought in on the right project at the right time.

The biggest regret of most traders in those days was that they had not bought a Bored Ape. Day-one investors had turned $200 into $200,000, which gave them license to hold court over Crypto Twitter. There was no longer a way to buy an Ape cheaply—but maybe one of these Ape knockoffs would hit it just as big. So NFT traders piled into projects that contained scant artistry, originality, or hope of success.

This FOMO-driven climate posed an enormous opportunity for NFT creators, who also stood to become extremely rich if they created a successful Ape replica, tapped the right influencers, and perfectly timed the crypto roller coaster. With just a little hype, creators could earn back any costs almost immediately thanks to the feeding frenzy around initial drops. "Toward the end of 2021, there would be thirty Bored Ape copycats a day," Keen says. "Even if they knew they weren't going to sell out, if they could sell five hundred of them for .08 ETH or whatever, it's still a good amount of money for doing nothing." (In late 2021, that was over $100,000.)

Some PFP projects went beyond the adjective-animal conceit and pandered to specific demographics, whether it was gender, ethnicity, or age. Given the overwhelming masculinity of the crypto space, several female-focused projects were created to incentivize more women to buy in. One of those was the Fame Lady Squad, which featured cartoon women with halos and laser eyes. The project listed its founders as "Cindy, Kelda and Andrea," and advertised itself as the "first female avatar project of all time." Christine Chew saw people talking about it excitedly online, and minted one of the avatars the day after launch for .05 ETH, or $95 (plus an $8 transaction fee).

"Almost every woman in crypto promoted this project," Christine says. "If you had it as your profile picture, you counted as in the in-group." But a month later, it was discovered that the Fame Lady Squad wasn't created by women at all: It was developed by Russian men who sensed a market opportunity. The same day that one of those developers admitted the truth, tweeting, "sorry for the lie," Christine sold her Fame Lady at a loss for about $62.

But for many of these PFP projects, no matter how shameless or shoddy, a funny thing would happen after launch: the NFT holders would form a genuine community on Discord, forging relationships across the globe that transcended their JPEGs. In August 2021, one Pudgy Penguin holder broke down in tears on a Twitter Space while talking about how his new community had provided an emotional safety net during a personal crisis. "My penguin is the reason I'm here. My penguin is me," he sobbed. In an era of alienation and lingering mental health taboos, PFPs had become a shortcut to solidarity—a pretext for lonely dudes to make friends online.

Owo Anietie's original goal had been to create a movie or a television show based on his artwork. In 2020, he had come up with the idea of AfroDroids, a project that practically epitomized the idea of Afrofuturism. In the year 3045, his story went, humans have gone extinct due to global warming and humanity's refusal to nurture the Earth. But before they were annihilated completely, an African scientist developed a method to upload human consciousness onto droids. Now the Droids are the only beings on the planet, and they walk around anguished by the disconnect between their metallic bodies and human consciousnesses. As they try to save the Earth, stray memories float across their screens: of scrambling up jungle gyms, falling in love, dancing, grieving for loved ones. The Droids were a metaphor for the blockchain itself: the resolute digital wardens of our human legacy.

Owo realized that he could take the idea of AfroDroids and turn it into an algorithmically generated project similar to the Bored Ape Yacht Club. If the rollout went well, continued sales could serve as the seed money for his bigger goal of building an Afrofuturist film franchise.

He first brought the idea to Esther Eze, a Nigerian writer and manager who had been helping him with freelance art and advertising projects. Owo showed Eze the Bored Apes and explained how they worked, with their clothing templates and algorithmic attributes, and told her that they needed to launch something like it as soon as possible. In August, Owo and Eze started crafting the AfroDroids PFP. Where there were ten thousand

Bored Apes to collect, there would be 12,117 AfroDroids, signifying the number of months until the Droids took over the Earth. Owo began animating dozens of different attributes that spanned African and global influences: colorful kente kufi hats, beads, streetwear puffer jackets. He pulled all-nighters, fueled by coffee and alcohol. His artistic output was relentless.

"You would be having a conversation with him, and during the course of the conversation, he must have drawn sixteen to twenty characters," his brother Nsikak remembers. "He was working too much, barely eating enough, drinking more than enough, and doing his designs at a speed that was astronomical."

Eze, who was working on creating content for the website and promoting the project, didn't sleep much that month either. "When we go to sleep, our American friends were waking up, and we had to answer their questions," she remembers.

As much as Owo liked his vision and artwork, he knew that he couldn't achieve viral success on his own. In the NFT world, marketing and rollout strategy were more important than the product itself. So he enlisted Michael Keen, the NFT marketer and a prominent collector of Owo's NFTs, to lead pre-launch strategy. Keen's burgeoning company, NFT Catcher, tracked project release dates on a calendar that had quickly amassed seventy thousand subscribers. He had a deep well of connections, including in the all-important NFT communities Veve and Vee Friends, the social club centered on the entrepreneur and influencer Gary Vaynerchuk, who broadcast motivational diatribes to his millions of followers. Keen hosted Twitter Spaces and understood marketing strategies. He also bought a Bored Ape for $2,300 in May 2021 and proudly wore it as his profile picture, which bestowed upon him authority and savviness.

Keen had long been a fan of Owo and became enthusiastic about AfroDroids after hearing Owo talk about the idea on Clubhouse. He cut a deal with Owo for a portion of every sale and brought aboard his whole NFT Catcher team to help Owo achieve his vision. Two of those builders included the generative artist Gary Geck and the smart-contract builder known as Wade, both of whom wore Apes as their Twitter profile pictures, once again reinforcing that project's ubiquity—as well as NFT Catcher's bona fides. Owo was convinced he was surrounding himself with all the right clout.

Keen made a series of suggestions to Owo, many of which were oriented toward emulating the Bored Apes. First, he encouraged Owo to actually incorporate Bored Apes into some of the artwork: to put individual Apes into some of the Droid's face screens. In the way that pale-blue "alien" CryptoPunks were highly coveted because there were only nine of them in the collection of ten thousand, Keen hoped the Ape Droids could attain a similar level of prestige. He licensed the image of his own Ape to Owo for free use in the project. (This was also a self-serving move, as the value of his Ape would rise if associated with a successful spinoff project.)

And just as the Bored Apes had maintained momentum by doling out NFT rewards to their holders, Keen encouraged Owo to airdrop giveaways of his *Everydays* artwork for Droid holders. This idea was controversial to some artists, who felt that Owo was degrading the value of his real art in order to boost a trading card collection. But it was an effective way to get buyers to feel like they would get additional rewards beyond the NFT itself. In the same vein, Owo also promised to send Droids buyers a companion "Drone" NFT, which would flit beside Droids in this new world just like R2-D2 accompanied Anakin Skywalker.

Owo was amenable to these suggestions, as he wanted the project to be as successful as possible. At the same time, he laid out plans to build a production studio for the eventual AfroDroids movie, dreaming that the fledgling brand could one day be as recognizable as *Black Panther*. AfroDroids holders, he pledged, would have "fractionalized ownership" of his studio and its creations.

Many NFT projects at this time were advertising similarly ambitious road maps filled with all sorts of perks for holders. What would set apart AfroDroids, Owo and Eze decided, would be its charity component. Eze had come across a tweet from the founder of a Nigerian arts school that was struggling to pay bills during the pandemic. The school, Dream Catchers

Academy, had been founded in 2014 by Seyi Oluyole, a screenwriter and educator who grew up in poverty and wanted to give young girls like herself an opportunity to pursue their artistic dreams.

Oluyole's Dream Catchers was housed in Ikorodu, a high-density city to the northeast of Lagos. It had scraped by for several years thanks to its GoFundMe page, receiving much-needed jolts of funding when videos of students dancing went viral thanks to re-shares from celebrities like Rihanna and Naomi Campbell. But social media attention did not always equate to donations. Fans of those celebrities would often just hit like, write a comment, and then move on with their lives.

In the fall of 2020, Dream Catchers was given notice to move out of the building the school occupied. As they searched for a more permanent home, Oluyole's funding ran dangerously dry. COVID-19 lockdowns had reduced dance performance opportunities, which had been a steady source of donations. Inflation in Nigeria had soared over 16 percent, its highest rate in fifteen years. Oluyole was forced to ration foods, cut the amount of milk she served in half, and limit protein to either one or two meals a day. "I have even considered running away out of fear," she tweeted in July 2021.

Both Owo and Eze saw themselves in the Dream Catchers' students. The power of NFT smart contracts, they felt, might allow them to help the students directly and continuously. They could code in a donation to the school every single time an AfroDroid was traded. If NFT enthusiasts swapped AfroDroids back and forth just like they were doing with CryptoPunks and Bored Apes, then the school would receive a constant stream of funding.

AfroDroids' combination of art, charity, and incentives was too powerful for the NFT community to resist. Here was a project that seemed to represent everything that crypto idealists wanted to believe in: They were using technology, community, charity, and culture to lift children out of poverty and fulfill their dreams.

Keen and the NFT Catcher team, for their part, were highly successful in rallying their connections toward AfroDroids. "It's important to have a road map, but at the end of the day, it's more about getting hype to the right people," Keen told me. After the project's announcement, Owo started receiving shout-outs from major Clubhouse rooms and podcasts, like Club Q and, of course, the *NFT Catcher Pod*. One minor influencer, Chris Verzwyvelt, hosted Owo on his podcast *Coffee with Chris* and told his listeners, "Not only are you potentially making yourself money, but you're providing for these kids." A massive global base of AfroDroids fans sprouted up from Mexico, Australia, Georgia, Sweden, and beyond.

Of course, the African NFT Community threw its weight behind the project. Liam Vries cohosted Owo in a Clubhouse room two days before launch. The following day, the AfroDroids Discord reached ten thousand members—and Liam devoted himself to "encouraging every single person on the continent" to buy into Owo's project.

On an individual level, Owo played the part of crypto salesman perfectly; it wasn't so different from his childhood storytelling days on the streets of Uyo in Nigeria. "We are offering so much value," he bragged on the CryptoNovo network. "We are buying land in the metaverse, because the metaverse is the future of not just the NFT space, but the future of humanity and how we're going to be interacting." After almost a year immersed in the NFT world, Owo fully understood that broadcasting his conviction was essential to his success.

On September 1, 2021, the day of launch, AfroDroids superfans who had registered in advance for a presale immediately stormed the site, buying up more than two-thirds of all AfroDroids NFTs. Twelve minutes after the public sale began, the entire collection had sold out. The 12,117 AfroDroids sold to 3,200 holders for .07 ETH—or about $250 a pop—netting more than $3 million worth of cryptocurrency. It was the biggest NFT drop from Africa ever.

Collectors ranged from first-time NFT buyers to degens to professional financial investors. CryptoWizard, an early AfroDroids fan and cybersecurity expert who would later become an adviser to Owo, says that he helped dozens of newcomers who were struggling to use their wallets buy into the project. The crypto novices included one seventy-year-old woman in Michigan, who excitedly bought one with the help of her niece's husband, and announced her intention to frame her Droid and put it up on her wall.

Once the sale was done, the charity component executed seamlessly, with more than $600,000 in crypto transferred to the Dream Catcher Academy's MetaMask wallet. This transaction was proof of the beauty of smart contracts in action. Six figures' worth of charity could be funneled from individuals around the world to a single account immediately and transparently. And since the donation was written into the AfroDroids code, there was no way for Owo or anyone else to reneg on their promises.

The sale made the AfroDroids by far the biggest donor to Dream Catchers in its history, generating far more hype and cash than Rihanna, Naomi Campbell, or Lady Gaga. Oluyole recorded a video of twenty of her students calling out the names of individual AfroDroids buyers and crowing, "we love you!" The video featured an augmented reality filter that turned some of the girl's faces into Droids while they danced joyously to the Nigerian pop singer Ayra Starr. Oluyole withdrew $100,000 and bought the girls crisp pink uniforms, laptops, and a school bus, so that they didn't have to trek to school or pile onto tricycles every morning. She was able to enroll twenty more girls, effectively doubling the size of the school, and pay for six full-time teachers, three part-time teachers, and a janitor. Crucially, she was able to expedite the building of a new two-story schoolhouse with a hostel next door.

"For weeks I have panicked about what to do," Oluyole wrote in a note to Esther Eze days after the sale. "How we'd feed the girls and stay sustainable. We are literally building this school now. Literally like a dream. . . . The girls are too excited."

For Owo, AfroDroids drop day was one of the strangest of his life. An unfathomable $1 million in crypto had materialized in his wallet, thanks to a combination of hard work, artistry, and a technology he had not heard of a year prior. He had become the success story he long dreamed about, and he sobbed with joy the whole night. "I was just crying, trying to reminisce on all of the shit I've taken from people just to get here, and how much things were going to change," he said. "I was so happy. Little did I know the universe had a bigger plan for me: that the universe was ready to fuck me sideways."

PART II

THE KINGPIN

CHAPTER 10

The Traditional Buyer

The day after the AfroDroids launch, Sotheby's began an NFT auction. The auction house had jumped into the NFT space in April following its rival Christie's success with Beeple. But in accordance with the shifting winds of crypto, this September auction did not consist of art but rather 101 Bored Apes and 101 Bored Ape Kennel Club dogs. A week later, the Apes sold for $24.4 million, or over $200,000 per Ape. This was double the amount of some pre-auction estimates and a record for an NFT auction at the house. Sotheby's head of contemporary art auctions, Max Moore, said on a Twitter Space that the buyer was a "traditional" buyer, according to multiple listeners who posted about it later. Evidently, savvy investors believed NFTs were a valuable long-term investment.

But, as it turned out, that undisclosed buyer was not a "traditional" art collector at all. The new owner of these Apes was Sam Bankman-Fried.

By this point, Sam was worth an estimated $16.2 billion and was quickly growing a reputation as one of crypto's smartest and most exciting entrepreneurs. His crypto exchange, FTX, had muscled into the top 5 of exchanges in just two years and had branded itself as the safe, dependable, and streamlined choice for crypto traders. NFTs, however, were decidedly not part of Sam's public strategy: He had criticized them on CNBC in August 2021 as "almost going mainstream faster than the mainstream understands what it is they're adopting." In a space full of profit-obsessed gamblers, Sam, at least in public, appeared the judicious architect of a more stable, regulated future.

At this point, Sam was not yet the main character of crypto. In its decentralized nature, crypto was not supposed to have a single protagonist but rather a series of disparate individuals working diligently to rise upward, like Beeple, Owo Anietie, and Christine Chew. The communities they formed and the ethos they carried aligned with Vitalik Buterin's hopes and dreams for Ethereum as a global computing system disrupting traditional power structures and spurring creativity and productivity worldwide.

But it's also possible to look back on crypto activity in 2021 and see a completely different and much more cynical story: one in which NFT artists were creating Potemkin villages that hid a far more greedy, nefarious strain of crypto bubbling underneath. This strain of crypto looked a lot like the brew of shadow banks and subprime mortgages that felled the financial world in 2008, in which traders built Jenga towers of risky assets bought with borrowed money.

Sam was the king of this crypto underworld—and its craziest gambler. His covert overpay for a bunch of monkey JPEGs, despite cautioning the public against them, is emblematic of the cutthroat and underhanded way he operated—and far from the strangest bet he would make. Even as good vibes largely reigned across the crypto and NFT spaces, Sam was well on his way to reshaping the movement in his own image—and then spurring its ruin.

Sam Bankman-Fried was born on March 5, 1992, the son of academic prestige. His parents, Joseph Bankman and Barbara Fried, were celebrated professors at Stanford Law School. Joseph Bankman was a trained clinical psychologist and a tax law professor, and Barbara Fried was a renowned ethicist who also ran an influential data-driven Democratic donor group. The pair had taught there since the late 1980s and regularly hosted Sunday dinners at their house on campus, which attendees likened to modern salons.

Sam also had a younger brother, Gabe, but they weren't close: Gabe later told the author Michael Lewis that he interacted with his brother "as another tenant in my house." Sam made few friends as a child and became incensed when he learned that other kids believed in Santa Claus and that he would be expected to play along.

Sam grew into a chubby, awkward, and anxious teenager. His mother, Barbara, would later write that Sam could seem "odd and off-putting" to strangers. George Lerner, who became Sam's psychiatrist in 2019, described him as "on the autism spectrum." But he made friends with like-minded math and science obsessives, creating puzzle hunts for them to solve. Some of his friends affectionately called him "Bank" or "SBF." He also found solace on internet message boards dedicated to utilitarianism, the philosophy of doing the most good for the greatest number of people. In particular, Sam was intrigued by the ideas of Peter Singer, who argued that people had an equal duty to save a faraway person from starvation as to pull out a child drowning in a pond three feet away. (Christine Chew was similarly persuaded by reading Singer to become vegan.)

Eventually, Sam developed a personal philosophy that his own mother described as "take-no-prisoners utilitarian": to be ruthless in fighting for the maximum good, even if it meant hurting people in the process.

The process of utilitarian decision-making revolves around the concept of "expected value," known colloquially as EV. In order to make sense of complicated decisions, Sam tried to turn pros and cons into numbers and then decide which number was bigger. Sam knew that this act of conversion was fundamentally flawed: "You can never be sure that you're calculating it right," he told the economist and podcaster Tyler Cowen in 2022. But for someone who struggled with reading emotions and social interactions, it seemed like the most logical way to tease answers out of a fraught, multidimensional world.

Sam attended MIT for college, where he joined a nerdy co-ed fraternity called Epsilon Theta and stayed up all night playing board games. Sam recruited some of his frat brothers to assist in activism against factory farming. He had become vegan after beginning to read about all the facets of ethical consumption—of grass-fed farming, humane animal rearing, and the pros and cons of eating certain types of meat over others. "The cognitive load was overwhelming," he would later describe. It was much easier for him to simply cut out all meat and be done with it; to choose an absolutist worldview and stick to it, rather than to grapple with any inconsistencies or intricacies of a compromised course of action.

In 2012, Sam started a blog called *Measuring Shadows*, writing rambling posts about ethics and baseball. Many of his writings explored how to make difficult decisions based on the tenets of utilitarianism. "It's true that utilitarianism occasionally incentivizes lying but in practice relatively rarely," he wrote in a comment. "And it's a good thing that it does so occasionally."

Sam devoted one blog post to a thought experiment called the "Utility Monster" popular among anti-utilitarians. The theory argues that because utilitarians only care about net happiness, then they might approve of the existence of a creature that derives immense pleasure when it causes others pain. Sam rejected this idea, arguing that the negative value of pain exceeded the positive value of happiness. But he didn't rule out that such a monster could be good for the world—especially if it behaved "fundamentally differently from any creature we've ever encountered."

When Sam started college, he thought he might become a professor like his parents. But he instead lurched toward finance after attending a talk at Harvard by leaders of the effective altruism movement, including the Oxford philosophy professor Will MacAskill. Before the talk, MacAskill met Sam for lunch in Harvard Square, where he convinced the college student to adopt the "earn to give" philosophy: to work within the capitalist system to maximize his earnings, and then give most of it away to vetted philanthropic causes. If a wealthy banker donated half their income to an organization fighting malaria in Africa, MacAskill argued, they could save ten thousand lives over the course of their career.

So in 2013, Sam accepted a summer internship at Jane Street Capital, a prestigious Wall Street trading firm that allowed its interns to expense multiple restaurant meals a day. Jane Street managers actively encouraged their interns to make all sorts of wagers against each other while at the office. These gambling games taught the interns to quickly assess risk and reward, to sniff out bad deals, and to feel like they had skin in the game before they were actually betting with millions of dollars.

"Taking on risk was a big part of the company culture," says Milo Beckman, another Jane Street intern who sat next to Sam all summer. "But Sam definitely took it further than your average intern."

All summer, Sam placed bet after bet against the other interns, many of them against Beckman as the duo sat at their desks. Sam won some, and Milo won some. But Milo's takeaway from their many wagers was that Sam was willing to risk a lot for a little. "He would risk fifty dollars on a bet, even if the positive EV [expected value] was only five cents," he recalls.

This type of bet stemmed out of a concept that Sam was obsessed with, called risk-neutrality. The term hides its true meaning, and in plain English signifies something much closer to "risk embrace." A risk-neutral trader embraces any bet that has a mathematical upside, even if the consequences for losing are huge. For example, if a risk-neutral trader had believed that Barack Obama had even a 52 percent chance of winning against Mitt Romney in the 2012 election, then they would be willing to put all their money into the trade.

Jane Street managers advised interns to adopt a risk-neutral mentality about trades but with limits: They warned that making the same plus-EV bet over and over could result in them losing all their money. "They would try to teach us that risk management goes both ways," says another Jane Street intern from that summer. "But Sam only really liked the first part of the lesson."

When the pair wasn't gambling, Milo Beckman tried to engage Sam in discussions about politics. Sam often asserted his commitment to effective altruism. But when it came to having actual opinions on specific issues (besides animals), his answers were often noncommittal and unspecific, Milo says. "It was really hard to get him to have a conversation about pretty much anything in the real world that felt substantive," Beckman says. "For him, it was kind of just like, 'Everything is a math problem to be solved.'"

Sam loved Jane Street: He returned there after graduating in 2014, and began raking in hundreds of thousands of dollars by making all kinds of risky bets for the company. He then gave away some of his earnings to the Effective Altruism Foundation, gaining their friendship and trust. To outsiders, he was becoming a poster child for how a young, enterprising brainiac could do good in the world.

CHAPTER 11

Dead Simple Arbitrage

After a couple years at Jane Street, Sam realized that his six-figure salary wasn't sating his ambitions and that he might be able to make a far bigger impact on the world elsewhere. So in 2017, he departed the hedge fund for San Francisco in pursuit of a new moneymaking opportunity that promised to blow traditional finance out of the water.

At the time, Sam knew virtually nothing about crypto: He confessed in 2019 that he "could maybe explain roughly what a bitcoin was, and that's about it." But when he learned about the crypto market from others in the EA world, he saw an opportunity to profit on much higher orders of magnitude, thanks to a classic trading technique known as arbitrage.

In arbitrage, traders take advantage of small differences in how assets are valued in different markets. Let's say the price of a global company is $10 on the New York Stock Exchange and $11 on the London Stock Exchange, due to exchange rate fluctuations and slight differences in demand in the two countries. A trader could buy the stock in New York and sell it immediately in London to earn $1, a tidy risk-free profit.

Price differences between traditional financial exchanges were usually tiny and disappeared fast due to market corrections. But in crypto, the pool of value was much smaller. So when whales—slang in cryptospeak for intimidatingly wealthy traders—moved their money in and out of certain coins, they could cause much bigger price jumps, leading to mouthwatering arbitrage opportunities. "In U.S. stock markets, it was like, maybe this thing is trading at the wrong price by a hundredth of a percent," Sam explained on a podcast. "Then you get to crypto and everything is multiplied by fifty. It seemed like one of two things were true: Either all of this data was fake, and nothing was going on here; it was just some mirage. Or it was an extremely exciting opportunity." For Ethereum founder Vitalik Buterin, moneymaking had been perhaps the least important part of crypto. For Sam, it was the entire point. If Vitalik was an early San Francisco settler working to build out the city's roads, schools, and democratic ideals, Sam was a prospector out for gold.

So in the fall of 2017, Sam arrived in the Bay Area and convened with Tara MacAulay, an effective altruist who had been inspired to get into crypto in part by seeing Vitalik Buterin speak in 2016. Together, they convinced earn-to-give believers to help them found a new crypto trading firm, called Alameda Research. The first people who came on board were effective altruists, Jane Street defectors, and eggheads from MIT and Berkeley. Much of Alameda's initial funding was loaned to them by influential EA practitioners, who hoped Sam would make even more money to donate back to EA-approved charities. Their involvement lent Sam a veneer of ethical legitimacy.

Very few of the early Alameda employees had traded crypto before. But they applied the same principles of arbitrage they had used on Wall Street. Sam and his team built algorithmic quantitative bots that would identify price differentials between crypto platforms. They would then rapidly execute massive trades before those differences disappeared.

The most successful of these arbitrages came from the difference between the price of bitcoin in the U.S. and in Japan. On Japanese exchanges, bitcoin traded at a 15 percent premium because demand for the cryptocurrency had spiked in the country. This meant that in theory, if someone bought $10 million of bitcoin every day in the U.S. and then sold it in Japan, they could earn a cool $1.5 million daily.

But getting the money in and out of these crypto exchanges was a headache. U.S. banks blanched at any transaction that involved crypto, while Japanese banks were suspicious of the frequency with which Alameda wanted to send overseas wires. Eventually, Sam put together a convoluted system in which a U.S. team spent three hours to make sure money transfers went through, and another team waited for hours in rural Japanese banks to wire the money back. It was "dead simple arbitrage," Sam said—and it brought in over $1 million a day.

The runaway success of the "Japan premium" invigorated Alameda's earn-to-give effective altruists. In order to maximize their philanthropic power, many of them became hopelessly consumed by crypto trading, routinely putting in fifteen-plus-hour days, glued to their desks. "I felt guilty every time I stepped away to do something else because I was like, 'I could be making tens of thousands of dollars per hour trading right now and then donating it to charity,' says one early Alameda employee. 'So is it worth going to my friend's birthday party for two hours?'"

Accordingly, the company built a reputation for its youth, brainpower, and doggedness. "Sam was incredibly creative. They were number one when it came to crypto-native, edgy, tech-forward innovations and new ideas," says Alex Pack, a crypto venture capitalist who invested in early-stage crypto projects and scouted Alameda's rise. One of Alameda's innovations was an automated trading system over the messaging app Telegram, which saved traders the time and energy it would take to coordinate with actual humans.

Sam, of course, was at the center of this relentless work culture, often sleeping less than four hours a night on a beanbag chair in his office. (This sleep schedule echoed that of the infamous 1980s corporate raider Michael Milken, who also bragged that he slept three to four hours a night and arrived at his desk by 4:30 a.m.) Sam had long battled insomnia and had undergone sleep studies as a teenager to try to find the root of his difficulties. In September 2019, he tweeted that his keys to success included "stimulants when you wake up, sleeping pills if you need them when you sleep." At work, Sam sat in front of six screens and constantly multitasked, even playing League of Legends during strategy meetings. He shuffled cards so vociferously he wore out a deck every week. He rarely took days off.

Sam's furious work ethic was making him rich but not happy. He wrote in his journal in his mid-twenties that "My highest highs, my proudest moments, come and pass and I feel nothing but the aching hole in my brain where happiness should be." "He talked very openly about his struggles with extreme depression," the Alameda employee says. "He had been through many different treatment options, trying to find something that would work at all."

The solutions that Sam landed upon were Adderall for his ADD and an Emsam patch for his depression. Adderall was an all-too-common drug for a twitchy millennial; Emsam was decidedly not. While early studies showed Emsam to be an effective antidepressant after its creation in 2008, its user adoption hit a major snag when researchers found that it could be lethal when ingested with certain moldy cheeses and fermented foods (not such a problem for a vegan). Emsam's primary substance, selegiline, has also been associated with compulsive behaviors, pathological gambling, and the uncontrolled spending of money.

Alameda's maximalist, high-stress approach was incredibly productive for a while. But predictably, it led to burnout. "We were all suffering from months on end of very little sleep in this pressure cooker environment," says the Alameda employee. "That was getting to Sam and affecting his decision-making."

Sam had promised his effective altruist creditors that Alameda was in the business of making safe, low-risk trades. But Sam, the employee says, started behaving more erratically and was attempting to pull off increasingly precarious trades behind their backs. He agreed to deals that other employees believed were sketchy; he tried to launch trading bots without implementing safeguards; he reneged on agreements. Sam's poor trading sometimes resulted in the company losing half a million dollars in a single day. "It got to the point that we were sleeping at the office because we were worried about what Sam might do if we're not there," says the employee.

Alameda's bookkeeping was terrible: It didn't distinguish between different streams of capital. In February 2018, the company lost $4 million worth of the cryptocurrency XRP due to sheer sloppiness. It took weeks for traders to track the tokens down, and by the time they had found them, their value had dropped drastically.

Sam claimed these errors and oversights were by-products of a bold risk-taking strategy that would pay off in the long run. Just as in the bets he had made with Milo, he was happy to risk a lot if the odds told him to. But many of Alameda's effective altruists were growing increasingly concerned that Sam wasn't aligned with their goals—and endangering the movement. "We had $150 million-plus in EA money at stake that, from our perspective, would have gone toward saving lives," the Alameda employee says. "If we lost the money, to some extent, it would feel like we were party to harming someone."

So in April 2018, about half a year after the company's founding, a group of employees tried to organize a coup, accusing Sam of "gross negligence" and "willful and knowing violations of agreements or obligations." "Sam will lie, and distort the truth for his own gain," they wrote in a memo. But Sam refused to step down, so those executives, including cofounder Tara MacAulay, resigned instead, along with roughly half of Alameda's thirty employees. Many of them were shocked by the callousness with which Sam shut the door on even the people he was close with and had known for years. "I think Sam is unusually willing to take actions that would directly harm people he cares about, if he thinks that's the best way to achieve his goals," the employee says. Sam had become a variant of the "utility monster" he had written about in college: a pain-inflicting creature that might be accepted by utilitarians due to his net utility being positive.

Before the schism, Alameda had been filled with idealists who were philosophically aligned with Vitalik Buterin and other crypto philosophers. There had even been Ethereum smart contract developers on staff. "But all those people left at the same time," says the employee. "The core that was left was just Sam and his pals."

Improbably, Sam and his posse weathered the storm and refocused around Sam's high-risk, high-reward mentality. Going forward, Sam owned 90 percent of the company, while the other 10 percent went to another cofounder, Gary Wang, an intensely quiet software engineer who Sam had known from high school math camp and MIT's Epsilon Theta. To boost their efforts, Sam successfully raised money from other lenders by promising "high returns with no risk" in letters that were laden with typos: "We guarantee full payment of the principal and interest, enforceable under US law," he wrote in 2018. "We are extremely confident we will be pay this amount."

Alameda was further propelled by new hires, including a mousy bookworm named Caroline Ellison, who had also previously worked at Jane Street. Caroline had wandered into trading mostly out of a lack of other ideas. In the summer of 2018, she and Sam began sleeping together. As the pair spent more time together, Caroline wanted a real relationship, but Sam kept brushing her off. They would drift in and out of romance and despair for the next couple years.

Half a year after the Alameda exodus, the venture capitalist Alex Pack, who was then the managing partner of Dragonfly Capital, took a meeting with Sam with the intention of investing in Alameda. Pack was impressed with Sam's trading strategies and his fearless embrace of decentralized finance (DeFi), an umbrella of financial services that offered lending and borrowing in crypto without the need for centralized banking intermediaries. After several meetings, Pack agreed in a handshake deal to invest $5 to 10 million in Alameda, pending due diligence.

But when Pack combed through Alameda's books, he became increasingly worried. "It was almost like a Russian doll, where we kept discovering more and more weird cons and red flags that were bordering on fraud or integrity issues," he remembers. Pack found out about how Alameda had lost track of the millions of dollars in XRP and about the attempted coup in April. He learned that Sam was being evasive about the fact that Alameda had been wildly unprofitable in February 2018, and had instead told Pack that Alameda "didn't have any good record keeping" from that time.

It seemed nearly everything Alameda did was laced with an eye-popping level of risk. "It was probably like Alex Honnold–level of risk taking," Pack says, referring to the climber at the center of the documentary *Free Solo*, who scales sheer rock faces without a harness. "To the point of, like, is there a part of his brain missing? Everyone would tell us this, including the heads of the exchanges that he traded on."

Pack also became concerned by the way in which Sam seemed to treat Alameda like a video game. In one meeting, Sam actually referred to Alameda's equity capital as a "hit points bar," as if he were playing a first-person shooter game. "He felt like trading was a game, and he was willing to take these really big risks," Pack says. "And if he died, then his hit points go to zero—but then he just re-spawns."

CHAPTER 12

FTX

By April 2019, Alex Pack and Dragonfly had been conducting due diligence research on Alameda for several months when they noticed something even more concerning. For the first time in months, Alameda was losing money. When they asked Sam about it, he gave them an answer that blindsided them: He and the main executives at Alameda were now spending most of their time not on Alameda, but on creating a new crypto exchange.

"The expected value of an exchange is huge, and we think it's worth it to spend our time on," Pack remembers Sam telling him. "So the trading algorithms have basically been running on autopilot."

Sam had decided he was unsatisfied with simply scooping up the change that had slipped through the cracks between markets. After all, the amount of money to be made by trading on a market doesn't compare to profits of the market itself.

The crypto exchanges that existed at the time were severely flawed. Most of them had clunky interfaces that dissuaded crypto newbies from opening accounts and their range of financial products was limited. Major crypto exchanges had also suffered devastating security lapses. In 2014, hackers had stripped $460 million from the first major crypto exchange, Mt. Gox.

Many crypto idealists, including Vitalik Buterin, felt that centralized crypto exchanges shouldn't exist at all and were oxymoronic: that the very act of trusting someone with your money went against crypto's core values. But Sam didn't care so much about those values. He felt that lack of an easy onboarding process into crypto was keeping many prospective users out.

So by late 2018, Sam and his Alameda employees had begun quietly building their own centralized crypto exchange: FTX, which stood for "Futures Exchange." His main collaborators on this project were Gary Wang, his taciturn Alameda cofounder, and Nishad Singh, an engineer at Facebook and friend of Sam's younger brother, Gabe. Sam, Gary, and Nishad were FTX's nerve center: They conceptualized and engineered its trading platform nearly by themselves, chatting often on a Signal group named "The Fantastic Three."

The trio soon realized that such an exchange would face too many regulatory hurdles in the U.S., so they decamped from Berkeley to Hong Kong, a global crypto epicenter. There, they fostered a relentless FTX work culture in which staffers were expected to work through holidays and even typhoon warnings.

This shift in focus from Alameda to FTX was the final straw for Alex Pack and Dragonfly—especially because Sam told him that FTX was outside the parameters of Pack's investment. "He was basically telling us, 'You're giving us money that we're going to use to do another thing that is actively harming the business. And this other thing, you have no rights to or information about,'" Pack says. The deal fell apart. A year later, Sam posted a scathing "horror story" on Twitter about an unnamed VC who had valued Alameda too low—and many people in crypto understood it was about Pack. It was a petty, thinly veiled attempt to blackball Pack from an industry in which Sam was gaining influence and power. "I don't know how to explain how unprecedented it is for a founder to write a thirty-tweet thread about how shitty you are for doing due diligence," Pack says. "I could have sued him for slander—but Sam was the golden child at the time, and I didn't want to piss him off."

FTX.com launched in May 2019. Its most basic feature was its spot market: a trading platform for customers to turn cash into crypto and then back again. Spot trading was easy for crypto novices to understand:

All they had to do was buy bitcoin with a bank account and hope that the price would increase, so that they could then cash out with a profit.

But FTX went a lot further: It allowed people to take the same kind of high-risk, high-reward bets that Sam did himself at Jane Street. FTX mostly functioned as a derivatives exchange, allowing experienced traders to not just buy bitcoin directly but bet on its future movement. FTX offered options, futures, and swaps: classic Wall Street financial products used by sharks to gamble big on which way the market was headed. These gamblers bet not just their own money but were able to borrow from the exchange itself, in order to maximize their victories—and their losses.

———

While promising big returns can help draw in new customers, brand-new exchanges face steep uphill battles to onboard people because of network effects. Traders want to be where the action is because exchanges without volume suffer from price volatility. In small pools of money, every big transaction can spur huge price swings.

But FTX had a crucial leg up in this regard: Alameda Research, which was trading hundreds of millions of dollars a day, was ready to inject lots of that capital onto the platform. At the time, Sam led both companies from the same Hong Kong office; they were essentially one unit. Alameda became FTX's main market maker, meaning it always served as a buyer or a seller for FTX customers, no matter the conditions. Caroline Ellison, who had become one of Alameda's most important traders, would later say that Alameda's primary goal in FTX's early days was to market-make for the exchange and stabilize prices. "It was not the most fun thing because the reward was if you do well, there's liquidity on FTX," she said on the FTX podcast in 2021. "As a trader the most fun thing is to, like, make money."

Sam also forced trading firms that wanted to trade with Alameda's OTC desk—for "over the counter" deals that were settled directly between two parties—to complete their transactions on FTX. This brought big traders onto the platform and gave the appearance that this new exchange was already facilitating major deals. By May 2019, Alameda accounted for half of all of FTX's volume.

The cozy relationship between FTX and Alameda raised many eyebrows. Such a dynamic would not be allowed in traditional finance, Mark, a crypto executive whose trading firm worked with FTX and who asked to be referred to by a pseudonym told me. That Alameda traded against FTX users while simultaneously running the exchange was akin to a major law firm running a courthouse. On July 31, 2019, a skeptical user wrote to Sam on Twitter: "How are you going to resolve the conflict of interest of running your own derivative exchange AND actively trading against the market at the same time?" Sam responded quickly: "Alameda is a liquidity provider on FTX but their account is just like everyone else's."

This was a blatant lie. The very same day, Sam directed Gary Wang to write a custom bit of code that allowed Alameda to carry a negative balance on FTX. Alameda could now borrow from the pool of FTX customer funds without anyone knowing about it.

The funds of Alameda and FTX customers mixed freely in several different ways. FTX didn't even have its own bank accounts for a year, because most U.S. banks were incredibly leery of crypto. Sam joked on a 2021 podcast that if he had named Alameda "We Do Cryptocurrency Bitcoin Arbitrage Multinational Stuff," most banks would have shut their doors. Even those potentially interested in taking Alameda on as a client would have forced it to undergo an excruciating due diligence process. But Sam did not want to endure any sort of costly and time-consuming due diligence, especially because his risk-management protocols were already so poor. So instead, FTX's top lawyer, Dan Friedberg, set up a bank account with the California crypto-focused Silvergate Bank called North Dimension, which didn't mention FTX in its filing papers at all. North Dimension, Friedberg asserted, was its own trading firm that held its own assets. This was not true. North Dimension was controlled wholly by Alameda, and existed for Sam to hold and control deposits from FTX customers. These customers had no idea that when they sent their hard-earned money to FTX, it was being controlled by Alameda, via a sham bank account.

By the end of 2021, the North Dimension account had received at least $1 billion in customer deposits, which were comingled with an assortment of other Alameda funds. Once the money came into the house, it didn't matter where it came from: It was all Sam's to play with.

———————

In 2019, FTX received a crucial mark of approval via an investment worth roughly $100 million from Binance, the leading crypto exchange. But FTX was still struggling to break through the middling pack of crypto exchanges despite Alameda's concerted efforts to prop it up. Even in the summer of 2020, FTX had about five thousand users and "practically no volume," Sina Nader, the company's head of partnerships, would later tweet. FTX's first adopters had been experienced day traders, large firms, and quant whizzes like Sam himself. ("By traders, for traders," went the company's tagline.) They provided action, but no excitement or outward growth. Sam needed FTX to expand, to be adopted not just by the whales but by the minnows as well.

So that summer, FTX acquired Blockfolio, a portfolio tracking app, for $150 million, in the third-largest crypto company acquisition ever. Blockfolio's mobile-only app was one of the first major crypto projects to break through with the masses, with more than 6 million cumulative downloads. FTX's intentions were clear: Blockfolio's CEO, Edward Moncada, predicted that the deal would precipitate a "big mainstream wave coming in" to the exchange. With the acquisition of Blockfolio, everyday people could use a streamlined interface that would allow them to easily take the same kind of high-flying risks that professional traders did on FTX. Sam's exchange allowed people to borrow one hundred times the amount they put in, opening up highly leveraged positions that could prove disastrous in the event of a margin call (the automatic forfeiting of funds after a failed trade using borrowed funds).

Sam encouraged this sort of behavior and not just because it would put more money into his pockets. He complained constantly to his friends and employees about how most people were too risk-averse. When Tristan

Yver, a future FTX employee, flew to Hong Kong for a job interview, one of the first things that Sam told him was: "If you really want to make a difference in the world, you can't do it by being careful and cautious."

Sam expounded on this mindset even more starkly on a 2022 podcast, when its host, Tyler Cowen, posed a thought experiment: Would Sam risk a 49 percent chance of the annihilation of the Earth if there was a 51 percent chance of doubling the Earth and all of its wonder? Sam immediately said yes. When Cowen asked if Sam would make the bet a second time if the first bet was successful, Sam said yes again.

Having such a mindset would inevitably destroy the Earth, Cowen argued. Sam replied evenhandedly that even if that was true, there was also a chance that placing the bet over and over could lead to an "enormously valuable existence."

In 2021, this sort of approach led the tech writer Mario Gabriele to describe Sam as the "prince of risk." And Sam's strategies were only getting riskier. Alameda had initially specialized in arbitrage, a strategy that is supposed to have no risk at all. But as crypto got bigger, and more sophisticated trading firms like Tower and XTX entered into the crypto market, Alameda's edge over other crypto traders began to shrink. "As real institutions get involved, they have massively better connectivity than we do, and we're just totally outclassed," Sam admitted on a 2022 podcast.

So Alameda began to traffic in bolder strategies. It offered yield farming—an opaque and Ponzi-like investment approach of depositing tokens in crypto protocols to generate passive interest—and debt and equity investments. "It was embracing the mindset of, 'Great, I'm gonna go out and look for whatever the weirdest, dumbest thing people are talking about today—and that's gonna be the thing I'm working on,'" Caroline Ellison said on *The FTX Podcast* in 2021.

One of Alameda's most common strategies during that era looked an awful lot like a vulturous practice commonly known as a pump-and-dump scheme. (Jordan Belfort, the subject of *The Wolf of Wall Street*, had deployed similar tactics a couple decades earlier.) Alameda would invest in a new crypto project and, in exchange, receive a stash of the project's crypto token. Alameda would use its social media presence and deep industry connections to generate hype for the project, thus raising the price of the token, and then list a futures contract of the project to trade on FTX. But once the project was on the public market, Alameda would then sell off its tokens at the inflated price for a profit, which would cause the token's value to plummet immediately.

"Every single time I saw Alameda being involved in a project, they'd launch at a very high price and then it would just be down only," says MacLane Wilkison, an early crypto founder who was heavily involved in DeFi (decentralized finance) at the time. Wilkison says that this practice was not necessarily illegal. But he described it as "just kind of crappy and unethical, and explicitly taking advantage of these retail [regular individual] investors that they would essentially dump these overpriced tokens on very quickly."

After observing these tactics, Wilkison says he started to advise his portfolio companies to avoid doing business with Alameda. He concluded they were "finance people who had no ideological alignment with the crypto space at all, and were just in it to extract as much money as they possibly could."

Christine Chew says that before she joined FTX, she understood Alameda to have a reputation of being "dumpers . . . that would just sell all of your coins." But still, she said that young crypto companies accepted Alameda's bargain because of the benefits of being listed on a platform like FTX and being associated with Alameda, which was generally respected—if not feared—in the crypto world by that point. By June 2019, Alameda was trading $600 million to $1 billion a day, making it one of crypto's largest liquidity providers.

"Alameda was always on the cutting edge of what's new," says Alex Pack. "And that could get risky, because what if you run out of ideas? What if you get sloppy?"

At the end of 2020, as Beeple was making his first millions, Alameda plunged into even riskier strategies. Instead of trading the minor ups and downs of a market, Alameda instead borrowed huge amounts of money to place massive long-term bets on parts of the crypto ecosystem, from altcoins to risky startups. To take the first route was "wasting time," Caroline Ellison wrote on Twitter in early 2021. "The way to really make money is figure out when the market is going to go up and get balls long before that."

This strategy was a lot less complicated than Alameda's previous hustle of finding arbitrage opportunities to squeeze money out of differences in valuations around the world. In 2021, for instance, Alameda co-CEO Sam Trabucco tweeted that the trading firm had bet on Dogecoin—a jokey meme cryptocurrency—simply after "noticing how it goes up when Elon tweets."

This type of thinking was emblematic of the most extreme type of crypto degenerate, says Mark, the anonymous crypto exec. "When you're investing in crypto, your mind is not thinking about what happens in the worst case scenario," he says. "Sam was always thinking about 'I just need the maximum amount of funds, because that gives me leverage for everything else I want to do.'"

Going "balls long" was an unusual route forward for a market maker in crypto and carried a lot more risk. If crypto continued to expand, then Alameda would rake in massive returns. But if crypto contracted significantly, then Alameda could be liquidated all at once. Essentially, Sam had stepped up to the roulette table and put all of his money on red. It was now his responsibility to do everything in his power to make sure the ball landed there.

CHAPTER 13

Shitcoins

I n earlier eras of Wall Street, day traders and stockbrokers could hide behind a veneer of respectability that seemed to set them apart from degenerate gamblers at craps tables or horse races in Las Vegas. But financial speculation and gambling are nearly identical in their psychologies, wrote the economist Edward Chancellor in his book *Devil Take the Hindmost*. Both, he wrote, are "addictive habits which involve an appeal to fortune, and are often accompanied by delusional behavior."

And in 2021, delusional behavior propelled the Wall Street Bets craze, when Reddit day traders sent the price of GameStop soaring upward in a way that had absolutely nothing to do with the profit margins of the video game store. Meme stocks like GameStop usually didn't have inherent worth. Investors understood that they could lose all their value if their community lost faith. But the right meme stock might multiply by ten, a hundred, or a thousand, as long as enough people kept believing.

Sam saw this behavior and decided to try to tap into its unruly and potentially profitable energy through the embrace of meme coins: crypto's answer to meme stocks. Sam not only listed these hyper-volatile coins with dubious staying power on FTX but also created a whole subgenre of them that became known as Sam Coins. The fate of his empire would soon rest upon them.

There are about twenty-three thousand cryptocurrencies in existence, and that number is ever climbing. Beyond the top two of bitcoin and ether, a slew of cryptocurrencies with random and varied origins have gained value. Some of their creators are idealistic; others shamelessly greedy.

Several cryptocurrencies exist to power their own blockchains, mirroring the way that ether powers Ethereum. AVAX, for the blockchain Avalanche, and ADA, for the blockchain Cardano—created by Ethereum cofounder Charles Hoskinson—are the coins of the realm for new digital frontier settlers, who hope to one day rival Ethereum with their own thriving communities.

Then there is a subset of cryptocurrencies known as meme coins— or more profanely, shitcoins—because their value derives not from any specific mechanics or attributes inherent to the coin, but from the whims of their admirers and detractors on social media. Dogecoin and Shiba Inu are two examples. Their health was not tethered to any larger blockchain or ecosystem, but instead rose and fell in sharp spikes in 2021 due to Twitter feeding frenzies and co-signs from figures like Elon Musk.

Meme coins, while flighty and often frustrating, were oddly empowering to some small-time investors, who now felt like they could impact markets for the first time. By buying into a meme coin and promoting it on social media, they could help perpetuate and extend its narrative— and make themselves richer. Every holder had a duty and incentive to convince the next wave of investors to buy in.

Illia Polosukhin, the cofounder of the blockchain NEAR, says that meme coins were a prime example of a phenomenon in crypto in which individual incentive ran counter to those of the larger group. "The individual incentive is to try to play the game. You know it's complete bullshit, and you know it's going to crash," he says. "But if you're not the last one out, that's great—you made money."

Vitalik Buterin mostly dismissed meme coins as a trivial and counterproductive part of the crypto ecosystem. When he was gifted $6.7 billion worth of Shiba Inu tokens in a marketing stunt in 2021, he immediately offloaded them, explaining that he wanted to give some to charity and surrender his role as a "locus of power." Sam Bankman-Fried also said publicly that meme coins probably didn't have any inherent worth. "There is no sense that any reasonable person could look at Dogecoin and say, 'yeah, discounted cash flow,'" he told the podcaster and economist Tyler Cowen.

But this lack of fundamentals actually intrigued him. "I think there is something bizarre and wacky and dangerous, but also powerful about that," he continued. "There is no pretense anymore that there is any real sense of how would you price this thing other than supply and demand."

Besides, the value of other traditional assets was nearly as hollow, Sam argued. The value of art fluctuated based upon wispy hunches and the endorsement of art influencers. So did many stocks that served as the backbone of the American financial system. As an example, Sam told Cowen that he considered Elon Musk's greatest achievement not Tesla or Starlink but the stock TSLA, whose growth far outpaced the actual number of cars sold, thanks to Musk's outsize bravado on Twitter. TSLA ostensibly tracked a real project, but Sam argued it was closer to a meme coin fueled by Musk's personal aura.

Sam hoped to take this idea to its logical, vacuous end: to conjure cryptocurrencies that surfed high upon the hearts and minds of their followers. Thus, the Sam Coins were born.

The first and most important Sam Coin was FTT. FTT was the native token of FTX and was spun up along with the exchange. Many other exchanges also created native tokens, like Binance's BNB, in order to get customers to aid their growth and feel some sense of loyalty. FTT allowed its holders to pay fewer fees on FTX Trading. Sam pledged to sweeten the deal for FTT holders by buying some of the coin and burning it (aka destroying it) every week, thus reducing its supply and increasing its value. This mechanism was seen as a very good deal for holders, who felt that the company was taking active steps to make their bags more valuable.

But while FTT did dole out minor perks for traders, its value was more psychological: It served as a pseudo-stock for FTX. To buy FTT was to buy into the idea that FTX's usage would continue to soar— and to bet on Sam himself.

Some minor traders did profit off FTT, at least in the early days. But the prime beneficiary was Sam himself, for reasons that he baked right into the project. First, Sam dictated that more than half of the total circulation of FTT would not be released to the public, but slowly meted out to

Alameda Research over several years. Because only a small percentage of FTT's total volume was actually available for trade, even a small amount of trading could drive up its price very fast and could make the entire ecosystem look huge.

To explain this dynamic: Let's say you bring five hundred oranges to a remote island but only sell one hundred of them to the people there. Because of the limited supply, people might be willing to pay $3 an orange. You could then boast that the rest of your four hundred oranges, sitting in your warehouse, are collectively worth $1,200. But if you had released all five hundred oranges at the same time, the island residents would probably have been willing to pay less per orange, due to the five-times increase in supply of the fruit. They might be only willing to pay 60 cents for each one, meaning your lot is actually only worth $300.

By holding on to the supply and then slowly unlocking coins, Sam could say that FTT was far more valuable than it actually was. The demand for FTT was low—but it looked much higher because its supply was artificially low. And unlike an orange that could be held and eaten, FTT had been literally created out of thin air.

Sam also used a much simpler method to goose the price of FTT: He directed Alameda to buy the token so that its price would increase. Caroline later testified that Sam told her that FTT shouldn't fall under a dollar for psychological reasons, and instructed that Alameda should buy the token if its value ever dipped below that threshold. This was market manipulation, plain and simple.

While not many people actually bought FTT, these strategies paid off for Sam handsomely. Because Sam controlled millions of FTT tokens and had taken steps to push their worth above a dollar, his perceived wealth ballooned into ten figures. Alameda Research came to own an enormous larger reserve—and the majority—of the token, as it was the recipient of periodic FTT disbursements from FTX's proverbial vault.

So as FTX burned FTT and increased its value—theoretically to the benefit of traders—it more acutely increased the enormous holdings of Alameda and Sam. While these stashes of FTT looked like billions of dollars on paper, they were worth much less in reality. If Sam had actually tried to cash them out, the token's shallow market would have been flooded, and its price would have plummeted immediately.

So how could Sam and Alameda weaponize this pile of crypto if they couldn't truly spend it? Sam found a clever solution: to allow traders on FTX to use FTT as collateral to trade futures on margin. Traders, including Alameda, could use this fake, inflated coin as collateral for other cryptocurrency bets made with borrowed money. If the value of those secondary cryptocurrencies increased, the traders could make an enormous amount of money extremely quickly.

Alameda also flaunted FTT to convince lenders to give them bigger loans. Sam directed Caroline to put Alameda's enormous stash of FTT on its balance sheet, despite her hesitations, in loan applications to lending firms like Genesis, which took the bait and started lending out billions to Alameda, securing FTT as collateral.

Around early 2020, Gary Wang ran a database query and found that Alameda had a negative balance on FTX of $200 million—some $50 million more than FTX's entire revenue. (This was allowed because Gary himself had coded in an exception into the system several months before that allowed Alameda to run negative.) Gary became worried that Alameda was simply taking the money of FTX customers and confronted Sam about it. Sam responded that it was fine, because FTX's loans to Alameda were collateralized by FTT.

That $200 million debt would soon balloon, as Alameda borrowed more and more money from the pool of FTX customers to make investments and pay back debts. Some of FTX's other major clients were also allowed to take out lines of credit from the exchange—but Gary had coded in limits so that they could not extract more than a specified amount, which rarely surpassed $25 million. Alameda, in contrast, was borrowing hundreds of millions of dollars, and Sam kept asking Gary to raise Alameda's cap so they could take out even more. After several requests, Gary set Alameda's credit limit so high that he would never have to move it again: $65 billion.

FTT was now a vastly important element of Sam's empire. He had spun up the coin and inflated its value by putting his finger on the scale of supply-and-demand mechanics. He gave oodles of the coin to himself and Alameda, increasing his perceived net worth and that of his hedge fund, and thus their stature in the world. Alameda used the coin as collateral to take massive, risky bets on other cryptocurrencies—and to borrow directly from FTX customers. "Maybe FTT should be the new global reserve currency," FTX tweeted in January 2021, alongside a graph displaying the token's recent dramatic increase in price.

FTT was just the first of the Sam Coins. In 2020, Sam became acutely interested in Solana, a small blockchain that prioritized speed and volume in a way that Ethereum, its more established rival, did not. Ethereum was experiencing major growing pains: the more people used the network, the more they had to pay in massive congestion fees in order for their transactions to go through. At the time, Ethereum was processing roughly twelve transactions per second. Sam argued that if the end goal was for blockchains to replace the key infrastructure that underpinned Visa, Google, Amazon, and more, it would need to process a million transactions a second.

To solve this problem, Sam could have tried to work directly with or fund Ethereum developers working on solutions to increase its throughput. But it was becoming clear that Sam held a very different vision of crypto than Ethereum's main founder, Vitalik Buterin. In December 2020, the two crypto titans had engaged in a polite (if strained) tête-à-tête on Twitter about the differences between Ethereum and Solana. Ethereum prioritized censorship-resistance and decentralization, but their users were paying the price (literally). Bankman-Fried, conversely, argued that growth was the whole point, telling crypto reporter Brady Dale in early 2021 that scaling was "closer to being the only factor that matters."

So in the summer of 2020, FTX and Alameda became primary drivers of the fledgling Solana blockchain, similarly to how Alameda had propelled

FTX out of infancy a year earlier. FTX and Alameda were among Solana's earliest and largest investors, accruing hundreds of millions of dollars' worth of SOL, the native token of the blockchain. FTX devoted engineering resources to building crucial parts of the ecosystem, including Serum, a decentralized and ostensibly independent exchange, and Sollet, a crypto wallet.

Solana also allowed Sam to create a slew of new Sam Coins that he could use to inflate his perceived worth in the same way that he used FTT. Four tokens—Serum, $FIDA, $MAPS, and Oxygen Protocol—were all launched within an eight-month span between August 2020 and March 2021. Alameda had served as their main investors, leading funding rounds of $50 million for MAPS and $40 million for Oxygen. Sam listed those coins on FTX and gave some of them away to FTT holders, both to reward FTT holders and generate interest in these new Sam Coins. As he'd done with FTT, he held back the vast majority of the total volume of Sam Coins from entering the public market—sometimes more than 90 percent—to make the demand for them seem much higher than it actually was. (As manipulative as this seems, many crypto projects used similar tactics.) Then, he used some of those coins as collateral to trade way above his weight.

The whole point of blockchains was supposed to be decentralization. But Sam had almost single-handedly jump-started the Solana ecosystem. "Honestly, Solana did not have its first big break until Serum," early Solana investor Chris McCann said on a 2022 podcast. Solana soon became home to a growing community of developers and entrepreneurs who convened in conferences around the world. Fans of the blockchain dubbed it the "Ethereum killer" on Crypto Twitter and declared that SOL's price would "flip" (become more valuable than) ETH any day. Sam was weaponizing Sam Coins to not only make himself rich but to launch a siege on Vitalik Buterin's crypto kingdom.

———————

Vitalik watched Sam's rise anxiously. Vitalik hated centralized exchanges like FTX on principle: They were essentially crypto banks that replicated the institutions that Vitalik and Satoshi had hoped to overthrow in the first place. "I definitely hope centralized exchanges go burn in hell as much as possible," Vitalik told the attendees of a blockchain conference in 2018.

But Vitalik was an innately trusting person—perhaps too much so. He felt that it was his duty to welcome newcomers into the crypto space, especially those who might help encourage wider adoption. And unfortunately for him, centralized exchanges did an awfully good job of making buying crypto almost as easy as buying a stock on TD Ameritrade or Robinhood. Vitalik was also intrigued by Sam's focus on effective altruism and charity. So at the end of 2020, as Beeple was making his first millions, Vitalik agreed to appear on a panel with Sam organized by FTX titled, "Effective Altruism: Giving in Crypto." Each of them, along with the venture capitalist Haseeb Qureshi, pledged $50,000 to whichever of their causes garnered the most votes in a Twitter poll.

During the conversation, the pair disagreed politely on a number of issues, including the give-now-versus-give-later debate, and Ethereum's security versus Solana's speed. Vitalik later shared with me that he came away from the conversation lacking respect for Sam, but didn't necessarily view him as a major threat, either. "He was willing to have a strong 'ends justify the means' mentality," Vitalik recalls.

After the panel, Vitalik immediately sent his $50,000 to the SENS Foundation, which researches aging and had topped the Twitter poll, and notified Qureshi, who also sent his money over to the foundation. But according to Qureshi, Vitalik messaged him after a few days, writing, "I think Sam still hasn't paid."

"Huh, that's weird," Qureshi said. "I'm sure Sam is the richest of the three of us. Fifty thousand dollars was like him pulling a quarter out of his pocket." After several weeks, Qureshi says he was finally able to track down Sam and get him to send over the money.

CHAPTER 14

Sam's APE SZN

By the fall of 2021, Sam Bankman-Fried's primary business strategy had become clear: chase the latest crypto trend, extract as much profit as possible through dubious tactics, and then move on. He took risks through big investments and attempted to squeeze every ounce of expected value from every situation.

At that moment, the big bucks were in NFTs. They were fun, culturally relevant, and the ideal entry point for newcomers. OpenSea, the biggest platform for buying and selling NFTs, had just recorded a stratospheric $3 billion in sales volume over a thirty-day period. Perhaps, Sam thought, he could divert some of those users away from OpenSea and onto FTX itself.

Sam didn't care a lick about NFT art—or any art, for that matter. "Paintings, in general artwork: I actually don't get it. They all look dumb to me," he told an interviewer in October 2021. (He was no fan of literature, either: He hated Shakespeare.) But he did know that others cared about art and NFTs in a way that might increase his wealth. "A lot of these NFTs mean a lot to the people buying them," he explained. So two weeks after he dismissed NFTs as "going mainstream faster than the mainstream understands what it is they're adopting," he announced the creation of an FTX NFT U.S. marketplace. Sam's first NFT—an image of the word "TEST," which he drew in Microsoft Paint—sold for $270,000. The social media frenzy around the drop contributed to the soaring price of FTT, which surged to an all-time high of $83, more than triple its price in July.

Sam now proclaimed to *Bloomberg* in November 2021 that NFTs were in the "top category" of "what brought a non-crypto native audience to crypto." He excitedly auctioned off an NFT of an image of a tungsten cube, a type of metal block that had become a meme on Crypto Twitter. Sam also retweeted FTX employee Tristan Yver—the same person he had chastised for not taking enough risks—who claimed that buying a microbe-like NFT called a "babyblob" from FTX would be "to own a piece of NFT history."

Sam augmented his own NFT marketing blitz with a general company-wide publicity campaign. Yver appeared on the *Crypto Round Up Africa* podcast, where he bragged that FTX's NFT platform was a "more accessible market for everyone" compared to its competitors. Brett Harrison, the head of FTX US, hosted a Twitter Space to promote FTX NFTs with the ascendant crypto trader Su Zhu, whose Three Arrows Capital (3AC) was doling out billions of dollars in funds to crypto projects.

Christine Chew, the FTX employee, was excited about Zhu's appearance on the Space, as he was one of Crypto Twitter's biggest celebrities. "He'd always post funny tweets and inflammatory comments that made you want to look at them," she says. "I assumed he'd be some big brain math genius to grow 3AC from nothing to billions within a short amount of time."

In November, FTX assigned Christine to fly to Lisbon for the conference Solana Breakpoint, where she stood at a booth gushing about FTX NFTs for hours. At night, she followed her colleagues to parties in massive villas in the Portuguese countryside, where Jet Skis sat inside giant pools.

Two years later, Christine would look back cynically on FTX's NFT campaign. "That was the height of NFT mania, and FTX wanted to hop on that trend," she says. "It was mostly to entice people to download the FTX app, because in order to buy an NFT on FTX, you needed an FTX account. That was direct traffic to the exchange."

One person who fell precisely for this bait was Anthony Boyd, an American artist who was active in the Black NFT art community and Crypto Twitter. Boyd eagerly signed up for an FTX account because the company was running a sweepstakes where all new users would be entered into a drawing for a coveted CryptoPunk. When he won, he was ecstatic.

"You guys are the best. FTX customer for life," he tweeted to the company on September 1—the same day as the AfroDroids sale. A couple months later, Boyd sold the NFT for $207,000 and used the cash to pay off bills, send money to his grandmothers, and buy other NFTs, especially from Black artists, including some from the African NFT Community.

Boyd had only set up an FTX account to enter the sweepstakes. But he soon found that he actually liked using the platform to trade crypto. FTX had lower platform fees than Coinbase, which ate into his profit margins. FTX had a more intuitive interface and allowed him to experiment with automated trading: He could preset commands for his FTX account to buy or sell when a token reached a stipulated top or bottom of a range. The exchange promised users 8 percent interest on deposits. And it also offered other types of products, like event tickets and luxury goods, which telegraphed Sam's end goal of turning FTX into a super-app like WeChat in China, where customers could buy virtually anything.

"It was just convenient," Boyd says. "You could handle your trades, do your deposits. They were getting ready to implement NFTs. Everything was just all in one place."

But FTX's NFTs endeavor once again proved how Sam Bankman-Fried centralized crypto tools for his own profit. A key property of NFTs is that each buyer owns their digital goods directly on the block-chain without an intermediary. But when someone bought an NFT on FTX, it stayed on the exchange. To own an NFT on FTX was no different than to post a photo on Instagram—it would vanish if the company disappeared.

––––––––

Just as Boyd opened an FTX account for a CryptoPunk, many more opened FTX accounts for the platform's Bored Apes. The same 101 Apes that had been sold at Sotheby's in September for $24 million material-ized on the FTX NFT platform three months later. Sources told me that Alameda initially purchased the Apes as a trading strategy. It fit into the trading firm's overarching approach of wielding huge amounts of capital to make big purchases that could boost consumer confidence and swing the market upward, allowing Alameda to sell those assets for a profit.

Sure enough, the Apes increased significantly in value after the Sotheby's sale. The sale was considered a blue chip event, as Sotheby's involvement had bestowed prestige and institutional commitment onto an NFT project that many outsiders had once dismissed as juvenile or outright stupid. Michael Bouhanna, the head of digital art at Sotheby's, bragged on Twitter that the sale was "a great indicator of the level of confidence in this amazing NFT project."

The sheer price tag of the Sotheby's sale was equally impactful. Analysts predicted that the eventual winner of the auction would nab a per-Ape discount for buying the whole bundle. But Alameda had bought the Apes at a premium: almost 69 ETH ($241,515) per NFT, compared to other Apes available for 40 ETH elsewhere. The Sotheby's sale had seemingly proved that the Apes' worth was growing, and galvanized new investors to buy into the collection at higher prices.

Alameda leadership had initially bought the Apes as their own investment. But after internal discussions, executives realized that selling them on FTX might bring a wave of action and eyeballs to their new NFT platform. The 101 Apes materialized on FTX in December 2021.

Sam Bankman-Fried didn't publicly comment on the sale or own up to his company's involvement. It was clear, however, that the Apes aligned with his no-holds-barred mentality. He even had an "APE SZN" sign on his desk, signifying an unholy mixture of savagery, gang mentality, and faux commitment. He would continue to support the project in major ways. Several months later, FTX Ventures invested $50 million in the seed round of Yuga Labs, Bored Ape's parent company.

———

After the Sotheby's sale, the Apes continued their dizzying, perplexing ascent into the cultural stratosphere. In September 2021, Jenkins the Valet—the Bored Ape everyman whose stories featuring other Apes went viral on Crypto Twitter—signed to Creative Artists Agency, joining the ranks of Beyoncé and Justin Bieber. (Yes, you read that right: The Ape, not his creators, had an agent now.) Jenkins's production company, Tally Labs, signed a book deal with the best-selling author Neil Strauss to pen the first Bored Ape novel centered upon Jenkins. The book, naturally, would be turned into NFTs that would make its investors money if it sold well. Jenkins's human owner, who went by Valet Jones on Twitter, told me that he wanted to make Jenkins "into the undisputed Web 3 Mickey Mouse."

The Apes took other routes to Hollywood. On November 10, 2021, Beeple appeared on *The Tonight Show Starring Jimmy Fallon*, where Fallon announced that he had bought his first NFT: a Bored Ape, which he had bought through the crypto payments company MoonPay, Fallon enunciated. In January 2022, Fallon dedicated several minutes of an interview with Paris Hilton to the Bored Ape Yacht Club, during which they each held printouts of their Apes aloft to a confused and nervously giggling crowd. Fallon's sailor cap–wearing Ape reminded him of himself, he said, because "I love yacht rock and being breezy."

Many *Tonight Show* viewers sensed something was amiss. Here were two celebrities using their platforms on national television to promote ugly cartoons, without being able to articulate in the slightest what they were or why they were valuable. Clips of the interview were crucified on Twitter. Almost a year later, Fallon, Hilton, Yuga Labs, and MoonPay were all hit with a class action lawsuit for promoting the asset without complying with disclosure requirements. The suit alleged that MoonPay had gifted the Apes to Fallon and other celebrities in exchange for promotion. Bored Ape had infiltrated Hollywood in part via Guy Oseary, Madonna's well-connected manager who had taken the Bored Ape founders Wylie Aronow and Greg Solano on as clients. (In a sign of how small the crypto world is, it was Beeple himself who introduced Oseary to Aronow and Solano.)

Fallon's shout-out, however vapid, reinforced the idea that the Apes had gone mainstream. They had just surpassed the CryptoPunks—long considered the king of PFP projects—in floor price value, with the cheapest Apes reaching roughly $217,000. Within months, the CryptoPunks bent the knee to their rivals: Their creator, Larva Labs, sold the rights to the whole Punks collection to Yuga Labs. The acquisition signaled that the Apes' "utility"-driven commercial model had triumphed unequivocally over the Punks' artistic, countercultural bent.

In December 2021, a Bored Ape Yacht Club party in Brooklyn featured performances from Questlove, Chris Rock, and the Strokes. From the stage, Strokes frontman Julian Casablancas expressed bewilderment about why, exactly, he was there. "This is kind of about art, right? NFTs? I don't know, what the hell," he said. "All I know is . . . a lot of dudes here tonight."

Casablancas's snark notwithstanding, the Apes were now the ultimate crypto status symbol: Celebrities who posted their Bored Apes on social media included Madonna, Steph Curry, Snoop Dogg, and Gwyneth Paltrow. Blockchain evidence shows that Paltrow, the rapper Lil Baby, and others received their Apes from MoonPay, with no on-chain sign of the celebrities actually paying for them. Still, other collectors who actually paid for their Apes were happy to pay the absurd prices for the prestige. This phenomenon is known as the Veblen Effect: the idea that luxury items paradoxically become more coveted the more that they cost. The Veblen Effect has long been present in the modern art world, causing wealthy collectors to buy works of art without any affinity for the art itself. Don Thompson wrote in *The $12 Million Stuffed Shark* that "there is almost nothing you can buy for £1 million that will generate as much status and recognition as a branded work of contemporary art—at that price maybe a medium-sized Hirst work." In crypto, Bored Apes were the new Damien Hirsts. Buyers gained instant access to an elite crypto social club full of celebrities and millionaires. And the centrality of art in the NFT world had been replaced by sheer wealth-signaling. In the first quarter of 2022, the volume of dollars traded on NFT collectibles like Bored Apes and CryptoPunks was almost ten times the size of NFT art sales.

The crypto devotees and NFT artists who had entered the space for more idealistic reasons sensed this cultural shift. "It was the greediest project ever," Liam Vries says of the Bored Apes. "It sucked up a lot of finance out of the system, and ended up monopolizing it."

Christine Chew attended a Bored Ape party in Singapore during a

2022 crypto conference called Token 2049. "It was a pretty boring bunch of people flexing on their diamond necklaces and watches," she remembers. "They made Bored Apes their entire personalities."

Michail Stangl, a curator at the alternative NFT platform Zora, was similarly disgusted with the Apes. "Nobody accounted for the moonboys and the Bored Apes, which immediately turned a technology with incredible potential to liberate into a toxic pile of dung," he said.

The Bored Apes had risen in part due to the self-serving machinations of Sam Bankman-Fried.

CHAPTER 15

Total Rug

The Bored Apes cast a long shadow over Owo Anietie's AfroDroids when they hurtled into the world in September 2021. Within hours of selling out, AfroDroids NFTs started getting flipped on OpenSea for thousands of dollars, with new investors FOMO-ing into the project in case it became the newest PFP project to go to the moon. One unique X-ray AfroDroid was sold for 10 ETH ($37,877), or 142 times the original sale price. Among the highest-selling Droids were those with Bored Apes on their face screens. Michael Keen's integration strategy had worked smashingly. Within two days, over $1 million in ether (284 ETH) was generated for Droids via OpenSea trades.

The enthusiasm continued for several weeks. Collectors excitedly created fan art and posted pictures of their Droids on Twitter, comparing their outfits side-by-side to those of celebrities like Snoop Dogg and Rihanna. Other holders tweeted as if they *were* their Droids: "We are very happy to be here meeting and learning from the remaining humans here on planet earth," wrote one collector on Twitter. "Hopefully we Droids can help to save this planet."

By mid-September, the AfroDroids Discord had over eighteen thousand members. Inside the group, holders excitedly joined smaller chat rooms based on their Droid's attributes, preening over their bucket hats and pizza icons. Droid holders attended virtual watch parties of sci-fi films like *Chappie* and *Galaxy Quest*. The fervor around the Droids swept up several celebrities, including the rapper French Montana and the actor Drake Bell, who both bought into the project.

Owo was hailed as the leader of a social movement. He was the dream of NFTs fulfilled in the flesh: an African artist who had independently created a globally beloved project without the support of Sotheby's, art galleries, or Hollywood, and who lifted up his community along the way. One buyer, a teacher in New York City, incorporated AfroDroids into their lesson plans to teach students about robotics and hereditary traits. Another superfan, named Krystal, compared hearing Owo talk about AfroDroids to listening to Martin Luther King.

Owo was grateful that Liam Vries, who had kick-started the whole NFT African movement half a year prior, remained central to AfroDroids. Liam had lent Owo an art piece—which featured a bejeweled crown and a pair of colorful wings—that appeared on the faces of some of the most valuable NFTs in the project. Liam also created a series of lush, psychedelic pieces inspired by the Droids, which sold for hundreds of dollars as NFTs on OpenSea. The pair usually chatted twice a week, giving each other advice about navigating their new leadership roles.

Owo felt dazed for the first few weeks, and he felt strangely afraid to touch his portion of the money, which was over $1 million worth of crypto. He worried that somehow if he tried to take it all out, the whole thing would be exposed as an illusion or a long con. Sometimes he woke up in the middle of the night and stared at the seven-figure number on his computer screen, wondering if it was real.

―――――――――

While AfroDroids lapped up public accolades, its financial peak, it would turn out, was launch day. Many degens who minted Droids turned around and sold them immediately. They didn't really care about the project, but had just seen it as a way to make a quick buck. Their sales pushed the price down, which caused others to scramble to sell their Droids. But because there was dwindling interest from new buyers on the secondary market, the price continued to dip every day.

Such a trend was all too common in the crypto space. Almost a quarter of all tokens with significant volume in 2022 exhibited pump-and-dump behaviors, according to Chainalysis. Especially at this peak of NFT mania, most projects found it extremely difficult to maintain interest from new collectors, since there was always a newer, shinier NFT to capture their attention.

As the AfroDroids price dropped, collectors started expressing their anger on Discord. They demanded that Owo do something about it. These demands initially perplexed the new million-dollar man. Previously, his collectors were simply fans of his work who had bought his art pieces with no strings attached. For months, NFTs had centered on artists like Beeple and the Vancouver-based creator Fvckrender, who sold artworks with no expectation they get involved with their value going forward. In contrast, many of the newfound AfroDroids holders—trained by the utility-driven model of Yuga Labs' Bored Ape Yacht Club—acted more like shareholders, who spent thousands of dollars specifically because they believed that they could eventually flip their Droids at a profit. They laid the responsibility for their investments' failure at Owo's feet.

Flummoxed, Owo reached out to the NFT Catcher marketing team, including Michael Keen, for solutions. He found them almost entirely disengaged. "After everybody got their money, the team we dropped with was radio silent," Owo says. "You thought you were really working with people who understood what we're trying to build. After the project went live, most of those people were like, 'Eh, whatever.'" The members of the NFT Catcher team had arranged that they be written into the smart contract royalties: Keen, for instance, had nabbed 6.99 percent of the sale, which netted him around $200,000 on September 1. After that, he and others had a much weaker incentive to stick around.

Keen would later partially blame the project's slippage on its aesthetics, which didn't quite match the public's demand. "I think the art might have been a tiny bit redundant throughout the collection," he says. "A lot of the ones that stayed relevant were little cute things: Doodles, Cool Cats, Pudgy Penguins. These were big, strong, brass-faced."

Macro-economic forces didn't help matters. In terms of sheer sales, AfroDroids could hardly have picked a better release date than September 1, which coincided with the top of a frenzied NFT bull run. Bitcoin hovered around $50,000, and ether around $4,000. September 2021 was the biggest month for NFT art ever, with $881 million in primary and secondary sales.

"That was the time when if you caught a mint, you were basically guaranteed profit," remembers Owo's adviser CryptoWizard. "You started to see a lot more degens passing themselves off as Web 3 technology enthusiasts. But it also meant that the focus wasn't about which project actually followed through and delivered something. It was just like 'there's always a new one to mint, and the mint's always a good flip during the bull run.'"

In mid-September, the market dipped once again, and the traders who had invested too ambitiously in the previous weeks found themselves over-leveraged. In order to cover their outstanding loans, many panic-sold projects at a loss, especially ones they felt would not succeed. That included AfroDroids.

The vibes among remaining holders soured, especially in the Discord channel. Owo had disliked spending time on Discord from the start: He wanted to spend time on art, not self-promotion. But the NFT Catcher team had instructed him to spend more time on Discord in order to keep his buyers engaged. To Michael Keen and his colleagues, the constant selling of the project mattered more to its success than its fundamentals.

So Owo dutifully logged into the Discord group, and found it filled with ire and accusations that he was a scammer. "This is a total rug LOL," wrote one buyer named Ely Trader, who had scooped up forty Droids on the day of launch for around $10,000 and found they couldn't flip them a week later. (A "rug pull" was a type of crypto scam in which a team of founders generated hype for an NFT project or crypto token, only to immediately run off with all the proceeds of the initial sale and disappear.)

"Charity was a big part why I invested, but also invested to make money. Anyone who says otherwise is lying," wrote the aptly named user ScroogeMcDuck. "We are stuck and can't get out. . . . It's not my job to do anything more, y'all got paid millions to be able to execute."

These investors wanted more from Owo: more visibility on Twitter, more free airdrops, different art, anything to get the price up. Perhaps more than anything, they wanted AfroDroids to be more like the Bored Apes. "In general, they needs more AGGRESSIVE look," one Discord user wrote on September 14. "MY BEST PROPOSAL for now is to do the step like in Bored Apes, at the beginning they were more friendly and cute, but later they had a chance to be mutated if someone wants it."

Looking back, Owo acknowledged that the project probably should have had a chief technology officer or a business development team. But that sort of investment was rare for NFT projects at the time, especially for creators coming from the art world. Instead, the burden of managing the project, and especially social media, fell almost entirely to Esther Eze, Owo's cowriter and manager. Eze would spend all day on Discord, Clubhouse, and Twitter, trying to soothe the nerves of angry buyers and entice potential new collectors to enter the project.

Eze was already resentful because Owo had squeezed her percentage of AfroDroids revenue from 15 percent to 5 percent to accommodate the NFT Catcher team's share. That team had taken their money and largely vanished following the drop—and Eze was not getting paid for her continuing work. "All of the bad vibes and vitriol were being directed at me. I was falling ill, and I couldn't handle it," she says.

As Eze tried desperately to calm the nerves of owners, Owo tried many tactics to improve the project's "utility" based on his community's wishes. He implemented a "liquidity pool," modeled after DeFi (decentralized finance) exchanges, which allowed AfroDroids owners to stake their Droids and earn rewards. (The model was something like the certificate of deposit that banks offer.) Owo bought a plot in the metaverse world Cryptovoxels, believing that virtual real estate would increase in value as people gradually spent more time in the metaverse. He announced the formation of the First Continent Art Collective, a Web 3 incubator and production studio that would be fractionally owned by AfroDroids holders, so that "everyone here can continue to profit," he wrote on the AfroDroids Discord on November 3.

None of these actions had any real impact on the AfroDroids' price.

When Owo spent thousands of dollars more on a new marketing agency to replace the NFT Catcher team that had left, he found their ideas to be harebrained and unhelpful. Eze tried to calm the mounting rage while also forming connections with major NFT influencers. Influencers, like Farokh of Rug Radio, had become all-powerful gatekeepers of this new and allegedly decentralized industry. Their co-signs and promotional efforts could make or break an NFT project.

But prominent NFT influencers did not respond to Eze's queries. "When you want to broker a deal, they need to see we have something to give to them," she says. "Owo was just another African creator to them."

Eze felt overworked and underappreciated and considered quitting several times. Her final straw was when she learned that Owo had used some of his portion of the project's proceeds to buy a Bored Ape and a CryptoPunk for $619,000. Owo hadn't consulted with Eze: He felt that it was his decision and his money, and that the PFPs would boost his status in the crypto world and give him access to moneyed investors. He proudly changed his profile picture from an AfroDroid to his new CryptoPunk, which featured stringy hair covering a bald head, shifty blue eyes, and a gold stud earring.

But the decision was immediately crucified by AfroDroids holders, who felt Owo was abandoning his own community in favor of a more famous, profitable one. How could Owo ask them to commit fully to AfroDroids when he couldn't himself? Eze was similarly disgusted by Owo's investment in two garish JPEGs that had nothing to do with their project, especially given that she was the one absorbing the current wrath of the fan base. "All hell broke loose," she says. "And I was like, 'I'm out. I can't do this anymore.'"

The Bored Apes had hypercharged the AfroDroids; now they were threatening to wrench the project apart. When Eze told Owo she was leaving, Owo was enraged. He felt like his creative partner of over a year had abandoned him at his time of most acute need. The pair had an angry conversation, and their fruitful creative partnership was mostly over.

Without Eze, Owo felt overwhelmed and isolated. He felt guilty that his bank account was so flush while so many people had lost so much on their investments and thought he might have committed a crime. "It was like I was in one empty room screaming by myself and nobody could hear me," he remembers.

Before the drop, Owo's *Everyday* art pieces were filled with Droids in glimmering futurist settings. In the fall of 2021, these characters were replaced by desolate, moody landscapes and terrifying, lurking beasts: a giant squid tentacle, a menacingly curling horn, a skeleton standing over his own grave.

Owo didn't even realize how dark his work had become. But when an NFT artist friend pointed out how drastic the change was, Owo was overcome with the realization of his mental fragility. "After I sold out, I was so happy. But I was suddenly overcome by so much darkness," he says. "I feel like I'm by myself. All the people I trusted, maybe I shouldn't have trusted them."

As winter arrived in the northern hemisphere, yet another unexpected macro force weighed down upon AfroDroids: the perverse and byzantine U.S. tax code. Savvy crypto traders realized that they could pay fewer taxes on their crypto winnings in the calendar year of 2021 by abandoning some of their struggling NFT projects and then marking them as a loss. Relinquishing the NFT would allow them to dodge the tax bill for the original value of the asset. And if the project remained dormant, they could then buy in again in the new year at the same price or less.

To jump through the loophole, many people listed their AfroDroids for sale on OpenSea for highly discounted prices. Some even listed them for 0 ETH, practically begging someone to take a distressed asset off their books. "I don't understand what the aim of listing for '0' is. It hurts the project and the holders," Owo vented on Discord.

Within just three months of launch, Owo saw that the current version of AfroDroids—which was now driven by shameless price obsession and obtuse crypto concepts like tokenomics and yield mechanisms—was nearly diametrically opposed to his initial vision of Afrofuturist storytelling and charity. "I felt really disassociated from this beautiful thing I built," Owo says. "At some point, I wanted to forget about AfroDroids. It brought so much pain and anguish to me."

So the day after he complained that a Droid was listed for free, Owo announced his intention to step back from the community and reorient the project's strategy. The initial end-goal of the project's road map, after all, had been to create a movie, not play stock market games with JPEGs. The criticism he received on Discord was impacting his mental health and filling him with anxiety. He received racial epithets, taunts, and accusations that he was just a Nigerian scammer.

"Every day, you go into the space and people say, 'You failed,'" he says. "If you were in my shoes, would you want to be around people constantly telling you you're a failure?"

Owo's absence inflamed the community further. "It's all an illusion guys," a Discord member wrote. "He left with all the ETH."

Esther Eze, meanwhile, departed AfroDroids for a job with a newly created Nigerian crypto startup called Nestcoin. Nestcoin was founded by the Nigerian entrepreneur Yele Bademosi, who had previously worked for Binance and hoped to bring crypto adoption to the African continent via gaming, social media, and other avenues. Like many crypto entrepreneurs in late 2021, Bademosi was riding high, having just secured a pre-seed round of $6 million. Nestcoin's investors included none other than Alameda Research, which invested $250,000 in the startup in October 2021.

That was a small amount for Alameda compared to many of its other investments—and was also offset by Bademosi's decision to take his millions in VC cash and store it back on FTX itself. Bademosi didn't have many banking options at the time. Many Nigerian companies struggled to obtain U.S. bank accounts because of the widespread perception that Nigeria was a haven for scammers. And crypto companies struggled to obtain Nigerian bank accounts due to the central bank's resistance to crypto. Those two realities made it nearly impossible for Nestcoin to find a bank that would take them on as a client. But FTX was happy to take their money. And Bademosi trusted Sam, given his overwhelmingly positive public image, so he deposited his newly earned millions on the exchange. It was an eerily similar reflection of how FTX had turned to extralegal approaches to obtain bank accounts in its early days.

"FTX was positioned as an institutional exchange, founded by an American, which had raised money from top investors and was very close to regulators," Bademosi says. "You don't think that this is gonna be a problem."

CHAPTER 16

Philanthropist and Colonizer

Yele Bademosi's Nestcoin, which had just received funding from Alameda, and Owo's AfroDroids were just two elements of a rapidly expanding African crypto ecosystem. A Chainalysis study found Africa to be the third-fastest-growing crypto region in the world, behind North America and Western Europe. The study also found that African crypto markets were propelled disproportionately by retail transactions (under $10,000), meaning that more people with less money were converting their hard-earned dollars into these new tokens.

Africa was central to Sam's vision. Investing in the Mother Continent allowed him to play the role of both selfless philanthropist and digital colonizer. He felt he could do a large amount of good for cheap while also profiting off the urgent ambition of many in a young generation desperate to break out of cycles of disinvestment, authoritarianism, and poverty.

Crypto, Sam argued, could solve actual problems across the continent, like cross-border payments—sending money to someone in another country—and runaway inflation. But his vision of crypto on the continent was very different from the high-minded idealism of Vitalik Buterin: Sam was happy to take shortcuts in terms of security and centralization if it meant that more people bought in. "Decentralized, on-chain, trustless . . . Those are buzzwords," he declared at the 2021 Blockchain Africa Conference. Most newcomers to crypto, he added, "don't give a shit."

So in the middle of 2021, Sam ramped up the activities of FTX Africa, a new wing of his company dedicated to onboarding as many Africans to his exchange as possible. Harrison Obiefule, FTX's new PR and marketing manager in Africa, led a marketing blitz in person and online, including hiring micro-influencers to create content, staging NFT event showcases, and organizing regular Twitter Spaces for curious audiences. As the world emerged from the pandemic, FTX Africa funded a continental crypto education tour on university and polytechnic campuses. Obiefule was given an enormous budget and a long leash. "If I wanted a partnership to be done, I was one approval away from getting it," he says. "Anything you wanted to do was approved super fast. FTX was just free-flow: move fast and break things."

Obiefule centered his efforts in his home country of Nigeria, which made sense for many reasons. Nigeria was the continent's most populous nation, boasted Africa's highest GDP, and was home to one of the world's highest concentrations of young people. It ranked sixth overall on Chainalysis's 2021 global adoption index, and a 2022 CoinGecko study found Nigerians searched for crypto-related keywords on Google more frequently than people in any other English-speaking country. While FTX users fanned out across South Africa, Kenya, Ghana, and other African countries, Nigerian adopters led the way.

FTX Africa made courting the Nigerian youth a huge priority. It enlisted college students as FTX ambassadors, who were given their own budgets to put on crypto conferences. These ambassadors typically framed the events as general blockchain education seminars. But they also offered cash incentives to people who specifically opened FTX accounts—and received a 25–40 percent commission for those who did. The system sounded suspiciously like a multilevel marketing scheme.

Harrison Obiefule didn't have to work hard to find willing evangelists to spread the FTX gospel. Many young people across the continent were deeply disillusioned by traditional educational systems, slim career pathways, and financial instability. Annaelechukwu "Anthony" Nduka was one of those people: While studying at the University of Nigeria, Nsukka, he discovered crypto as a potential alternative to his daily grind and soon became an FTX campus ambassador at the public university. Ambassadors like Nduka earned $1 for every student who attended the meetups.

Nduka put on all-day events, attracting hundreds of people both from the college and across Enugu State. He led a seminar about blockchain basics, helped people set up FTX accounts, and gave away FTX shirts and hats. Thanks to events like these, FTX swag made its way across the continent in the form of tees, hoodies, and sweatpants. The company even distributed FTX condoms, which cheekily bragged on the wrapper: "Never breaks, even during large liquidations."

But as Nduka brought other students onto FTX, he was actually floundering in his own attempts to trade crypto profitably. At one juncture, he lost $500 in one day trading volatile cryptocurrencies. He realized that his crypto investments had lost more than they had earned overall. "I saw how stressful it is, and I made the decision to quit," he says. He would depart his FTX job in February 2022 in favor of jobs at various other blockchain companies that prioritized infrastructure and decentralization.

———

Another Nigerian who enlisted in Sam's continent-wide campaign was Anthony Olasele, who went by the online moniker Groovy. Olasele and a friend hosted a recurring Twitter Spaces show called *Crypto Round Up Africa*. Olasele was a crypto evangelist because the technology had already removed several barriers in his own life. In 2012, Olasele was one of over fifty thousand Nigerians studying abroad. When he arrived at Stamford International University in Bangkok to study mass communications, he found it was a headache to send money home. PayPal transactions were littered with fees. TransferWise, another global payments company, worked for a while—but stopped serving Nigeria after its government changed a fiscal policy in late 2020. The World Bank found that by late 2022, the average global fee of remittance payments was 6.3 percent. These fees essentially served as a "poor tax" levied on people in emerging economies. Crypto, in comparison, transferred instantly across national borders, and at any time of day, regardless of business hours. During the pandemic, when Olasele's college classmates had lost their jobs and were struggling to make money, he was able to send them lifelines via crypto without having to navigate a labyrinth of international banks.

Olasele also believed in the transformative power of stablecoins: cryptocurrencies that are designed to hold the value of a U.S. dollar. Stablecoins aren't all that useful for the average Westerner, who has unfettered access to real dollars or euros. While those currencies do suffer from inflation, they're still generally a good bet to hold value over time, especially compared to currencies in more volatile economies, like the Nigerian naira. In 2011, $1 USD was worth about 150 naira. A decade later, a dollar was worth 400 naira and rising. Any Nigerian family who kept their savings accounts in naira over that time frame would have seen their nest eggs shrink by over 60 percent.

Some people chose to hedge against inflation by buying U.S. dollar notes and stashing them in their mattresses. This rankled the Nigerian government, which felt this sort of behavior would only further devalue their currency. In 2016, the Central Bank of Nigeria proposed an amendment to make holding dollars illegal. Stablecoins provided another escape hatch. Starting in 2020, Olasele converted naira into stablecoins and stopped depositing money into Nigerian bank accounts altogether. "It became that my whole entire financial needs were being met by crypto," he says.

Stablecoins brought Olasele stability. Shitcoins brought him welcome surges of chaos. Olasele had become interested in meme stocks during the Wall Street Bets craze. He loved being on Twitter in all its raucous enthusiasm and tribalism, especially as he saw people making money hand over fist.

In May 2021, Elon Musk appeared on *Saturday Night Live* and delivered an entire *Weekend Update* spiel about Dogecoin, his meme coin of choice. Dogecoin had been created by two programmers as a joke in 2013, but it had jumped in value as people posted memes about it and bought in over the years. Musk called it an "unstoppable financial vehicle that's going to take over the world" before admitting to host Michael Che that it was a "hustle"—which perhaps allowed him to escape any accusations that he was giving unambiguous financial advice on national television.

Olasele watched the segment from his apartment in Madrid, Spain, and bought some Dogecoin. He thought it was obvious that Musk's speech would gain worldwide attention and boost the coin's price. Unfortunately, the exact opposite happened: The price of the coin immediately plummeted, perhaps because while newcomers bought in, even more Dogecoin holders rapidly cashed out in hopes of capitalizing on the newbies.

Olasele lost money on Doge. But many other coins rose dramatically during those halcyon bull run days, and Olasele's digital wallet ballooned. He didn't care much about whether his investments had inherent value: after all, the official currency of his homeland didn't seem to hold inherent value, either. "There are a lot of poor countries, and a lot of people in search of a better life would play sports betting," he says. "But there was definitely this other thing you could do, which was investing in crypto. So a lot of people started buying these shitcoins."

The shitcoins were skyrocketing. "If you buy $1,000 worth of a coin, you could have maybe $5,000 in a week or two. There was a lot of euphoria," he remembers. Olasele partied harder, dined at fancy restaurants, and sent money back home to his family. "You feel invincible, actually," he remembers. "You feel that you're such a genius: You just buy, and numbers go up."

Major unrest in Nigeria also convinced more young people to turn to crypto. In late 2020, a series of massive protests called the #EndSARS movement began in Nigeria, with the country's youth demanding the disbanding of the country's special anti-robbery squad (SARS). For decades, SARS was responsible for frequent brutality and the extrajudicial killings of citizens; they operated in plain clothes and would extort and torture civilians, according to Amnesty International. On October 20, 2020, tens of thousands of Nigerians gathered in Lagos, where the army shot dead at least a dozen peaceful protesters. They jailed many more and blocked the bank accounts of people and organizations they believed were linked to the campaign.

With no way to receive traditional funds via traditional banks,

#EndSARS organizers turned to bitcoin donations. Olasele sent bitcoin to the Feminist Coalition, one of the main organizations that provided financial support to the movement. This transaction served as fulfillment of one of Satoshi's promises: that bitcoin would be a censorship-resistant tool of financial freedom; a way to rebel against an unjust government oppressing its citizens.

By 2021, Olasele was using his social media platforms to praise blockchain technology, broadcast his trade strategies, and help his friends buy in. Olasele felt American tech titans had always viewed Africa as an afterthought in technological development, a charity case that needed saving. Crypto presented an opportunity to be on the front lines of a global revolution, to self-determine a brighter future.

One of the brightest parts of the African crypto ecosystem, Olasele believed, was FTX. The FTX Africa team was putting on exciting events and doing good work in the community, helping Nigerian schools raise money for tables, books, and chairs. On a September 2021 episode of *Crypto Round Up Africa*, Olasele and his cohost Oloye joked that Sam Bankman-Fried would soon amass enough power to buy the nation of Nigeria.

Previously, Olasele had done all his trading on Binance, FTX's largest rival. But in the fall of 2021, Olasele switched to FTX. He wanted to be part of Sam's rapidly expanding orbit. And FTX offered all sorts of perks. It advertised free withdrawals, while other platforms incurred fees. In the wake of the GameStop stock craze, FTX was one of the few major crypto exchanges to offer tokenized stocks, which track the value of shares in companies like Tesla and GameStop, giving Olasele the chance to participate in the global financial system.

FTX also allowed Olasele to trade futures: derivative assets whose value hinged on whether a cryptocurrency went up or down in the future. Olasele liked trading futures because it allowed him to make bets with borrowed money: to gamble far above the amount of crypto he actually owned in his account. In futures trading, he could very quickly multiply his winnings—or his losses. "There was a lot of dopamine to it," he says.

In order to borrow crypto for futures trades, exchanges required that Olasele put down collateral, which he would lose if the market turned against him. But while Binance required he use stablecoins as collateral, FTX allowed him to use all sorts of meme coins as collateral, some of which were even shadier and more speculative than Dogecoin. That included Sam Coins like Serum. "They didn't care: Everything was accepted," Olasele says.

This was a risky proposition. When Olasele had traded futures on Binance, there was only one volatile variable: the price of the asset he was betting on. When he traded futures on FTX, there were two: both the price of the asset and the collateral, which could also collapse overnight. "Your entire account can get blown up," Olasele says. "You can't really manage whatever exposure you have."

Alex Pack, the venture capitalist, says that the option to use meme coins as collateral on FTX—also known as cross-asset margining—was one of the features that made FTX so appealing. "That was how they got users," he says. But cross-asset margining was also extremely dangerous for the exchange itself: If it didn't liquidate users whose collateral had evaporated fast enough, then FTX could lose a lot of money. "You can start losing track of things. It can get very bad, very fast," Pack says. But in 2021, the prices of these meme coins and many obscure cryptocurrencies kept increasing—and Olasele, other traders, and FTX kept making money.

Olasele was so enamored with FTX that before long, he had turned *Crypto Round Up Africa* into a de facto FTX podcast. Olasele hosted FTX employees Tristan Yver and Tina Chen, FTX's head of global expansion, for free-flowing conversations that drew hundreds of listeners. "We were just using *Crypto Round Up Africa* to kind of shed more light on FTX," Olasele admits.

In October 2021, *Crypto Round Up Africa* pulled off a major coup and booked Sam Bankman-Fried himself. Olasele and his guest host Victor Asemota asked Sam for his opinion on African governments' regulatory stances, and how he was approaching getting more Africans to invest in cryptocurrency. "We're focusing more on ways we can make our brand stronger and more powerful," Sam told them. "How do we get not just people to have seen an advertisement, but to actually feel strongly about it?"

Olasele came away extremely impressed. "He seemed to have a good grasp on issues, especially with those that concerned Africa and crypto," he says. "He had really good answers and good visions for how to tackle some of these cross-border problems. I thought, 'This is a genius right in front of me.'"

There was something strange about the interview, however. Whenever Sam would speak, his answers would be accompanied by loud, frenetic plastic tapping. "I definitely cannot forget that constant clacking of the keyboard," Olasele says. "It gives this impression that he was multitasking: looking after a multibillion-dollar company while still giving you the benefit and time to have a conversation."

At the end of the call, Olasele referenced the crypto rallying cry "WAGMI," asking Sam for reassurance: "Are We All Gonna Make It?"

"I think it's looking pretty good," Sam replied.

CHAPTER 17

Playing Games

Yele Bademosi, the Nigerian cofounder of the crypto startup Nest-coin, who had just hired AfroDroids' Esther Eze, was feeling good, too. Flush with millions of dollars from venture capitalists and trading firms like Alameda Research, he began investing in a slew of different projects that he hoped would serve as crypto on-ramps for Africans. One of the on-ramps he believed in most fervently was a crypto game called Axie Infinity, a cartoon battle game that looked a lot like Pokémon at first blush.

Bademosi had started playing Axie Infinity a couple months earlier after seeing conversations about it dominate Crypto Twitter. He paid several hundred dollars to buy three cutesy monsters that resembled axolotls, the Mexican salamanders that held a hallowed place in Aztec lore. He started battling with them and recouped his initial investment in a couple months. Bademosi was amazed: Playing Axie seemed to be a money printer. "It was a no-brainer," he says.

In the middle of 2021, Bademosi was far from the only person to have come to this realization. Anthony Olasele raved about it on *Crypto Round Up Africa*. New Axie players around the world jumped into the game and earned thousands of U.S. dollars a month in crypto, allowing many to leave dead-end jobs and support their families. These new crypto gamers didn't have to understand complex concepts like proof of work or the blockchain; all they had to do was lead floating blob creatures in battle.

The success of Axie gamers seemed inarguable proof that crypto was maturing into a society-altering technology. "[Axie] empowers gamers to really own the things they're creating," Alexis Ohanian, a cofounder of Reddit and an Axie Infinity investor, told *Bloomberg* in August 2021. "This play-to-earn model is going to become the new normal. And what it's doing to empower people all over the world is actually really remarkable."

The "play-to-earn" model of gaming was a new-ish concept in crypto that aimed to revolutionize a gaming industry that was already worth billions of dollars in revenue every year. Elite gamers who played popular games like Fortnite or Dota 2 could make a living through sponsorships and revenue from streaming their games to online viewers. But these elite gamers made up a small fraction of all players, most of whom spent hundreds of hours leveling up their characters or collecting rare items with little to show for it except pride and bragging rights. In some games, like World of Warcraft, black markets sprouted up in which players bought and sold virtual items. But the games' watchful creators waged war on them in continual games of cat and mouse.

Crypto entrepreneurs believed they had a solution that let players earn money. What if characters and items inside games were NFTs: unique digital properties to be bought and sold? That way, if a gamer spent months leveling up a character to make it more powerful and then lost interest, they could sell it to another gamer and be rewarded for all their hard work.

Of course, these crypto mavens weren't only looking out for gamers' best interests. They also believed that gaming could provide an easy bridge to onboard people into crypto. Gamers were ideal potential customers because they were technologically savvy, chronically online, and reflexively understood concepts like digital value and scarcity. Gamers were growing in number and influence: Metaverse-like open worlds, including Minecraft and Fortnite, were serving as increasingly vital social spaces for tens of millions of teenagers. Entwining crypto with video games could spark the interest of young future investors while adding a badly needed element of fun to the crypto world.

It didn't hurt that gamers populated the highest ranks of crypto. Sam Bankman-Fried had been devoted to League of Legends as a teenager, while Vitalik Buterin was a World of Warcraft obsessive. They saw the world through the lens of solvable quests and strategic battles, and were inclined to shine a light on crypto games they liked and thought could succeed. Vitalik didn't have much time for games, but Sam did: He played League of Legends and other games during Zoom interviews and work calls. In the summer of 2021, Sam poured millions into crypto gaming projects. FTX paid $210 million to sponsor a professional e-sports team and inked a seven-year branding deal with a League of Legends tournament.

In August 2021, FTX cut a deal to support Axie Infinity. In Axie gameplay, each monster has certain strengths and weaknesses in battle. When Axies win face-offs or complete other tasks, their owners earn in-game currency called Smooth Love Potion (SLP), which can be exchanged for other cryptocurrencies. Players can also sell their Axies or spend SLP to breed new, more valuable monsters. Crucially, each Axie is an NFT. They are all unique and owned by players as opposed to the game's Vietnamese game maker, Sky Mavis. "We believe in a future where work and play become one," Sky Mavis declared on the Axie Infinity website. "We believe in empowering our players and giving them economic opportunities. Most of all, we have a dream that battling and collecting cute creatures can change the world. Welcome to our revolution." Sky Mavis earned money by taking a cut of in-game transactions and by sitting on a large stash of tokens that increased in value as the game increased in popularity.

For much of 2021, the company succeeded wildly in realizing its rousing vision. The game caught on like wildfire in the Philippines and other Southeast Asian countries, where local economies had been devastated by the pandemic. People left their call center jobs and pawned their delivery bikes to devote their lives to the game, sometimes earning thousands of U.S. dollars a month. In the beginning, few questioned whether the gold rush would last.

———————

One Axie player who entered the game in early 2021 was Samerson Orias, a twenty-five-year-old Filipino working as a line cook on the outskirts of Manila. Orias was earning about 4,000 pesos a month (about $80, less than half the national minimum wage) making takoyaki—Japanese octopus balls. But he desperately needed an escape from his financial woes: His mother had had a stroke and required medication, and electricity and grocery bills were stacking up.

Orias heard that his friends were earning money from Axie Infinity. But he did not have the hundreds of dollars of cash on hand needed to buy three Axies to enter the game. Instead, he heard about new in-game structures that had sprouted up called guilds, in which Axie owners leased out their monsters to "scholars," who actually played the game in order to level up the monsters and earn SLP. Scholars took a cut of those earnings without having to make a big initial investment. "Managers," as the Axie owners called themselves, would pocket 30 to 50 percent of the scholars' earnings without having to do much at all.

So in May 2021, Orias signed up to be a scholar with a manager based in Australia. The manager required Orias to earn a minimum of 120 SLP a day—which took five to six hours of game play—and pocketed half of Orias's earnings. Whether or not it was a fair business model, Orias didn't have much choice. His family needed money, and this slice of SLP was still better money than other job opportunities available to him. So he plunged into Axie, doing battle deep into the night. The SLP he earned allowed him to pay grocery bills and buy medication for his mother.

Khai Chun Thee, a twenty-one-year-old from Kuala Lumpur, Malaysia, also jumped headlong into Axie in May 2021. Thee had heard about Axie the previous year but hadn't loved the gameplay. So he was shocked when the game's popularity started rising in May 2021. "Everything else was crashing, but the only things that were pumping were SLP and AXS," he says. (AXS was the native token of Axie Infinity, kind of like the game's version of Sam Bankman-Fried's FTT.)

Thee decided to take the crypto he had earned from previous bull runs and create his own Malaysian Axie Infinity guild, with managers and scholars. Like the Philippines, Malaysia was still in the throes of the pandemic in the spring of 2021, with many businesses shuttered. The World Bank had found in a 2020 study that 64.5 percent of Malaysian jobs could not be performed from home, which especially harmed low-income, low-education workers.

When Thee started posting about his new guild, his posts were swarmed by prospective players who hoped to earn crypto from home. Within weeks, Thee's new organization, called Hooga Gaming, was flush with dozens of Axie scholars. These scholars were essentially unregulated, unprotected employees who played Axie for hours a day—and were making money for Hooga in heaps and gobs. The twenty-one-year-old Thee says he could earn $400 to $500 a day, marking the first period of his life in which he had a daily inflow of earnings.

As Hooga Games raked in cash through its scholars' efforts, Thee put that money right back into the game, buying more Axies for more scholars. "We got into euphoria mode: just making money, growing fast," Thee says. "We injected personal money into it and it grew way faster. I would say after the initial amount I put in, I put in five or six times that. It was really, really crazy."

Yele Bademosi, some 6,700 miles away in Nigeria, concocted a similar strategy. He decided that one of the main initiatives of his new company Nestcoin would be its own Axie-focused gamer guild, called Metaverse Magna. He hoped to spend over hundreds of thousands of dollars to assemble a team of a thousand Axies. "If I can make money from two NFTs, what if I could do it with three hundred thousand?" Bademosi reasoned. "And if this is sustainable, could we potentially create a world whereby people on the continent could be employed in these digital worlds and make a reasonable income?"

By August 2021, Axie Infinity had over nine hundred thousand daily active users, many of them from the Philippines, like Samerson Orias. Over a seven-day stretch in August, Axie raked in $218 million in sales thanks to ninety-seven thousand individual buyers. The game sat atop CryptoSlam!'s revenue leaderboard, generating $30 million in sales a day. Trailing far behind were Art Blocks, a generative art project, in second, CryptoPunks in third, and a still-ascendant Bored Ape Yacht Club in fourth.

That month, FTX joined the Axie fray, an unsurprising move given

Sam Bankman-Fried's penchant for glomming onto the latest money-making crypto fad. On August 5, he announced a partnership with one of the biggest scholar providers in the world: Yield Guild Games, which already employed over four thousand scholars. FTX announced its intention to breed 137 new Axie teams, which would then be leased out to scholars around the world, including eighty-one from the Philippines, twenty-five from Indonesia, and fifteen from Latin America. In a statement, Sam said that FTX had funded the scholars "as fans of both gaming and making a positive impact." Two months later, FTX invested $2 million in a $152 million funding round for Sky Mavis, the company that had created Axie, giving Sky Mavis a valuation of around $3 billion.

Khai Chun Thee in Malaysia, Yele Bademosi in Nigeria, and Samerson Orias in the Philippines were all making money from Axie. But where was it coming from?

When economists analyzed the game, they found a pretty clear answer: The money was coming from new entrants buying in, which is the same model as how a Ponzi scheme works. The makers of the game, Sky Mavis, didn't even bother to try to hide this dynamic: The company acknowledged in Axie Infinity's white paper that the game was "dependent on new entrants." In August 2021, cofounder Jeff Zirlin defended this economic structure on FTX's own podcast. "All of crypto is growth-dependent. If you're not growing, you're kind of dying," he said. He contended that this was more so a feature than a bug—"because everyone knows that growth is important, and everyone is working towards growing the network."

Thee, who had poured thousands of his own dollars into Axie from Malaysia, was suspicious of the game's economic sustainability. "It feels very Ponzi," he remembers thinking. "But as a crypto investor, you kind of always know that when you buy something, if you think you come in early, you always have some people that come in later that help you to move the price." This was an overwhelmingly common sentiment among crypto investors: that there would always be a "greater fool" to take a risky asset off their hands.

By the fall of 2021, Axie Infinity had more than a million daily active users. But so many scholars thrust themselves into the game, harvesting SLP for fiat, the value of each SLP token began to slide. It was textbook inflation in action: Just as libertarians had accused the Federal Reserve of meddling with the money supply during the pandemic by recklessly printing cash, far too much SLP was flooding the market, reducing its value. In July, SLP was worth as much as 40 cents a piece. By November, it was down to 6 cents—and average earnings for Axie scholars dropped below the Philippines' minimum wage. Scholars who depended on Axie to feed their families were grinding more hours for less money.

But many of the big-money backers in Axie's orbit, including FTX, carried on as if nothing were amiss. In November 2021, FTX partnered with Lightspeed Venture Partners and Solana Ventures to create a $100 million Web 3 gaming investment initiative. (Not so coincidentally, Mark Zuckerberg had changed Facebook's name to Meta a week earlier to signal his commitment to these new virtual worlds.) FTX also sponsored an Axie Infinity tournament centered in Malaysia, whose organizers included Thee's Hooga Gaming. Thee and the other organizers had seen SLP prices sliding downward and hoped to open up another source of revenue. An e-sports tournament, they thought, might bring them venture capital investments, ad money, and livestreaming audiences. The resulting FTX Galaxie Cup, as it was called, featured gamers and prominent influencers livestreaming Axie matches for audiences around the world. There were streams in five languages, including Tagalog, Thai, and Japanese, for audiences both on YouTube and Twitch. Tournament organizers also raffled off a highly coveted Mystic Axie, which was worth $130,000 at the time.

FTX's six-figure investment in the Galaxie Cup was a small drop in the bucket in their vast marketing budget, but nonetheless a miraculous figure to Thee and the other organizers, including Ian Tan, a fellow Malaysian and the head of another Axie guild, Lorcan Gaming. "Things like conferences were not big in Malaysia, so exposure was scarce," Tan says. "Having the opportunity to speak to the likes of FTX, back then, it was like living a dream."

An FTX staffer told me the company's sponsorship of the tournament was part of a larger partnerships campaign to convert people in various parts of the global crypto ecosystem into FTX users. And Tan and the rest of the organizing team were happy to help them achieve this goal: They diligently prepared FTX user acquisition strategies and pushed their community to sign up for FTX accounts. During the Galaxie Cup, they stipulated that anyone who won one of its prize pools would receive it on an FTX account. "So you've gotten SLPs from playing Axie Infinity, but what's next?" read one tweet sent from the Galaxie Cup's official account in November 2021. "Trade, buy or sell cryptocurrencies on platforms like FTX to expand your crypto investments."

Tan, Thee, and other organizers loved their FTX Galaxie Cup experience: They were proud to prove their entrepreneurial and organizational abilities on the global stage. But the tournament had not brought in its own revenue: It relied on the largesse of FTX and other sponsors. So over the next few months—as the price of SLP continued to dip—the team prepared for a second Cup, pouring thousands of dollars into a sequel that they hoped would forge a lasting business model.

CHAPTER 18

The World's Richest
Twenty-Nine-Year-Old

The FTX Galaxie Cup was far from the only way in which Sam Bankman-Fried spread his tendrils across the world. In Japan, he bought out a rival crypto exchange in order to win market share. In the Middle East, he created a subsidiary that offered crypto futures to investors in the region. And he inked a partnership with the International Cricket Council, with the FTX company logo emblazoned on broadcasts around the world.

By October 2021, FTX accounted for around 10 percent of the crypto derivatives trading market, facilitating over $10 billion in trades a day. Sam landed on the cover of *Forbes*, which anointed him the world's richest twenty-nine-year-old, with a net worth of $22.5 billion. Crypto prices were surging all around him: Bitcoin hit a record high of $66,000, becoming one of the best-performing assets of the year. With crypto ascendant and seemingly invincible, venture capitalists rewarded FTX with their biggest funding round yet: $420 million in capital, to go along with a $25 billion valuation.

How had Sam managed to attract so much VC capital despite the many red flags that Alex Pack and other entrepreneurs had spotted early on? Christine Chew, based on her experience working at the venture capital firm GBV, says it was rare for venture capital firms to conduct rigorous research about the companies they invested in. Even a project with dubious fundamentals could rake in profits for VCs, especially in the frothy bull market. Many venture capitalists weren't focused on long-term growth at all. They could invest in a project, receive tokens in exchange, watch the value of those tokens rise thanks to their investment, and cash out within months or even days. "The decision criteria was basically, do we think the coin is going to pump or not?" she says.

Mark, the crypto exec, tells me that FTX's staggering fundraising numbers were the result of their immaculate public image. Many prestigious firms were leery of putting money into specific tokens, which could be volatile. A poorly timed bet on a cryptocurrency as silly as Dogecoin, for example, could lead to a public relations disaster for a Wall Street trading outfit. Sam, on the other hand, seemed trustworthy and regulator-safe. And because Sam's business was mostly in futures trading as opposed to the actual assets, this gave these non-crypto firms another level of separation while still giving them exposure to the fastest-growing asset class in the world.

"Sam's status of being enshrined as the world's youngest billionaire gave some of those firms a way to put a foot in the door, through an exchange they thought was clean," Mark tells me. "And this was a self-fulfilling prophecy: because he had successfully raised money from reputable firms, others bought in."

This was ironic, because just a couple years before, crypto insiders had widely considered Sam "the king of the shady side of crypto," Alex Pack says. But Sam had since built a hallowed public image, thanks in part to a gargantuan marketing and PR blitz. Before 2021, FTX hadn't paid for a single advertisement. Crypto marketing overall was mostly confined to targeted online campaigns, which could pique the interest of handfuls of crypto enthusiasts. But Sam wanted to take over the entire world. "If a crypto company you've never heard of runs an ad on Google or Facebook, it's not very compelling," he told *Yahoo Finance* in November 2021. "You probably assume it's basically just a scam. So rather than just try to mass acquire a ton of retail users with advertisers—it probably wouldn't have worked—what we've really been focusing on is trying to communicate to the country and the world, like, who we are as a company."

FTX embarked on this strategy in March 2021, paying $135 million to slap its name onto the Miami Heat's arena, formerly known as the American Airlines Arena. American Airlines had posted four straight quarterly losses during the pandemic, when travel plans were eviscerated around the world, and had decided to let the spot go. After the name change, even people who didn't care in the slightest about crypto would be forced to say FTX's name in the same breath as the Heat, a powerhouse franchise that had muscled its way to the NBA Finals a year before. At the Heat's season opener at FTX Arena, Bankman-Fried sat courtside, beaming in front of the TV cameras as 2020 league MVP Giannis Antetokounmpo dribbled a few feet away. Everyone in attendance received an FTX T-shirt with a code that allowed them to redeem an NFT—as long as they downloaded the FTX app, of course.

This was just the beginning of a $900 million deluge of multiyear sponsorship deals. In the fall of 2021, FTX forged partnerships with some of the best and most famous athletes in the world: NBA champion Stephen Curry, MLB MVP Shohei Ohtani, and the Mercedes Formula One team anchored by Lewis Hamilton. On the opening night of the NFL season, defending Super Bowl champ Tom Brady and his wife, Gisele Bündchen, shared a commercial together for the first time, in which they phoned all of their friends and implored them to sign up for FTX. (FTX ended up outlasting Brady and Bundchen's marriage by about a month.) In many ads, FTX advertised itself as the "cleanest brand in crypto."

The Commodity Futures Trading Commission (CFTC), which regulates the derivatives of oil, crops, and other goods, would later allege that these commercials, and the Miami Heat sponsorship, were paid for in part by FTX customer funds. But in the moment, the ads instantly elevated FTX's brand awareness into households across the country. FTX didn't need to explain to the public what they did; they simply hovered in the back of people's minds. If a football fan learned their friend had made money in crypto and wanted to try it out for themselves, why wouldn't they sign up for the exchange they had seen on TV—the one that was endorsed glowingly by (arguably) the greatest quarterback of all time? FTX's relentless marketing campaign earned them a spot in *Ad Age*'s Top Ten Marketers of 2021. The commercials also drew the interest and respect of the artist Liam Vries all the way in Zimbabwe. "The normal human brain is assuming something is safe because it is associated with bigger brands," he says. "I never saw Binance at Formula One." Liam would open an FTX account the following year.

———

Sam appeared on TV and media more and more often those days. Natalie Tien, FTX's head of PR and marketing, says that he was wholly uninterested in press until the release of the October 2021 *Forbes* 400 magazine cover. "That's when he really started to see how impactful PR can be toward changing a brand and himself," Tien says. Sam soon became a near-constant presence on CNBC, explaining the fundamentals of crypto to curious hosts over and over again. With his slumping shoulders and nasally voice, Sam, now widely known as "SBF," did not look or sound the part of a classic alpha male. But he did fit into the Silicon Valley mold of the eccentric genius, whose social limitations and lack of aesthetic pretense allowed him to optimize his business.

On TV, Sam was enthusiastic, generous with his time, and patient with crypto novices. With his fast-talking demeanor and emphasis on global good, he developed a cult of personality in a crypto world that, by design, had a power vacuum. Especially to the outside world, he seemed a refreshing change of pace from materialist crypto mavens who begged for attention with their Lambos and gold watches. Sam, in comparison, drove a Toyota Corolla and wore cargo shorts and faded New Balances.

But Sam did, in fact, care deeply about appearance: His shagginess was crafted. To be clear, Sam had always been a schlub, even as a non-famous teenager. But he had since realized that his aesthetic carelessness could be a visual calling card. One investor told me that Sam would brag in pitch meetings about how carefully he had cultivated an image for the press. Caroline Ellison similarly testified that Sam asserted that his unruly mane carried a financial value of its own. She added that Sam chose to drive his Corolla not for comfort, but because he said the optics were better than driving the luxury company car that FTX had bought for him.

As Sam courted TV news programs, he fashioned himself into a main character on Crypto Twitter, offering outspoken and seemingly nuanced analyses on a variety of topics, from coronavirus prevention to football. In each of his meandering tweet threads, he cast himself as a sensible wonk who transcended partisan talking points in favor of quantifiable truths. "The moral of the story is: always do the math," he scolded the *Atlantic* about a COVID-19 article in October 2021 that contended that the virus was a "forever problem," and which Sam dismissed as "lazy" and "incoherent." On November 4, he published a twenty-tweet thread on hubris, writing, without a trace of irony: "Each year, the world stands witness to a giant company, felled by its own arrogance."

Often, the math that Sam offered was completely made up. On the *80,000 Hours* podcast, he estimated his odds of giving away below $1 billion to charitable causes over his lifetime were "less than 1 percent," compared with "fifty-fifty" odds that he would give away $50 billion. There was no way for him to calculate these future percentages. But by framing these wildly optimistic guesses in terms of expected value, he made it seem like he was bringing a quant trading approach from Jane Street Capital to every aspect of his life and the world; that he was making decisions on a higher plane of analysis.

———————

By this point in time, there was plenty of evidence that Sam was not as successful or altruistic as he claimed. The discrepancy between Sam's checkered trading history and his wunderkind persona should have raised suspicion from journalists. But Sam slid right into a unique moment in the media landscape, in which both crypto media and the mainstream press were ill-equipped to treat him suspiciously or uncover his misdeeds.

The crypto publications proved easy for Sam to initially win over. Crypto publications were often staffed with ardent crypto supporters who did not hide their quest to evangelize the technology. They were often heavily funded or outright owned by crypto moguls. Sam himself secretly funded *The Block*, a major crypto news outlet, starting in 2021.

The readers of these publications liked hearing good news about their investments. They also had a habit of turning vicious the moment they believed an outlet was promoting FUD (which stood for "fear, uncertainty, doubt"). These dynamics rendered it unlikely that a crypto outlet would actively seek to uncover the wrongdoings of a crypto leader, especially one who was doing so much to bring their beloved industry to the masses.

Much of the mainstream media, in contrast, was predisposed to be skeptical of crypto, due to its many frauds and scams. But many journalists were just learning the ins and outs of crypto technology—and wholly un-equipped to duel with Sam on his home turf. Sam was an eager interview subject who picked up the phone at almost any hour. He was a master at deflecting tough questions with jargon-filled monologues that ranged from merger and acquisition strategy, to blockchain staking, to philosophy. And he made for a fascinating character portrait, with his beanbag sleep sessions and fidget-spinning restlessness. Sam was strange, to be sure, but he also came off as charming, astonishingly smart, and principled. He wasn't like the *rest* of those crypto bros. He was the good guy changing everything. He was a "capitalist monk," wrote *Bloomberg*, who hoped to make FTX the "biggest source of financial transactions in the world." Sam said that his goal was to keep about $100,000 annually—1 percent of his earnings—and then donate the rest.

It didn't hurt that Sam was throwing money at mainstream publi-cations, just like he was on the crypto side. His family foundation sent grants to Vox Media and ProPublica, and he contributed to the seed round of the news platform Semafor. So in short, the crypto journalists who might have had the technical chops to unveil Sam's misdeeds were disincentivized to do so. And the mainstream journalists who were supposed to be questioning his rapid success didn't quite know what they were looking for—and enjoyed the access he gave them a little too much.

Sometimes, small rays of truth peeked out. While Sam was giving away millions of dollars to an array of causes, including global poverty mitigation and AI safety, *Forbes* pointed out that his charity proportional to his net worth was "the rough mathematical equivalent of a typical 29-year-old American stuffing $15 into a Salvation Army bucket." When presented with that analogy, Sam defended himself by claiming that he didn't actually have access to his fortune: that he had "certainly well under" a million dollars in his bank account. The rest of his billions, he explained, were contingent on equity valuations of FTX and other companies, which meant that his philanthropy was "not a short-term goal" but a "long-term one."

―――――――――

As Sam's public persona took more of his time, he decided that holding leadership positions at both Alameda and FTX was untenable. Alameda, a trading firm betting on volatile assets and companies, was playing a much different game than FTX, which aimed to be the world's most trusted crypto bank and trading platform. Sam needed to at least give the impression that the two were operationally divided. So in August 2021, he stepped down as CEO from Alameda and appointed the traders Caroline Ellison and Sam Trabucco as co-leaders. But their promotions were little more than a facade. Sam was the final decision-maker at Alameda, advising Caroline on big trades. The two companies still shared office space, systems, accounts, and communications channels. "SBF did try to tell the public that he had nothing to do with Alameda," says an Alameda employee who declined to be named. "But he was on all the Signal chats where the major things happened."

Those "major things" included a growing number of loans. Sam instructed Alameda traders to borrow as much money as they could, from whatever sources they could find, at whatever terms they offered. This money then went to high-risk trades and investments that could make Alameda even more money. This was Sam's belief in the philosophy of expected value taken to its most violent extreme. By late 2021, Alameda had borrowed $10 to $15 billion from third party lenders—and much of those were open-term loans, meaning they could be recalled by their lenders at any time.

But Sam wanted more. And he thought creating a new venture capital wing of FTX to fund startups might make him even richer. But before he pulled the trigger on the project, he asked Caroline Ellison for a report on Alameda Research's finances, to see if they could afford to inject several billions of dollars more into the crypto ecosystem.

When Caroline tallied up Alameda's assets and liabilities, the result worried her. Far too much of Alameda's balance sheet was made up of Sam Coins like FTT and Serum: $10 billion on paper. If she disregarded the Sam Coins' value—a smart calculation given their flimsiness— the company's net asset value would be -$2.7 billion. If the crypto market crashed, Caroline realized that FTX would have very little choice but to dip into customer funds. "It was the only available large source of capital I could think of if all of the rest of our loans were being called," she later testified.

Caroline shared her results with Sam. He proceeded to go ahead and create FTX Ventures, with a seed fund of $2 billion from Alameda.

———————

At this point, Caroline and Sam were dating once again. Few people, not even Alameda insiders, knew about their relationship. Sam preferred that they kept it a secret, which made Caroline unhappy. But many people in the industry did have a loose understanding that the two companies they ostensibly led were a lot closer than Sam let on. Mark, the crypto exec, says that many financial players assumed that Alameda was front-running most of the larger orders coming onto FTX: viewing the exchange's internal real-time data to see how the market might shift in the following minutes and locking in more advantageous prices before its edge disappeared.

Mark and other traders could have walked away to another exchange. "But it's a trade-off: You got, it was assumed at the time, the most compliant, reliable, legitimate exchange that offers derivatives and other services," he says. "And FTX had good prices. So maybe I get a few percent of bips stolen here and there, but it doesn't matter overall."

Caroline and Sam consistently denied that they were front-running trades. Whether they were or weren't, it was still telling that major financial players weren't scared off by the potential conflict of interest. The bigger FTX got, the less volatile it became, and the better it was to trade upon. The *Forbes* cover story reported that over the previous twelve months, FTX had made $350 million in profit, while Alameda had pocketed $1 billion. Sam's two entities had simply become too big to criticize or ignore.

CHAPTER 19

Island Boy

On October 8, 2021, Sam Bankman-Fried stood in the bright Bahamas sunshine, his fingers running over his ill-fitting azure tie. Sam's formal suit was a far cry from his usual T-shirts and shorts. But today was no ordinary day: He was being celebrated by a head of state for his decision to move his company nine thousand miles across the world.

After a couple months of scouting from FTX employees like Christine Chew, Sam had decided to officially move FTX's headquarters from Hong Kong to The Bahamas. Sociopolitical tensions had intensified in the Chinese city: Pro-democracy protests in 2019 and 2020 had been quashed by the mainland government, and the city was now firmly under Beijing's thumb. Western companies that had long relied on the port city as a safe haven for U.S.-friendly business were quickly pulling back, fearing the prospect of more invasive surveillance or even coercion. Crypto companies, in particular, found themselves in the crosshairs. The Chinese government, in the process of rolling out a digital yuan, acted with mounting hostility toward cryptocurrencies. Beijing wanted total oversight of the money supply: to track every dollar and to control inflation. Bitcoin and other cryptocurrencies threatened to undermine its unwavering authority.

Previously, Chinese proof of work "miners" had been a crucial part of the Bitcoin ecosystem. These "miners" were the watchdogs of the blockchain who validated new transactions—and their efforts to keep the blockchain active and secure required an enormous amount of energy. China had hosted around 75 percent of the world's bitcoin mining capacity due to its long-established technology supply chains and cheap electricity.

149

But in May 2021, China began a crackdown on crypto mining, which triggered a $400 billion bitcoin downturn and sent miners scrambling to set
up shop in other energy-rich areas of the world, from Kazakhstan to Texas.

Hong Kong still had a separate financial system, currency, and regulators from the mainland—but crackdowns were coming there, too. In
August, in the face of pressure from the city's regulators, Binance prohib-
ited its Hong Kong account holders from trading derivatives. This decision boded very badly for FTX, whose business relied heavily on crypto
derivatives trading. In September, regulators in Beijing banned crypto
transactions outright.

Living in Hong Kong was also wearing on Sam personally: He chafed
at the COVID-19 lockdowns that continued to stifle the city. Sam wanted
the freedom to fly around the world to conferences and investor meetings,
evangelizing for FTX as he pleased. But governmental COVID-era travel
restrictions required masks in public places and three weeks of quarantine
locked in a hotel room every time he left and came back.

More concerning was Alameda's strained relationship with the Chinese government. Alameda stored crypto on Chinese exchanges like OKX
and Huobi, and found one day that $1 billion worth of crypto on those
accounts had been frozen. Officials told them that the freeze was related
to an investigation into the possible money laundering of a third party.
(The U.S. Department of Justice would later charge Chinese companies
with using crypto to facilitate their fentanyl trades to the U.S.)

Caroline later testified that Sam tried several approaches to freeing the
money. He hired an attorney to negotiate with the Chinese government.
He tried to create sham trades so that Alameda would lose all its money to
other accounts that they also secretly controlled. (Those accounts were
owned by "Thai prostitutes," Caroline testified, without elaborating
further.) Finally, an Alameda employee named David Ma suggested Sam
send a bribe to officials of around $150 million. The tactic worked, and in
November 2021, the money was released. Alameda employees who learned
about the transaction became worried that they had violated international
rules and were going to be prosecuted.

The Bahamas seemed like paradise in comparison. The temperature in Nassau, the country's capital, rarely fell below 75 degrees Fahrenheit even in the winter, which was oncoming. Bahamian companies did not have to pay taxes on income, capital gains, or wealth. And the Bahamian government was also working hard to make its country hospitable to fintech companies. A year prior, the government had passed the Digital Assets and Registered Exchanges (DARE) Act, making it one of the only countries in the world to create a licensing framework for crypto exchanges to legally set up shop and offer a slew of financial products, like crypto derivatives. After the DARE Act passed, FTX struck fast, becoming the first registered exchange under this new regime. They would now be able to offer derivatives and all sorts of other high-risk, high-reward financial products without worrying about the Chinese government breathing down their necks.

On October 8, FTX staffers threw a welcoming party for themselves, and invited members of the Bahamian government. Sam instructed his staff to dress formally for the occasion, which amused Christine: "That was really funny because we joined crypto hoping we could escape dressing up," she says. Nobody seemed less comfortable with the dress code than Sam himself. His tie hung loose around his neck and barely crossed past his belly button; his black suit was covered with wrinkles. His face mask sagged below his nose.

Philip Davis, the prime minister of The Bahamas, didn't seem to mind. After arriving on-site, he pulled Sam into a hug. He sported a company logo pin that matched Sam's, and beamed as he and Sam used giant ceremonial scissors to cut through a bow hanging on the front door. "The Bahamas begins its rise as the next global fintech hub," Davis said onstage. "The arrival of FTX is proof positive that we are headed in the right direction."

Other Bahamian entrepreneurs shared their prime minister's enthusiasm. Memes were created of Sam dancing and playing the saxophone to the TikTok song "I'm an Island Boy." When Sam changed his location on Twitter to The Bahamas, Tyler Gordon, a member of the crypto organization Bahamas Masterminds, tweeted at Sam, "One of us!! One of us!!"

"Everyone was like, 'Okay, we have a big dog here now!'" Michael

Armogan, the president of the Bahamas Esports Federation, says. "A lot of people were expecting and wanting The Bahamas to become a tech hub."

"Couldn't sleep, back to the office," Sam tweeted on October 16 at 6:44 a.m., alongside a photo of the Nassau dawn. "Gm to those that'll never take work off." In fall and winter of 2021, crypto pushed into uncharted territory over and over again. Bitcoin hit its all-time high of around $69,000 in November, with the global crypto market cap peaking at almost $3 trillion, surpassing the market valuation of Apple, the world's largest publicly traded company at the time. (It's worth noting that "market cap" is something of an imaginary number: There's no way all of that crypto could have been cashed out for that amount.)

SOL—the native cryptocurrency of Sam's preferred blockchain, Solana—had climbed all the way to $259 from its 2021 starting point of $2.16. Beeple's NFT record was broken, too: An anonymous artist named Pak sold a collection called *The Merge*, which consisted of gray spheres morphing into bigger gray spheres, for $91.8 million in December. Over the course of 2021, $44 billion was collectively spent on NFT marketplaces and collections, up from $106 million (with an "m") in 2020, according to Chainalysis. Collins Dictionary named "NFT" word of the year.

In November, crypto's mainstream wave crested in a strange saga known as ConstitutionDAO. When Sotheby's put an early copy of the U.S. Constitution up for auction, a group of crypto enthusiasts declared their intention to buy it collectively. ConstitutionDAO was a DAO, or decentralized autonomous organization: an organizational structure that came into vogue in 2021 as crypto's reformulation of the corporation. DAOs, crypto enthusiasts advertised, would be owned and governed by their members, who could vote on decisions that would trigger smart contracts on the blockchain. Compared to traditional companies or organizations, DAOs would be more egalitarian, more streamlined, and allow people from across the world to come together to raise money seamlessly in order to create real-world change.

ConstitutionDAO attempted to fulfill those promises. Its bidding target of the U.S. Constitution was symbolic: It suggested that the rise of DAOs was just as much of a revolution in global coordination as the creation of American democracy. Within a week, about eighteen thousand people contributed more than $47 million in ether to the project.

But the DAO's public fundraising process also proved to be a fatal flaw, because other bidders could see the exact price—a little over $43 million, after taxes and fees—that would trump the DAO's war chest. Sure enough, ConstitutionDAO lost the auction to the hedge fund CEO Ken Griffin, who spent $43.2 million after expressing doubt to the *Wall Street Journal* that "a large decentralized group would be able to manage the responsibilities necessary to protect this rare document." Earlier in the year, Griffin had become degens' foremost public enemy for his role in the Wall Street Bets craze: When the hedge fund Melvin Capital bet against GameStop and racked up billions in losses, Griffin simply used his vast fortune to bail them out. Crypto's "We the People" moment had been crushed by a Wall Street kingpin.

Despite the loss, crypto boosters declared ConstitutionDAO a triumph in crypto coordination, and the harbinger of a new era in which DAOs would replace corporations as the go-to organizational structure. Detractors dismissed it as a quixotic quest that reinforced crypto's obsession with memes and shallow symbolism while failing to actually accomplish anything in the world.

But the vast, frivolous wealth on display for the ConstitutionDAO project—combined with the proliferation of Lambos and six-figure Swiss watches in the crypto community—betrayed a troubling trend. A growing faction of crypto skeptics questioned whether the crypto boom was really helping to democratize finance or was just the latest tool to consolidate it. A December 2021 study by professors at MIT and the London School of Economics found that 0.01 percent of bitcoin holders controlled 27 percent of all coins in circulation. To those researchers, it seemed that the main purpose of new bitcoin buyers was to increase the wealth of early investors. Mark, the crypto exec, agrees. "2021 is the story of everyone in crypto profiting off retail [investors]," he says. Translation: As minnows flooded the crypto market, the sharks went on a feeding frenzy.

Mark adds: "Coming out of COVID, all of a sudden, your friends are making tens or hundreds of thousands of dollars on tokens you've never heard of. And the FOMO gets in. So a lot of crypto companies make a lot of sense in 2021, and their business models work."

In 2021, there were many crypto businesses that found they could do no wrong: Everywhere they turned there seemed to be a pot of digital gold. And because the prevailing mindset of crypto encouraged innovation and audacity—"Fortune favors the brave," Matt Damon declared in a 2021 ad for Crypto.com—many of these companies decided to go full degen, engaging in riskier practices that would either lead to domination or ruin.

Here's a very rough sketch of how a sizable chunk of the crypto ecosystem worked at the end of 2021. There were crypto lenders, like Celsius and Voyager, which accepted billions of U.S. dollars in customer deposits and promised their creditors returns. In order to fulfill those promises, they lent out those billions to crypto hedge funds like Alameda Research and Three Arrows Capital (3AC), which was run by the ruthless arbitrage trader Su Zhu.

These hedge funds used those loans to make big bets on various parts of the crypto ecosystem: shitcoins, DeFi strategies, NFTs, random start-ups. Harper Reed, Obama's ex-CTO who was at this point the founder of a Web 3 company, General Galactic Company, watched the money whiz around with bemused amazement. "The craziest stuff was watching all these weird fuckers like 3AC and FTX write these giant checks that seemed irrational," he says. "It was like, 'How are you possibly gonna get that money back?'"

In 2021, Reed's General Galactic Company had created a few different Web 3-related projects, but with not much financial success. One of those projects was an NFT search engine that sorted NFTs across the many marketplaces and exchanges. But by the fall of 2021, "the people inside the NFT space didn't need to search for them, and new people weren't arriving," Reed says. Eventually, Reed realized that he should be focusing his efforts on trying to make crypto useful for everyday people. "Our takeaway was 'This is totally fucked if we can't figure out how to actually use this for real shit,'" he says. "NFT artists who have a lot of crypto are still poor: They can't pay rent, unless they convince their landlord to take crypto. But then the landlord has to figure out what to do with crypto, so you basically keep pushing the problem down the line."

Reed decided his company would build a crypto debit card, which would connect to a user's crypto wallet and convert funds directly to U.S. dollars when they made a payment. At the top of 2022, his team—which included engineers who had built Venmo—began building out the card, raising money, and forging alliances with banks. "We wanted people to easily pay for groceries and childcare with crypto," he says.

But while Reed got some traction from crypto VCs and hedge funds, the projects that received much more funding were often those that peddled get-rich-quick schemes to everyday investors, encouraging them to pump in money for big rewards. The prime example of this model was the Terra-Luna project, which had grown to $8 billion by the end of 2021, and offered an absurd 20 percent yield to those who locked Terra stablecoins away into a specific vault, called Anchor. Christine Chew had heard about the project earlier in the year, as it gained widespread support on social media. "Su Zhu and another big VC, Delphi, backed it, so I thought it must be a decent project," she says.

Christine was also enticed by the massive interest it offered, which was far higher than what traditional banks were paying—or pretty much anything else in the crypto ecosystem. "The guarantee did not make financial sense. But I thought, 'This is crypto, and anything is possible. I cannot use my traditional finance mindset to think about APYs [annual percentage yields],'" she says. "So I put money into Anchor, and was super proud of myself for discovering it."

Many people on Crypto Twitter made audacious decisions this way. Every time they opened social media, there seemed to be a new billionaire at the top of the scrap heap, hawking a new project that was making everyone they knew thousands of dollars (on paper, at least). These companies built empires in the span of months, all feeding voraciously off the same money pool, all stacked on top of each other. They all supported each other's efforts and looked like geniuses at the top.

But these super-denegerates seemed awfully reminiscent of financial gamblers of eras past, most notably the corporate raiders of the 1980s like Michael Milken and Jeff "Mad Dog" Beck, who inflated the stock market before it all came crashing down on Black Monday, the largest one-day drop in the history of the Dow Jones. Beck, after the fall, described Wall Street in the 1980s this way: "Each of us in the deal game fed the next person's ambitions to the point of insanity; we were all magicians creating wealth and power from thin air."

Back at FTX, cracks were emerging in The Bahamas, in a similar way to how Alameda had splintered a few years prior. Some FTX staffers felt that because Sam was spending so much time on promoting his image in marketing and the press, the actual product was suffering. Brett Harrison, the president of FTX US, was especially concerned. Harrison had been hired that spring to head up FTX's new stateside exchange, which was much smaller and more limited than its parent company due to U.S. financial regulations. Sam wanted to profit off of the massive population of casual traders in the U.S., who bought stocks on Robinhood and Ameritrade. But pesky regulations kept him from offering crypto derivatives and other more advanced products to American customers: FTX first needed to gain certain crucial licenses and approvals from the CFTC.

Harrison's hiring was a part of Sam's effort to convince regulators of FTX's respectability. Harrison resolutely belonged to the traditional finance world, having previously worked at Jane Street (where he overlapped with Sam) and Ken Griffin's Citadel Securities. He had barely spent any time with crypto before his FTX appointment, admitting on a podcast that he joined partly due to the sheer boredom of working with "tradfi" (traditional finance) firms that were all "roughly doing the same things, chasing that quarter tick." He was proud to be part of this wave of fence-jumpers and encouraged others to join him: "Crypto is the ultimate brain drain," he bragged in April 2022.

Harrison cared very little about crypto's promise of decentralization. In fact, one of his main arguments was that the traditional finance world was not centralized enough: that the ecosystem was inefficient because it was splintered into too many different parts, from matching engines (which paired up buyers and sellers) to clearinghouses (which finalized transactions) to prime brokerages (which serviced hedge funds and other large firms). FTX could streamline all of those bit components into a single, contained ecosystem, he argued.

"Given the opportunity to make it all over again, I think you would do exactly what crypto did, which is just to say, 'the exchange does it all,'" he told the *On the Brink* podcast in March 2022. "We'll hold your funds for you, do all the risk and liquidation. . . . We'll be your iPhone app and it's all vertically integrated." Harrison, like Sam, hoped FTX would grow far beyond crypto. One of his main initiatives was to build a stock trading platform on FTX US. His "grand vision" was that retail traders could use FTX US for everything: to hold their savings, deploy funds to buy Tesla stock, Ethereum, or a Bored Ape, all the while using Solana or Serum tokens as collateral for risky trades.

Harrison's tradfi bona fides made him an asset to Sam and his mounting ambition to influence U.S. policy. Harrison also served to keep FTX leadership within Sam's old social circles; to keep his inner circle tight and loyal.

But while Harrison deeply respected Sam and his vision, he was also used to working at firms with real structures and checks and balances. FTX had none of those. Sam prided himself on the leanness of his organization: FTX US had less than one hundred employees in early 2022, compared to thousands at rival Coinbase. There was no CFO or HR department. There were no senior executives experienced in accounting, information security, or cybersecurity. There were fewer than ten engineers at the company, and they were severely overworked.

In late 2021, FTX was already suffering a "malaise," Brett Harrison says, due to a shortage of workers, a lack of leadership, and growing interpersonal tensions. Harrison voiced these concerns to Sam on his first visit to The Bahamas, in November 2021. He told Sam, to his face, that Sam was spending too much time on PR; that his developers were being overworked; that there needed to be a clearer separation between the executive, legal, and developer teams of FTX US. Harrison tells me that Sam responded angrily to him, and immediately dismissed all of the concerns as unimportant. "He was worked up and emotional," Harrison says. The eager, charming twenty-one-year-old he remembered from his Jane Street days was gone. But Harrison had nowhere else to turn in the company with his complaints. Sam had built a kingdom around himself in Nassau, and he was the all-powerful sovereign. Harrison returned to Chicago to run FTX US embittered, and the gulf between the two men would widen in the months to come.

Despite the internal problems, FTX was making mountains of money. The exchange earned revenues from fees of about $950 million in 2021. But this wasn't good enough for Sam, who believed that crossing $1 billion was an important psychological threshold. If he could tell potential investors and media outlets that he was running a billion-dollar company, that fact alone would spur even more investment and growth.

So Sam asked Nishad Singh, the head of engineering at FTX, to come up with a solution that would allow them to appear to cross the $1 billion mark. In the last two days of the year, Nishad dutifully went into the FTX database and backdated a slew of sham transactions throughout 2021, to make it seem like the company had generated $50 million more in revenue than it had. Sam then signed his name to a sham contract which was dated as having been written a year earlier. It was at this point, Nishad would later testify, that he first realized he was part of a criminal enterprise. But Nishad also felt this faked $50 million wasn't such a big deal in the scheme of things: FTX had genuinely produced $950 million in revenue in 2021, a staggering amount for a company run by a bunch of people who hadn't yet turned thirty.

There was another big problem. While FTX was earning lots, Alameda was spending even more. At the end of the year, Alameda's secret debt to FTX was over $2 billion—and was about to increase dramatically, due to Sam and Caroline taking increasingly risky bets in an increasingly volatile market that had already peaked.

"When you start playing with billions, risk management does not scale linearly," says VC Alex Pack, meaning that the bigger the bad bets you make, the more likely you are to cause ripple effects across the industry. "If the market is moving against you, you're gonna destroy the entire market."

CHAPTER 20

NFTs for Good

At the top of 2022, FTX Africa and Owo Anietie were on opposing trajectories. FTX Africa was happily expanding: It had just successfully launched FTX Africa NFT Week in Lagos, a series of talks, events, and educational sessions. Artists minted their works on the FTX NFT platform and attended a gallery showing in the city. Olufemi Akola, a Lagos-based 3D artist and architect, won 1 million naira ($200 USD) in an art competition, and tweeted: "FTX Africa came at a time when African artists and creatives needed them the most. There is no better time to get on the FTX NFT marketplace actively supporting African creatives than now." At another event, a Sip & Paint party, dozens of attendees painted Bored Apes—the de facto symbol of crypto success—in a penthouse high above the city.

One of the pieces of art that came out of FTX's Africa week was a tribute to Sam himself: a PFP in the Yoruba Demons NFT project, which was created by Nigerian artists and developers and minted on Sam's preferred blockchain, Solana. The NFT showed Sam in elegant red robes that matched his red laser eyes, signaling both his commitment to Bitcoin and his otherworldliness. His usually messy hair was rendered tightly curled and immaculately coiffed like Sly Stone's; he sported high cheekbones and a regal posture. "He's a force to be reckoned with in crypto," the artist wrote on Twitter, "that needs no introduction."

Owo Anietie, on the other hand, was still mired in the debris of Afro-Droids' collapse. He had largely disengaged from the project's Discord, with all of its anger and accusations, and was instead trying to focus on making his own art and forging inroads in Hollywood for the AfroDroids movie. In public interviews, he still waxed poetic about the transformative power of crypto. "We need to get to a space where NFTs are equivalent to using social media. I think it's going to happen," he said to the blog *Culture Custodian* in March 2022. "Everybody's going to be selling NFTs in a couple of years."

That month, Owo's utopian vision of NFTs was partially fulfilled when the Dream Catchers Academy opened up a brand-new school building funded mostly by AfroDroids NFTs. Before AfroDroids, founder Seyi Oluyole had only raised about $20,000 on GoFundMe, a far cry from the $100,000 needed to build a new school. Minor construction had dragged on for months with little progress. The success of AfroDroids in September changed Dream Catchers' trajectory immediately. Oluyole did not hold her new stash of crypto with "diamond hands," as crypto degens were supposed to: She immediately withdrew the entire amount needed for construction.

On March 24, just six months after the AfroDroids drop, Owo took a boat across the Lagos Lagoon to the neighboring city of Ikorodu and was picked up in a colorful school bus that had been bought with AfroDroids funds. The bus took him to the new Dream Catchers Academy, which was housed in a structure that looked nothing like the drab, squat houses surrounding it. The school rose two stories and was painted in bold blocks of lavender, periwinkle, sapphire, and tangerine. This was the first free formal arts academy in Nigeria, declared a Lagos governmental bureaucrat who had come to celebrate the building's opening.

The building housed six classrooms that could fit sixty students total, a dance studio with a barre, a library filled with new textbooks, and a computer room with new laptops. Murals painted by the children lined the walls alongside motivational posters with phrases like "If I can dream it, I can achieve it."

During the ground-breaking ceremony, Dream Catchers' students danced to Afrobeats songs and sang "We Are the World," wearing matching purple jerseys emblazoned with the phrase "One child, one hope, one dream." Oluyole, in a tearful speech, explained how her impoverished upbringing had led her to commit herself to this mission; how Nigerian girls were often married off at early ages and forced to carry the brunt of housework compared to boys. She explained how many Nigerian schools had slashed art and music funding, and that the influx of donations would soon allow her to expand her number of students from thirty to one hundred. She thanked Owo and the AfroDroids community for their "massive support and encouragement," adding, "Today is the beginning of a new chapter in our lives."

Owo was swarmed by reporters from local news outlets. "I've seen the girls, and can attest to the fact that I've never experienced something like this ever," Owo told one reporter. "Today has been a dream." As drones flitted overhead, capturing the school's vibrant colors, Owo and Oluyole unwrapped a plaque that read, "This building was commissioned by the AfroDroids community." Over the next few months, the students would move into the school, record covers of famous songs, learn to play trumpet, and farm corn and sweet potatoes.

This massive real-world achievement did little to assuage the fury of angry NFT buyers on the AfroDroids Discord. For starters, some people didn't even believe that the school was real. They claimed that Owo had somehow paid an existing school to take fake photos. Others dismissed the school as unimportant compared to the state of their investments. "[Owo] did do the school which is great," wrote a user named CLXRB. "but he just another scammer who happens to have talent in art."

CryptoWizard, the pseudonymous AfroDroids superfan, had essentially replaced Esther Eze as AfroDroids' communications liaison. He, too, was getting burned out from the constant criticism. He now argued that the project couldn't have done much more to satisfy its holders and that both AfroDroids' initial success and long-term failure were the products of the timing of its rollout. "At that time, pretty much everyone was following Bored Apes," he says. "Every project's road map was based less on what they could deploy and more on trying to one-up the last project. It wasn't until the end of 2021 that people realized that maybe overpromising and then crashing is a bad idea."

In early 2022, the number of dead-end NFT projects started to pile up. Both Owo and Liam Vries were commissioned to create art for a project called the Meta Art Club, which promised to be an exclusive curated collection of fine art. But they and many other artists were never paid, and the project essentially vanished upon arrival.

Around the same time, Owo became involved in another mission-driven NFT project called Meta Water. The project was the brainchild of a Nigerian photographer and activist named Mayor Otu, who was also from Owo's home state of Akwa Ibom. Over the previous couple years, Otu had become a feel-good viral sensation in his own right for helping to raise awareness and funds for the water crisis in Nigeria. An estimated 60 million Nigerians—or more than a quarter of the country's total population—lacked access to basic drinking water, according to the World Bank. This shortfall was particularly felt in rural communities, where local governments couldn't afford the high-powered hydraulics needed to tap into clean water deep underground.

Otu had spent years traveling the country and photographing its residents, and was shocked by how many communities drank brown, muddy water from streams, ponds, and rivers. The dirty water contained all sorts of bacteria and contaminants; it caused rashes and other skin ailments. In 2021, UNICEF determined that more children died from lack of access to safe water than violent conflict. So Otu started photographing residents on the outskirts of the Nigerian capital, Abuja, holding muddied water bottles. After Otu posted the photos on social media, they went viral, prompting a local bank to donate the roughly $1,300 needed to drill a new well in the village. Within months, residents had access to clean water thanks to Otu's social media campaign.

Otu was amazed that his photos and accompanying words had transformed a community. Before long, his inbox was flooded with leaders from other villages, pleading for him to broadcast their own plight. He soon formed a nonprofit called Give Water, with the aim of using his photography and social media donations to bring water to Nigeria, one village at a time.

While Otu was raising money in dribs and drabs, he was bowled over by the comparatively gargantuan success of AfroDroids. It seemed like his fellow Nigerian had cracked a new model of sustainable fundraising from a new donor base. Maybe, Otu thought, the pair could use their influence and joint knowledge to create an NFT project that would lead to the digging of wells not just in Nigeria but around the world. "Instead of begging and crowdfunding, you can have people collect this art—and it becomes permanently yours while you have the utility of helping someone somewhere get access to clean drinking water," Otu said.

When Otu reached out to Owo asking him to collaborate, Owo was immediately on board. He had grown sick of the rampant status-chasing and greed in the crypto space and wanted to join another project that actually improved people's lives. The Meta Water Project, the pair decided, would turn Otu's photos of children from the Uzamagu community in South East Nigeria into NFTs. The images of the children showed them holding murky water bottles—but if an NFT was bought, it would turn clear, thanks to the magic of smart contracts and Owo's graphic design skills. Once enough money was raised, a new well in the village would be dug, and a stone would be placed alongside it with the names of the NFT collectors who helped fund the clean drinking water.

The introductory paper for the project used the same lofty rhetoric of many Web 3 projects, arguing that it could "change the way in which humanitarian aid is being managed, redefine the role and value of the NGOs (nongovernmental organizations) under this new structure and decentralize the governance of the most basic human needs projects." Mayor Otu, who previously had no exposure to the NFT space, agreed to promote Meta Water on Twitter Spaces and Discord day and night. But Otu, like Owo, quickly found that he disliked pandering to NFT holders. "It was tiring for me," he says. "I learned that people give out of pity, not empathy."

Otu was a successful artist who sold physical prints of his photographs to collectors around the world for thousands of dollars. But here, in NFT-based Twitter spaces, people were asking him to sell his photographs for $5 or $10 apiece. "Sometimes you would wait for hours in the spaces—and then you talk, and people are trying to look down on the art," he says.

The pessimism wasn't surprising given the larger crypto climate. In early 2022, the NFT space had cratered again. Secondary sales and search volume both collapsed. Ether, which had climbed to $4,800 in November, sunk below $3,000. At the end of February, Sotheby's planned a Crypto-Punks sale, hoping it would be just as successful as the Bored Apes auction won by Alameda Research a few months prior. But on the day of the auction—which had drawn a packed house at the Sotheby's salesroom in midtown Manhattan—the owner of the CryptoPunks withdrew from the auction block, shut down the proceedings, and posted a meme mocking Sotheby's on Twitter. Experts speculated that the owner had pulled out after realizing that his target price of $30 million was not going to be reached.

If CryptoPunks auctions at Sotheby's were failing, then Meta Water had no chance. AfroDroids had made more than $1 million in one day in September 2021. The Meta Water project—which had hoped to transform NGOs and donations—registered a single sale on OpenSea in April, for $1,600. With flipping NFTs no longer particularly profitable for traders, the Uzamagu community would have to wait for clean water.

PART III

THE POWER STRUGGLE

CHAPTER 21

Vitalik's Warning

Despite recent downturns, the general forecast for crypto still looked bright in February 2022. The price of Ethereum was double what it had been a year earlier, and the recent dips were just "corrections" from unsustainable highs, crypto backers assured investors. FTX had just been valued at $32 billion, and Sam had just testified confidently in front of Congress to explain the crypto phenomenon that had enveloped the nation and brag about his company's overwhelming successes. He didn't face much resistance. New Jersey Senator Cory Booker jovially teased Sam about his wild hair: "I'm offended you have a much more glorious Afro than I once had," the bald Democrat joked.

A couple weeks later, I packed my bags for ETHDenver, a yearly Ethereum-based crypto conference at a sagging former Sports Authority now dubbed the Crypto Castle. Like many people there, I went to try to grab some facetime with Ethereum's founder, Vitalik Buterin. As Ethereum had become the central hub for most crypto activity, Vitalik had become a hero to many, and a kind of cypher for this new, strange digital society. The philosophical and technical treatises he posted on his blog, *vitalik.ca*, were hotly debated and served as the backbones for many crypto projects.

But Vitalik was notoriously elusive with both fans and the press, even at conferences that ostensibly existed to celebrate him and his ecosystem. For days during the conference, I wandered around the packed halls aimlessly as if trekking through the Himalayan wilderness in hopes of a Yeti sighting. All around me, a giant crypto bacchanalia raged, full of sunnily

169

strummed guitar songs, garrulous one-on-one business pitches, high-flying NFT sales, and late-night poker sessions.

On the last day of the conference, I was sitting alongside thousands of attendees at the conference's closing ceremony, when a man who was sitting onstage and wearing what appeared to be a half-unicorn, half-buffalo costume removed his furry head, revealing brown cowlicks and a pair of unblinking, unfocused eyes. He looked dazed, like a disgruntled minimum-wage employee gone rogue after hours in costume at a theme park. But the crowd roared in recognition, as it was Vitalik himself. As soon as the ceremony was over, a scrum gathered outside his greenroom, hoping to perhaps pitch an idea, seek wisdom, or just snap a photo with the mythological founder.

But when Vitalik finally emerged from within, he began to trot through the crowd nervously, past astonished selfie takers and venture capitalists, ignoring calls of his name. Once outside the venue, he broke out in a full sprint down the street, in the opposite direction of the enormous queue waiting to get in. His boldest fans chased him down the street, both on foot and scooters, shouting after him. But he outran them all, and disappeared into the privacy of his hotel, alone.

Vitalik had plenty to celebrate that night. By virtually every metric, Ethereum had become a juggernaut: a trillion-dollar ecosystem that rivaled Visa in terms of money moved. Vitalik was beloved and insanely rich; he could land a meeting with just about any politician in the world. Ethereum had energized thousands of artists around the world, including Beeple, Owo Anietie, and Liam Vries.

So why was Vitalik so uncomfortable and anxious? Why did he flee his own community like a refugee?

———————

The first reason was personal. Vitalik had always been an introvert who struggled in social situations. He had actually been walking around in the mascot costume for days before revealing himself, which allowed him to anonymously revel in the conference's giddy energy.

But there was a more theoretical reason for his discomfort. Vitalik had created Ethereum precisely so that no one man should have all that power. Ethereum was supposed to dislodge powerful individuals and extractive middleman: to convey the will of its builders, investors, and ever-sprawling community. Vitalik was actively trying to reduce his own importance inside of the ecosystem. "The good news is that I feel like Ethereum depends less on me than it ever did at any previous point in history!" he tweeted in September 2021.

That hardly mattered: The bigger Ethereum grew, the more Vitalik seemed to receive hero worship wherever he went. And for the past year, during the frenzied bull run, Vitalik watched helplessly as Ethereum became overrun with values and practices he abhorred. For years, Vitalik had tried to tune out the day-to-day price movements of crypto in favor of a long view of the blockchain. He preferred to see the good in people and to use his megaphone to emphasize positive developments. "My general view is there's a lot we can do to reduce the bad and to amplify the good. Sometimes amplifying the good can even crowd out the bad," he told me in his hotel room the morning after the ETHDenver party. (After days of indecision, he had finally agreed to meet with me through a representative for the Ethereum Foundation.)

But the bad was becoming too big, too loud, and too powerful for him to ignore. He worried about the dangers to overeager investors, the soaring transaction fees, and the shameless displays of wealth. Some of the major utopian concepts of his vision, including DAOs (decentralized autonomous organizations) and DeFi (decentralized finance), were turning into localized hellscapes. And other leaders like Sam Bankman-Fried and Binance's Changpeng Zhao were building their prestige and power, hawking their own agendas that actively eroded Vitalik's decentralized dreams for the space.

At this point, it was easy for many people, even those who understood the crypto world, to mistake Vitalik and Sam as the same archetypal man. Both were millennial founders, painfully awkward white-male math genius billionaires who loved monologuing about social good and technological transformation, and whose eccentricities inspired both revulsion and worship. But the decisions they made in terms of leadership and technology were almost diametrically opposed. Vitalik compared Sam's "personalistic style" to that of "1930s dictators." It was clear to Vitalik that Sam was moving crypto toward centralized platforms that encouraged gambling, shitcoins, and new gatekeepers.

So in early 2022, Vitalik shifted course, and began to rail against the industry's faults, hoping to coax crypto away from craven capitalism and toward the renovation of broken systems. My interview with him, which became the cover story for *Time* magazine's March 28 issue, was representative of his change in mindset. Vitalik definitely wasn't enticed by the allure of being a cover star on some legacy mainstream media outlet. But he agreed to talk to me because he hated crypto's current trajectory.

"Crypto itself has a lot of dystopian potential if implemented wrong," he told me. "If we don't exercise our voice, the only things that get built are the things that are immediately profitable. And those are often far from what's actually the best for the world."

So what did Vitalik believe was best for the world? His views had changed significantly over the years. In 2008, before he conceived of Ethereum, he spent some time in an anarchist commune near Barcelona, where about three dozen radicals were building a "postcapitalist eco-industrial colony" in an abandoned factory. Many of his Ethereum cofounders—who had come aboard the project to lend money, industry connections, or technical expertise—held libertarian views: They were consciously trying to build a pathway out of a corrupt financial system and automatically detested any sort of regulation or initiatives that resembled welfare.

But as the 2010s went on, Vitalik grew disillusioned with libertarians and conservative thought. His blog posts increasingly engaged with collectivist ideals, and the ways in which blockchain technology might automatically redistribute individual wealth through novel tax ideas or public goods initiatives. Blockchain shouldn't just exist to dislodge the status quo, he argued: it could be used to create mechanisms that would make society fairer.

DAOs, for example, could restructure power so that instead of a wealthy board controlling an organization, its stakeholders or employees could vote on its direction through the blockchain. NFTs could fund artists in far-reaching parts of the world. Because of the blockchain's transparency and ease of digital organization, it could spur fairer voting systems, urban planning, public works projects.

Walking around ETHDenver, it was hard not to see a community of builders created in Vitalik's image. The conference itself was organized by a member-owned cooperative. Its halls were filled with exhausted coders working on zero-knowledge proofs (a cryptographic technique to increase online security); environmentalists touting the advantages of putting carbon credits on the blockchain; developers touting "solarpunk" values of sustainable, communal building. Given the importance of NFTs to Ethereum's mainstream growth, art also had a major presence, with floors filled with galleries of trippy, undulating work.

But many of the bright ideas that Vitalik championed in the abstract were collapsing under real-world pressures. Vitalik liked the idea of funding NFT artists and democratizing pathways to success. But the center of the NFT space was now the Bored Ape Yacht Club, which he found vacuous and bad for crypto's brand. "The peril is you have these three-million-dollar monkeys and it becomes a different kind of gambling," he told me dismissively. "There definitely are lots of people that are just buying yachts and Lambos."

DAOs, or decentralized autonomous organizations, were supposed to make organizational structures more efficient and equitable. But almost all of the DAOs that had formed in the past year had relied on coin voting, a one-vote, one-coin process in which wealthy venture capitalists could buy up all the tokens of an organization and make self-interested decisions.

A 2022 study showed that across several major DAOs, less than 1 percent of the holders held 90 percent of the voting power. "It's become a de facto standard, which is a dystopia I've been seeing unfolding over the last few years," Vitalik said.

Vitalik was unhappy with crypto's political valence, which was tilting heavily toward the right. Although he hoped radicals from both poles could find something appealingly disruptive in crypto—because that meant it could serve as a flexible, all-encompassing system—he wished individualist libertarians weren't dominating the branding and public perception of the industry. "There's definitely signs that are making it seem like crypto is on the verge of becoming a right-leaning thing," he said. "If it does happen, we'll sacrifice a lot of the potential it has to offer."

Vitalik was similarly aggrieved by El Salvador's rollout of bitcoin as legal tender. Crypto maximalists had celebrated President Nayib Bukele's decision as proof that crypto was making governments more efficient and uplifting developing countries. But the rollout had been riddled with identity theft and volatility and had allowed Bukele to concentrate financial power around his own administration. And within just a few months, barely anyone in El Salvador was actually using their bitcoin to buy everyday stuff.

Finally, there was DeFi, or decentralized finance, which aimed to provide the financial services of banks without the need for an intermediary. Vitalik had long championed DeFi as a superior alternative to the hyper-restrictive financial system, which concentrated wealth and stifled cross-border monetary flows. DeFi, in contrast, could facilitate fairer loans for college students or medical patients, and simpler ways for immigrants to send remittances back home to their families.

But in reality, DeFi was mostly being used by a very small group of day traders—around 5 million people total—who were leveraging it to gamble on borrowed money. Their manic activity was being propelled by trading firms like Alameda Research, which drove up gas fees on Ethereum that cannibalized more well-intentioned yet low-flying projects.

One of the blockchain projects that Vitalik publicly supported, for instance, was Proof of Humanity, which aimed to generate a universal basic income to anyone who signed up. Proof of Humanity had been created in part by Argentineans, where reliable flows of income were desperately needed in the face of continued inflation and economic collapse. In 2022, the project was paying each user about $40 per month. But Ethereum gas fees took such a huge percentage that the project's UBI (universal basic income) payouts were essentially useless for anyone who actually needed them to pay for groceries. "When everything costs $8.75 [in fees], the only way people are willing to pay that is if they're gambling and they think that there's higher profits down the road," Vitalik said.

Fees were high; plutocracies were forming; public works projects were being drowned out. Sam Bankman-Fried was not the root cause of these problems. But he did encourage and calcify many of them. FTX stood for centralization; for trusting third-party systems; for meme coins and meaningless pumps. Vitalik saw crypto as a framework upon which to build new systems; Sam saw it as a means to his own private ends. Sam hoarded power; Vitalik relinquished it at almost every turn. And in February 2022, Sam's vision of crypto was winning.

It didn't help that Vitalik had a self-presentation problem. He sniffled and stuttered through his sentences, walked stiffly, and struggled to hold eye contact. He put almost no effort into his clothing, mostly wearing Uniqlo tees or garments gifted to him by friends. He was tense around strangers and prone to going off on long, technical tangents that would lose anyone but the most devoted developers of Ethereum. He was not an ideal face of Good Crypto, in part because he did not want to be.

When the *Time* magazine issue with Vitalik's vacant grin on the cover was released in March, it caused all sorts of social media firestorms. Many NFT holders felt that Vitalik's comments about the Bored Apes were overly harsh, and accused him of promoting FUD (fear, uncertainty, doubt). Others disliked the fact that the negative aspects of crypto were even mentioned in the article. "Why does legacy media select people who hate

& misunderstand crypto to cover it?" wrote Jeff Roberts, the editor of the crypto publication *Decrypt*.

Above all, social media users insulted Vitalik's appearance. "How is it possible to be this rich and still be ugly?" wrote one commenter. "This is if Tom Brady was on dog food," wrote another.

Vitalik had taken a stand—and had been met largely by jeers and vicious insults. He continued to stump for values-based crypto on various podcasts, but it was clear that his vision was being overwhelmed by the self-interested and status-obsessed. That month, Sam partnered with Stocktwits, a platform that allowed regular joes to trade meme stocks and meme coins in real time, on a new crypto trading service. The move was celebrated by degens on social media, and served as another example of how Sam had read the cultural pulse of the world better than Vitalik had. People didn't want to read treatises about land use or zero-knowledge proofs. They simply wanted to use the internet to get rich.

Sam was also winning the war for cultural supremacy. That month, headlines raved about his charitability, his D.C. aspirations, and his FTX Super Bowl ad, which starred the comedian Larry David and compared the arrival of crypto to that of the wheel or the lightbulb. The ad, which netted David a cool $10 million, described FTX as the "safest and easiest way to buy and sell crypto."

Sam was now part of the Hollywood elite. He watched the Super Bowl in Los Angeles from box seats just in front of Steph Curry, an FTX endorser, and dined at a Beverly Hills mansion hosted by Hollywood power broker Michael Kives, where Hillary Clinton, Jeff Bezos, Leonardo DiCaprio, and Kendall Jenner were also in attendance. Sam raved in a note to FTX executives that month that Kives could serve as a "one-stop shop for relationships that we should utilize," and invested $700 million in Kives's venture capital firm. Others at FTX were horrified by the investment. "That crew was blatantly grifters, and everyone else saw through it other than Sam," says one FTX employee. "We couldn't understand it. I think he was blinded by the celebrity access, which was also wasting his time and distracting him from the business."

But the PR onslaught was working. The day after Kives's dinner, Katy Perry posted on Instagram that she was "quitting music and becoming an intern for @ftx_official." And flipping through Vitalik's *Time* magazine issue, readers would have been hard-pressed not to see the one crypto ad inside of it, which took up a full page. "All of the excitement of crypto. Now with the added thrill of low downtime, market-leading liquidity and a commitment to regulations," the ad read. "FTX: Get into crypto with confidence."

CHAPTER 22

Christine and Amy

FTX didn't only intrude upon Vitalik's print space in *Time*: It showed up at ETHDenver itself.

FTX wasn't really a part of the Ethereum conference. The company did not pay for a booth or a sponsorship, or appear on any panels. But it did furtively send a coalition of employees to Denver, including Christine Chew and Amy Wu, the new head of the $2 billion FTX Ventures fund. (This was the venture money that Caroline had warned Sam in the fall of 2021 FTX could not afford.) "FTX just wanted to have our own private events. We didn't want to mingle, as FTX events were usually quite exclusive," Christine says. "We only invited executives and their friends."

FTX hosted a happy hour and a private dinner. Both were such hot tickets that Christine was tasked with telling uninvited people to leave. Once the riffraff had been escorted out, only VIPs remained. There was Illia Polosukhin, the cofounder of the blockchain NEAR, sitting next to onetime presidential hopeful Andrew Yang. Everywhere you looked was a crypto founder or executive, from Sandeep Nailwal (Polygon) to Steven Goldfeder (Arbitrum) to Don Ho (Quantstamp). Christine says that the goal for the FTX dinner at ETHDenver was to solidify FTX Ventures' reputation as the nexus of crypto's elite. And by all accounts, the dinner was a huge success. FTX had swooped into a rival's conference and poached the starriest attendees for its own exclusive gathering. The heavyweights there were forced to acknowledge Sam's centrality in the crypto universe.

Polosukhin had a complicated relationship with Sam and FTX. NEAR was a direct competitor with Solana, and Sam's heavy investment in the latter blockchain had diverted developers and entrepreneurs in that direction. But Sam was also directly funding NEAR's growth, with Alameda and FTX Ventures investing a combined $80 million toward NEAR funding rounds. "At the time, partnering with FTX and Alameda seemed like the right way to propel ecosystem growth for NEAR," Polosukhin says. "It did feel like we needed to have that support to continue growing."

After the dinner ended, Amy Wu asked Christine to come back to her hotel room. This invitation surprised Christine, as Amy outranked her by several levels, and the two were not close. When Christine arrived, Amy started crying. "She was really sad and looked extremely in pain," Christine says. "She said that she felt a lot of pressure from Sam; that Sam said she doesn't work hard enough. I think Sam was quite verbally abusive to Amy."

Just a few months prior, Amy had been one of the leading Web 3 venture capitalists in Silicon Valley as a partner at Lightspeed Ventures, injecting millions into crypto and gaming projects. Now she had been reduced to one of Sam's whipping posts, crying to a near-stranger in a Denver hotel room. Another FTX employee says that while Amy had ostensibly been hired to run investments, that department was really led by Ramnik Arora, who refused to share control with her. "People were really anti-Amy. She was totally on the outs very quickly," this employee said.

It was another example of the dysfunction ramping upward at FTX, and how different Sam's public persona was from his private one. The merry-go-round of his court would continue to spin.

CHAPTER 23

Axie Fatigue

I t didn't help Amy that Web 3 gaming—one of her areas of purview at FTX—was sinking like a stone. The summer before, she had jumped excitedly into Axie Infinity, spending $1,000 of her own money for a team. On social media and in interviews, she cheered on Axie for its real-life impact around the world. "After spending more time in the Axie Infinity ecosystem, I feel that the heart of the play-to-earn (P2E) model lies in the new guild system," she tweeted in July 2021. "The alternative for these players is not playing Fortnite. The alternative is driving Uber."

For much of 2021, Axie had been beneficial for everyone in the ecosystem and was causing positive real-world uplift. In December 2021, Super Typhoon Odette, the second-costliest typhoon in Philippine history, devastated the nation, killing over four hundred people. Several Axie guilds sprang into action, including YGG Philipinas, which raised 31 million pesos ($620,000) to rebuild over a thousand homes.

When Amy joined FTX, she argued that gaming could be the impetus for crypto adoption overall. "We think games can onboard the next 100 million, even 1 billion people into Web 3," she told *Blockworks* on the day of the founding of FTX Ventures in January 2022. But a month after that, Axie, the leading Web 3 game, was fading, with the value of its in-game currency, SLP, dropping to one-thirty-third of what it had been worth seven months earlier. The influx of hundreds of thousands of "scholars" who joined Axie solely to earn money had changed the dynamic of the game completely. Not only had their arrival opened up an exploitative power dynamic that was akin to digital sharecropping—

in which owners profited directly from their labor—but their extractive approach to the game meant that enormous quantities of SLP were being sold for cash on the open market, causing its dollar value to plummet.

"All scholars are just gonna dump the token: That's the name of the game," Ian Tan, the cofounder of the Malaysian guild Lorcan Gaming, which co-organized the FTX Galaxie Cup, says. "We play Axie Infinity to make money. We don't play because we enjoy the game."

The creators of Axie tried to counter this slide with all kinds of economic tricks, but nothing worked. Samerson Orias, the Axie gamer in the Philippines, had long bowed out of the game. In the summer of 2021, he had developed a daily routine in which he cooked takoyaki from 3 p.m. until midnight, came home, and played Axie through the wee hours of the morning. His play earned him badly needed cash: about $29 a week, after giving the same amount to his manager. But his relentless schedule, and the game's randomness, exhausted and frustrated him. "At first I was happy. But after some time, I noticed I was slowly getting weaker. There was sleeplessness and the stress of the game," he says. "I felt fatigued all the time. I became more aggressive in every aspect of my life."

Toward the end of the summer, Orias's mother died of a heart attack. Her funeral wiped out his savings, including the $200 he had saved up playing Axie. He drifted away from the game, as it no longer paid his bills. "I felt regret that I wasn't able to provide for my mom," he says.

At Hooga Gaming in Malaysia, Khai Chun Thee watched the number of his scholars dwindle from hundreds to dozens. "I see a lot of sad stories: people who bought something on mortgage, and they couldn't pay for it after one to two months, after their earnings slipped so fast," he says. Jeremy Ng, the COO of Lorcan Gaming, witnessed a similar downfall. "Many people would spend two to three hours a day grinding, knowing that they might not even earn from it. It became a toxic environment for a lot of people," he says. "It was devastating for a lot of them, because we had people quitting their jobs just to play Axie, trying to support their family or studies."

As Lorcan's and Hooga's scholar pools dwindled, the organizations poured more time and effort into a second season of the Galaxie Cup, which they announced in February. If players weren't earning money in day-to-day gameplay, maybe the organizers could incentivize them to join the tournament, which would draw viewers and thus sponsors. Thee hoped a well-financed Cup would host not only Axie tournaments but also other games and eventually become an entire Web 3 gaming convention.

But FTX decided the tournament wasn't worth the additional investment. Sam had initially said his interest in Axie was "making a positive impact," but he jettisoned it once its expected value was no longer positive. No other crypto companies picked up the slack, so Thee, Tan, Jeremy Ng, and other organizers paid for expenses out of their own pockets. "We were having meetings after meetings, looking how to manage the crisis," Ng says.

Ng says that eventually, the combination of the sinking of SLP price and FTX's decision not to reinvest in the tournament led to Lorcan Gaming winding down its operations. Hooga Gaming shuttered its guild program, too. "Many of the guilds failed to provide a return toward their investors," says Ng. "Many of the investors lost 80–90 percent of their portfolio when the whole economy really tanked." Some of those investors were hurt even more than the players themselves. The players had started with nothing and had been let down by a promise. The investors had pumped thousands of dollars into Axie, only to watch it all disappear.

In Nigeria, the decline of Axie was hurting Nestcoin, Yele Bademosi's startup dedicated to bringing Africans into crypto. The number of scholars in Nestcoin's Axie guild rapidly declined, leaving Nestcoin with a significant loss on the six-figure investment it had made in buying Axies. ("You only lose when you sell, and we're still holding them," Bademosi told me wryly a couple years later. "Nobody knows the future.")

The company pivoted to prioritize other projects. "When Axie was up high, the value proposition was very clear," says Sonia Amadi, the growth manager at Nestcoin. "It would resonate especially in a place like Nigeria, where a lot of young people are eager to find something to make money from. But we had to really count the dollars when Axie plunged. We weren't as eager to sponsor certain communities unless they were so crucial."

As Axie fell, scholars across the world climbed on any raft they could find, which meant joining similar schemes in knockoff crypto games that borrowed Axie's structure to lure in new players. But every single one of those play-to-earn games—Pegaxy, Crabada, StepN, the last of which Alameda bought millions of tokens of—followed the same peak-and-crash trajectory. "A lot of the games that would come out during the time were overflow from Axie," Thee says. "They were purely driving the token price to generate FOMO for other people to come in. It's a very bad thing. Eventually it crashes."

In March 2022, Axie was hit with one final, humiliating blow: The game was hacked for $624 million. Hackers targeted the "bridge" upon which money was transferred between game developer Sky Mavis's blockchain and Ethereum. Bridges between chains are notoriously vulnerable and were exploited several times by hackers in 2022.

While blockchains are supposed to breed transparency because all of their history is public, no one noticed that hundreds of millions of dollars had been drained from the ecosystem for almost a full week. Two-thirds of that money belonged to the users themselves, which caused an even bigger panic among traders and another drop in SLP price. The U.S. Treasury Department accused the North Korean hacker group Lazarus of perpetrating the attack as part of a larger effort to help Kim Jong Un pay for test launches of ballistic missiles.

After the hack, Sky Mavis made a hard pivot, de-emphasizing Axie's play-to-earn nature and introducing a new version, Axie Infinity: Origin, that didn't involve crypto at all. The dream of wielding crypto gaming to uplift striving workers in developing countries, for now, was dead.

Even Amy Wu, the head of FTX Ventures, admitted in the spring of 2022 that Axie and its inaugural class of crypto games hadn't exactly panned out as planned. "There's definitely been last year a lot of activity in gaming followed by, maybe, entering in a trough of disillusionment with play-to-earn specifically," she said. "The world has yet to see a lot of really fun games."

CHAPTER 24

Sam Pays Off the Umpires

In early 2022, Axie was but a minor outpost in Sam Bankman-Fried's empire. At this point, he was shuttling from Nassau to Washington, D.C., every week or two to meet with lawmakers and regulators, making a power play for control of the nation's capital.

Sam's dalliance with Washington was partly a PR strategy: to flood the public with brand awareness. Before 2020, Sam had no history of political giving. He roared into action during that year's presidential election, donating $5.2 million to Joe Biden's campaign—making him the president's second biggest personal donor, surpassed only by Michael Bloomberg. The eye-popping contribution proved an easy route to press coverage: *New York* magazine, for instance, ran an interview with Sam, describing him as a "mysterious crypto magnate."

Around this time, Milo Beckman, the former Jane Street intern, started hearing about Sam's political generosity. Beckman had left finance and written about politics and data science at *FiveThirtyEight* for a spell—and was shocked to hear that his co-intern, who had barely seemed interested in politics at all, was now one of the country's top donors. "I had a mini panic spiral. I was like, this guy should not have as much power as he does," Beckman remembers. "He was the classic case of someone who has STEM [science, technology, engineering, and mathematics] talent and thinks they're smart at everything else."

After FTX's crash, theories would fly about Sam's larger designs on Washington. Some speculated that he had been angling to move FTX from The Bahamas back to U.S. soil, where he could carve out concessions for the company that would make FTX the top dog in the country. Others believed he was laying the groundwork for a political career himself. (Caroline Ellison testified in court that Sam had boasted there was a 5 percent chance he would become president one day.) A less charitable theory was that he hoped to preemptively seek federal leniency for the illegal activity he knew he was already committing.

Whatever Sam's long-term goals in Washington, he made his short-term aims plenty evident: He stumped for a more lenient regulatory climate for crypto companies in the U.S., so that he could sell more crypto products to Americans. The wider crypto community obviously wanted more crypto in the U.S., too, so they largely rallied behind his efforts. And getting favorable legislation seemed feasible in 2022, given how much national excitement there was about crypto—and how little lawmakers actually understood it.

Sam's approach to Washington was two-pronged. The first was a charm offensive by Sam, involving high-profile hearing appearances and countless closed-door meetings with members of Congress and regulatory officials. The second was a donations blitzkrieg for crypto-friendly candidates, which was led by Sam's younger brother, Gabe Bankman-Fried.

Sam's money and sudden omnipresence in Washington sent shock waves through the Democratic Party establishment. "Washington is a place where the power structure is more or less set," says a former member of the Treasury Department. "And Sam disrupted it."

———————

Sam testified in front of Congress multiple times, with his first appearance in December 2021. At this point, around $15 billion in assets were traded daily on FTX, and its market share was rapidly growing.

Sam used his testimony to both argue that crypto improved upon traditional finance, and that FTX improved upon crypto. First, he explained the 2008 financial crisis using the jargon of an economic wonk: "You saw a number of bilateral bespoke non-reported transactions happening between financial counterparties, which then got repackaged and re-leveraged again and again and again, such that no one knew how much risk was in that system until it all fell apart," he said. (Translation: Shadow banks pretended bad assets were valuable and spread them around the financial system in increasingly risky ways.) FTX, Sam reassured lawmakers, operated with "complete transparency about the positions that are held."

In subsequent speeches and statements to Congress, Sam emphasized FTX's so-called "risk engine," a suite of automated tools to minimize unforeseen losses for customers. FTX calculated its traders' margin levels every few seconds and could automatically margin-call reckless accounts, constantly weeding out bad actors in the system, he claimed. He added that if too many customers made bad bets, FTX had a $250 million insurance fund to absorb customer losses. FTX's financial cushion and its cutting-edge technology, he argued, would "ensure a customer without losses can redeem its assets from the platform on demand."

Many lawmakers found his speeches persuasive. "It sounds like you're doing a lot to make sure there is no fraud or manipulation," Representative Tom Emmer, the GOP's majority whip, told him at the December 2021 hearing. FTX would become one of Emmer's top donors during the 2022 election.

Congressional staffers across the Hill came away from the hearings impressed and intrigued, says Devina Khanna, who was working for Representative Stephen Lynch, a Massachusetts Democrat, at the time. "There were a lot of stars in people's eyes watching that: folks on both the Democratic and Republican sides that were very taken with SBF," she says.

But there was a big problem: Virtually none of the above descriptions about Sam's business, which he made under oath, were true. While he attempted to portray FTX as the opposite of the shadow banks of the 2000s, he was mirroring their actions with his Sam Coins: leveraging and repackaging dubious assets, which were worth a lot of money in theory but lacing the system with untold risk. While FTX's risk engine was innovative and mostly effective, Sam knew that a single account was exempt from ever getting auto-liquidated: Alameda Research. Sam had directed Gary Wang to write into FTX's code that their trading firm could rack up as much debt as it pleased without getting flagged for internal review. Caroline Ellison's team could take virtually an unlimited line of credit from FTX and use it to make bigger and bigger trades.

Lastly, the insurance fund that Sam advertised to Congress as the final line of defense was fake, too. While the FTX website stated at the time that the platform had $250 million stashed away for a rainy day, that number was completely made up, and generated by a bit of code created by Gary that divided FTX's twenty-four-hour trading volume by a billion, and then multiplied it by a random number around 7,500.

By 2022, it was hard to walk around Washington without seeing Sam Bankman-Fried's face. While the press often praised him for his humility, he plastered ads of himself all over the city, and particularly in areas where congressional staffers might walk to work, including Gallery Place and Union Station.

Sam hoped that if he won the trust of regulators and Hill staffers, they might forge crucial policy changes that would allow him to grow his business in the world's largest economy. Crypto had long existed in a regulatory gray area in the United States. In 2011, the FBI explicitly stated that it was illegal to "create private coin or currency systems to compete with the official coinage and currency of the United States." But authorities mostly stood on the sidelines during the 2010s as crypto companies emerged, choosing to wait and see how the industry developed rather than snuff it out at the root.

Many early crypto companies didn't quite know if their actions were legal or not. But they largely made the economic calculation to forge ahead: to try to make millions before the government granted them a formal stamp of approval, just as major players in other industries—from Citigroup to Microsoft to Facebook and Uber—had done before them.

By 2021, however, this uncertainty had become increasingly problematic for these crypto firms, as the Securities and Exchange Commission

(SEC) began to take action against companies it deemed to be violating federal laws. The leaders of these companies complained they were playing on a field with invisible sidelines, on which refs declared them out of bounds at random. Regulators, on the other hand, felt that crypto companies were running headlong into areas marked "illegal trespassing" and then complaining when they got arrested.

Either way, something needed to change. And Sam's biggest lobbying goal was for the crypto industry to be regulated by the Commodity Futures Trading Commission (CFTC), as opposed to the SEC. "They know their shit, care about details, and display an approach that today's partisan climate could learn something from," he tweeted in May.

Crypto skeptics dismissed these arguments as disingenuous and hiding a much simpler motive. The CFTC was a much smaller organization than the SEC: It had one-third of the budget and one-seventh the number of full-time staffers. SEC chair Gary Gensler had long cast skepticism upon crypto. The CFTC, in contrast, appeared to be a much friendlier watchdog that possessed less bandwidth to wage regulatory battles or punish wrongdoers.

Timi Iwayemi, a senior researcher at the Revolving Door Project, which tracks the unholy interplay between industry and government regulators, says that the idea of CFTC oversight of crypto never made much sense to him. The CFTC focused mostly on industries with big, institutional players, like corn, wheat, and oil. The SEC, on the other hand, dealt often with investments from everyday retailers—which was exactly Sam's target market. "To put the CFTC, with its several hundred full-time workers, to deal with an ever-growing number of retail traders, seemed ridiculous," Iwayemi says.

Still, the CFTC/crypto narrative gained traction in Washington, especially thanks to the industry's intensive lobbying push, which included heavy advocacy from a plethora of new organizations with solemn names like the Chamber of Digital Commerce. These lobbying groups received funding from deep-pocketed crypto millionaires and billionaires. While they were somewhat effective, D.C. insiders argue that crypto talking points did not stick until Sam Bankman-Fried made himself the face of the effort.

Sam didn't approach Washington as a one-man band. He bolstered FTX's roster with former CFTC staffers like Mark Wetjen, who led FTX's public affairs and regulatory strategy, and Ryne Miller, a former legal counsel to then-CFTC chair Gary Gensler who became general counsel at FTX's U.S. exchange. Together, they back-channeled with current regulators while drafting industry-friendly regulation. "If you get enough smart lawyers and former regulators that know how these agencies work, you can write a draft that is appeasing to different segments," Iwayemi says.

The culmination of these efforts was a bill written by Senators Debbie Stabenow, a Michigan Democrat, and John Boozman, an Arkansas Republican, called the Digital Commodities Consumer Protection Act (DCCPA). The bill promised to create a crypto regulatory regime that would give the CFTC oversight of the industry. Sam pushed the bill so wholeheartedly that some people simply referred to it as the "SBF Bill."

Once the bill was drafted in August 2022, Sam launched into an aggressive ground game to convince congressional staffers of its merits. His powers of persuasion became evident to congressional aides—and to those hoping to strengthen regulation of the crypto industry. Rohan Grey, a law professor at Willamette University, was working on the ECASH Act, a bill that aimed to develop and pilot a digital federal dollar. Such a technology would stand in direct competition to crypto and FTX's dreams of creating their own widely traded stablecoin, which would hold the value of a U.S. dollar.

But when Grey showed up to the offices of Democratic legislators to lobby them on the merits of the ECASH Act, he found many of them had already taken meetings with FTX and absorbed their talking points. "In the land of the blind, the one-eyed man is king. And FTX is coming in with detailed legislation at a time when most elected representatives have absolutely no idea about any of this stuff," Grey remembers. "Every time we go into a room, that language is going to be at the top of everybody's head. And the first question those people have is 'Well, why shouldn't I use it?'"

Khanna, the staffer for Massachusetts Democrat Lynch, says that many representatives' offices were "falling into those kinds of traps" in part because the crypto lobby was so much louder than the public policy groups that argued for stricter regulation, including Americans for Financial Reform. "Many of the policy groups are understaffed, underfunded, and going up against this giant industry," she says. "So I think part of the issue was that a lot of these younger staffers were only hearing from the industry side."

Another one of Sam's central goals was to give FTX US retail investors the ability to trade crypto derivatives on margin. Derivatives are financial instruments that inherit their value from another asset. Someone might buy a derivative of bitcoin, for example, to bet on the price of bitcoin going up without having to actually own the asset on the blockchain. Trading on margin means borrowing money from the exchange itself in order to bet more than you have.

Under the existing governmental rules, any trade with crypto derivatives needed to be fully collateralized; that is, the investor needed to put the full amount of their bet on the table. But Sam and FTX US president Brett Harrison wanted traders to have more freedom to punch above their weight. Harrison argued that aggressive trades on margin were precisely the edge that Wall Street traders had over the public. Easing rules around collateral would simply level the playing field, he said on the crypto podcast *Wolf of All Streets*. He described this policy change as the company's "holy grail."

Derivatives are an umbrella of financial instruments that include options, swaps, and futures, the latter of which was FTX's specialty. (Remember that "FTX" stood for "futures exchange.") Derivatives can be used by traders in two ways: either to maximize their risk by betting which way the market will move, or to minimize their risk by shielding themselves from future price volatility. To give an example on the latter, let's say a corn farmer sees a major drought on the forecast that will decrease his production. He can then try to offset those losses by "shorting" corn futures on a futures commodities exchange, that is, betting that corn production will be lower than market value. So even though he sells less actual corn, he has won some money back thanks to derivatives.

Vitalik Buterin even suggested that Ethereum be used this way in the blockchain's white paper: that farmers in Iowa could easily hedge against bad weather via Ethereum derivatives without having to go through a centralized commodities exchange. Crypto derivatives, he argued, would *protect* against volatility and make trading safer.

But more often, derivatives have been used by aggressive traders for the opposite reason: to speculate on assets with the hopes of growing their money faster. Anthony Olasele, the Nigerian host of *Crypto Round Up Africa*, loved trading futures for exactly this reason. And when too many people place their money in derivatives, risky financial bubbles can grow. In 2003, Warren Buffett called derivatives "financial weapons of mass destruction, carrying dangers that, while now latent, are potentially lethal." In 2008, the downfall of Lehman Brothers was exacerbated by its status as counterparty to almost 1 million derivatives contracts.

After the 2008 financial crisis, the economist Alan S. Blinder wrote an analysis of the disaster in his book *After the Music Stopped*, in which he argued that while derivatives had been sold to the public as a tool for safety, they were actually central to the crash. "Instruments that are originally designed to hedge away risk typically become innovative ways to create risk where there was none before," he wrote.

Nevertheless, FTX plowed forward with its derivatives quest, purchasing LedgerX, a derivatives firm, in August 2021. LedgerX was a U.S.-based company that had been approved by the CFTC to offer fully collateralized futures to traders, allowing them to bet on future price movements of cryptocurrencies, albeit only with money they actually had on hand. By absorbing a reputable company, Sam believed he would get a fast track toward winning over the CFTC and being able to offer all sorts of financial crypto products to American traders.

After the deal went through, FTX US's general counsel Ryne Miller relayed the news to Dan Berkovitz, a former CFTC commissioner who had just been appointed to an SEC post by President Biden. The FTX team was aggressively courting Berkovitz's good graces, and had just wined and dined him at the D.C. hot spot Rasika.

Berkovitz, in response to Miller's email—which was made public via the Freedom of Information Act—noted that he had seen FTX's logo while watching an MLB baseball game. "I'm not sure why MLB needs to have a cryptocurrency exchange, but glad to see that it has one that supports regulation!" he wrote.

Sam wrote back: "We are the natural choice to be the 'umpires of the crypto industry.'"

Sam participated in a CFTC roundtable in May 2022, in which he tried to persuade regulators and giants from the derivatives industry that FTX US should be allowed to offer derivatives on margin without having to go through traditional intermediaries. One skeptical futures brokerage executive predicted that FTX's automatic liquidation system, which was supposed to keep traders safe, would "create a cycle of flash crashes."

Sam responded impatiently. "Most of the traders on our platform know a lot more about these contracts than many of the people in this room, including many of the people who are condescendingly talking to them about what they do and don't know," he barked.

In 2021 and 2022, Sam met with top CFTC officials more than ten times in the hopes of scoring favorable regulation. While he threw his weight around at the CFTC, the SEC was proving much more of a challenge. The month before Miller and Berkovitz's dinner at Rasika, SEC chair Gensler called crypto a "highly speculative asset class" and argued that many cryptocurrencies should be closely regulated as securities under his purview. In March 2022, the SEC filed an inquiry into crypto firms like FTX to examine their "unique risks."

The agency's decision to investigate, however, was met with swift blowback from a bipartisan group of eight members of Congress, known as the Blockchain 8, who penned a critical letter suggesting that the SEC might be breaking the law and overstepping its boundaries. They were Republicans Emmer (a Minnesota Republican and later failed House speaker candidate), Representative Warren Davidson from Ohio, Representative Byron Donalds of Florida, and Representative Ted Budd of North Carolina, and Democrats Representative Josh Gottheimer of New Jersey, Representative Jake Auchincloss from Massachusetts, Representative Ritchie Torres of New York, and Representative Darren Soto from Florida. In the coming months, five of the eight signees would receive campaign donations from FTX employees ranging from $2,900 to $11,600. Budd alone received half a million dollars from a Super PAC created by FTX co-CEO Ryan Salame—a sign that Sam was not just courting members of the Democratic Party.

But the SEC didn't budge. The same month, March 2022, Sam met with Gensler in Washington. Miller, the general counsel who had just been hired straight from the CFTC, came along with Sam as a friendly face.

The pitch, Gensler later said, was for FTX to receive approval for a new crypto trading platform. But the SEC head says he rebuffed the group within minutes of the meeting's onset, telling them that they should stop their presentation on the second slide. "I indicated to them," Gensler told *New York* magazine, "that it was not a valuable use of their time."

CHAPTER 25

More *Veep* Than *West Wing*

If Sam couldn't crack Gensler's defenses, then maybe he could get Congress to write legislation that would allow him to bypass the SEC altogether. As he personally met with senators, he enlisted his younger brother, Gabe, to help bring new crypto-friendly faces to Congress's halls.

Gabe had lived in Washington with a bunch of effective altruist friends for several years and had served as a staffer for Illinois Representative Sean Casten, a Democrat on the House Financial Services Committee. Given Sam's penchant for hiring family and friends, Gabe was the obvious choice to head up his new political outfits. That included a nonprofit called Guarding Against Pandemics and an affiliated Super PAC called Protect Our Future. Sam quickly funneled $27 million to the PAC, whose ostensible goal was to promote candidates who prioritized anti-pandemic research and prevention.

"He thought it was very effective, that you could get very high returns in terms of influence by spending relatively small amounts of money," Caroline Ellison testified about Sam's fundraising.

Sam and Gabe were not the first generation of D.C. operatives in their family. Their mother, Barbara Fried, was herself an influential Democratic party operator who had cofounded Mind the Gap, a California-based fundraising operation that Fried described as "risk-neutral"—one of Sam's own very favorite terms—in a letter to potential investors in January 2018. Mind the Gap operated stealthily, often donating to candidates in secret so as to escape the detection of Republicans. Their tactics worked: In 2018, Mind the Gap raised millions for dozens of candidates from Silicon Valley's young, rich, and Democratic elite, helping to secure a blue landslide in the midterms that year.

When Sam and Gabe jumped into politics, Barbara was ready to teach them a few tricks of the trade—including obfuscation. In April 2021, Barbara asked Sam to give $1 million to Mind the Gap but to mask the source of the funds. "I'm assuming Nishad would be the better person to have his name on it," she wrote in an email that was later published by FTX's bankruptcy team. "We don't want to create the impression that funding MTG is a family affair, as opposed to a collective effort by many people (including some mystery guy Nishad Singh :))." Sam agreed to front the money, and Nishad, FTX's director of engineering, agreed to put his name on it.

In 2022, the Bankman-Fried boys were flush with cash and energy, and had a keen understanding of how to spread money around in secret. As the primary election cycle heated up, Protect Our Future doled out unprecedented amounts of donations to races all over the country. Gabe also found a willing collaborator in the pollster Sean McElwee, a rising star in the Democratic Party. Together, they held court at many Washington meetings with prospective candidates who sought Gabe's endorsement and fat checks. "It was still a pretty scary show of force," says Rohan Grey, the Willamette professor who was campaigning for a rival digital currency bill. "It was very clear how much money they were throwing around, and everybody was salivating."

———————

Protect Our Future purported to be a one-issue PAC: to guard against future pandemics. Their early donation choices seemed to align with this mission. One of the first candidates they threw money at was Carrick Flynn, a political newcomer running in the Democratic primary for Oregon's 6th Congressional District. Flynn had spent years studying the risks of artificial intelligence and pandemics, and had ties to effective altruism circles. Sam rewarded him with a cool $11 million, which shattered previous records for single-group spending in a single House primary race. Flynn's campaign manager, Avital Balwit, would join the FTX Foundation a few months later.

But Flynn had few local political connections and failed to engage with local media or resonate with Democrats in the district. He proceeded to get crushed in the May primary election, receiving just thirteen thousand votes, or 18 percent of all ballots. Essentially, Sam had spent $850 per vote to lose in a local primary. For someone who aspired to be a heavyweight political influencer, his first attempt was laughable, with pundits all over the country skewering the attempt as ill-spent and quixotic.

Despite Flynn's loss, the race put Bankman-Fried on the map as an eager donor with nearly unlimited pockets. "One, it was an announcement that 'I'm a big player in this room. This is how much money I can give to you,'" says Iwayemi, the researcher at the Revolving Door Project. "Two, it was a test case to see how much money can actually influence an election, especially one that doesn't have much national press."

From that point on, Protect Our Future would be no less generous but slightly more tactical with their donations. It soon became clear, however, that the group's spending didn't relate to pandemic prepared-ness at all. Instead, it seemed the PAC was increasingly supporting can-didates who fell into at least one of two buckets: moderates who would preserve the Democratic establishment and overwhelming favorites who would undoubtedly walk the halls of Congress in the years to come. If Bankman-Fried couldn't get effective altruists into power, maybe he at least could buy the ear of lawmakers.

Nida Allam fit into neither of Sam's preferred categories. In 2020, Allam had become the first Muslim woman to hold an elected office in North Carolina when she was voted a Durham County commissioner. Two years later, she decided to run for the open congressional seat in North Carolina's 4th Congressional District, hoping to foment a more progressive and inclusive Congress.

Allam declared that she would not accept any campaign donations from PACs or Super PACs, as a rejoinder to the dominance of big money since the *Citizens United* Supreme Court decision in 2010. By March, she had rallied passionate grassroots support to raise $700,000, far outpacing her main primary rival, Valerie Foushee. Allam was also boosted by endorsements from major Democratic figures like Senators Bernie Sanders and Elizabeth Warren.

But in April, Allam learned that Foushee had started to receive a flood of money from Protect Our Future. Over three weeks, Sam's PAC dumped a little over $1 million into pro-Foushee ads and mailers. PAC-funded commercial spots started popping up on the airwaves, while registered Democrats in Durham received a deluge of flyers every week. At the same time, AIPAC, the American Israel Public Affairs Committee also poured more than a million dollars into Foushee's campaign. The combined contributions made the race for North Carolina's 4th District the most expensive Democratic congressional primary in state history.

AIPAC's contributions made some amount of sense, as Foushee had argued for Israel's right to defend itself, while Allam had long criticized Israel's treatment of Palestinians. But if Protect Our Future really strove to prevent pandemics, Allam felt its massive support of Foushee was strange. The PAC gave scant explanation as to why they felt Foushee was the best choice on pandemics. The group's ads for Foushee didn't mention the topic at all. Other candidates in the race included Duke University climate expert Ashley Ward and virologist Richard Watkins.

And Allam was currently serving on the state's Board of Health during the pandemic. She had been part of the official team overseeing vaccine rollout, tracing hot spots, and deploying vaccine education to marginalized communities.

Allam didn't question Valerie Foushee's commitment to stopping the next pandemic. But nobody at Protect Our Future had reached out to Allam to ask about her opinions in that arena. And for the PAC to pour so much money into the primary, as opposed to the general election, seemed, to her, unhelpful to its stated purpose. "If you really cared about that, you should go invest in beating Republicans who have refused to provide funding for masks or families struggling to care for their kids during the pandemic," she says.

By the day of the primary, Allam had raised a total of $1.2 million, around the same amount that Foushee received from Protect Our Future alone. Foushee had barely done any campaigning and skipped several of the candidate forums. But she ended up prevailing over Allam by eight thousand votes, or 9 percentage points.

"Anyone would be delusional to believe that significant of an investment flooding TV, email, digital did not impact this race," Allam says.

———

Protect Our Future spent millions more in dozens of races across the country, often siding with moderates. The Foushee-Allam race was one of fourteen primaries in which one of Sam's PACs and an AIPAC-affiliated outfit put money toward the same more moderate candidate. Ten of those candidates won, including Shontel Brown (Ohio), Morgan McGarvey (Kentucky), and Sydney Kamlager (Illinois).

One exception for Sam's moderate bias was Florida's progressive rising star Maxwell Alejandro Frost, whom Sam spent almost $1 million on in TV and digital ads. But Frost was already an overwhelming favorite in his race, and as a Gen Z candidate he was predisposed to Sam's pro-crypto message. Shortly after the PAC gave him money, Frost announced the formation of a crypto advisory council, which included Gabe's close political ally Sean McElwee.

D.C. insiders say that late in the campaign cycle, a clear pattern emerged—of Sam and Gabe Bankman-Fried giving donations not based on ideology but likelihood of victory. "At that point in the cycle, they had switched to 'We'll give $500,000 to anyone who already has this locked up—that way, they'll be forever in our debt,'" a D.C. operative tells me. "There was no ideological consistency to who they gave money to in the last four to five months. It was a lot more silly than strategic: More *Veep* than *West Wing*."

Sam ended the 2022 election cycle as the third-biggest public Democratic donor of the midterms, trailing only Michael Bloomberg and the infamous financier George Soros. He sent huge amounts to the Democratic establishment: $6 million to the House Majority PAC, which focused on helping Democrats hold on to the House, and $500,000 to the Senate Majority PAC, a similar group aimed at Senate races. At more local levels, Sam donated to thirty-nine state Democratic parties and executive committees.

It was easy for some centrist Democrats to look at Sam and see everything they hoped their party would become. Here was a young entrepreneur with deep familial party roots, who was proselytizing about effective altruism and the power of fintech to facilitate financial inclusion. Over the prior decade, prominent Democrats, including President Obama, had enjoyed a cozy relationship with the tech industry and relied on its power players as a major source of campaign cash. Bankman-Fried seemed to be a younger, fresher version of the Jack Dorseys of the world. "He was the perfect poison pill inside the rot of the party," Rohan Grey says.

While some Democrats embraced him, others questioned his goals and tactics, and raised the same questions that Nida Allam did. If Sam was such a big booster of the Democratic Party and pandemic prevention, then why had a hundred percent of Protect Our Future's donations been spent in the midterms? Why was he not funding the Democrats to flip red seats blue?

The answer was that he was secretly funding the Republicans, too— and for a very predictable reason. Leaders of Sam's pandemic-preparedness-oriented Super PAC Protect Our Future repeatedly denied that their aims had anything to do with crypto lobbying. But a private, typo-laden text from Ryan Salame, CEO of FTX Digital Markets and one of Sam's closest allies in The Bahamas, to a confidant, told a different story. "Sam wants to donate to both democtratic and republican candidates in the US but cause the worlds frankly lost its mind if you dontate to a democrat no republicans will speak to you and if you donate to a republican then no democrats will speak to you. We wont be flipping any red seats blue or blue seats red," he wrote in a November 2021 message that was later admitted as evidence in Sam's trial. "But we will be heavily putting money to weed out anti crypto dems for pro crypto dems and anti crypto repubs for pro crypto repubs."

The Blockchain 8 was proof that Sam could win crypto allies on both sides of the aisle. But he felt that he couldn't give money directly to Republicans because of the optics. "Reporters freak the fuck out if you donate to Republicans," he told the content creator Tiffany Fong in November 2022, after his empire had fallen apart. "They're all super-liberal, and I didn't want to have that fight."

So instead, Sam turned to hidden donations, just like his mother had. Virtually all of the political donations coming out of FTX were part of one coordinated influence campaign, which largely unfolded over a Signal group chat called Donation Processing. Sam was on the chat; so was Nishad Singh, who was made the face of the center-left donations, giving out $14 million to Democrats—even though he grumbled in messages about having to donate to "explicitly-woke stuff" like the LGBT Victory Fund. When Gabe Bankman-Fried's team decided to donate to a Democrat, they would send a request on the group chat prompting Ryan Salame, who had access to Nishad's personal bank account, to initiate the transfers. All Nishad had to do was click a button to approve the transaction. At one point, to expedite this process, Gabe's assistant flew to The Bahamas with Nishad's checkbook, so that he could sign a whole book of blank checks for Gabe to send out however he wished.

Ryan Salame, in turn, happily became the mouthpiece of the Republican side. He flowed more than $23 million to Republicans in 2022, a figure approaching the $35 million given out by conservative mega-donor Peter Thiel. (FTX also doled out $200,000 to New York Republican Michelle Bond, a Donald Trump Jr.–endorsed congressional candidate who happened to be Ryan's girlfriend.) Financial forensics experts would later trace much of the money for political donations—ostensibly given by Singh and Salame—back to Alameda bank accounts, and then back to transfers pulled from customer deposits.

Sam was playing both sides: a logical end point to his nihilist approach, in which the only thing that mattered was expected value. The ideological principles of the candidates he gave money to didn't matter. All that mattered was that he continued to amass power himself.

So Sam took meetings with Mitch McConnell and Ron DeSantis.

While he was publicly directing a million dollars to Democrat Valerie Foushee in North Carolina's 4th Congressional District, he was also using Salame to funnel six figures to North Carolina Republican Ted Budd, a Blockchain 8 member who was on his way to being elected to the Senate. And Budd didn't exactly have a sterling record on pandemic preparedness: At the start of COVID-19, he had been one of only a handful of Republican representatives who voted against the bipartisan Families First Coronavirus Response Act.

Ultimately, a majority of the candidates that Protect Our Future donated to expressed meaningful pro-crypto sentiment or held committee positions related to crypto regulation. And many other crypto executives saw Sam's successes in Washington and followed his lead: More than $26 million flowed from crypto companies to political races in 2021 and the first quarter of 2022, outpacing spending from Big Pharma, Big Tech, and the defense industry.

All in all, an astounding 196 members of Congress—more than a third of all senators and representatives—received cash from Sam Bankman-Fried or other senior executives at FTX. And Sam announced that he had only scratched the surface of his largess: that he was aiming for a $1 billion "soft ceiling" for the 2024 election. A new kingmaker had arrived in Washington.

CHAPTER 26

"FTX Will Always Be Here"

The irony of Sam Bankman-Fried's Washington influence campaign was that his company still operated offshore. Sam said that he had chosen The Bahamas for its innovative crypto regulation. But he was also using the island nation in the same way that many outsiders had done before him.

The Bahamas has had a long, complicated relationship with foreign money. The nation is now among the most stable in the region: It's the third-oldest democracy in the Western Hemisphere and celebrated its fiftieth anniversary of independence in 2023. But The Bahamas and the wider Caribbean region have "repeatedly functioned as a Frankenstein laboratory of global capitalism," the Columbia history professor Adam Tooze wrote in 2022.

Brits colonized The Bahamas in the seventeenth century; the islands were frequently battered by skirmishes among European naval powers. In the 1920s, The Bahamas was a prime staging ground for bootleggers shipping rum to the U.S. during Prohibition. The first wealth management offices opened in Nassau during that era and grew post–World War II, when new international monetary rules forced global elites to search for cheaper ways to move and store their money. The islands of The Bahamas were an ideal landing spot to park money and dodge taxes, as they had relatively stable politics, high income due to tourism, and familiar financial and cultural vestiges from their time as a British colony.

The Bahamian government eagerly courted foreign money over the years, creating rules to guarantee anonymity for new bank account holders. As business boomed in Nassau, so did money laundering.

According to a 1979 Ford Foundation study, drug money and tax evasion routed $20 billion a year from the U.S. into The Bahamas. A 1991 study asserted that in the decade prior, 40 to 80 percent of the cocaine and marijuana in the U.S. had come by way of The Bahamas. In the nineties, the former Chilean dictator Augusto Pinochet laundered at least $4 million through two offshore Bahamian shell corporations.

In recent years, The Bahamas has floated on and off various European blacklists naming countries with insufficient measures against tax evasion and money laundering. But the country's economy has become much more reliant on another industry: tourism. By 2022, tourism and related services made up about 70 percent of the country's GDP. This made the country extremely susceptible to macro-economic downturns in the rest of the world. Bahamian tourist seasons were hit hard following 9/11 and the 2008 financial crisis. The one-two punch of Hurricane Dorian, a Category 5 storm that ravaged the Bahamian islands in 2019, and the pandemic was even more devastating. As government spending surged to meet the needs of the people, and incoming tourists cancelled their vacations, the debt-to-GDP ratio shot above 100 percent; the country was $9 billion in debt.

In October 2021, FTX gave The Bahamas a chance at a fresh start: to be the nucleus of a new crypto era. The country's brand-new prime minister, Philip Davis, met with Sam within a month of being sworn in. The Bahamian real estate mogul Mario Carey predicted that FTX's arrival would "catapult the country to the top of the world stage," and crowed that FTX was "the holy grail of financial services that we have been waiting for." Sure enough, FTX spent over $243 million on real estate in the island nation, including a $16.4 million mansion bought in Sam's parents' names. Most of the purchases were in the gated community of Albany, which sits a forty-minute drive from Nassau's downtown.

Just like in Washington, Sam plastered his face—and his money—all over the island nation of four hundred thousand people. FTX ads popped up everywhere, including at the Nassau airport hall where tourists disembarked. To ingratiate himself with the community, he gave away millions collectively to local charities and government efforts for agriculture and coronavirus masks. Another recipient was Bishop Lawrence Rolle, a Pentecostal preacher known for singing his sermons, who received $50,000 to restore a food storage trailer and donate food to those in need. "This more than Emancipation Day, I feel like hollering," Rolle told local outlet *The Tribune*.

"FTX became the gold mine, the new thing everyone wanted to get a slice of," says Travis Miller, a Bahamian business and technology consultant. "So much money was flowing from them. But little to no one was paying attention in terms of exactly how this money was actually being generated."

Sam also hired a handful of Bahamians onto his staff, mostly to head up the compliance team stipulated by the DARE Act, the law that made The Bahamas a crypto haven. One of them was Valdez Russell, FTX's new vice president of communications and corporate social responsibility. Russell, a mellifluous public speaker, waxed eloquently about FTX's commitment to the island and the way it would uplift a country long over-reliant on tourism. "FTX belongs in The Bahamas. FTX will always be here," he told the local radio host Nahaja Black in January 2022. "We will be a vital part of our economic growth and touch the lives of every Bahamian, one way or another."

While Sam did give to The Bahamas, the country had something that Sam desperately needed: cover for his financial shell games. Bahamian government officials argued that the DARE Act propelled innovation and financial inclusion. But some crypto regulatory experts held a different opinion. In 2022, the Cambridge law professor Ann Sofie Cloots was approached by a UK crypto company to examine whether it was a good idea for them to incorporate in The Bahamas. After reviewing the DARE Act and its application process, she ended up advising them against it. "My impression was, if you fill in the paperwork and check the boxes, nobody really knows if you have these policies or how rigorously they're enforced," she says. "It was like it was made for FTX. Most other people that were serious about crypto stayed clear of The Bahamas."

The Black Bahamians who FTX did hire mostly did not become fully integrated into the company's work culture. They worked in a separate building and didn't mingle much with the international staffers. Disputes arose over whether the Bahamian employees were matching the work ethic of their international peers. It was an eerie shadow of a long history of racial segregation in Nassau: In the 1930s, a prominent American bootlegger built an eight-foot-high wall that would come to essentially separate the white and Black parts of town.

Sam came to The Bahamas not just to extract, but also to proselytize. The population of The Bahamas was a small fraction of the population of Hong Kong, his previous home. On an effective altruism blog forum in October, Caroline Ellison noted that its smallness could allow them to make EA a "somewhat influential force in the country." That month, Sam announced the creation of EA FTX fellowships in The Bahamas, in which he would fly utilitarians out to the islands to work among his crypto developers and spread their ideas. Sam, like the generations of colonizers before him, had settled in the Caribbean and intended to remake the country in his own image.

CHAPTER 27

Trouble in Paradise

While the philosophy of effective altruism centered on giving money away, it seemed like all that FTX did in The Bahamas was spend. In December, after months at the SLS Baha Mar hotel, Christine Chew moved into a massive $6.75 million apartment in the Albany, a resort complex in one of the ritziest areas of The Bahamas. The billionaire's playground included an eighteen-hole golf course designed by former World No. 1 golfer Ernie Els, a mega-yacht marina, and exclusive restaurants closed to the public. A full-size replica of the Wall Street charging bull statue sat on the marina, near a Rolex store.

Christine's new apartment was ostensibly owned by Ryan Salame but was more so just another property in the company's sprawling real estate empire. As CEO of FTX Digital Markets, Salame was Christine's boss, but they weren't too far apart in age and had been among the first FTX settlers onto Bahamian shores the previous summer. While many FTX employees were hardworking introverts who relaxed over board games, Ryan was different: He often hosted parties for employees in his apartment, filled with food and booze and revelry. FTX paid to keep restaurants open around the clock, hire DJs for parties, and allow employees to expense cars—including BMWs—to chauffeur them around the island. "It definitely felt a little bit crazy and extravagant. It feels like no one is keeping track of how much we were actually spending—the food, the cars, the benefits," says an FTX staffer.

FTX staffers who didn't live in The Bahamas could fly in and stay at luxury hotels in the Baha Mar, with all expenses paid. Executives flew the company's private jet on trips abroad. FTX chartered planes to fly Amazon packages from the mainland to employees in The Bahamas. At the Paris Blockchain Week Summit in April 2022, FTX threw a party across from the Eiffel Tower and rented a boat down the Seine, and their employees stayed at luxury hotels.

While Christine's new lifestyle didn't exactly fit into effective altruism principles, she was able to rationalize the expenses in comparison to FTX's seemingly ceaseless success. "The lavishness was justified in the assumption that we are making tons of money—and we're probably spending 0.1 percent of what the company makes in a day," Christine told herself.

Christine's apartment was stunning. But it was nothing compared to the crown jewel of FTX's new Bahamian real estate empire: a $30 million, 11,050-square-foot penthouse in the Albany's seaside Orchid residence. The sixth-floor residence consisted of five bedrooms, and included a private elevator, a spa, a pool, a grand piano, and Italian marble floors. A private balcony looked out onto the gleaming blue-green ocean below.

The penthouse, of course, belonged to Sam Bankman-Fried. For all his talk of living modestly and giving money away, he had chosen a palace that would have befitted the bootleggers and kingpins who had come before him. Initially, Sam's friends had blanched at the prospect of spending so much money on housing. Nishad Singh thought the penthouse was "super ostentatious," and wanted them to find a cheaper place. But Sam told him that he would pay $100 million for the drama of the house-hunting to be done, so Nishad stopped arguing and agreed to move in with him.

Five couples (or ex-couples) lived in the Albany penthouse: Gary and Cheryl Chen; Nishad and Claire Watanabe, an FTX executive; Leila Clark, an FTX developer, and Ross Rheingans-Yoo, a FTX Foundation staffer; FTX developers Adam Yedidia and Andrea Lincoln; and Sam and Caroline, who dated on and off. After the FTX crash, many outside voyeurs of the scandal came to believe that the penthouse's residents were polyamorous, and all dated each other openly. This belief stemmed from a widespread misinterpretation of a *CoinDesk* article—which stated that its residents were in relationships—and the unearthing of Caroline's blog posts from two years earlier, in which she had written about her previous forays into polyamory.

"I've come to decide the only acceptable style of poly is best characterized as something like 'imperial Chinese harem,'" she wrote. "None of this non-hierarchical bullshit; everyone should have a ranking of their partners, people should know where they fall on the ranking, and there should be vicious power struggles for the higher ranks." Polyamory was widely practiced in effective altruist circles, particularly in their communities in the Bay Area, where Caroline lived for a spell.

Christine says that it was clear that Sam's brain trust was very close, and that they would all get in the hot tub together to talk philosophy and effective altruism. Other reports would claim that Sam had dated multiple FTX employees in The Bahamas. "But I don't think there were any orgies going on," Christine says. "Every time I hung out, it was the most boring conversations ever. A bunch of nerds talking about card games, chess, board games, philosophy, and math."

Christine was first invited to the penthouse in December 2022, for an FTX community dinner and walked about a block along the marina from her apartment to get there. The inside of the penthouse was messy, stuffed with video game monitors and cheap bookshelves filled with board games. The view looking out from the giant balcony, however, was breathtaking. "I thought it was quite luxurious and over the top, and not what Sam claimed to be about, which was about being humble and choosing a Toyota over a Beamer," she says.

At dinners like this one, Sam cooked vegan meals of Beyond burgers and sausages. He and his friends talked endlessly about effective altruism, and considered expected value trade-offs even when making the most mundane decisions, like how much food to order. "Sam always encouraged taking risky decisions," Christine says. "He thought people were too risk averse. He said that you need to make decisions that can move you three steps forward or half a step back."

FTX employees, including Sam, were driven to work in private cars. It was a short twelve-minute ride to the Veridian Corporate Center, where FTX had spent at least $10 million on office space. FTX didn't just work there but served as a landlord to other crypto companies that hoped that proximity to FTX's overwhelming successes would rub off on them. FTX's Veridian offices mostly lacked decoration, but they were comfy and functional, filled with couches and beanbags. Sam sometimes slept in one of those beanbags rather than going home to his penthouse or his other apartment in the Albany that even some FTX executives didn't know about. His desk was often cluttered with the detritus of a college student: a stick of deodorant here, a Morton salt canister there. He munched on Nutter Butters and chickpea korma, and showed up to meetings with sauce stains on his khaki shorts. As he Zoomed into meetings with investors and journalists around the world, he played the crypto game Storybook Brawl, which FTX had recently acquired, on a different window of his computer.

As Brett Harrison had complained, Sam was spending more and more time on PR and self-promotion rather than the actual day-to-day operations of his company. But he still was running on an all-hours, all-consuming work schedule, and his employees were likewise expected to embrace this mentality. Many employees worked for upward of twelve hours a day, seven days a week, albeit with breaks to play padel tennis at courts downstairs. FTX's offices were stocked with vegan egg substitute and bottles of Soylent, which employees would sometimes drink for entire days so as to not waste time with food decisions or eating.

"He doesn't believe in taking vacations," says Natalie Tien, FTX's head of PR and marketing who also served as Sam's assistant. "If you're not in his visible sight for more than two weeks, just assume that you're not in the company anymore."

Sleeping at work was ingrained into the company culture: Nishad Singh also made a bed under his desk. One night, Gajesh Naik, a precocious teenage developer from Goa, India, who worked at the FTX campus for most of summer 2022 before getting hired as an intern in September, slept on a beanbag in the office in the hopes of channeling his relentless boss. "Some people got burnt out and left. But for most of the people at

FTX, it was like one person was worth twenty people," he says. "They were that strong."

Many FTX employees were forced to work this hard because they had to. FTX's staff of around three hundred people was now managing a multibillion-dollar company that held the wealth of people around the world. But Sam still treated the company like a scrappy startup: He placed people in jobs for which they were not qualified and expected them to figure it out. Other roles were simply unfulfilled. "We would hire a lot of people in random, unimportant roles, like logistics, operation, and product management," Christine Chew says. Christine was in one of those random roles herself, as a quasi utility player who sometimes helped put on events, but overall had to work much less hard than the engineering and customer support teams. Gary Wang, FTX's cofounder, was getting so burned out that the coder Adam Yedidia implemented a rule for staffers to stop waking up Wang in the middle of the night to fix the inevitable bugs that arose.

On the other hand, Sam had no problem with hiring people he was close to—including his own father, Joe Bankman. Sam put him on payroll in December 2021 as an adviser on corporate and tax matters, and bought him and his mother, Barbara, a $16 million, thirty-thousand-square-foot waterfront house in The Bahamas using funds from an FTX Trading bank account. Yet his father still complained about the size of his new paychecks. "Gee Sam, I don't know what to say here. This is the first [I] have heard of the 200K a year salary!" he wrote in an email that was later unearthed by FTX's bankruptcy team. "Putting Barbara on this."

By the middle of 2022, stress and sleeplessness had transformed FTX's new headquarters from a Caribbean paradise into a hornet's nest. The lack of an HR department or real job titles meant that employees fought over job territory and worked furiously to curry favor with Sam. "It all boils down to what Sam thinks is right or wrong: He is basically the monarch and the dictator," Christine says.

One employee got the sense that Sam liked being the nexus of office gossip and tension, since it gave him more emotional power over everyone—and that he would confront employees with accusations made by their colleagues. Natalie Tien says that the company's so-called "flat" structure led to people getting very territorial. "It's sort of creating a very toxic vibe that people feel like they have to fight for their job," she says. "Your colleagues became your friends, enemies, roommates, and your social circle." Employees who had no discernible role one day were suddenly giving out performance reviews and firing people the next.

The mood turned so sour that Sam decided to put his own psychiatrist, George Lerner, on payroll. Lerner would hold calls with employees, serving as a pseudo company coach. Lerner told the *Wall Street Journal* that he saw about a hundred of the company's three hundred employees for coaching, and that he tried to help them go out on dates. Employees said that Lerner was open about his ability to prescribe Adderall or Xanax to treat anxiety. (Lerner told the *Journal* that he only prescribed medicine to patients when medically necessary.)

Lerner's presence did little to reduce the growing stress of working in FTX's pressure cooker. Natalie Tien was working eighteen hours a day in order to field all of the incoming requests from people who sought Sam's charm and expertise. Natalie asked Sam several times to hire a second PR person—but Sam liked the way Natalie ran things, and declined. "There were just so many times I told George [Lerner] I felt like I wanted to rage-quit because of these many little incidents of Sam agreeing to something, and at the last minute, backing out," she says.

As Lerner listened to the employees' many grievances, he also became increasingly concerned about Sam's own mental health and advised him to improve his sleep, diet, and physical activity. Sam responded that he didn't care about his long-term health—and that he felt he had a five-year window to make as much money in crypto as he possibly could.

In the middle of 2022, long-promised employee bonuses were put off for months. Sam justified their delay by saying he was simply too busy to organize them. He was excelling in presenting himself to the world. But in being a competent internal company leader, he was failing disastrously.

Christine Chew says she began to feel increasingly lonely and isolated. Work and play blended together; her teammates and superiors were inescapable. "I believe I'm not the only one who felt this way," she says. "That's why many people, when they have time, they're just drinking excessively until they cannot handle it anymore." Christine and other colleagues coped with the stress by binging on tequila, cocaine, and weed.

Christine told Lerner about her problems at the company and feeling a lack of purpose. "He told me, 'Everyone feels lonely in FTX,' so you're not alone," Christine says. He also wrote Christine a prescription for anti-depressants.

Christine realized she had strayed extremely far from her initial mission to help people. She wasn't even donating her salary to charitable causes, as many effective altruists at FTX, including Sam, no longer believed it made rational sense to give away money from each paycheck. Instead, they thought that it was more effective to take the money they earned and invest it—so they'd be able to give far more money later on.

Christine eventually realized these actions looked identical to those of any money-obsessed trader with no higher purpose. She bounced around from project to project, unable to break into FTX's power structure. She worked for a while on the planning of Crypto Bahamas, a massive conference held at the Baha Mar resort in Nassau. Christine's job was to work with SALT, an events organization run by the famously short-lived Trump press secretary Anthony Scaramucci, to book speakers and organize panels.

But in April, just before the conference, Ryan told her she had been fired. Christine wasn't exactly surprised. But the news still stung, especially because Christine still lived in Ryan's apartment—and he gave her a one-week notice to move out. Over a couple days, Christine packed up everything she could in her suitcase, leaving behind a couple boxes of summer clothes and an electric skateboard. She spent the next couple weeks traveling Europe, trying to make sense of her eight-month stay in The Bahamas. She knew that FTX was poorly run and dysfunctional in many ways. But she still believed in Sam Bankman-Fried's vision of becoming the Robin Hood of the American financial system.

CHAPTER 28

Coronation

To most people outside of FTX, Sam was still a golden boy, only growing in stature. In April 2022, Sam and Prime Minister Philip Davis broke ground on a planned $60 million headquarters for FTX overlooking the aquamarine water at Bayside Executive Park. Ryan Salame had asserted at a Nassau town planning meeting that within three years, the campus would rival Google's or Apple's in Silicon Valley. Plans featured a thirty-eight-room boutique hotel, after-school facilities, gymnasiums, outdoor dining, and commercial and retail stores. Prime Minister Davis was thrilled. "Since moving to our shores, FTX has left positive footprints throughout The Bahamas," he tweeted. He predicted that the new headquarters would create hundreds of jobs for Bahamians.

FTX surpassed Coinbase—a more cautious, U.S.-focused crypto exchange—in market share to become the second-biggest crypto exchange in the world behind Binance. The company's U.S. wing, led by Brett Harrison, opened a new headquarters in Chicago, where Mayor Lori Lightfoot praised the company for challenging "the traditional banks and financial lenders to get on board with a new reality." She added: "Crypto has the ability to advance financial inclusion by reaching and benefiting those who are unbanked." (Lightfoot would be voted out of office the following year.) And in May, I myself (gulp) wrote an admiring entry about Sam for the *Time* 100 2022, which celebrated the year's most influential people.

The culmination of Sam's many victories was Crypto Bahamas. In the last week of April, thousands of crypto enthusiasts, venture capitalists, and

Wall Street veterans flew into Nassau to schmooze, pitch, invest, drink, and dance. Celebrities, political heavyweights, and financial titans were everywhere you turned: Bill Clinton and Tony Blair; Katy Perry and Orlando Bloom (who had come by way of Sam's Hollywood connector Michael Kives); Andrew Yang and Olympic gold medal speed skater Apolo Ohno; and Tom Brady.

But there was no doubt as to the true star of the show. "This was the coronation of the youngest billionaire in the world," says Mark, the crypto exec, who attended the conference and stayed at the Baha Mar for the weekend. "Everyone else at the conference was a spectator, here to witness their grandeur."

Sam made several on-stage appearances and was met with raucous applause. He wore a white FTX tee, cargo shorts, and crew-length white socks, even when sitting next to the former world leaders Clinton and Blair, who wore full suits and patted him jovially on the shoulder. Many people who saw photos of the trio on social media ridiculed Sam's outfit. But it signaled a sartorial power play in which the two world leaders were clearly on his turf.

While onstage with the Brazilian supermodel Gisele Bündchen, Sam announced a $1 billion charity fund and unveiled a new ad that featured a photo of him surrounded by the quote "I'm in on crypto because I want to make the biggest global impact for good." He shot a TikTok with Brady, feigning impatience with Brady's simple-minded self-promotion: The nerd getting the last laugh on the jock. Later, Sam told the *New York Times* that he hoped to buy a football team together with the quarterback. (Brady and Bündchen were paid about $56 million for their FTX endorsements.)

Sam was then interviewed onstage by Michael Lewis, the esteemed best-selling financial journalist who had previously memorialized heroic, math-driven rebels in books like *Moneyball* and *The Big Short*. Lewis was there reporting out his upcoming book, *Going Infinite*, on Sam himself. "You're breaking land speed records," Lewis told him. "I don't think people are really noticing what's happened, and how dramatic the revolution has become. There's a status upheaval in the financial world. And you're sitting right in the middle of it." The crowd cheered wildly.

Lewis asked Sam if his entrance into crypto had been financially motivated as opposed to idealistic. "Yeah, absolutely," Sam replied. "It was only over time that I started to get an appreciation for why it had value in the first place." As he spoke, his arms and legs visibly shook, and he rubbed his hands over his elbows as if beating back a chill.

The compliments for Sam poured in all weekend. Miami Heat captain Udonis Haslem described Sam's track record as "fucking amazing." Anthony Scaramucci, the conference's co-organizer, called Sam an "exceptional thinker" who "knows more about politics than anyone." He said that FTX might one day turn all stocks into crypto tokens.

These were high times for mainstream crypto adoption: Fidelity, the nation's largest provider of 401(k) retirement plans, announced that weekend that it would allow a portion of participants' contributions to be held in bitcoin. And the city of Buenos Aires announced it would start letting its residents pay taxes in crypto.

The number of superstars at Sam's conference, combined with its big-tent branding—it wasn't FTX Bahamas, but rather Crypto Bahamas—made it seem like the conference represented the best and brightest of all of crypto. In reality, Sam had built the bill around his financially entangled web of business connections, including Solana, the blockchain that Sam had bankrolled, and the VC funds Jump and Multicoin, which often partnered with Alameda on fundraising rounds. Exactly zero Ethereum representatives were booked as speakers.

One of the prominent members of the Sam multiverse was Su Zhu, the haughty cofounder of the powerful crypto hedge fund Three Arrows Capital. In this bull run, Zhu was an essential voice on Crypto Twitter, where he offered brash proclamations about the demise of banks and gold and sparred contemptuously with nonbelievers. He urged his five hundred thousand followers to keep buying tokens in order to spur crypto's "supercycle," or an everlasting bull run. Onstage at Crypto Bahamas, Zhu predicted that "all the new businesses that will be built will be crypto-native by nature." He marveled at how fast crypto had grown, proclaiming: "We're entering an exponential age of things. Someone can introduce an idea, and six months later it can be the most dominant idea in the world. I mean, Apes came out a year ago."

––––––––––

The actual Bahamians who were able to attend the conference were few and far between. The conference was invite-only, with tickets starting at $3,000. "We're not on their radar," Tyler Gordon, a member of the Bahamas crypto group Bahamas Masterminds, says. "We would have to have someone from outside of The Bahamas vouch for us and sort of bring us into the fold, but that didn't happen."

One of the exceptions to the rule was Melissa Alcena, a Nassau-based photographer. Alcena had carved a decent career as both a photographic artist and a photojournalist, with her work appearing in the *New York Times*, *Time*, and *GQ*. Alcena specialized in shooting portraits of Black Bahamians that were at once regal, stoic, and vulnerable. She hoped to shatter the colonial gaze that her countrymen were so often viewed through by creating portraits full of bright color palettes and vitality. She almost never took a picture of a Black subject from above, believing that it furthered a long history of demeaning portrayals.

In early April 2022, Alcena got an assignment to photograph Sam Bankman-Fried for an upcoming *Bloomberg* feature article. While Alcena knew virtually nothing about NFTs and crypto, she had heard of FTX. She knew that her Bahamian friends in tech were psyched about FTX's arrival, and had heard through the grapevine that the company offered lavish perks to its staff.

So on one sunny morning, Alcena reported to Bankman-Fried's compound in Albany. He was far from the ideal portrait subject. His hair had grown into a tangled, messy mop, and his FTX T-shirt, which slumped over his protruding belly, had some schmutz on it. But what Sam might have lacked in glamour he made up for in calm friendliness,

Alcena says. He was gently responsive to her prompts and suggestions. The ensuing photographs, which showed him covered in the shadows of a palm tree, appeared in *Bloomberg*'s crypto issue, next to a story titled "A 30-Year-Old Crypto Billionaire Wants to Give His Fortune Away." "He's a kind of crypto Robin Hood, beating the rich at their own game to win money for capitalism's losers," wrote *Bloomberg*'s Zeke Faux.

A couple weeks later, Alcena received a message from a man named John Darsie, who said he was co-organizing the Crypto Bahamas conference. Would Alcena be interested, Darsie asked, in releasing an NFT project in conjunction?

Alcena barely knew what an NFT was and didn't understand many of his words. But the limited freelance photography opportunities on the island had left her strapped for cash. "I was like, 'I need X amount of dollars and I don't know how that's gonna happen,'" she remembers. So she sent over a few photos from her portrait collection, *People of the Sun*.

Alcena's NFT drop was released on the third day of Crypto Bahamas—the same day she was scheduled to be a speaker on a panel titled "Art, Community & Culture in Web 3." Alcena was bewildered, as she knew nothing about crypto.

They day before, Alcena went to meet her panel-mates, who promised to give her a primer on crypto and NFTs. Instead, the group wanted to party, and took her aboard the yacht of Brock Pierce, a crypto investor and onetime child star from *The Mighty Ducks* and *First Kid*. Alcena filmed Pierce jumping off the side; she marveled at the boat's gleaming elevator and the gobs of food and liquor flowing from every corner. "It was a bunch of millionaires, billionaires, and people who just want to be millionaire- and billionaire-adjacent," she says. While the vibe was bacchanalian, Alcena says she also sensed a desperation emanating from many of the partygoers. "When you can see other people make such immense wealth with such a small contribution, it drives people a little mad," she says.

The next morning, as Alcena was getting ready to go onstage, she looked at her phone and saw that her collection had sold out within twelve minutes. The amount of crypto sitting in her wallet was now almost $100,000. "That really just happened," she said onstage, laughing, her eyes widening.

She listened intently as her fellow panelists extolled the virtues of the blockchain for artists. "As you build, as you create, you will be rewarded pretty much directly because of Web 3 and the blockchain," crowed the crypto builder William Tong.

Every night of the conference, parties raged up and down the island. DJ Steve Aoki led a hard-charging dance party at one club. At the birthday party of the German bitcoin billionaire Christian Angermayer, former One Direction member Liam Payne brought Amy Wu, the embattled head of FTX Ventures, onstage and serenaded her with Disclosure's "Latch," taking off his shirt and handing it to her with a wink.

Another one of the few Bahamians who got to attend was Lamont Astwood, a member of Bahamas Masterminds. Astwood had snagged a pass via Solana's Hacker House, which provided a space for crypto developers to build out tokens, games, and NFTs on the Solana blockchain. Every morning of the conference, Astwood would wake up, head to the Baha Mar for a full day of seminars, network with crypto luminaries he recognized from Twitter or TV, and then stroll into the wide array of extravagant parties that were taking place all over Nassau. "You had beach parties, pool parties, nightclubs, parties at residences off-site. It was just nonstop," he says. "It was truly probably one of the best weeks of my life."

Given the number of VC power players on the island, money whizzed to anyone with an idea and some charisma. Outside the conference's halls, Gajesh Naik, the fourteen-year-old developer from Goa, India, told people about his idea for a startup for a DeFi application called a cross-chain yield aggregator, and quickly racked up investments tallying $1.3 million. (Naik would later admit to me that "yield farming is basically a Ponzi, if you really see it. . . . I would rather put my money in treasury bonds.")

Illia Polosukhin, the cofounder of the blockchain NEAR, remembers being in a conversation between an Alameda employee and a representative of a pension fund. The Alameda employee, Polosukhin says, confidently pledged that if the pension entrusted the crypto hedge fund with billions of dollars, the investment would yield annual returns of 12 percent. "That was insane," Polosukhin says. "The only way that could happen is if the economy is growing exponentially, and you are able to capture that very effectively. Even real estate bubbles don't grow that quickly."

Crypto enthusiasts flew back to the mainland full of euphoria and also envy of Sam's sunny empire. "The biggest alpha [advice] from the Crypto Bahamas conference is buy real estate in Nassau, Bahamas," the crypto entrepreneur Tegan Kline wrote on Instagram. She added that Sam and FTX were "working to make this the location for the future of Wall Street. Not just crypto, but all of finance."

Melissa Alcena came away from the weekend grateful, but also bewildered. All of these new self-professed fans of hers had simply packed up and headed to the next crypto conference and NFT drop. "It felt like a rush because you're just swept up into this space. Everyone is helping you out and is like, 'Yeah! Good for you!' And they pat you on the back—and then they're just gone."

Within eight months, Sam and the rest of FTX would be gone from The Bahamas, too.

PART IV

THE FALL

CHAPTER 29

Have Fun Staying Poor

Crypto Bahamas had reinforced the dominance of a crypto vision that was diametrically opposed to Vitalik's: centralized, hyper-financialized, status-obsessed, and enthralled to cults of personality. But its primacy was already coming to an end.

Case in point: Su Zhu, the cofounder of Three Arrows Capital. Zhu left The Bahamas gloating: "I'm followed by @katyperry now," he wrote on Twitter.

Within two and a half months, he would be in hiding—and would come to be known as one of the Four Horsemen of the Crypto Apocalypse.

These doom-bringers are Su Zhu, Do Kwon, Alex Mashinsky, and Sam Bankman-Fried. They had all risen rapidly during 2021, building crypto empires whose fates became helplessly entangled with each other. In hindsight, their businesses were built precisely for meteoric rises and catastrophic falls. They exemplified the worst impulses of the degenerate wing of crypto, and their hubris would burst the crypto bubble and lose millions of people billions of dollars in the biggest U.S. crash since the Great Financial Crisis. And how did they blow up crypto? To paraphrase Ernest Hemingway, gradually and then suddenly.

Su Zhu had a lot in common with Sam. In the mid-2010s, Zhu's hedge fund Three Arrows Capital made a killing by chasing arbitrage opportunities to gain even the smallest of financial edges. Three Arrows' relentlessness earned them a shifty reputation, and when banks began to cut Zhu off, he moved into crypto in 2017, the same year Sam found that the arbitrage opportunities in the space were far more plentiful and profitable than in traditional finance.

Also like Sam, Zhu soon graduated to managing some $10 billion in funds, which he used to bet on shitcoins and risky startups like Axie Infinity, which Zhu called his "best venture investment to date" in early April 2022. Alameda and Three Arrows often moved in tandem. They both were major supporters of the stablecoin Tether, which had earned many skeptics in the crypto industry—including Vitalik Buterin—for its lack of transparency around whether it actually held enough hard currency reserves to justify its peg to the U.S. dollar.

Zhu got all of that money to play with from the same place Sam did: lenders. A cottage industry of lenders emerged during the bull run to help move money around the crypto ecosystem. Retail crypto enthusiasts who had a little extra cash, thanks to stimulus checks and low interest rates, wanted to stash it somewhere it would grow. Trading firms like Three Arrows Capital, in contrast, needed immediate money in order to make even bigger bets. Enter Celsius, a crypto bank led by Alex Mashinsky, the Second Horseman.

Mashinsky enticed customers to deposit money by offering an interest rate of up to 18.6 percent—far above the rate of any traditional bank—and then loaned out that cash to trading firms. At its peak, Celsius built a war chest of more than $12 billion in deposits. Mashinsky assuaged any doubts about his business model by telling the press that Celsius was "probably one of the least risky businesses that regulators worldwide have ever seen."

But just like the lenders of the 2008 crisis, lenders like Celsius had stopped bothering with due diligence checks and instead threw money at pretty much anyone who asked. Zhu's Three Arrows, for its part, often resisted showing its lenders audited financial statements or even posting collateral for the millions it was borrowing. As Caroline Ellison admitted to her Alameda colleagues in an all-hands meeting a few months later, when it all was crashing down: "Did you ever read about Celsius or Three Arrows? The crypto lending space was kind of wild for a long time. People had a lot of money, and didn't really read your balance sheet. They would just lend you a lot of money."

So customers gave Mashinsky their money. He then loaned it out to Sam (at least $13 million), Zhu (at least $75 million), and others. These traders, in turn, gambled the funds on crypto startups with increasingly outlandish ideas, which claimed that with just a little momentum, they could upend the global financial system and forge a more decentralized, equitable future. The poster child of this level of the pyramid was Do Kwon, the Third Horseman, who set off a chain reaction that accelerated until it had engulfed all four of them—and wiped a trillion dollars from the crypto economy.

Kwon was a Korean entrepreneur who displayed an outsize ego from an early age: A former classmate remembers him flipping a table one time when he didn't get his way. Eventually, Kwon made his way to Singapore for tax purposes, where he became pals with Zhu. There, they each built massive followings on Crypto Twitter, becoming micro-celebrities, king degenerates, and crypto gurus. Zhu mocked Vitalik, dismissing him as a hapless idealist. ("Ethereum has abandoned its users," he tweeted in November 2021 in the face of mounting gas fees.) Kwon mocked just about everyone: He told critics to "have fun staying poor" to the delight of his million-plus followers.

Do Kwon's main creation was the stablecoin TerraUSD (UST). Stablecoins are meant, by design, to be one of the least sexy parts of the crypto ecosystem. Because they purport to be pegged 1:1 to the U.S. dollar, they serve as havens for investors who want to park their money when markets get choppy, without transferring their funds out of crypto into the traditional banking system. But Kwon designed UST with two wrinkles that caused buyers to rush in.

The first was the 20 percent interest rate he offered to anyone who bought UST and then locked it away in the Anchor Protocol. Anchor was intended to work like a crypto bank, lending Terra UST "deposits" to interest-paying customers. But Anchor quickly became the main reason people bought UST at all. By April 2022, almost three-quarters of all the

UST stablecoins in existence were deposited with Anchor and earning almost 20 percent interest—a rate of return that not even Bernie Madoff dared offer.

The second wrinkle was that UST was not backed by hard cash. This was intriguing to crypto fanatics who preferred that their tokens operate independently from real-world money. Most other major stablecoins were backed by hard currency, with dollar reserves being held in a bank to support the coin's value on the blockchain. UST, on the other hand, was billed as an "algorithmic" stablecoin, designed to hold its value due to a complex link with its sister cryptocurrency, Luna.

Luna wasn't pegged to the dollar: Like any good shitcoin, it could rise or fall depending on supply and demand. But Kwon designed it so that one UST could always be redeemed for $1 worth of Luna, and vice versa. He argued that due to this algorithmic relationship, people would be incentivized to continually look for arbitrage opportunities and cash in one currency for the other when the value of Luna or UST rose or fell. In December 2021, Kwon told *CoinDesk*—which named him one of crypto's most influential people of the year—that UST "just offers a fundamentally better experience that other money is lacking right now."

If this all sounds ridiculous and unstable, it was. Even as many crypto fans were praising the ecosystem and pumping billions of dollars into it, economists and crypto experts who examined it were highly skeptical. Over the years, many crypto developers had tried to make an algorithmic stablecoin that would rely on technical and mathematical ingenuity to hold their peg to a dollar. None had ever lasted. The comedian John Oliver later summed up the Terra-Luna system like this: "Imagine if someone came up to you when you're at the ATM and said, 'Give me that money, and I'll give you blorps. One blorp is always worth one dollar, and the reason I can guarantee that is I'll sell as many fleasles as it takes to make that happen. Also, I make the fleasles.' Most people would say no. But if they then said, 'I do it with a special algorithm,' suddenly you might think that they know something that you don't."

Kwon gleefully brushed off critics on social media, wielding not math but schoolyard taunts. When one skeptic wrote on Twitter that "Self-correction mechanisms that rely on financial incentives do not work when panicking humans are stampeding for the exit," Kwon responded back: "I don't debate the poor on Twitter, and sorry I don't have any change on me for her at the moment."

Kwon's growing community of UST investors started to mimic his cruel, unflappable confidence. They called themselves the "Lunatics," and spammed anyone who cast doubt on Kwon or the project. The Lunatics were perhaps the most extreme version of the crypto degens who treated their investments with a religious zeal. It didn't matter whether their beliefs were supported by economic realities. Their faith transcended logic. One prominent crypto executive, Galaxy Digital's Mike Novogratz, even got a giant Luna tattoo on his shoulder.

James Block, a psychiatrist and blockchain analyst, compared some crypto belief systems to end-times narratives put forth by religious sects like the Seventh Day Adventists, who preach that true believers will be rewarded with eternal paradise and all others will be destroyed utterly when Jesus returns to Earth. "There's this idea that Bitcoin or whatever will be the basis for a new financial system—and anyone who holds it will ascend to the promised land of Infinite Wealth," he says.

By May 2022, the Lunatics were feeling blessed. UST had hit a $17 billion capitalization, making it the third-largest stablecoin behind Tether and USDC. But there was one big problem: Earlier users were starting to cash out the 20 percent yield they had earned from depositing their UST in Anchor. Simple math dictated that if enough people cashed out at the same time, Kwon wouldn't have nearly enough money to pay them all back.

To further complicate the story, Kwon created an organization called the Luna Foundation Guard (LFG), which raised $1 billion to buy bitcoin, which would act as a kind of insurance fund in case the ecosystem started to crash. Kwon followed this up by announcing his (outlandish) intention to become the single largest holder of bitcoin in the world; he imagined a bitcoin treasure trove worth $100 billion. "In that case, within the crypto industry, the failure of UST is equivalent to the failure of crypto itself," he said in an interview, grinning wide, his eyes sparking mischievously. It was crypto's equivalent to Heath Ledger's Joker walking into a mob hideout strapped with grenades, daring Gotham City's gangsters to kill him—and risk killing themselves. If Kwon's behavior was alarming, the other crypto mavens on his wavelength didn't seem to mind. In fact, Su Zhu likened Terra-Luna to "the holy grail" on Twitter—and his Three Arrows Capital invested $200 million into the LFG, irrevocably sewing the fates of Three Arrows and Terra-Luna together.

While Su Zhu and Do Kwon talked of financial revolution, all they were doing was putting a new spin on the behaviors and structures of the banks and lenders before the 2008 financial crisis. As Princeton economics professor Alan S. Blinder wrote in *After the Music Stopped*: "A financial system that is highly leveraged and betting massively on the continuation of bubbles is a two-pronged accident waiting to happen."

Unlike government-issued money, bitcoin is supposed to be resistant to inflation and geopolitical crises. Because bitcoin has no central issuer or authority controlling it, the coin should hold its value through economic dips, international wars, or drastic policy changes, its supporters argued. They actually hoped that times of crisis would lead to the increased value of bitcoin, and thus greater adoption.

But this idea was forcefully debunked in the spring of 2022. Russia's invasion of Ukraine upended supply chains, caused oil prices to spike, and exacerbated inflation. Slowing growth in China as it tried to quash COVID-19 outbreaks there contributed to financial anxieties. Prices for gas, rent, and groceries continued to rise rapidly across the world.

Agitated economists loudly called for central banks to reverse the monetary policies that had in part caused there to be a surplus of money floating around, making each greenback worth less than it used to be. The U.S. Federal Reserve listened and, in March, raised interest rates for the first time since December 2018. They hoped the move would slow consumer spending and business' borrowing, which would drive inflation back down to normal levels.

The decision thrust the crypto industry into uncharted waters. For the last decade plus, crypto had basically always existed in an era of cheap money. When interest rates were low, it was much easier—and more profitable—for people to make risky decisions using borrowed cash. But now the last place that belt-tightening consumers wanted to put their money was in a wildly volatile asset. In fact, Anchor's rise was proof of this shift: People were increasingly choosing to park their money in what seemed like a safe, steady asset rather than betting on tokens that could either multiply by a hundred or sink to zero. Do Kwon actually used this logic to coax non-crypto believers into Anchor: "In a world where the baseline interest rate is getting decimated, it's one of those things where you can protect yourself against inflation," he promised in March 2022.

But crypto, once believed by some to be inflation-proof, was now hurtling downward in tandem with stocks like Zoom and Peloton. Many crypto investors decided to leave the market entirely: to withdraw the ether and bitcoin they earned in the year prior and reinsert it into the traditional financial system in the form of bank deposits or bonds. When once-ambitious investors cut their losses, the crypto market started to contract, creating a reciprocal cycle of jitters and downward prices. The days of "HODL" and "diamond hands" were fading fast. The bear market was just one jolt away.

On May 7, Caroline Ellison wrote an update document about Alameda's operations and sent it to Sam, as she did several times a year. She noted that one of her main worries was Alameda's leverage—meaning the enormity of the borrowed funds they were trading with, including their debt to FTX customers—and how they might present this shaky financial position to lenders. Alameda owed around $3 billion in crypto and $10 billion in U.S. dollars to FTX.

Sam wrote back with a simple comment: "yup & could also get worse."

It got worse immediately. That very day, the value of Do Kwon's stablecoin UST slipped to 98 cents as holders exited the project. But

UST had wobbled before, so surely the algorithm would work its magic and return its value back to a dollar, the Lunatics declared.

It didn't. In this newly tense economic climate, the two-cent drop in price caused a full-fledged run, as people who had deposited funds in Anchor scrambled to withdraw their money. The fact they were selling each UST below the dollar they had bought it for didn't matter, because they had been earning an unprecedented 20 percent interest all along. Even when UST continued to sink—to 90 and 80 cents in the next two days—many people were still able to pull out more than they had deposited.

This mass panic was exactly the reason Kwon had bought all of that bitcoin in the first place: so that he could sell it and buy back UST to push its price back up, engaging in a financial tug-of-war. "Deploying more capital—steady lads," Kwon wrote on Twitter on May 9. "Steady lads" soon became a meme signifying crypto's false assurances and irrational exuberance.

But Kwon's bitcoin sell-off caused an even greater ripple effect. When the Luna Foundation Guard dumped more than $750 million worth of bitcoin onto the market, the glut pushed bitcoin itself downward, decimating not just the holders of UST but nearly everyone in crypto. On the evening of May 9, the price of bitcoin fell below $30,000, its lowest price since the previous July and less than half of its November peak. And the bitcoin ploy didn't even work to save UST. People who had called themselves Lunatics just days before were now selling off the stablecoin at lower and lower prices, hoping to get out before it was too late. This, in turn, sent Luna, UST's algorithmic sister, into a death spiral. "You had this one stablecoin that's collateralized by some other coin you also made up," says MacLane Wilkison, the founder of the encryption system NuCypher. "Once one of them starts going down, the system is literally programmed to go to zero."

Luna's $41 billion market cap shrunk to $1 billion in two days. Each token had been worth as much as $116 in April. On May 12, they were each worth fractions of a cent. The stablecoin UST hit 43 cents on May 12, and the entire blockchain it rested upon, Terra, was halted as exchanges like Binance and OKX suspended trading of UST and Luna or delisted them entirely. (Curiously, FTX chose not to delist UST or Luna during its crash, allowing its users to continue to bet on the carcass of the crypto project.) UST was soon worthless, marking the largest collapse of a stablecoin ever.

Some savvy trading firms actually made money off Terra by getting out of the project before everyone else. In 2023, the SEC alleged that Jump Trading, a firm that sent delegates to Crypto Bahamas, had made more than $1 billion in profit off of Terra. "All of the traditional trading shops were sitting around laughing about how this was obviously a Ponzi scheme," says a former Alameda trader. "But they were certain that they were technologically savvy enough to recognize the signs of it starting to break down and get their money out before the retail folk. And they absolutely did." Christine Chew, the former FTX employee, had somewhere between $10,000 and $20,000 in UST; she wrote it off as a loss. "It definitely made me have a very bad mood for a week," she says. "I tried to cheer myself up by not thinking about it—and telling myself, 'at least I still have money on FTX and Ethereum.'"

Some of the crash's hardest-hit victims were small retail investors who had gotten sucked into the frenzy of optimism that Do Kwon had whipped up on social media. A Korean family of three was found dead in their car at the bottom of a lake, and the father's recent online searches included "Luna coin" and "ways to make an extreme choice." The r/Terraluna subreddit online community filled with people opening up about their mental health issues and contemplating suicide. "I'm going through some of the darkest, most severe mental pain of my life. It still doesn't seem real that I lost $180,000," one poster wrote. And because crypto lacked regulation, these investors had no recourse to get their funds back.

After that, the Horsemen fell like dominoes. Su Zhu's Three Arrows Capital saw its Luna holdings—once valued at $500 million—shrink to a paltry $604. This was very bad news across the crypto industry, because Three Arrows had borrowed hundreds of millions from some of crypto's most prominent companies. When those nervous lenders began to call back their loans, Three Arrows didn't have enough money on hand to cash them out. In their efforts to pay off their margin calls, they frantically asked investors and executives to borrow even more money. But in late June, Three Arrows defaulted on a loan to Voyager—a crypto lending firm—worth more than $670 million and subsequently filed for bankruptcy. Voyager itself was insolvent by July 1, and the savings of millions of its customers disappeared. Three Arrows owed an additional $270 million to the crypto exchange Blockchain.com. In all, Three Arrows was in hock for more than $3 billion.

Zhu and Three Arrows cofounder Kyle Davies went into hiding, and wouldn't even share their whereabouts with Three Arrows advisers. They told *Bloomberg News* they were on the lam because of death threats, and sheepishly added that they had failed to consider the possibility that Terra-Luna's failure would "catalyze a credit squeeze across the industry that would put significant pressure on all of our illiquid positions."

Celsius, the crypto bank run by Alex Mashinsky, had lent millions to Three Arrows, and froze withdrawals. While Mashinsky had bragged that his company was "one of the least risky businesses" in 2021 and that the company straight up didn't have leverage, Celsius was leveraged about 19 to 1, meaning for every $95 it declared in assets, it had $90 of debt and $5 in equity. (The median leverage ratio for North American banks was about half as risky.) Celsius had lost some $350 million in customer funds on high-risk leveraged trading. Its marketing had vehemently mocked the traditional banking system, but its internal processes were just as centralized as banks—without any regulatory safeguards. (The SEC had begun scrutinizing Celsius and Voyager earlier in the year, however.) On July 13, 2022, Celsius filed for bankruptcy, reporting $5.5 billion in liabilities compared to $4.3 billion in assets that were mostly illiquid, in part because selling them off would crash their value. Regulators contended that the company had been technically insolvent since 2019, and it owed money to hundreds of thousands of customers who had trusted Mashinsky with their savings. A shepherd in Ireland lost his farm; a Pennsylvania bank manager and father of two reported seeing his entire retirement savings of $205,000 evaporate.

Ultimately, the entire crypto economy began to look like a shell game.

The collapse of one company with dubious financials exposed the precarious state of another, leading to its collapse, then another and another. It was a reprise of the 2008 financial crisis, but on the blockchain—and with no regulators and no federal bailouts. "One or two things get really big by having very high risk, and they blow up the whole space—and even the ones that were relatively low risk get blown up too," says the crypto venture capitalist Alex Pack. "A few bad apples, a few bad risks, and some out-and-out fraud blew up the entire industry."

Within one week of Terra's fall, over $400 billion in value was wiped from the crypto ecosystem. That included Ethereum. Because crypto firms had sold off their ether in their own attempts to defend UST's peg to the dollar, ether plunged below $2,000 for the first time since July 2021. As many investors tried to cash out their Ethereum-based stablecoins, the sheer number of transactions caused Ethereum's gas fees to spike, causing people to forfeit even more money.

Coinbase, a major crypto exchange especially popular among U.S. users, slumped 35 percent in revenue and rescinded job offers it had already handed out. Gemini, a crypto exchange founded by the *Social Network*–famous Winklevoss twins, conducted multiple rounds of layoffs. From mid-May to mid-June, NFT sales volume plunged 75 percent.

The market crash delivered a decisive blow to the aspirations of Khai Chun Thee and other Southeast Asian gamers, who were already treading water following the Axie Infinity crash. "Some of the gaming companies had part of their assets in someone that got affected by 3AC. We started to see the winding down of a lot of operations," Thee says. "Gaming has not established a core position that it is a strong store of value—so people dumped those tokens first, and that caused a lot of games to end." Within weeks, the dozens of potential partnerships that his company Hooga Gaming had been exploring with nascent Web 3 games all but vanished. A 2023 study from the gaming DAO Game7 later found that while 2022 had brought 640 blockchain games into the world, 157 were also halted.

Before the Terra-Luna crash, the Bahamian photographer Melissa Alcena possessed almost $100,000 worth of ether from her Crypto

Bahamas NFT sales. But as a newcomer to the space, she had no idea how to get it out. Due to The Bahamas' history as a haven for laundering, most banks there wouldn't touch crypto. When Alcena tried to take $500 out of her bank account, it was flagged as suspicious, and the transaction was denied.

While Alcena tried to figure out how to extract her money, Terra-Luna collapsed, bringing ether down with it nearly 50 percent. Approximately $40,000 of the crypto that she had supposedly earned off NFTs had vanished by the time she was finally able to convert her ether into cash. Alcena was still grateful, because it was money that had been created out of very little work on her part. But she was left bewildered by the whole experience—and was further turned off upon learning that the Ethereum blockchain used an enormous amount of energy and was bad for the environment. She decided to never mint an NFT again.

"You're like, 'What the fuck just happened?'" Alcena says. In the summer of 2022, millions of people around the world who had invested in crypto were asking themselves the same exact question.

CHAPTER 30

Bulletproof?

The only crypto mogul standing atop the wreckage, it seemed, was Sam Bankman-Fried. On June 6, 2022, he posted a gloating Tweet thread about why FTX would "keep growing as others cut jobs." He scolded the public for believing the "mass enthusiasm, excitement, and—frankly—marketing and memes" of Terra-Luna, when it was clear that it was "going to falter according to publicly available information." (Never mind that FTX itself had listed UST on its exchange—and kept its trading active far longer than other exchanges.) Sam flung blame at the Federal Reserve and its decision to aggressively increase interest rates. "The core driver of this has been the Fed," he told NPR in a June 19 article. "People with money are scared."

Because of his confident tweets and formidable reputation, many people assumed that he and Alameda CEO Caroline Ellison had profited at everyone else's expense during a moment of crisis. But in reality, Sam was deep, deep underwater.

Alameda had invested directly in Do Kwon's UST, to the tune of about $100 million, all of which had vanished. That was chump change compared to the cascading loans that were being recalled in the wake of the crypto crash. Alameda, like Three Arrows, had heavily relied on the freewheeling crypto loan ecosystem to borrow billions of dollars in order to make huge trades and invest in startups. For example, Alameda had borrowed over $6 billion from the major crypto lender Genesis using FTT as collateral. On June 13, a Genesis representative sent a flurry of Signal messages to Caroline and company, demanding that Alameda repay $250 million, then another $150 million, then another $125 million. Caroline's team quickly sent back the $525 million. But the requests kept coming from other major lenders. Caroline was panicked: This was the bad situation she had warned Sam about last fall in her spreadsheets.

To assess the severity of their problems, Sam asked his inner circle of Caroline, Gary Wang, and Nishad Singh to put together a spreadsheet of Alameda's balances. The results were grim: Alameda was already borrowing around $10 billion from FTX customers. Some of the money had been smuggled over via the secret line of credit that Gary and Nishad had coded into the system. Billions more had come through North Dimension, the bank account with a deliberately misleading name that had been opened to hold FTX user deposits when the crypto exchange first launched and couldn't get bank accounts.

The spreadsheets showed that Alameda had billions' worth of other theoretical assets, like investment stakes in startups and Sam Coins. But cashing out the former was impossible at the moment, while cashing out the latter would tank their value and bring down the whole company. There was only one thing to do, as Caroline later testified: "In order to repay all of our loans, we would have to borrow money using our FTX line of credit. That would be coming from customer funds." With lenders hounding her, Caroline asked Sam what to do.

Sam was now faced with one of the most consequential decisions of his life. He could own up to the fact that he didn't have the money and walk away from the roulette table with his tail between his legs. Or he could try to keep the game going with one more shady gambit, and bet that the continued growth of crypto would turn his fake dollars into real ones.

Sam had come this far precisely because of how many times he had chosen the riskier path. Leaving Jane Street for a crypto Wild West, starting FTX when other crypto exchanges were flailing, jumping from Berkeley to Hong Kong to The Bahamas—at each juncture Sam ruffled feathers, then ascended to new heights. The crypto and venture capital ecosystems, which themselves thrived on risk, had continually rewarded him for his behavior.

So Sam directed Caroline to pay back the lenders in full. In the next two weeks, Alameda returned several billion dollars to lenders including Genesis. And much of it came from unwitting FTX customers. FTX had specifically promised its users that it would never lend out the funds they put on the exchange. "You control the Digital Assets held in your account," promised the platform's terms of service. "Title to your Digital Assets shall at all times remain with you and shall not transfer to FTX." By this point, customers had deposited about $13 billion in U.S. dollars into their FTX accounts, assuming that their money would be safely stored away. But now only about $3 billion remained.

Caroline was in a constant state of dread. She was worried that customers would start withdrawing their funds en masse, just like they had from Terra-Luna, and that the whole thing would soon collapse. She became especially stressed when the co-head of trading and lending at Genesis, Matt Ballensweig, asked her on June 18 to send over an updated version of Alameda's balance sheet for reassurance that they were on stable ground. Caroline understood the potential ramifications if Ballensweig saw the real numbers.

So, on Sam's direction, she prepared seven "alternative ways" of presenting the information. Each version removed a different crucial aspect of Alameda's debts, like how much it was relying on FTT and other Sam Coins, or the fact that Alameda had given $4.5 billion in personal loans to FTX executives, including Sam and Gary. "I didn't really want to be dishonest, but I also didn't want them to know the truth," Caroline testified.

In the end, Sam told her to send the seventh version, which hid the personal loans and nearly $10 billion borrowed from FTX customers. In this seventh version, Alameda was relatively risk free and happily sitting in the green—while hiding over $4 billion in liabilities. The spreadsheet seemed to mollify Ballensweig. "Appreciate it. Just caught up with Sam," he texted Caroline. "Let's keep in tight comms this week."

Because Sam and Caroline were sending out misleading documents, and because much of the money was not sent over public blockchains, nobody realized that Sam had secretly taken his customers' real dollars and left them an IOU for Monopoly money. But Adam Yedidia, Sam's roommate in the Albany penthouse and an FTX developer, caught a whiff of the scheme. Yedidia had been tasked with fixing a bug in the FTX system and stumbled across this multibillion-dollar debt to FTX customers. One day in June, after a game of padel, Yedidia told Sam he had seen some worrying numbers in the system, and asked if everything was okay.

"We were bulletproof last year, but we're not bulletproof this year," Sam responded, according to Yedidia's testimony in federal court. Sam seemed nervous, the coder told prosecutors.

"How long until we're bulletproof?" Yedidia asked.

"Maybe something like six months to three years," Sam responded, in another one of his galaxy-brain numerical calculations that meant absolutely nothing.

CHAPTER 31

Crypto's J.P. Morgan

S am was staring down the barrel of his debts and had two possible escape routes. One was to raise an enormous amount of money to fill the hole. The other was for crypto itself to skyrocket upward, so that all of his assets would increase in value. For either to happen, Sam had to play a confidence game: to convince everyone that he was not just okay, but thriving. Sam, obviously, was crypto's Fourth Horseman, and its most damaging in the long run. But in June 2022, he pretended instead that he was its White Knight.

In late June, Sam announced he was bailing out Voyager and BlockFi, two of the crypto lenders hit hardest by the Terra-Luna collapse. The move appeared heroic to many in the crypto industry. Not only was Sam seemingly the only trader savvy enough to escape the damage but he was also going out of his way to help others who had failed. Analysts called him the "J.P. Morgan of crypto," a nod to the way that Morgan had intervened twice to prevent major economic collapses at the turn of the twentieth century. In August, Sam's smiling face appeared on the cover of *Fortune* above the title, "The Next Warren Buffett?"

Sam cast his bailout in an altruistic light. "We're willing to do a somewhat bad deal here, if that's what it takes to sort of stabilize things and protect customers," he told *Forbes*. On June 27, just weeks after he started secretly sending billions in his own customers' funds to pay back lenders, he tweeted: "Backstopping customer assets should always be primary. Everything else is secondary."

Of course, Sam's core motivation was self-preservation. He told Caroline that the deal with BlockFi might allow him to transfer that platform's assets onto FTX's, which would shore up his own balance sheet and let him take out even more loans. Sure enough, BlockFi itself lent an additional $800 million to Alameda over the next couple months.

At the time of Sam's buyout of Voyager, Alameda actually owed it $377 million. This debt did not go unnoticed by Sam's chief rival, Changpeng Zhao, the CEO of Binance, who pointed out the discrepancy. "If you have the ability to move markets, why do you still need a loan?" he asked Sam rhetorically on Twitter.

Zhao had a lot of questions about how FTX, now the second biggest crypto exchange in the world behind Binance, operated. After Sam's highly lauded bailouts in the summer of 2022, Zhao ramped up his public criticism of his rival. "Bailouts here don't make sense. Don't perpetuate bad companies," Zhao wrote in a blog post. "Let them fail. Let other better projects take their place, and they will."

Whether these critiques had merit, some people in the crypto world dismissed them as jealousy. Zhao had long been perceived as the cutthroat older brother to Sam's affable brainiac. And in this instance, his messaging suggested he was willing to leave behind his crypto colleagues for his own benefit, as opposed to Sam who was making personal sacrifices to save the entire industry. Ryan Salame, Christine's former boss, framed the contrasting approaches on Twitter as "one company trying to lift others up, one company trying to take others down." He also gloated publicly as FTX sent lifelines to their struggling former competitors. "While my condolences go out to all those being affected across the industry, I'm unabashedly proud to say that we were right," he tweeted. To twist the knife, he gleefully announced the return of Crypto Bahamas, scheduled for April 2023, as "the crypto event of the year."

In the ashes of Do Kwon's house fire, FTX seemed to be the phoenix. The scapegoats—Kwon, Zhu, and Mashinsky—were cast aside; the diseased branches of the crypto world pruned. Sam had long wanted FTX to become a hub for virtually every type of financial transaction online. His latest acquisitions brought him that much closer to his infinite goals.

———————

While Sam was secretly drowning in debt, the summer of 2022 marked the zenith of his public stature and perceived heroism. Sam was lauded for signing the Giving Pledge, a promise made by the world's richest people to give away most of their money to philanthropy. The same month, a Nigeria-based community decided to ramp up their efforts in celebrating Sam and spreading his gospel. They called themselves FTT DAO, based on FTX's native token. Some of the members were former FTX ambassadors who had worked under FTX's bombastic Africa comms chief, Harrison Obiefule. Members of FTT DAO called themselves "BFFs," which stood for "Bankman-Fried's friends, followers and fans." In July 2022, FTT DAO put on their first event in Uyo, Akwa Ibom, Owo Anietie's hometown. Organizers constructed a ten-foot-tall banner showing SBF's face looking down peacefully upon them. "The participants of the event should be able to go back home with a turning point experience," Emmanuel Godswill, a founding member of FTT DAO, said on-site. That summer, FTT DAO raised $7 million worth of FTT, which it said it would spend on crypto education.

But Damian Williams, the U.S. attorney for the Southern District of New York, took notice of Sam's swelling empire. Williams was the first Black person to lead the vaunted fraud-fighting office, known for policing Wall Street as much as for prosecuting terrorists and drug traffickers. In May, he announced charges against fund managers who misled investors about the security of their funds, leading to $5 billion in losses. Williams declared that his office would be "relentless in rooting out corruption in our financial markets."

"If you are someone who has ripped off investors in the past, is ripping off investors right now . . . we are not asleep on the beat," he said. Within months, his office would quietly open a probe into FTX, examining how the company's international exchange, which was not licensed in the U.S., might be illegally serving American customers.

CHAPTER 32

We're Not All Gonna Make It

S am had momentarily saved FTX from annihilation. But the crypto market remained depressed following the Terra-Luna crash: Its market cap had been slashed in half, shedding nearly a trillion (yes, with a "T") dollars in value a month and a half following the start of May. And many of the artists who had served as the movement's pioneers found themselves abandoned. The NFT movement had shifted from art to tacky, meme-able profile picture projects like the Bored Ape Yacht Club. The collector pool had evaporated along with the war chests of Terra, Three Arrows, and the other centralized crypto giants.

In early 2022, both the African NFT Community, led by Liam Vries, and an offshoot group called Cyber Baat DAO attempted fundraising campaigns, which they hoped to use to scale their efforts and pay artists. Both failed miserably. Cyber Baat, which aimed to support African creators of fine art, hoped to crowdfund 57.5 ETH, or $155,000, through an auction. "We believe in the power of web3 in revolutionizing how Africans share and consume works of art," read the campaign summary. The auction included a piece from Liam, who was part of the DAO. But all in all, the artworks only sold for 7.55 ETH ($20,000), or 13 percent of what they had hoped. Liam's own African NFT Community's campaign did even worse. It made just $2,500, from six backers, a far cry from its $19,000 goal.

If there was a silver lining, it was that the bull run from months prior had allowed both Liam and Owo to do something that had previously been unthinkable: to emigrate out of Africa based on the income they had made as artists. Owo left Lagos for Dubai, while Liam left Harare for

Nottingham, UK. Both journeys were bittersweet fulfillments of long-held dreams: They both loved their countries, but had become fed up with their unpredictability and lack of opportunity. "Africa is such a rough landscape, the way you look at life: It's very crabs in a barrel," Owo says. "For the first time in my life, if I want to work for an entire day without having any issues, I can."

———————

But as African NFT artists left the continent for more stable situations, the African NFT Community was disintegrating. Many artists, especially those who had not become renowned during the bull market, found themselves unable to sell any NFTs at all. "I've had a dry spell for months now," wrote the Nigerian artist Taslemat Yusuf on Twitter in September 2022. "I think I'll cry if I make a sale." While many African artists simply departed the NFT space for lack of opportunities, those who remained were snagged in a vicious personal disagreement that ballooned on social media. In August, a female photographer was asked by the African NFT Community to cohost a Twitter Space with a male animation artist. But the photographer had recently been alerted to a few of the animator's old tweets in which he made crass and tasteless jokes about false rape accusations. She told members of the African NFT Community that she would not participate unless he was removed from the panel.

The disagreement turned ugly with the animator threatening the photographer with legal action for defamation. Instead of investigating him, the African NFT Community opted to instead cut ties with her, and wrote a statement accusing her of attacking them with "deep-rooted psychological tactics." Liam felt like it was not his responsibility to adjudicate what he saw as a personal squabble. "You never expected social constructs coming into an industry that was art-based. My whole life I lived in a prison, and then you finally have this freedom," he said, referring to the authoritarian state of Zimbabwe. "I'm not HR."

But the note from the African NFT Community appalled some members, particularly women, who felt that the photographer was unfairly targeted. They felt that the board had brushed off serious concerns about the animator while using their megaphone to attack the photographer's credibility. After the incident, several African female NFT artists distanced themselves from the community, including Taslemat Yusuf.

"Everything was childish," Yusuf says. "It was a really messy situation. After that, I left: I can't keep struggling to try and make myself feel welcome in a place I'm obviously not welcome."

"I think it was really negative and reflected really badly on people like Liam, who I know to be a very loving and respectful person," says Linda Dounia, a member of the community and the founder of Cyber Baat DAO. "Without any structure to address something like that, it was just so terrible, because what always happens in the space happened: The man gets away scot-free, and the women end up being the ones who have to leave the space."

Cyber Baat and the African NFT Community had been founded on the principles of community, uplifting marginalized voices, and celebrating culture. A year in, it was clear that many NFT artists possessed a different set of characteristics and motivations. These were risk-embracing, fiercely independent autodidacts who prided themselves on swimming against the tide. They prioritized ambition over prudence. They acted quickly and decisively, and their hunger sometimes veered into desperation. These qualities catapulted them forward in the beginning—and then led to massive rifts when hard times hit.

Crypto enthusiasts promised their new industry would be an equalizing force across the world. "If the spread of technology truly makes the world 'flatter,' then Web 3 will be a steamroller," wrote the blockchain evangelist Alex Tapscott. The only problem with his thesis was that the wrong people were getting flattened. "Right now the mood in the NFT space is betrayal," Liam told me in late 2022. "Web 3 is very, very, very brutal. People are angry. I can't remember the last time I saw WAGMI on the internet."

That unifying catchphrase, which stood for "We're All Gonna Make It," had helped propel NFT sales. It now rang hollow at a time when many crypto customers had lost thousands due to the carelessness or greed of entrepreneurs like Do Kwon and Alex Mashinsky. Crypto was supposed to be an ever-growing self-sustaining city, but it was looking a lot more like a zero-sum casino. Crypto Twitter was filled with former high-stakes poker players and other former gambling addicts, who goosed the pot in the middle of the table with reckless abandon. Now much of it was gone.

"'WAGMI' is mostly BS," says Michael Keen, the NFT Catcher marketer who had initially helped Owo with AfroDroids. "It's mostly people that don't want you to sell because they want theirs to go up in value. It's a nice sentiment. But when you're investing, not everybody's going to make it."

The NFT market was not only failing economically but also failing to live up to the technology's most central promises. The unique thing about NFTs, everyone said in 2020, was that they allowed for absolute ownership of digital goods without the need for an intermediary. But in 2021 and 2022, most NFTs didn't even store their data on a blockchain. Instead, they contained a URL that simply pointed to the data on a web server. Anyone with back-end access to that server could change the image associated with the NFT. Someone who bought a Beeple NFT for a million dollars risked it getting replaced by a poop emoji if the server was compromised.

Most NFT buyers didn't have enough knowledge to interact with the blockchain directly, anyway. As far as they knew, their NFTs were located on platforms like OpenSea and Foundation—a strange development for a technology whose exact purpose was to dislodge these sorts of intermediaries. "To make these technologies usable, the space is consolidating around . . . platforms. Again," wrote the Signal cofounder Moxie Marlinspike in a widely read critique of NFTs.

This centralization had more insidious effects. Many artists from countries with oppressive governments, including Cuba and Iran, had originally flocked to NFTs as a way to create political art without censorship. But artists from both countries soon found themselves delisted from OpenSea, due to U.S. sanctions of their countries. There was little point in these protest artists continuing to mint their work on the blockchain if mainstream crypto users couldn't see it or buy it.

And what of the dream of NFTs promoting diversity and democratizing artistic production? A November 2021 study found that at least 77 percent of the money generated by NFT art sales in the previous twenty-one months on Nifty Gateway had gone to male artists, with just 5 percent definitively going to female artists. Fifty-five percent of all the money generated by NFT art sales went to just sixteen super-successful artists—a list unsurprisingly topped by Beeple.

Another study showed that CryptoPunks investors preferred buying white, male avatars as opposed to female ones or those with darker skin. These buyers, who tended to be white and male, were willing to pay thousands of dollars more on average for avatars that looked more like themselves. Crypto was supposed to level the playing field for historically marginalized groups, because no one could see anyone's face, the argument went. As the market for CryptoPunks showed, that wish was hopelessly naive.

NFTs had enabled nobodies from around the world to get rich. But celebrities also flooded into the industry, sucking up attention, cheapening it with lazy concepts, and once again imposing a top-down attention economy. While some celebrities profited nicely off their NFT projects, many of their forays ended up being much more trouble than they were worth. Stoner Cats, an NFT-animated web series starring voice acting from Ashton Kutcher and Mila Kunis—as well as Vitalik Buterin—was slapped with a $1 million SEC fine for selling unregistered securities. Kim Kardashian was forced to pay a $1.26 million SEC fine after she promoted a cryptocurrency called EthereumMax—which had no relation to Ethereum—without disclosing she had been paid to shill for it. And Logan Paul was pilloried for promoting and then abandoning several crypto projects, including the Pokémon-like concept CryptoZoo, after convincing his die-hard fans to buy in.

The number of NFT-related lawsuits, often between former collaborators, piled up. Two factions of cofounders of a neon, psychedelic Bored

Ape spin-off called Caked Apes sued each other for control of the project, which tanked in value in the months later. And Vignesh Sundaresan, the buyer of the $69 million Beeple NFT at Christie's, sued his former partner at the crypto fund Metapurse.

––––––––––

Questions also began to arise about whether all the money in the NFT ecosystem had been real in the first place. Yes, a lot of money had been spent on NFTs during the bull run, benefiting many artists. But new analyses showed that what had looked like a massive influx of mainstream adoption had been grossly exaggerated, thanks to a technique known as wash trading.

Wash trading is when someone sells an asset to themselves at increasing prices. By creating fake trades, you can simulate a heightened demand for an asset, thus enticing more people to buy in. This technique proved remarkably easy on the blockchain. All wash traders had to do was buy an NFT, create new wallets, and then pass the NFTs back and forth between them. This left a trail on the blockchain suggesting that the asset had increased in price, creating value through a funhouse mirror illusion. And code-savvy traders could create automated programs that allowed them to wash-trade at scale.

Wash trading is illegal in securities and futures markets but exists in a "murky area" with regard to NFTs, the blockchain analytics firm Chainalysis wrote in a report. Because NFTs were so new and their jurisdiction was yet unclear, very few regulators took enforcement action against these self-deals. Virtually every player in the crypto ecosystem was incentivized to either engage in wash trading, or to pretend like it wasn't happening. Cutthroat traders used the technique to conjure value out of thin air. Normal NFT holders were happy to see their asset class appreciate in value. And NFT marketplaces like OpenSea relied on rising trading volumes for both brand awareness and profit from transaction fees.

So wash trading proliferated wildly. One blockchain analysis found that NFT wash trading made up 58 percent of all trades in 2022—and a shocking 80 percent of trades during the NFT January peak. A Chainalysis report found hundreds of habitual wash traders conducted hundreds of trades, netting more than $8 million collectively.

The National Bureau of Economic Research found that wash trading made up over 70 percent of total crypto volume on unregulated exchanges. (Coinbase counted as one of the few regulated exchanges; Binance fell into the unregulated category.) Crypto exchanges incentivized customers to wash-trade by offering rewards through fee rebates—and the exchanges themselves engaged in wash trading as a shortcut to increase brand awareness and acquire clients, the NBER report asserted.

Wash traders especially loved NFT projects that didn't stipulate built-in royalties for every secondary sale. While other NFTs automatically sent a percentage of each trade to the NFT's creator, these projects allowed traders to cleanly sell an NFT to themselves at inflated value without giving up a cut every time. As these types of projects grew in volume and profit, NFT marketplaces like Magic Eden and LooksRare came to the conclusion that guaranteeing royalties for creators was no longer a viable financial option. By the end of 2022, many platforms had removed royalties, which incensed artists, as royalties were the exact reason many artists had believed in the first place that NFTs were a more sustainable system for them as opposed to the traditional art market. "The only reason we do NFTs is for secondary sales and digital sovereignty," Liam said. He told me that collectors of his work were even writing to him asking him to rip up the original smart contract—and to agree to a new one that cut him out of any future sales. Unsurprisingly, he angrily rebuffed them.

Liam also became worried that some of his collectors were less interested in enjoying his art than in using it as a tax haven. That concern was shared in much loftier corners—including by Charles Rettig, the IRS comissioner. Rettig told Congress in 2021 that the U.S. was failing to collect as much as $1 trillion in crypto taxes due to the difficulty of tracing and tracking transactions. NFTs, Rettig said, were "not visible items by design."

The greed in crypto was overwhelming in 2021 and 2022, and manifested in all types of crime. According to Chainalysis, there was $18 billion in illicit crypto transactions in 2021—including scams, stolen funds, and crypto sent to sanctioned addresses—and $20 billion worth the following year. As newcomers flocked into the bull market, the lack of safety precautions in crypto combined with the growing number of scammers amounted to newcomers essentially "walking down a dark alley carrying bags of cash," Philip Martin, the chief security officer at Coinbase, described at a 2023 crypto conference.

Scammers especially made a killing on Discord, a social media platform and a central hub of crypto social activity. While NFT buyers were less likely to click on a random Twitter link, they had a higher level of trust for links posted on Discord, where users were grouped into smaller, more tight-knit communities. If a scammer posed as the lead for a new crypto project and put up a link purporting to give the community exclusive access to a new NFT, many people in the Discord would immediately click due to FOMO. The attached malware would immediately drain their crypto wallets. Between May and July 2022, over one hundred reports of NFT-related Discord hacks were filed to the blockchain analytics company TRM Labs, to the tune of an estimated $22 million. And people who had lost their NFTs or crypto had no legal recourse to get them back.

CryptoWizard, Owo's adviser, says that when he warned NFT teams of these Discord vulnerabilities, those teams would wave him off, worried that arduous security measures might slow incoming sales. "So a lot of hackers and scammers figured out that there was not just money in crypto Discord, but dumb money," he says. "It was fish in a barrel."

Scammers used "pig butchering" techniques—i.e., pretending to befriend victims before promising them investment returns—to extract crypto, particularly the mostly unregulated stablecoin Tether, from victims, which they then turned back into real cash. Reporters in Cambodia found that many of the scammers themselves were being held against their will in vast office parks by human traffickers, and forced to turn over their crypto winnings to crime bosses. Tether, the reporters contended, made it very easy for crime rings to steal money undetected.

While some scammers targeted people randomly or lurked around the edge of crypto communities, others were embedded inside the heart of the industry. In June 2022, an employee at the premier NFT market-place OpenSea was charged with insider trading. The employee, Nathaniel Chastain, was accused by the U.S. Attorney's Office of buying NFTs he knew were about to be featured on OpenSea's homepage, which inevitably led to a massive jump in their price. He then cashed out for two to five times his initial buy-in, at virtually no risk. Chastain was carrying out these machinations during the height of the NFT frenzy in summer and fall of 2021, right when Owo and Liam were raking in thousands. While the artists themselves were not harmed by Chastain's actions, the buyers who purchased NFTs after him certainly were. Chastain was later convicted by a jury of wire fraud and money laundering and sentenced to three months in prison. The U.S. attorney leading this case was Damien Williams, who was getting a handle on crime in cryptocurrency and would soon move on to a much bigger target.

CHAPTER 33

The "Next Level" Alliance

NFTs had allowed Liam Vries to move to a country with more stability and more opportunity. But his sales had slowed to a trickle. So over the summer of 2022, he decided to start trading crypto. "As an artist, I wasn't selling as much, but knew my money could make money," he says.

And the exchange he chose to start on was FTX. He had seen and internalized all of FTX's aggressive advertising, including at Formula One. American friends he trusted had recommended it. And Liam soon found that FTX was easier to use than its competitors. Its interface was more streamlined and intuitive, and the app had fewer barriers to entry, especially as a recent migrant without a UK driver's license. "With Coinbase, you needed to provide your proof of address and all this other kind of stuff," he says. "With FTX, all I needed was my national ID and a bank account."

Owo, now in Dubai, also became interested in FTX. Any revenue stream that had previously trickled out of AfroDroids was now essentially dry. He was looking for ways to "double his money, being the typical Nigerian that I am," he described to me, laughing. For months, Owo saw videos about Sam Bankman-Fried popping up on YouTube accounts he followed. "There was a period where FTX didn't exist, and then, boom! Every YouTuber was talking about them," he says.

Sam seemed to be trustworthy and profitable. So Owo decided he wanted to create his own token and list it on FTX. AfroDroids community members had come up with the idea of a token called $RAM, based off an idea from the AfroDroids universe that the Droids need RAM storage space. Owo liked the idea, and excitedly brought it to his adviser

CryptoWizard, who had long had suspicions about Sam Bankman-Fried and told him to junk it. "I told him to get his money off there and run for the hills," CryptoWizard says.

"If I didn't have Wizard, I would have led three thousand people into the hands of Sam Bankman-Fried," Owo says, exhaling deeply. "And I would be solidified as a scammer."

———

But FTX certainly did not need Owo, because it was in the process of forging a much, much bigger NFT partnership. Sam and his team were working on building an NFT platform that might dethrone OpenSea as the industry's top dog and allow it to corner the market. And FTX's collaborator in this quest was none other than Yuga Labs, the creators of the Bored Ape Yacht Club.

At this point in 2022, both FTX's NFT efforts and the Bored Apes were sliding backward. FTX's strategy to peddle the Sotheby's Bored Apes in late 2021 hadn't helped. The company's NFT platform had failed to gain any traction from NFT enthusiasts. Sam had barely touched the project, instead off-loading it to Brett Harrison and his small, overworked team in Chicago. Harrison's team found it nearly impossible to build out an entirely new infrastructure while trying to lure customers away from OpenSea, which had hundreds of employees devoted exclusively to NFTs. Alameda's attempts to trade NFTs had also gone nowhere. "Did like a bit of trying to buy some, seems like it didn't go great," Caroline Ellison wrote in an internal memo that summer.

Individual Bored Apes were still selling for more than $100,000. But the prices of the cheapest Apes had fallen to half of their peak in April 2022. And the collection was also increasingly a punch line rather than something to boast about. The actor Seth Green had his Ape swiped from him in a hack, rendering him temporarily unable to proceed with the cartoon TV show he had created with the Ape's IP rights. Green's show was supposed to be just one in a constellation of Bored Ape content that would turn the brand into a "decentralized Disney," as one executive at Universal Music Group, who had created and signed a band of Bored Apes to her label, put it to *GQ*. As opposed to Disney movies, which were controlled by one company behind closed doors, the Bored Ape Cinematic Universe would be built piece by piece by thousands of Ape holders who would be able to profit directly from their creations.

But especially after the NFT market turned south, some investors found it harder than expected to turn their Apes into profitable businesses. One of the Apes' first major success stories had been Jenkins the Valet, the Ape that now had both a CAA agent and a book deal. The company behind Jenkins, Tally Labs, had raised $12 million in seed funding, and hoped to cash in with an array of media products, from a novel to a TV show to a metaverse world with new characters. Jenkins's owner, who went by Valet Jones, argued that his Ape would prove that the next generation of beloved characters and worlds would be built on the blockchain. But one key element was missing: artistry. When Tally Labs proudly released their designs for their spin-off alien NFT characters, they were roundly mocked: "If I was a deformed cat lizard, I too would drape myself in blankets," wrote one Twitter user. "Did you hire a blind artist?" wrote another.

The same month, September 2022, the Jenkins book, called *Bored and Dangerous*, was released to the world via a digital reader. While the book's byline belonged to the best-selling author Neil Strauss—who had previously written about another strange, noxious subculture in *The Game: Penetrating the Secret Society of Pickup Artists*—Tally Labs had set up a system in which Ape owners could pay to suggest ideas to Strauss, and have their Apes written into the book's plot. Unsurprisingly, the result was less a coherent narrative than a shameless two-hundred-page commercial. Nobody outside the Jenkins community seemed to read it, and many within it disliked the book both for its writing quality and the fact that it was failing to make their Apes more valuable. One community member on Discord described it as an "endless name-dropping of Apes," adding: "It's so distracting and the writing gains no flow."

Strauss himself emerged out of the Jenkins experiment disillusioned. "I began this phase of the crypto cycle very utopian," he told me in the summer of 2023. "Before, I was telling artists and musicians, 'there are so many cool opportunities here.' And now I'm not having those conversations. I think that says it all.

"The question is, did we have a great thing—and did greed ruin it? Not just the villains of it, but everybody? Did this pervasive atmosphere of greed really ruin what could have been an incredible revolution in art?"

While individual Ape owners struggled to make money, Yuga Labs, the centralized company that had created the Apes, was still flush with cash. In March 2022, the company had raised $450 million in a seed round that gave them a valuation of $4 billion. Because Yuga had bought out two of Bored Apes' biggest rival NFT projects, the CryptoPunks and the Meebits, Yuga-owned NFTs now made up more than 30 percent of the total NFT trading volume.

The more that Yuga consolidated assets and rolled out new projects, including a cryptocurrency tied to a metaverse world, the more it became clear that the "decentralized Disney" idea was largely a myth—because Yuga itself was crypto's Disney, and it was still dictating the value of its products. And in mid-2022, the company turned to FTX for a partnership each company hoped would elevate them further.

FTX had already invested $50 million into Yuga's seed round. In the middle of 2022, the companies started devising a plan to build a marketplace that would be just as easy for crypto novices as shopping on eBay or Amazon. FTX, with its Super Bowl commercial and stadium, was becoming *the* name-brand crypto exchange. The Bored Apes were *the* flagship NFT brand. It seemed like the ideal partnership to truly bring NFTs mainstream. "We felt like with killer content from them, moving their inventory onto the platform, and encouraging their community to move onto the platform, we thought we could really build a for-retail NFT experience to bring it to the next level," says one FTX employee who worked on the project.

Greg Solano, the cofounder of the Bored Apes, told me the project had stemmed from a pervasive feeling of being "let down" by OpenSea. "In order for this ecosystem to thrive, there does have to be a creator-centric marketplace that respects royalties," he says.

But the FTX-Yuga partnership only reinforced how centralized the space was getting, and how Web 3 was simply emulating Web 2 in worse ways: full of quasi-mergers leading to hyper-centralized gatekeepers. An FTX-Yuga exchange was akin to Amazon and Nike creating a new shoe marketplace. They might sell Adidas and Sketchers, and claim that the partnership would benefit the consumer—but it's clear who would profit the most in the end.

CHAPTER 34

Vitalik's Breakthrough

I n September 2022, as crypto continued to slog through its doldrums, Vitalik Buterin experienced two major breakthroughs. One of them was technical, and would forge a greener future for Ethereum. The other was philosophical, and would cause him to shift course yet again in his approach to crypto leadership.

The technical breakthrough was a long-awaited software upgrade for Ethereum known as the Merge. The Merge solved one of the loudest and most pervasive criticisms people had about NFTs and crypto in 2022: that they were extremely bad for the environment.

When the person or persons who went by the pseudonym of Satoshi Nakamoto created Bitcoin, they needed some way to safeguard the system without relying on a single watchdog. Trust and authority needed to be dispersed throughout all the network's participants. The solution was to use a system called proof of work—a peer-to-peer network that authenticated transactions by using computers to solve complex computational puzzles. The "miners" who put their computers to work in this way were rewarded by occasionally finding bitcoin. The more puzzles their computers solved, the more likely they were to find bitcoin. Anyone could become a miner, provided they had the right computational equipment. But bitcoin was designed to become harder and harder to mine the more of it was discovered. Conversely, the more activity on the blockchain grew, the more computing power it took to authenticate. The result was a functional decentralized system that was nearly impossible for hackers to penetrate, where the guardians were paid in ever-more-valuable cryptocurrency tokens.

Collectively, these crypto miners earned billions of dollars a year. But their activity was also wildly energy intensive. In 2022, crypto miners burned through energy at a faster rate than the entire country of Argentina. In the U.S., when power-thirsty crypto mining companies moved in, coal plants that were on the verge of being retired sprung back to life, pumping out fumes that debilitated those who lived nearby. In Texas, crypto miners' usage of the state's grid drove up its cumulative electricity bills by $1.8 billion annually. In one Texas town, the constant low roar of a new bitcoin mining plant voraciously consuming energy caused migraines, vomiting, and nosebleeds among local residents.

As the public learned about this destructive element of bitcoin, backlash grew. How could a new technology that was used by relatively few people consume more energy than the populations of whole countries—especially as climate change–induced disasters wreaked havoc all over the globe? One Twitter poster snarkily described proof of work being as if "keeping your car idling 24/7 produced solved Sudokus you could trade for heroin."

Vitalik and the other founders had initially built Ethereum on proof of work, partially because it was the main blockchain security mechanism that they knew worked. But Vitalik called proof of work an "utter environmental and economic tragedy" in 2014, and stumped for Ethereum to transition to an as-yet untested mechanism called proof of stake, which consumed 99.9 percent less energy. In proof of stake, energy-guzzling miners are replaced by watchdogs known as "validators," who deposit a significant amount of money (32 ETH) into the Ethereum network in order to be able to approve or deny transactions. Like miners, they earn financial rewards for doing so. Under this system, a hacker or bad-faith actor would need to put an obscene amount of money into the system in order to game it—and, in doing so, risk losing that money if they were discovered and kicked out. But the transition from proof of work to proof of stake was a highly technical and arduous one, akin to swapping out a car's gas engine for an electric one while it was barreling full-speed down a freeway. (Oh, and the car was worth $400 billion.) Repeated delays over the years turned proof of stake's implementation into a *Waiting for Godot*–style drama.

But in September 2022, Ethereum researchers, client teams, and users collectively switched the network over to proof of stake, without a hitch. For Vitalik, the Merge's success represented an ideological victory for Ethereum: that a group of dispersed developers and engineers who self-organized and collaborated for years around the world could pull off such a complicated technical maneuver without a board of directors or CEO. The Merge proved that Ethereum was malleable (albeit over the span of years) and responsive to criticism. And people could no longer write off NFTs or any financial activity on Ethereum simply for environmental reasons.

———

While the Merge was a powerful step forward for Ethereum, it was still an internal process. But the same week, Vitalik witnessed firsthand the transformative effect cryptocurrency could have on the lives of people in desperate need. On September 8, 2022, he boarded a train in Warsaw headed east to Kyiv, Ukraine. Vitalik, joined by a film crew shooting a documentary about him, spent eighteen hours on the train, writing a highly technical blog post about Ethereum domains before passing out in the bottom bunk. When he awoke, he found himself in a city that had been badly bombed six months earlier, and in which air sirens rang out regularly.

Most billionaires would do everything in their power to stay away from a war zone. But the war was personal to Vitalik: He had both Russian and Ukrainian ancestry and had spent the first six years of his life under an unstable post-Soviet government. Vitalik had actually met Russian president Vladimir Putin in 2017 to talk about the potential for Ethereum usage in Russia. When Putin launched a full-scale invasion of Ukraine in February 2022, Vitalik still had relatives living in Russia, which made speaking out extremely risky. Nevertheless, he condemned Putin on Twitter and personally contributed millions to Ukrainian relief efforts.

In Kyiv, Vitalik traveled in an armored car to the ministry building, where he met with Mykhailo Fedorov, Ukraine's minister in charge of digital transformation. Over a game of chess, Fedorov told him that in the early days of Russia's invasion of Ukraine, the country's national bank had banned international transactions, so the Ukrainian government instead used crypto to receive funding and buy weapons and military supplies. "We saved the lives of hundreds—maybe thousands of our military. So it was highly important," Fedorov told him.

In the first couple weeks of the invasion, almost $100 million in crypto donations had poured in from around the world, offering fast relief and easy, direct transactions. It might have taken weeks for a regular NGO to receive money and set up their organizational efforts. In contrast, a multi-signature crypto wallet—which requires multiple people to sign off on transactions, making it more secure—could be set up in ten minutes and instantly begin to collect crypto donations for people already on the ground.

Illia Polosukhin, the cofounder of the blockchain NEAR, is from Kharkiv—a city that borders Russia to the east. When the invasion began, Polosukhin searched for ways to get his family out of the country. He eventually arranged a car to drive them some thirty-six hours to the Romanian border, and paid the driver in crypto. He also sent his family and friends stablecoins to pay for supplies like gas on either side of the border. "Sending money via a regular bank would not really help because it doesn't work on the weekends, or if they shut down," Polosukhin says. "Crypto was there and it worked." In the following months, Kharkiv was heavily bombed: The windows in Polosukhin's childhood home were blown out, and a school three buildings over was partially destroyed.

In April 2022, the Ukrainian crypto organization Unchain Fund created a crypto-funded debit card for displaced Ukrainian mothers. The cards were loaded with €25 worth of crypto a week converted into fiat, and could be used for regular payments like food and gas. The Unchain Fund was flooded with requests from those in need and eventually distributed 7,754 cards. One of the women, Natalia Bulba, used the card to buy food, toilet paper, and shoes for herself and her children after they fled their home. "It was very easy and clear to use the card . . . never had any problems," Bulba wrote to me on the instant messaging service Telegram. "When we found ourselves in a very difficult financial situation, it helped a lot."

Donations were not the only use case for crypto during the war. As the invasion stretched on and accusations of Russian atrocities against Ukrainians mounted, Starling Labs, a nonprofit backed in part by Stanford, began to register videos containing evidence of alleged crimes against humanity onto distributed storage networks and blockchains. Starling Labs hoped to preserve these videos for prosecutors or war tribunals far into the future, free from tampering, manipulation, or deepfakes, especially given the rapid rise of artificial intelligence tools. Starling also submitted these cryptographic dossiers to the prosecutors at the International Criminal Court in the Netherlands and the United Nations for review. The latter body acknowledged the submission as part of an "emerging" movement of "good practices."

Back in Fedorov's office, Vitalik barely looked up from the chessboard as he made a stark admission: "For the blockchain community itself, this was the first opportunity to make a real difference with blockchain and cryptocurrency." Ethereum had existed for the better part of a decade. Over that time, Vitalik had proposed so many ways in which he hoped it would transform the world. Yet here he was, acknowledging that its first real impact was to help a country buy ammunition and survive invasion. After a lengthy game, Vitalik beat Fedorov by a single pawn, playfully chasing Fedorov's king around the board with his own king until Fedorov conceded with a laugh.

Vitalik had always been obsessed with games like chess and World of Warcraft. Standing in war-torn Ukraine, he was flooded with the realization of how much crypto had to grow up. When Fedorov asked him how Ukraine could become more involved in Web 3, Vitalik deflected the question, saying that the technology and infrastructure first needed to be improved. All of Web 3's current use cases seemed to pale in comparison to the needs of a country at war. "I think in the last decade it was really a LARP [live-action roleplay] in a lot of big ways," he later told me. It was then, standing in the streets of Kyiv, that Vitalik realized that crypto "can't just be a game anymore."

CHAPTER 35

Unknown Unknowns

In September 2022, about a week after Vitalik left Ukraine, Sam Bankman-Fried embarked on a trip of his own. But unlike Vitalik's Ukraine journey, Sam's was purely about money: He needed a lot of it, fast. The number on Caroline's Alameda spreadsheet notated "FTX borrows" had crept up to around $14 billion. FTX also owed more than $1 billion to lenders, including BlockFi, Genesis, and Voyager.

So Sam flew to the Middle East to plead for money from the Gulf's richest investors. He was an experienced and effective fundraiser; he had already raised $400 million so far in 2022. But he now needed to raise orders above that.

The Middle East seemed like a promising place to find allies. FTX had gained approval to operate its exchange in Dubai, and was scaling up its FTX MENA (Middle East and North Africa) operations to try to capture that rapidly growing market. Anthony Scaramucci—Sam's co-organizer of Crypto Bahamas—had spent years cultivating ties with powerful Middle Eastern businessmen. He offered to help Sam navigate the region, and brought him to dinner at the palace of Saudi Arabia's Crown Prince Mohammed bin Salman, where former secretary of the treasury Steve Mnuchin and Trump's son-in-law Jared Kushner were also in attendance. Sam spent the trip pitching potential investors—and badmouthing rival Changpeng Zhao, the head of Binance, to regulators, Scaramucci later remembered. While he didn't return with any concrete cash, Sam thought investors were "interested" and "going to do more diligence."

In an interview in late September 2022, CNBC called Sam the

"Michael Jordan of crypto." In the interview, Sam was asked if FTX had enough cash on hand for another industry bailout. "Yep, yeah," he responded. "We try not to empty the coffer." He said that FTX was ready with a "ballpark billion to deploy, completely unencumbered."

"It's not gonna be good for anyone long term if we have real pain, real blowouts," he said. "It was important for people to be able to operate in the ecosystem without being terrified that 'unknown unknowns' were going to blow them up somehow." Sam grimaced as he said this and blinked nervously.

Sam, of course, was in deep financial trouble. Alameda Research had been saved by the funds of FTX customers, but it was still flailing from the massive bets it had placed on the crypto economy going up, up, up—which it was decidedly not. In August, Sam took his anger out on Caroline in a one-on-one meeting in their apartment, yelling at her that their massive debts were her fault, because she hadn't hedged enough. They decided to protect themselves from future losses by hedging against the crypto market. But hedging cost $2 billion in collateral, which they did not have on hand. So they simply borrowed more from FTX customers.

With Alameda on the skids, Sam considered shutting it down completely. "It was probably time to do that a year ago," he wrote in a memo to Gary and Nishad. He also blamed Alameda as "hilariously beyond any threshold of any auditor being able to even get partially through an audit," and wrote that employees would "sometimes find $50m of assets lying around that we lost track of."

"Such is life," he wrote with a shrug.

Nishad suggested over Signal messaging that instead of shutting down completely, Alameda simply close down all accounts on FTX, and stop trading on the platform. This would lessen the conflicts of interest between the two companies and forge a badly needed organizational separation that Sam had been advertising for a year. Sam added that some of Alameda's market making on FTX could be replaced by another company: Modulo Capital, which just happened to be co-run by another one of Sam's exes, Lily Zhang. Caroline hated this idea for several reasons. First, it seemed that Sam was trying to replace her both professionally and romantically. Second, shutting Alameda's accounts on FTX was impossible, she wrote back, because of money that Alameda owed to FTX. Gary, in the chat, noted it was $13 billion.

Of the quartet, Nishad believed most wholeheartedly in effective altruism and doing good in the world. And as he came to understand the gravity of the situation, he started to panic. He demanded a meeting with Sam that evening on their penthouse balcony, which was ironically the most private place in the house given how rarely any of the roommates thought to swim or take in the view.

As Nishad paced back and forth on the balcony, Sam explained that Alameda had borrowed billions of dollars from FTX customers. But he assured Nishad that if the customers didn't try to take their money out all at once, everything would be fine.

"Jesus fucking Christ," Nishad spit at Sam, standing next to their turquoise-tiled hot tub, which melted into an infinity pool. "This is going to do a lot of damage to me."

"Yeah, I was worried about this," Sam replied, reclined on a cream-colored chaise. "In hindsight, it might have been a mistake for me to circulate that document this morning. People are going to freak out."

And Nishad was freaked. "I knew that customers were betrayed," he testified in October 2023 about that moment. "So many customers had to put their trust in us."

But Sam assured him he had many strategies to right the ship. He would sell off illiquid assets and fundraise from investors. He was working the CFTC so that they might be allowed to offer crypto derivatives on margin to U.S. customers, which would surely open up a new consumer base and bring in billions more in funds. And of course, the crypto market would rebound in due time. FTX, supposed to be a pillar of trust, now rested on little more than pure hope.

Virtually every part of Sam's empire was cratering. Solana, his preferred blockchain, was supposed to be the "Ethereum killer," a faster, more efficient answer to the network Vitalik had created. Instead, it was besieged by frequent outages that froze transactions for hours or days at a time. And in August 2022, *CoinDesk* published a report that found that much of Solana's financial activity was fake. According to the report, two brothers, Dylan and Ian Macalinao, had built a system of shell projects on Solana pretending to be a whole network of developers. Using pseudonyms, they created an array of trading and staking services that stacked on top of each other, double and triple counting the same dollars. This Russian nesting doll of fake trades accounted for more than half of the billions of dollars in the Solana DeFi ecosystem.

The purported success of the Macalinaos' projects had helped spur the price of Solana's coin from under $22 in July 2021 to $259 that November. But by the autumn of 2022, Solana was hovering miserably around $30. The brothers would later face an investigation from the U.S. Department of Justice for their actions, *CoinDesk* reported. And Solana's price drop further dented Sam and Alameda's balance sheets, as they had put hundreds of millions of dollars into the coin.

Then, there was the biggest liability of all for Sam and his co-conspirators. Damian Williams had assembled a team of federal prosecutors in the Southern District of New York, including Nicolas Roos and Samuel Raymond, who had worked on crypto-related cases and understood the intricacies of the blockchain. Together, they steadily collected evidence of FTX's shady practices.

CHAPTER 36

Withdrawals

Ultimately, it wasn't prosecutors who moved first against Sam, but a crypto news site that had cheered him on for years. *CoinDesk* had covered Sam's rise extensively, including a fawning profile in April 2022 subtitled "The Man, the Hair, the Vision."

But on November 2, the *CoinDesk* reporter Ian Allison published a leaked PDF of Alameda's balance sheet from June. Allison wouldn't say who had leaked it, but the balance sheet showed that $3.66 billion, or a quarter of Alameda's $14.6 billion in assets, were held in FTT. Another $2.16 billion was listed as "FTT collateral." The balance sheet was also rife with other FTX-related Sam Coins, including Serum and MAPS.

Sam had long admitted that much of his fortune was illiquid. But the public had not been made aware how illiquid, exactly, it all was. The massive FTT stash was especially concerning because the entire market of FTT tokens in public circulation was worth about $5.1 billion, which meant that Alameda held a majority of all the tokens in existence. If Alameda ever tried to sell off its FTT, that very action would flood the market, causing the FTT price to plummet. Essentially, the article insinuated that Alameda had billions of dollars less than anyone realized and that large portions of its balance sheet were effectively conjured out of thin air.

Many in the crypto world dismissed the report as FUD (fear, uncertainty, doubt). The leaked balance sheet wasn't real—or if it was, it lacked crucial details, they said. The PDF purported to be from the summer, so Sam must have sorted out his problems by now. Besides, Sam had just bailed out the rest of the crypto world. How could he have done that if he was insolvent himself?

This sort of denial, backpedaling, and deflection was all too common among crypto enthusiasts when confronted with evidence of a scam. Because so many speculative crypto assets depended almost entirely on other people having faith in them, it was immensely important that crypto minnows mobilize to support sharks like Sam on social media.

A few months prior, Anthony Olasele, the host of *Crypto Round Up Africa*, had kept much of his crypto on KuCoin, another exchange. But in June, a rumor spread on social media that KuCoin was insolvent. The crypto community was already wracked by anxiety following the Terra-Luna and Three Arrows crashes. Bankman-Fried himself had thrown fuel on the fire by telling *Forbes* that several "third-tier" exchanges were already "secretly insolvent." So Olasele decided to move his assets off of KuCoin—and onto FTX. Bankman-Fried, he believed, was a "giga-brain," charting a path through harrowing turbulence. When the *CoinDesk* article with the balance sheet was released, Olasele dismissed its veracity. The claims about Alameda made no sense to him given the company's track record. So he left his assets—which amounted to nearly $100,000 at the time—on FTX.

Olasele and other skeptics were right on one count: The balance sheet wasn't accurate. But that's because it vastly *understated* the full extent of Alameda's problems. Caroline had created it to send to lenders to mask the massive debts that Alameda owed to FTX, as well as to hide the $4.5 billion that Alameda had loaned out to Sam, Gary, and others. The balance sheet made Alameda look bad—but in reality, the company's financial situation was much, much worse.

Caroline and Sam hoped that the report would blow over. Instead, it sparked alarm in one of the few people in the world who had the ability to topple Sam's empire: Changpeng Zhao, the CEO of Binance. Binance had long been the world's biggest exchange, buoyed by a huge head start, a much larger staff, and a strong presence in Asia. Its widespread usership made Zhao the richest man in crypto, with *Bloomberg* listing his fortune at $96 billion—at least four times the size of Sam's. Binance had actually been FTX's first investor: In November 2019, it acquired a roughly 20 percent stake in Sam's fledgling exchange for about $100 million, with the goal of "grow[ing] the crypto economy together," Binance said in a statement at the time. But FTX had come on hard and fast, especially through its marketing campaign. While Binance had more customers, FTX had increasing name recognition and regulatory support, especially in the western hemisphere.

In July 2021, just as the competition between FTX and Binance was really heating up, Sam unwittingly gave Zhao a powerful tool to undermine his crypto empire. In order to strip Zhao of any power over him, Sam decided to buy back Binance's stake in FTX, which was worth about $2 billion. Sam later described the process as a "very acrimonious negotiation" and claimed that Zhao threatened to walk away from the buyout unless FTX kicked in another $75 million, which it did.

Caroline vehemently disagreed with Sam's decision to buy out Zhao. She didn't think they had enough money to front the whole $2 billion and warned Sam that if they went through with the deal, about half the funds would be money borrowed from FTX customers.

Sam went through with it anyway—and ironically placed himself in an even more vulnerable position. Not only was Alameda now much deeper in debt to FTX customers, but Sam paid back Binance, in large part, in FTT tokens as opposed to dollars. Changpeng Zhao now sat on a huge pile of Sam Coins, which he could use as a weapon of corporate warfare.

In 2022, Sam and Zhao increasingly feuded in public and private. Caroline wrote in a fall 2022 internal memo that one of Sam's highest priorities was "getting regulators to crack down on Binance," because he thought enforcement action might result in Binance customers switching over to FTX, which would be the easiest way to increase their market share. "Various regulators had been promising him that this would happen for a while," Caroline testified. "But it never happened."

On Twitter, Sam thumbed his nose at Zhao, insinuating in October that Zhao's potential ties to the Chinese government might make him unable to travel to Washington, D.C., to participate in crypto regulation efforts. The tweet was later deleted, but successfully drew a sharp contrast between Sam, who positioned himself as the regulation-embracing American, and Zhao, the shadowy foreigner.

So when Zhao read the *CoinDesk* balance sheet report and saw a chance to move against a foremost competitor, he did, swiftly. On November 6, Zhao publicly questioned FTX's financial stability and announced his intention to sell off at least $580 million worth of FTT that he had acquired in the buyout the previous year. Zhao wrote that the decision was "risk management, learning from LUNA."

Zhao's comparison of Luna, an unmitigated financial disaster, to FTX, one of the world's most trusted crypto institutions, at first seemed laughable and petty. But cautious traders decided to take their money out of FTX all the same, and their withdrawals soon ballooned to $120 million every hour. In a Signal group chat with Caroline and Nishad, Sam responded to the outflows with a simple "oof."

Sam summoned his executive team to devise a damage control strategy. Together, they workshopped a response for Caroline to tweet out, in which she cheerily declared that Alameda was willing to "happily" buy all of Zhao's FTT for $22 a token—slightly under the market price, but a good financial deal for Zhao considering how much the value of FTT would inevitably slide during the sell-off he had sparked. She then directed Alameda traders to buy as much FTT at $22 as they could, in an attempt to build a price wall. Caroline's tweet reassured Anthony Olasele, in Madrid. In fact, he bought even more FTT after seeing it, thinking he was grabbing a valuable asset during a minor blip in its market.

Caroline's tweet, combined with her traders' fierce defense of the $22 wall, stabilized prices for about thirty-four hours. But their efforts were akin to patching an overflowing dam with duct tape: Far too many people were trying to get rid of their FTT at the same time. When Caroline and Sam relented and stopped buying FTT, the price nosedived to $5. They had blown tens of millions of dollars to preserve the value of a token that was approaching worthlessness. Little did customers know that the wasted cash could have helped pay back Alameda's debts to the customers themselves, who were fast cashing out of the exchange.

Customers' fears became a self-fulfilling prophecy. On the day of Zhao's tweet, FTX clients requested roughly $5 billion of withdrawals. FTX's stablecoin reserves sunk by 93 percent of what they had been just two weeks prior. As withdrawals cascaded, FTX's major clients and partners frantically contacted the company for reassurance. But Sam went silent, both outside and inside the company. Employees suggested a war room to coordinate public relations, but were told that FTX and Sam were already all set. The customer and client teams were kept in the dark.

Sam was shocked by the crisis, but still carried an optimism that veered into delusion. On Twitter on November 7, he played off the accusations as pure mind games. "A competitor is trying to go after us with false rumors," he wrote. "FTX is fine. Assets are fine. FTX has enough to cover all client holdings." Every part of the statement was false. Just a few hours later, he sent a spreadsheet to a group chat of FTX executives acknowledging a shortfall of $8.1 billion in customer assets. They needed money, fast.

The first place to rifle through for cash was Alameda. After all, that's where the money had gone in the first place. At the time, most of Alameda's staff was in their Hong Kong office. Caroline directed traders to close out all of their positions and grab all the cash they could from various exchanges to send straight to FTX. "She was using a more frantic tone than I'd ever heard from her," remembers the former Alameda software engineer Aditya Baradwaj. "So we basically drained all of our capital, and got to the point where we weren't even trading anymore, because we had no capital to trade with." Alameda employees dredged up money that was parked in yield farms (a DeFi mechanism for earning interest) or stationed as collateral on exchanges. "I thought that we would be happy if we found $10 million," one Alameda employee who was there for the sell-off tells me. "But we found all of the $10, $20, and $50 millions we could find. It was still not enough. Withdrawals kept coming."

With Alameda tapped out, Sam picked up the phone and tried to find someone—anyone—who would give him a loan. He drafted talking points for himself and his colleagues to use on potential investors, which included blaming Binance for the collapse. "What we need is a few billion of USD. We will take whatever we can get, at whatever terms make people comfortable," he wrote. His first entreaties went to recipients including Sequoia, the firm that had published a blog post speculating that Sam could become the first trillionaire; Dustin Moskovitz, a Facebook cofounder and prominent effective altruist; and Pete Briger of Fortress Investment Group.

But the FTX spreadsheets that Sam showed to potential investors revealed an absolute mess. FTX International held just $900 million in easily sellable assets against $9 billion in liabilities. FTX's biggest asset, the spreadsheets said, was $2.2 billion worth of Serum, a Sam Coin created in 2020. But almost two-thirds of the entire volume of Serum was held by Alameda and FTX. Only 3 percent of Serum was even on the open market, which meant that if any new parent company of FTX tried to actually sell off its Serum holdings, the token's price would turn to dust. Around two-thirds of the billions that FTX owed to customers was backed by crypto assets Sam had invented, which were now depreciating rapidly amid this public crisis. FTX's holdings of Sam Coins (FTT, SRM, SOL, and MAPS) had shrunk in value from $14.4 billion to $4.3 billion in one week. Unsurprisingly, even Sam's foremost allies were not interested in striking a deal with a company with billions of dollars in debt.

With all other options exhausted, Sam swallowed his pride and turned to his nemesis: Changpeng Zhao, whose FTT sell-off had triggered the crisis. Sam offered to sell Zhao FTX Trading in its entirety, understanding that Binance, the biggest crypto exchange in the world, was one of the only companies that would be able to absorb such massive debts. On Tuesday, November 8, Zhao accepted, for a price tag of several billion dollars, a steep discount from FTX's $32 billion January valuation, sources told Reuters. Zhao had essentially performed a hostile takeover of his greatest rival. Zhao hoped that Binance's own deep coffers would allow him to cover the enormous shortfall. In exchange for refunding FTX's customers in full, Binance would emerge with another crucial piece of crypto infrastructure.

On Wednesday, November 9, Aditya Baradwaj and the rest of the Alameda staff showed up to their Hong Kong office and sat around all day apprehensively. There was no more capital to trade. One Alameda employee told me that their funds were so depleted, they weren't even able to order delivery to the office. "That's when I knew it was over—when we couldn't afford food," they said. And the one person who had answers for them, Caroline Ellison, was locked in a conference room all day on the phone with her boss and ex-boyfriend, Sam Bankman-Fried. Alameda employees could see her crying through the glass.

At the end of the day in Asia, Caroline called everyone onto the trading floor and told them the secret she had been holding on to for years: that Alameda had been borrowing FTX customer assets and had used them to make venture capital investments and repay loans that had been recalled during the Terra-Luna crash. The only people who had known about this arrangement, she told her employees, were herself and the self-anointed "Fantastic Three": Sam, Gary Wang, and Nishad Singh.

Within hours, most of Alameda's staff resigned.

———————

Sometimes, nature provides metaphors that are too on the nose even for Hollywood. As the East Coast of North America awoke the morning of November 9, a massive tempest named Tropical Storm Nicole made landfall in The Bahamas. Winds whipped up to seventy miles an hour, and swells caused flooding across the island of New Providence. Inside the Albany, Sam led a group of executives trying to track down the money somewhere, anywhere.

At the same time, Zhao and his team at Binance were combing through FTX's financial statements. They found the problems to be even more extreme than they had anticipated. That day, reports circulated that FTX faced a federal investigation over whether the company mishandled customer funds. So instead of placing himself at the helm of a sinking ship, Zhao instead decided to walk away. He announced the news on Twitter, jabbing at Sam by saying that FTX's issues were "beyond our control or ability to help." Hours later, bitcoin sank to its lowest price of the year: $15,742, down 77 percent from its November 2021 high. It was now the level it had been at when Beeple minted his first NFT in November 2020. The gains made during crypto's miraculous pandemic-era run had been wiped clean.

At 4:30 a.m. the following morning, under strong pressure from his legal counsel, Sam clicked a button on DocuSign and relinquished his company to longtime crisis manager John Ray III, who had led the unwinding of Enron two decades prior. "I fucked up," Sam wrote on Twitter. To his "sparring partner" Zhao, he wrote: "Well played; you won," as if they had just finished a rather intense game of Axie Infinity.

A few hours later, FTX and 133 related companies filed for chapter 11 bankruptcy.

CHAPTER 37

Doomscrolling

Just two years earlier, Sam Bankman-Fried had described crypto as "sort of a collective fiction that we're writing." Sam had penned an epic saga of fiction: of made-up coins, faked balance sheets, overstated charitable efforts, and a Toyota Corolla. But now, the pain around the world was all too real.

Christine Chew was in Malaysia visiting her dad when FTX combusted. She initially blamed the entire situation on Changpeng Zhao thanks to the conditioning of her FTX colleagues, who had constantly bad-mouthed Zhao as a cold-blooded, conniving enemy dead set on destroying their sunny Caribbean hideaway. In this lens, Zhao's sell-off of FTT seemed little more than a ruthless corporate chess move.

It was only after FTX declared bankruptcy, with Sam admitting publicly that he was missing billions in funds, that Christine started to accept the truth. Even though her time at FTX was fraught, she had truly believed in Sam's overarching vision of wielding crypto for global good. Sam had flaws as a boss, but he was young, driven, and seemingly hell-bent on improving the world. She felt her entire belief system shattering before her eyes.

Sam's fraud had decimated Christine's bank account, too, as she had placed 80 percent of her savings into an FTX account. She had been lured by the rewards of doing so, including earning Serum, a Sam Coin, and the ability to buy into new tokens for low prices. "I thought it was the safest place to put my money," she told me.

But Serum was losing value every day as confidence in Sam plummeted:

from 86 cents a token all the way down to 18 cents. By the time she realized what was happening, the $63,795 in various cryptocurrencies that Christine had saved up over the years had dwindled in value and then became inaccessible when FTX halted withdrawals. When Christine finally came to grips with the fall of her former employer, she wept for hours. She was unable to sleep or eat for days, instead glued to her computer screen watching the horrors unfold in real time. "The entire week, I was not me," she says. "All I could do was doomscroll on the latest news. And also just be angry at myself for not withdrawing money."

Christine had joined FTX and the crypto world because she saw it as an alternative to the avaricious mainstream financial world. Sam was supposed to be a hero of this revolution. "A lot of us wanted there to be a Sam," she says. "That's why we ignored a lot of the shaky parts of the entire orchestration."

Many other FTX employees had similarly used FTX as their bank. They received their paychecks directly into their FTX accounts, deposited their savings there, and received their bonuses in FTX equity. Natalie Tien, FTX's head of PR, reported losing $500,000. Harrison Obiefule, the Lagos-based marketing manager of FTX Africa, lost everything, too. For two years, he had worked tirelessly to paint the image of FTX as safe, reliable, and transformative for Africans. Now that FTX had been exposed for a fraud, people assumed Obiefule was too. He started receiving threats from strangers and friends who had lost money in the FTX crash and was forced to go into hiding. "I lost everything from my savings, from my employee stock options," he told me in 2023. "Everything that I owned was in FTX."

FTX's island paradise in The Bahamas turned Ozymandian within days. "It quickly went from 'Is Binance going to let us run independently?' to 'The Bahamian government is going to evict us?'" says Natalie Tien. "Everyone pretty much fled as soon as they could." The $30 million penthouse where Sam Bankman-Fried, Caroline Ellison, and their closest companions lived was quickly vacated. Dozens of shoes and boxes of Legos were left behind, strewn on the floors.

But it was hard to feel too bad for those in FTX's inner circle when their mistakes and greed caused so many average crypto investors around the world to lose so much. Bankruptcy filings indicated that the company potentially owed over $3 billion to 1 million creditors. For comparison, Bernie Madoff defrauded some thirty-seven thousand clients. Social media flooded with posts from distraught FTX investors, who voiced varying stages of grief.

As much as Sam wanted to return to the U.S., FTX was an international exchange by design. He had aggressively courted users in developing markets like Nigeria and India, who felt like their national economic systems had left them with few other options. "My family is asking if I have converted the money yet and I can't bring myself to tell them there is no money to convert anymore," wrote one Reddit user from Iran, who said they put their money into FTX to avoid the volatile Iranian banking system. "My life is over. See you on the other side," wrote another investor who said they lost $40,000.

In his new home in Nottingham, Liam Vries lost $2,260, an important chunk of cash for an immigrant artist searching for steady income. Two weeks earlier, he had participated in a panel at the NFT London conference, telling the crowd how NFTs had changed his life. He hadn't told them that his sales had slowed to a trickle—he was making 10 percent of the income he earned the prior year—or that he was growing frustrated with trying to be a leader in a space full of fierce individualists. Overall, NFTs had fallen 97 percent from their January peak. Now Liam feared the psychological impact that such a massive crash would have on the African crypto movement as a whole. Crypto builders across the continent were slowly making progress toward creating all sorts of decentralized alternatives to exploitative financial systems. FTX's spectacular meltdown threatened that momentum. "Many were already skeptical in Africa, and this is not going to help," Liam said. "It's going to backdate the Third World countries even further." A year later, Liam estimated that half of the people in the African NFT Community left in the wake of the FTX crash.

FTT DAO, the Nigerian organization that had ebulliently promoted Sam as a force for good on the continent, quickly shuttered its operations. Izuchukwu Offia, who had both served as an FTX campus ambassador and a FTT DAO member, was wracked with guilt. "I don't have the words: It affected Nigerians negatively, a lot," he says. "It's my fault for giving advice. It's affected so many people."

Nestcoin, the Nigerian crypto startup that had kept its assets for operational expenses on FTX, was forced to lay off thirty people. Over the next couple months, the company shelved four of its five products and separated from Metaverse Magna, the Axie Infinity guild that Yele Bademosi had hoped would provide stable incomes for Africans. "I genuinely believe that no individual or business should have the experience that we had with FTX," Bademosi told me. A year later, however, Nestcoin was able to raise another $1.9 million in funding and launch a crypto debit card that allowed its users to pay for goods in 160 countries.

Owo's AfroDroids NFT project essentially lay dormant through 2022 aside from monthly virtual dance parties for faithful AfroDroids believers. In those dance parties, robot-like avatars waved their mitts to Afrobeats music under a spinning AfroDroid head and videos of Dream Catchers students dancing euphorically. But after the FTX crash, Owo shuttered the dance hall's virtual doors. The hype around the metaverse had died down almost entirely, and Owo didn't see the point in forcing communal enthusiasm for a project whose secondary market essentially no longer existed. CryptoWizard, his adviser, says the market got so bad after the FTX crash that it didn't even make sense for them to release new NFTs for free, since people wouldn't be willing to pay the $15 in gas for the transaction to go through.

Over the course of a single year on the AfroDroids Discord, optimism had given way to anger and then resigned disappointment. "It's astonishing how many people fell for scams and rugs, clearly most of the projects were in only to make money and didn't have the knowledge or [interest] to keep and sustain them," wrote a user named Alpha01 at the end of 2022. "Every 'diamond hand' was left holding the bag and without their ETH. Only the owner and the quick 'paper hands' flippers profited . . . I only trust Yuga [the Bored Apes company] and a handful of established blue chips."

At the Dream Catchers Academy, the school's founder, Seyi Oluyole, didn't know much about FTX: She had used Coinbase to receive and withdraw the funds from the AfroDroids sale. All she knew was that following the Terra-Luna crash, the ether that she had kept in her wallet for the school had lost hundreds of thousands of dollars' worth of value. Nobody had told Oluyole that crypto was so unstable, or that it could depreciate so much. "We believed it was a way to safekeep the money while we gradually did everything piece by piece," she says. "We didn't get enough education on how volatile the market can be." After the FTX crash, Oluyole was forced to postpone construction of the hostel next to the school, where she had hoped to house homeless students. Her initial dreams of increasing enrollment from twenty to one hundred was delayed. By the end of 2022, Dream Catchers still only enrolled forty girls. The funds from the AfroDroids drop had fulfilled Oluyole's initial dream of opening a physical school, and saved her from having to make devastating cuts. But there were still so many girls who needed help, which Oluyole was now unable to provide.

The impacts of the crash rippled across the world. The Ontario Teachers' Pension Plan, one of Canada's largest pension funds, was forced to write off its $95 million investment in FTX and announced it would steer clear of crypto investments going forward. A promised grant of $600,000 from FTX to the nonprofit Equity and Transformation, which assists formerly incarcerated Chicago residents, went unfulfilled. The Miami Heat quickly cut ties with FTX. By the time the team returned to the NBA finals several months later, they would be playing in the newly christened Kaseya Center—named after a corporate sponsor that makes security and IT software.

Farther south in The Bahamas, the island nation that was supposed to be the biggest beneficiary of Sam's generosity was left to do some deep soul-searching. Prime Minister Philip Davis's dreams of overseeing Nassau's rapid ascension to a global tech hub withered away. The Bahamian government had been the first in the world to roll out a central bank digital currency: the Sand Dollar, which it hoped would solve problems of financial inclusion. But adoption of the new technology was painfully slow, and FTX's fall only increased Bahamians' skepticism. "Reputationally, it has affected us," says Nicholas Rees, the CEO of Kanoo Pays, a Bahamas-based digital payments system that worked to increase Sand Dollar adoption around the island. "The fear of technology is something that we've had to address significantly in The Bahamas and in the Caribbean [more broadly]. And when FTX collapsed, it made investors and customers look at technology companies as a whole, particularly in the financial services space, with a certain level of caution."

At a Nassau church, the Bishop Lawrence Rolle, who had received $50,000 from FTX, wailed to his congregation: "FTX! The money is gone. FTX! The money have done gone."

———————

Just a few months earlier, Sam Bankman-Fried had been hailed as the J.P. Morgan of crypto and the industry's selfless savior. Now, the firms that he had bailed out during his power grab collapsed. BlockFi filed for bankruptcy, and Voyager scrambled to find a new buyer. Crypto auditors, including those serving companies as large as Binance, decided to jettison their crypto clients and stop serving the industry.

Institutional investors grew leery of an industry that once again became mostly associated with crimes, and venture capital for crypto startups dried up. Alex Pack, who had started his own crypto venture capital firm, Hack VC, says that in the months following the bankruptcy, Sam's name came up in almost every single investor meeting. "The reputational harm that he did to the industry is ironically much greater than the actual harm on paper," he says.

Haseeb Qureshi, a managing partner at Dragonfly Capital who had encountered Sam on the "Giving in Crypto" panel in 2020, agreed, in an August 2023 interview. "No question it basically stands shoulder to shoulder with Theranos as being one of the most significant frauds that had VC involvement," he says. "It has led to a chilling effect on the enthusiasm for crypto, because LPs [limited partners, who supply capital] in general don't want to get embarrassed by having money in a fund that is affiliated with one of the biggest financial frauds of the decade." By March 2023, one study found that crypto financing had dropped 80 percent compared to the previous year. And the data company PitchBook found that Sam had caused more venture investing losses than any other founder: double the $1.1 billion that Elizabeth Holmes had vaporized with Theranos.

Harper Reed, Obama's ex-CTO, was just about ready to bring his crypto debit card to market when FTX crashed. Shortly after, the financial institutions supporting the project pulled out. "When FTX happened, a lot of the bankers were like, 'Wait a minute. You mean the young, white wunderkind is the bad guy?' I think that fucked with them." After several months of futility, Reed shut down his crypto startup and moved on. "As I reflect on it, it was fucking bonkers: all the hype, the churn, the wildness, the scams," he says.

The reputational damage extended to Washington, D.C., the town that Sam had so desperately hoped to conquer. He had worked hard to paint himself as the trustworthy, regulation-friendly face of crypto. Behind the scenes, he used all sorts of underhanded methods to shovel money from FTX's unwitting customers to pro-crypto candidates while also attempting to tarnish the reputation of his competitors like Binance. His true feelings about D.C. emerged during his late-night exchange with the *Vox* journalist Kelsey Piper in November 2022, as everything was crashing down around him: "Fuck regulators," he wrote to her in a Twitter DM. "They make everything worse."

Washington, unsurprisingly, did not take kindly to this heel turn. Representative Maxwell Alejandro Frost, who had received nearly a million dollars from Protect Our Future and had expressed enthusiasm about seeing crypto "thrive," stopped mentioning crypto altogether. Senator Debbie Stabenow, a cowriter of the 2022 pro-crypto bill that many referred to as the "SBF Bill," announced she would not seek reelection. Representative Ritchie Torres, one of Congress's foremost crypto advocates, glumly told *Roll Call* in May 2023 that FTX's collapse had crushed any ability for the two parties to find common ground on potential crypto legislation: "The gulf is much wider than it's ever been." FTX's new management declared their intention to claw back over three hundred political contributions to members of Congress.

With Congress on the sidelines, SEC chair Gary Gensler took center stage and waged an all-out war on crypto companies. The SEC's crypto actions surged 183 percent in the six months after the FTX collapse. In June 2023, the agency tagged Binance, Sam's biggest rival, with charges that looked eerily similar to those leveled against FTX. By this point, Binance had become frightningly central to crypto, accounting for over half of all trading volume. The SEC alleged that Changpeng Zhao had ascended to that level in part through mishandling funds, lying to regulators, and using market makers to manipulate trading volumes on Binance US. In November 2023, Zhao pleaded guilty to Justice Department criminal charges including money laundering violations and agreed to pay a $50 million fine and step down from the company. The SEC investigation is still ongoing.

The law came for the other three Horsemen too. Do Kwon was arrested in March 2023 in Montenegro; Alex Mashinsky in July 2023 in New York; and Su Zhu in September 2023 in Singapore. The men who had bragged they were revolutionizing finance and told their haters to have fun staying poor were now in jumpsuits facing fraud charges. (Zhu was released from prison a couple months later, however.)

And effective altruism—the purported reason that Sam wanted to make so much money in the first place—found itself at a crossroads. All the members of FTX's Future Fund—all of whom were effective altruists and had given away more than $160 million over the course of 2022—resigned. "Many people have been saying that EAs culturally are likely to follow naive utilitarianism into dark corners. I thought this was too cynical, but feel incredibly humbled by this event," tweeted Dustin Moskovitz, one of the most prominent advocates of the movement.

CHAPTER 38

House Arrest

For as long as Sam had been in crypto, he had always been surrounded by a tight-knit circle of friends and collaborators who fought for him and his vision. But in November 2022, after the collapse of FTX, Sam found himself in a luxury seaside resort all by himself. "You were my family," Sam wrote in a self-pitying note to FTX employees. "I've lost that, and our old home is an empty warehouse of monitors. When I turn around, there's no one left to talk to."

To fill his time, Sam booked a slew of interviews—from the *New York Times* to random Twitter Spaces—to try to convince the world that the lost billions were a result of mistakes and market movement rather than intentional fraud. Sam had long been able to manipulate the press for his own benefit. He developed a hangdog look and tried to appear as ashamed as possible while stopping short of actually taking responsibility for the crash. "I wasn't spending any time or effort trying to manage risk on FTX," he said in an interview with George Stephanopoulos. "If I had been spending an hour a day thinking about risk management on FTX, I don't think that would have happened."

In private documents, he brainstormed different shameless ways to garner public support. "Go on Tucker Carlsen, come out as a republican. . . . Come out against the woke agenda," he spitballed. "Talk about how the cartel of lawyers is destroying value and throwing entrepreneurs under the bus."

On December 12, Sam was still trying to talk his way out of legal jeopardy—and preparing for a congressional appearance he had booked before the crash—when a squadron of Bahamian cops banged on his door. His arrest came at the request of Damian Williams, the U.S. attorney for the Southern District of New York, whose team had amassed enough evidence over the past few months to suggest that Sam knew full well that he was swiping money from FTX customers to pay Alameda's debts.

Sam spent eight days in the medical wing of a Bahamian prison, so as to be separated from its general population. After he was extradited to the U.S., he pleaded not guilty to all criminal counts in a Manhattan federal courthouse and geared up for a vicious legal battle against the U.S. government. Neither side was much in the mood for compromise. Williams and the U.S. Attorney's Office were determined to make Sam a poster child for cryptocurrency's ills. They, however, did reach out to Sam's lawyers, asking if Sam wanted to talk over potential plea deals. But Sam, ever the gambler, said no: He didn't even want to hear their offer.

Initially, Sam had one major asset in his fight for freedom: his parents' money. On December 22, he was released on $250 million bond, with his parents' Stanford home put up as collateral. He spent the next few months in that comfy house, writing blog posts explaining his innocence and meeting with his new high-powered lawyers Mark Cohen and Christian Everdell—who had previously defended Jeffrey Epstein's longtime girlfriend and sex trafficking accomplice Ghislaine Maxwell.

But Sam's allies were shrinking by the month. His inner circle of Nishad, Gary, and Caroline were fed up with Sam leading them down paths of recklessness and financial ruin. And their complicity in FTX's fall meant that they were staring down the barrel of decades in prison, too. So within the next couple months, all three of them met with federal prosecutors and the FBI, pleaded guilty to an array of financial crimes, and agreed to cooperate in the case against their curly haired roommate in the hopes of earning more lenient sentences.

The trio became the backbone of the prosecution's case against Sam. They sat for what must have felt like endless interviews over the course of 2023 and relinquished their phones, laptops, and handwritten notebooks to the government's lawyers, who pored over them and eventually assembled 6 million pages of documents and other evidence.

Sam, from the solitude of his parents' home in Palo Alto, tried to fight back in the narrative war. In July 2023, he leaked to the *New York Times* Caroline Ellison's private writings, in which she questioned her own leadership ability and expressed jealousy of Modulo Capital, the hedge fund co-run by Sam's ex Lily Zhang. This tactic—of publicly undermining a nemesis—was reminiscent of how he had attempted to blackball the venture capitalist Alex Pack. But this time, it backfired spectacularly, because he was under the thumb of the American justice system. When prosecutors argued that Sam's ploy against Caroline was an attempt at witness tampering, Judge Lewis Kaplan agreed, and revoked Sam's bond in August 2023. Whatever defense preparation that Sam hoped to complete before his upcoming trial in October, he now would have to complete from the Metropolitan Detention Center Brooklyn, one of the worst-regarded prisons in the city, infamous for its staffing shortages, power outages, and maggots. When Ghislaine Maxwell had stayed there two years earlier, her lawyers complained that raw sewage had seeped onto the floor of her cell.

The prosecution, meanwhile, received another stream of evidence against Sam from FTX's new management team. John Ray, the company's new CEO, criticized Sam repeatedly, publicly airing all of FTX's failings and incompetencies, big and small. Ray declared that "in his 40 years of legal and restructuring experience," he had never seen "such a complete failure of corporate controls and such a complete absence of trustworthy financial information as occurred here." Sam's crypto empire, Ray wrote, seemed to be an enormous shell game of different interlinked companies across jurisdictions, with fifty-six of them failing to produce financial statements at all.

Ray's first forty-eight hours at the company, he said, seething, were "pure hell." Employees submitted expenses over Slack—which were approved via emoji—and relied on QuickBooks, a system designed for small businesses, not multibillion-dollar financial corporations. Loans were handed out without documentation. FTX employees stored the private keys—essentially passwords—to over $100 million worth of crypto in unencrypted plaintext documents, practically begging scammers to abscond with their funds.

But while Ray's proclamations about FTX were damning, many of them only reinforced Sam's own narrative entering his trial: He wasn't a criminal, just an overwhelmed and incompetent manager. In order to walk away a free man, Sam needed to convince a jury that he had acted in good faith; that he believed all the money was there until it wasn't; and that his co-conspirators Caroline, Gary, and Nishad were lying in order to save their own skins.

CHAPTER 39

One Last Roulette Spin

On most mornings in October 2023, a line of dozens of people snaked outside 500 Pearl Street, the federal courthouse in lower Manhattan. The first of them had shown up as early as 11 p.m. the night before, leaning on stone barricades and shivering in the autumn cold. Up the block, in state civil court, Donald Trump was facing a trial of his own, accused of fraudulently inflating the value of his assets. But for these people waiting in the cold for hours, the trial of Sam Bankman-Fried was an even bigger deal. They had come to see the "Prince of Risk" spin the wheel one last time.

Faced with the prospect of more than a century in prison, Sam could have thrown himself on the mercy of the court, admitted his crimes, and asked the judge for leniency. The act of pleading guilty alone would have lessened his recommended sentence. And forgoing a trial would have spared his friends and family the humiliation of such a public spectacle. But Sam's brain does not work like that. Sam, the king of risk neutrality, preferred the dangerous path that might lead to enormous reward. To plead guilty was a clear negative-EV play: It would render him a white-collar criminal, put him in jail for years, and significantly hamper his ability to make an impact on the world. But if he went to court, there was still a chance he could convince the jury of his innocence. And maybe that would allow him to take charge of FTX again—or build some kind of other project that would also rake in billions. And he believed in himself: He told the content creator Tiffany Fong before his trial that he thought he had almost a 50 percent chance of walking away a free man.

So here he was, sitting in a twenty-sixth-floor courtroom of 500 Pearl

Street, trying to worm his way out of another tight situation. One of the first tactics his legal team tried was to argue that the customer money that Sam had lost was actually recoverable. Some of the big bets that Sam had made with FTX funds had paid off—most notably the AI startup Anthropic, which had vastly increased in value during the AI boom that was now capturing Silicon Valley's wallets in crypto's stead. Thanks to that bet, a gradual increase in crypto prices and months of painstaking asset recovery from John Ray's team, it now seemed possible that FTX creditors would be able to recover much, if not all, of their lost funds.

This development was great news for creditors whose lives had been upended by Sam's carelessness and greed. But in court, the line of argument did not hold up because—like much of Sam's logic—it was predicated on the idea that the only variable that truly mattered was outcome. When Sam's lawyers asked for permission to tell the jury about Sam's savvy Anthropic bet, Judge Lewis Kaplan responded with a cutting analogy. "This is like saying that if I break into the Federal Reserve Bank, make off with a million bucks, spend it all on Powerball tickets and happen to win, it was okay," Kaplan told the lawyers. "The crime is the misappropriation. That's it, it's finished, the minute the misappropriation happens, whether it's used wisely, foolishly, or whatever."

The trial would only get worse for Sam, as his former friends and confidants proceeded to rip him to shreds. The most scathing of all was Nishad Singh. Not so long ago, Sam and Nishad were billionaire roommates who had built one of the fastest-growing companies in the world. They seemed to embody the wildest dreams of earn-to-give philosophers, who hoped that these bright, enterprising young men would turn crypto's chaotic markets into an everlasting wellspring for charity.

But on October 16, 2023, the two men sat across from each other in the courtroom, with Nishad unleashing a brutal torrent of accusations at Sam, which were designed precisely to land him in jail for decades. "I was blindsided and horrified," Nishad said, his voice rising as he recounted confronting Sam in September 2022 on the balcony of their apartment about the billions missing from FTX account holders. "I felt really betrayed, that five years of blood, sweat, and tears from me and so many employees, driving towards something that I thought was a beautiful force for good, had turned out to be so evil."

Sam stared past Nishad, stone-faced and motionless. The thirty-one-year-old FTX founder wasn't doing so well, emotionally or physically. He had lost a lot of weight. His lawyer Mark Cohen said he was being served a "flesh diet," and was instead subsisting on bread, water, and peanut butter. Cohen added that Sam was experiencing withdrawal from his lack of access to Adderall, which he had relied on for virtually all waking hours of his adult life.

Sam's once-scaturient mane, which he had let grow wild as a symbol of his overflowing genius and resistance to norms, was shorn off. (I sat a few rows behind him in the public seating area of the courtroom for much of the monthlong trial.) Under his now-visible neck and ears, Sam wore a purple tie and a gray, boxy Macy's suit that hovered uncomfortably over his shoulder blades and wrinkled across his lower back. He could no longer play the trump card of being too rich and powerful to have to look nice: Pleading for his life in court, he was just another criminal defendant in a cheap suit and a rushed haircut.

Sam's physical diminution was nothing compared to his reputational one. Every day in October, he faced withering testimony from his inner circle. Nishad's monologue was the emotional climax of the trial, but Gary Wang and Caroline Ellison scored plenty of their own jabs, systematically destroying the pristine image he had worked so hard to build.

Gary, shaky and mumbling, testified that Sam had ordered him to code in special privileges that allowed Alameda to secretly siphon money from the pool of FTX customer funds. Wang quietly admitted that he knew what he was doing was wrong: "The money belonged to customers and the customers did not give us permission to use them for other things," he said.

Caroline opened up about her tumultuous and unhappy relationship with Sam. The pair had first slept together in the summer of 2018, not long after Sam had hired her to work at Alameda, but they didn't start "dating" until two years later. Even then, Sam instructed her to keep their relationship secret from even their closest friends; they broke up and got back together again several times. Caroline described Sam's dominance and callousness in both their professional and romantic relationships. "If I messed something up at work and Sam gave me negative feedback on that, that would affect our personal relationship as well and sort of vice versa," she said. "It made me feel like sort of an unequal partner in our relationship."

Caroline accused Sam of misleading auditors and directing her to produce balance sheets with phony financial numbers to send to lenders. When she recounted FTX's collapse a year earlier, she broke down in tears, calling it "overall the worst week of my life." She also offered a stark analysis of what had led Sam to steal his customers' money. "He thought that the only moral rule that mattered was doing whatever would maximize utility," she explained. "He didn't think rules like 'don't lie' or 'don't steal' fit into that framework."

In addition to their verbal barrages, the trio walked prosecutors through a bevy of documents that showed Sam had known about Alameda's overwhelming debt to FTX customers for months before the crash. More damning evidence was produced by the accounting professor Peter Easton, who had run forensics on Alameda's books and determined that Sam had used FTX customer funds to pay for the Bahamas penthouse apartment, millions of dollars in political donations, and a slew of random investments including $700 million to K5, the company run by the Hollywood power broker Michael Kives, who had given Sam a taste of the celebrity high life.

None of this seemed to trigger any visible remorse or self-reflection in Sam. In fact, after three weeks of being ripped apart by his former friends, Sam decided to take the stand himself. This decision was one more risky choice atop of a life defined by them. Most lawyers advise their criminal defendants against it because it opens them up to an onslaught of cross-examination from prosecutors, in which they risk admitting to their wrongdoings or perjuring themselves.

Sam was on the stand for three days. At first, he easily handled his lawyers' softball questions, casting himself as a self-deprecating, inexperienced visionary who had gotten in way over his head. While he was busy growing FTX into a $32 billion company, he contended, he left many important business decisions to Caroline, Gary, and Nishad, so he was ignorant of his companies' financial troubles until it was far too late. "There were a lot of things that happened that I was either not informed of, or after the fact, sort of summarily informed of," he said on the stand. He even managed to blame FTX's customers for their own misfortune, arguing three-quarters of traders on the platform used spot margin trading, which allowed them to make highly risky leveraged bets that could wipe them out entirely. (He failed to mention that this same tactic helped to incur the massive losses that brought down Alameda and then FTX.)

But fielding softballs from his own lawyers was a completely different game than facing down the prosecutor Danielle Sassoon. Sassoon had clerked for Justice Antonin Scalia and served as a litigation attorney at Kirkland & Ellis. As an assistant U.S. attorney in the Southern District of New York, she had led successful convictions of street gang leaders and a sex abuser. "You can't get anything by her," Tim Howard, a former federal prosecutor at the SDNY, told me before the trial began.

Sassoon was champing at the bit to grill Sam and had a powerful weapon to refute his narrative: Sam's own words, which he had freely spewed at length to journalists over the years during his quest for media saturation. Over and over, Sassoon pressed him on discrepancies: between what Sam had testified and what he had told the press; between what he had said in public, including in congressional testimony under oath, and how he acted in private.

In one exchange, Sassoon asked Sam if he recalled saying Alameda had "more leeway" than other traders on the FTX exchange. "Not in those words specifically, and I don't know what context it was in," Sam responded.

Judge Kaplan, visibly frustrated by the non-answer, interjected: "Sir, do you remember saying that in words or in substance?" Sam, now cowed, garbled his way through a halfway concession: "Referring to some particular things in some particular time periods, yes."

Sassoon then presented Sam with a copy of the *Bloomberg* journalist Zeke Faux's book *Number Go Up*, in which Faux wrote that Sam, in December 2022, told him that Alameda did not follow the same margin rules as other traders and had more leeway on the exchange. The admission contradicted Sam's long-held position that Alameda did not have special privileges on FTX. "Did you tell Faux this?" Sassoon asked Sam.

"I don't remember," Sam responded sullenly.

Sam's many contradictions and evasions were on full display to the jury, and there was nowhere for him to hide. In press interviews, Sam excelled in deflecting tough questions with obtuse jargon or meandering vignettes, or simply lying. But now he was constrained by the court's unyielding format, which was enforced by the rigid Judge Lewis Kaplan. The man who would be responsible for deciding Sam's sentence, should he be found guilty, was growing increasingly irritated with Sam: He chastised him for non-answers and ordered him to answer questions directly. (Kaplan would tangle with Donald Trump in a civil case brought by E. Jean Carroll just a few months later.)

But Sam squirmed side to side, furrowed his brow, scratched his face, took agonizingly long pauses. Over three days on the stand, he said "I don't remember" sixty-one times, "I don't recall" thirty-nine times, and "I'm not sure" seventy-nine times. He waffled on whether he had attended a private dinner with Bill Clinton and Tony Blair just a year before: "There was something like a dinner with them. I don't remember whether there was food." His demeanor resembled a petulant teenager fibbing about breaking curfew. Judge Kaplan later found that Bankman-Fried gave perjured testimony multiple times under oath.

During Sam's testimony, the twelve jurors deciding his fate watched his duel with Sassoon, swiveling their necks back and forth between them rapidly as if at a tennis match, at times frowning at Sam and slightly shaking their heads. On November 2, two days after Sam finished on the stand, they took just over four hours to unanimously find Sam guilty on all seven counts, including wire fraud, money laundering, and conspiracy to defraud customers and lenders.

Sam had tried to hide behind his co-conspirators and the jargon of the blockchain. But in the end, his undoing in court wasn't his ex-girlfriend or the prosecutors but himself: his penchant for publicity, his arrogance that only he could fix things, and the casualness with which he had deceived others. The jury saw through all of that. It had taken Elizabeth Holmes's jury seven days to find her guilty. It took Martha Stewart's jury three days. Sam's jury convicted him on all counts after finishing their suppers.

As the foreperson stepped to the microphone and repeated the word "guilty" seven times, Sam's dad Joe Bankman doubled over, while his mom Barbara Fried covered her face with her hands. Sam did not turn around to look at them, and was instead whispering to his lawyers Mark Cohen and Christian Everdell. After the verdict, he turned around, gave his parents a small nod, and was led out of the courtroom by a marshal. The man who was supposed to guide crypto into the mainstream was now a convicted felon headed back to prison, where he is expected to spend the next 25 years of his life.

CHAPTER 40

Mania at Work

G old rushes tend to encourage impetuous investments," Bill Gates wrote in *The Road Ahead* in 1995, his treatise on the incoming internet revolution. "A few will pay off, but when the frenzy is behind us, we will look back incredulously at the wreckage of failed ventures and wonder, 'Who funded those companies? What was going on in their minds? Was that just mania at work?'"

After the collapse of FTX, many crypto leaders quickly declared that Sam's failures had nothing to do with their beloved technology. In some ways, they were right. Sam's actions mirrored those of countless old-school hucksters who took advantage of the frenzies of their times. Bernie Madoff, too, built an empire based on wildly speculative stocks, with underlings promising investments that were "100 percent" safe, similar to claims Alameda had made in its early days. Madoff, like Sam, spent lots of time with regulators and built a highly respectable reputation.

Like Enron, Sam used an in-house asset (FTT) as collateral for loans. (Amusingly, Enron commercials once bragged that the company was "creating an open, transparent marketplace that replaces the dark, blind system that existed.") Like Lehman Brothers, FTX used accounting subterfuges to conceal huge swaths of its debt. And like the Bank of Credit and Commerce International (BCCI) in the seventies and eighties, FTX used customer funds to finance its growth, shuffled money among different affiliates, and cozied up to politicians. Michael J. Hsu, U.S. acting comptroller of the currency, argued in 2023 that there were "strong parallels" between BCCI and FTX in their ability to "carry out and obfuscate fraudulent activity and operate with a stunning lack of basic risk management."

In the 1980s, the financier George Soros wrote a rebuttal to the idea that markets were rational and efficient in his first book, *The Alchemy of Finance*. Instead, he argued that economies followed a theory of reflexivity, which included the idea that optimism during good financial times led to people investing irrationally in worse investments, which then led to crisis and instability. Crypto's slide into shitcoins, Bored Ape knockoffs, and dodgy lending schemes was illustrative of this theory.

In some ways, the 2022 crypto crash closely mirrored the 2008 financial crisis. The 2008 bubble had been caused by risky mortgage loans repackaged into financial derivatives. The 2022 crypto crash was likewise brought down by hidden, interconnected chains of leverage, in which hedge funds, exchanges, and lenders played dangerous money games because they thought the market might keep expanding forever.

"Human psychology stays pretty much stable throughout history," James Block, a psychiatry resident and blockchain analyst, says. "And that's why we keep having speculative bubbles like this. It's just because people are the same. With the right environment, incentives, and narratives, people will take risks they shouldn't."

But while Sam may just be an old-school scammer in a new suit (or more accurately, pair of cargo shorts), crypto as a whole should not escape scrutiny, because most of the ideals it held dear failed miserably during its biggest mainstream moment yet.

Cryptocurrencies were supposed to be independent assets, yet their values rose and fell with inflation, central bank movements, and other traditional market pressures. The blockchain was supposed to facilitate decentralization, yet virtually every part of the crypto ecosystem relied on centralized entities—a company, an exchange, a marketplace, a lender, a dev team. It was supposed to be about code, but instead it coalesced around cults of personality.

While crypto advertised returns for small-scale investors, it mostly benefited a small group of early adopters. An April 2023 study by business school professors found that influencer-backed cryptocurrencies typically resulted in a 19 percent loss for investors after three months. A November 2022 study from the Bank of International Settlements found that three-quarters of bitcoin investors had lost money. Mark, the exec who went to Crypto Bahamas, admitted that the whole game for many crypto businessmen around him was to send crypto out—often to everyday consumers—and take actual dollars back in. "The real business was selling crypto for real money," he says.

DeFi was supposed to bring all sorts of unbanked people into financial systems. Instead, it was mostly used to create new tokens that were used as collateral for loans, which were then circuitously used to amass more crypto wealth. And even that usage failed to scale in any meaningful way. By the start of 2022, there were only five hundred thousand or so daily active users on DeFi platforms, one prominent analyst estimated, which paled in comparison to the stunning rise of the AI application ChatGPT, which accumulated 100 million users in just two months. The vast majority of crypto users remained in centralized exchanges, which hoarded power just like the banks and Wall Street barons they had claimed they would dislodge.

"The promise of decentralization is a complete joke," says Christine Chew. "The coins are concentrated around a few VCs, and they can manipulate the price." After her adventure in The Bahamas and witnessing the FTX crash, she decided she didn't want to be in crypto at all. Instead, she got a job with Impact HK, an NGO dedicated to providing food, shelter, education, and job opportunities for homeless people in Hong Kong. "I want to start doing what I actually wanted to do in the first place: make a positive change," she told me a year after she left FTX. "I feel so grateful to be helping people directly instead of thinking that my money will go to helping people one day."

Christine says that after several fraught months of processing, she is no longer angry at Sam, Do Kwon, and other crypto scammers. "One of my biggest lessons through Terra and FTX was learning to forgive people, even though they have lied to me and taken my money because of my naiveness," she says. "I can't really decide what happens to me. But I can decide if I am going to be happy or not."

———————

DAOs were supposed to reorganize human coordination and replace every major mainstream corporation. If you listened to crypto enthusiasts in 2021, you might have believed there would soon be fully functioning DAO alternatives to Uber, Facebook, Twitter, and Spotify. None of those ideas were realized at scale. Instead, DAOs mostly devolved into plutocracies or hyper-elite investment clubs manipulated by their wealthiest members.

Crypto metaverses and play-to-earn gaming both plummeted in value and usage. Axie Infinity retreated back to the purview of hardcore gamers, and no other play-to-earn game replaced it in building a large, sustainable economy. Many of the gamers in the Philippines and Malaysia simply drifted to the next moneymaking opportunity they could find. "Axie Infinity became a huge bellwether in the gaming industry and spawned billions of dollars of investment into Web 3 gaming," says Cordel Robbin-Coker, a founder of the African mobile games publishing platform Carry1st. "Companies who weren't oriented toward the space were pushed into it by investors and shareholders. But basically, none of them ever launched anything."

Blockchain technology was supposed to be an ironclad version of history. But over the course of 2021, these so-called immutable records became laced with transactions caused by scams and mis-clicks, which were now irreversible. After the crypto crash and FTX's collapse, entire blockchain initiatives were abandoned. The Australian stock exchange gave up an attempt to transition its database to blockchain after seven years of effort; so did IBM and the shipping company Maersk. The Universal Basic Income token, which Vitalik hoped might redistribute wealth to crypto users around the world, crashed from 20 cents to fractions of fractions of a penny. Once-exuberant developers left crypto for other opportunities. One study found that blockchain development activity descended right back to the level it had been at before the bull run.

"After FTX went down, it really changed my thinking about everything," Anthony Olasele told me in March 2023. "Why are we here? What are things that actually have value? I think about the average person that's close to me: Would any of them even want to use this technology, with all of the different barriers, the fees? It feels like the light of my optimism just dies down every day."

The majority of the NFT world, which was supposed to uplift artists, jettisoned royalties on secondary sales and instead promoted thinly veiled Ponzi schemes for degenerate gamblers. One 2023 study found that 95 percent of NFT collections had become effectively worthless. When FTX filed for bankruptcy, every NFT purchased on the company's system vanished. The whole point of NFTs was that they were supposed to be owned without an intermediary. But links to FTX NFTs simply redirect to a restructuring page with information on the bankruptcy. Beeple, once hailed as the king of NFTs, vehemently distanced himself from the craze after the FTX crash. "I was never an NFT evangelist," he told the online news publication *Vulture*. "I am not some crypto bro, because there is actually substance to what I have been doing."

In February 2023, OpenSea was overtaken as the number one NFT trading platform by Blur, an even more shameless marketplace that essentially incentivized its users to wash-trade by offering token rewards for executing trades. The NFTs on Blur had minimal artistic value or royalties for artists. "Blur has shown what this space is really about: Just throw up a picture and trade it like shitcoins," says Owo. "Nobody's looking at the art anymore."

In the summer of 2023, the Bored Ape Yacht Club, the flagship NFT brand, fell 88 percent from its April 2022 peak. The Yuga Labs–FTX NFT platform that was supposed to corner the market died along with FTX. And in August 2023, a group of Bored Ape investors sued Sotheby's and other celebrities for "misleadingly" promoting Bored Apes in a way that inflated their prices. (Greg Solano, the cofounder of Yuga Labs, told me in January 2024 that there was "a lot of absurd stuff" in the lawsuit, and argued that the Bored Ape Yacht Club had caused more people to "enjoy crypto, express themselves with it, and build businesses off it than most other things on the CoinMarketCap Top 100.")

So while Sam was an easy target for crypto enthusiasts to blame, the rot came from all over. It came from a nascent industry so desperate for mainstream success that it was willing to repeatedly overlook red flags. It came from token mechanics, which distorted actual value or created it out of thin air. It came from regulators, who took too long to act on a market frothing with illegal activity.

In the end, the complex, robust design of the blockchain was no match for an unholy twenty-first century brew of FOMO, greed, and status-signaling. The 2022 crypto crash proved that no matter how elegant and idealistic the technical systems we create, they are never beyond the reach of our worst impulses.

"When I first heard someone say that Ethereum isn't a token, it's the internet, my life changed," says Owo. "When I first started AfroDroids, my idea was that the blockchain was a tool to free humanity. But in the middle, it became a financial instrument because of the people I was surrounded by. I had to ask myself, 'Why did I get into this thing in the first place?'"

After taking an extended break from NFTs, Owo began to make art every day again: to re-spark the joy he once felt in creating, without any financial burdens. And when he found his mojo again, he dove back into the whole reason that he had created the AfroDroids NFTs in the first place: as a pathway to create the AfroDroids movie. "I'm not doing any business or tokenomics: I don't care about any of that," he told me in late 2023. "I just want to make beautiful art and tell good stories."

EPILOGUE

Zuzalu

In May 2023, Vitalik Buterin sat in a villa overlooking the Adriatic Sea, pondering how central crypto should be to his vision for human betterment.

Vitalik had gathered some of his closest collaborators and allies to Lustica Bay, a remote resort in Montenegro that typically hosted Russian oligarchs and Saudi oil tycoons. Vitalik had chosen Montenegro due to its geographic centrality to Europe and Asia, its seclusion from prying eyes, and its pro-crypto government. Perhaps fittingly, Do Kwon, the creator of Terra-Luna, was in the country, too, albeit sitting in a jail cell: He had been arrested by authorities at the Podgorica airport when trying to board a flight with forged documents.

Vitalik called this retreat "Zuzalu," a word with no meaning at all, so as to signify an entirely fresh start. This gathering had crypto folks as well as a collection of leading thinkers from other disciplines: artificial intelligence, longevity, and, most centrally, human coordination, or the science of how to best align humans to enact positive change. Vitalik hoped that this gathering would grow into a new kind of micro city, built on shared values, pooled resources, organically emerging group projects, and noninvasive technology.

Zuzalu, in its multidisciplinary construction, was a different path forward for this crypto guru, and an acknowledgment of a hard truth that he realized over the course of 2022: that shrewd technological systems alone could not create better versions of society. As a teenager, Vitalik had believed that he could use clean mathematical systems and flawless code to tame an unjust, unruly world. But those pesky humans always seemed to get in the way and corrupt it all.

"Especially with everything that happened in the last year, I feel like I get the extent to which even psychologically normal people just have this great ability to just create stories that justify things in pretty much whatever direction they want, pretty much without limits," he told me at Zuzalu. Vitalik had initially believed that Sam was not so different from him—and that he could persuade lots of people to act on their principles, not just in the short-term interest of their wallets.

After Sam's downfall, Vitalik decided to take a different approach. He would try to test out new ideas and methods in smaller groups, rather than putting them in front of the entire world. He would emphasize building not only with expert programmers but also thought leaders from different disciplines. And he would actively rail against the return of high crypto prices, because with good deals would come destructive, predatory traders like Sam Bankman-Fried.

"My biggest fear is a bull market," he said. "If a bull market happens, then all of that energy obviously just comes back."

Sure enough, at the end of 2023, the bull gently stirred, and then roared back into action a few months later with gleeful vengeance. In March 2024, bitcoin hit its all-time high of over $70,000, while ether broke $4,000 for the first time since 2021. Volatile, speculative meme coins like BONK surged in waves. Filipino gamers started harvesting new digital crops for new crypto tokens. Enthusiasts declared that this post-SBF era would be a chance at a gleaming fresh start, just like many had declared after Do Kwon and Su Zhu were discarded.

Had anything really changed? There were glimpses of progress, forged by the thousands of builders who had been busy diligently trying to forge better blockchain systems even at the market's nadir. The Merge drastically decreased Ethereum's environmental impact and proved that a lot of sincere crypto believers working together can pull off incredible things. People continued to use stablecoins for reasons beyond sheer gambling; their market cap reached $150 billion in 2024. And some DAOs persevered through the crypto winter, including Gitcoin, which deployed innovative crypto voting systems to hand out over $59 million in grants for projects that seek to build public goods, both inside and outside the crypto ecosystem.

Crypto folks argue that it's still early yet for the technology in the grand scheme of things. As a comparison, ARPANET, the precursor to the internet, sent its first message in 1969. HTML and the first globally accessible websites didn't appear until twenty-two years later. Seven years after that, in 1998, the economist Paul Krugman predicted that the internet's economic impact would be "no greater than the fax machine's."

Many still believe in the possibility of crypto's ascension to internet-level influence. Despite harboring deep skepticism about the financial side of crypto, the artist Beeple continued to mint NFTs and bought a $200,000 CryptoPunk in the summer of 2023. "We're coming off a crazy sugar high where it was like 'Whee! Money!' It was a bit nutty," he said in August 2023. "But the idea of virtual ownership is real: that there are going to be virtual things that have value because they provide value or entertain you. I don't see the world becoming less digital."

Liam Vries reformulated the African NFT Community into a smaller group with a more streamlined vision, called ANCurated, which curates art shows and offers blockchain education. In Nottingham, he pays for groceries with his CL card: a crypto debit card created by Visa and Ledger that converts his ether into the British pound instantaneously during every transaction. "We are sharing our life's work on the blockchain. Years from now, we will never question what was happening in Africa the same way how some people question the pyramids," he says. "We're writing our own history—and we've never had the opportunity to do that."

Liam and Beeple are just two disciples in crypto's constantly expanding and contracting flock. Crypto, like many other religions, has canonical texts, disciples and preachers, and digital congregations. Religions can exist for thousands of years, even in the face of overwhelming evidence debunking their central claims. They just need to give their followers something to believe in. And crypto has transcended code to become a belief system and a way of life.

But crypto faces many challenges ahead in its quest to become a lasting force for good. Powerful incumbents across the industries that crypto is trying to disrupt—government, finance, Big Tech—are working hard to suppress it. "There's a wall in front of it called the SEC," says Harper Reed, Obama's ex-CTO. He adds that in the gaming world, "the Roblox generation has proved that NFTs are real. But the problem is if you said to Roblox, 'This is great, but what if you didn't control this?' Roblox would just be like, 'Why would I ever make that decision?'"

Then there are the threats from within. In 2024, despite pledges to reform, much of crypto is still driven by gambling mechanics and people who just want to see the price keep going up, no matter their assets' hollowness. Many bitcoiners have even abandoned the idea of bitcoin actually being useful as currency in the real world, as its creator Satoshi imagined. "The idea that bitcoin is a global payment system has more or less disappeared," Haseeb Qureshi told me in March 2024.

Instead, many more people in 2024 are thinking about bitcoin just like any other high-risk, high-reward investment, thanks to an improved macroeconomic climate as well as the SEC's grudging acceptance of a bitcoin ETF (exchange-traded fund), an investment vehicle that allows mainstream institutional investors to bet on bitcoin's price on popular trading platforms like the Nasdaq. Institutions like BlackRock and Fidelity issued their own bitcoin ETFs, resulting in more than $4 billion in trading on their first day of availability. The irony is that the value of bitcoin is now being propelled by the traditional finance overlords that its original idealists had hoped to dislodge.

This newfound alliance has market watchdogs worried. When the Four Horsemen felled crypto in 2022, there was almost no contagion with the rest of the financial system because regulators had kept the crypto industry at arm's length. "What we're going to be seeing over the next months and years is increasing interconnections with the core of the financial system,"

Dennis Kelleher, a cofounder of the financial reform advocacy group Better Markets, told me in February 2024. "So the question is, how broad will the connections be? And will the crypto crash bring down the financial system, just like derivatives brought down the financial system in 2008?"

One Alameda trader, who left the company in 2018 but remains in crypto, says that many of the shamelessly opportunistic but less public-facing power players of the last cycle still remain. "I had hoped that there would be repercussions for some of the trading firms in the space," they say. "I hoped they would not want to participate in that same kind of predatory activity. But I think unless they're prevented from doing so by regulatory changes, they'll continue to do so."

Sam Bankman-Fried won't play a role in crypto going forward. But there are a dozen more Sams waiting in the wings, casino chips in hand, ready to bet everything that they and others own for a shot at digital glory.

ACKNOWLEDGMENTS

Cryptomania rests on the shoulders of the dozens of crypto and business reporters who concurrently covered this tragicomedy with tenacity and judiciousness. I learned a lot from reading the previous SBF books by Brady Dale, Ben McKenzie and Jacob Silverman, Zeke Faux, and Michael Lewis. I will never forget the interminable hours I spent with my colleagues in the SBF press corps in October 2023, who provided sorely needed camaraderie and intimidatingly sharp insight.

My first partner on this project, long before I knew it would be a book, was former *Time* editor Michael Zennie, who stayed up late and rose early in Hong Kong to edit my crypto articles as we tried make sense of this crazy world together. A year later, he made time in between his job and caring for two toddlers to wring a passable narrative out of *Cryptomania*.

Todd Shuster, my agent at Aevitas, was the first person to take my dreams of becoming an author seriously. He and Jack Haug whipped my germ of an idea into shape.

Stephanie Hitchcock took a chance on me and provided invaluable edits. The rest of the Simon Acumen team, including Erica Siudzinski and Jason Chappell, were equally impactful. Amy Stephenson was the first reader and editor of this book; she lent an exacting eye and positive reinforcement even when unwarranted. Chad de Guzman contributed reporting from Manila. Jordan Levy and Mark Nacinovich researched and fact-checked; Rick Willett copyedited; Nikhilesh De, John Pelosi, and Luke Strathmann offered crucial suggestions. Hannah Gadway proofread. Elizabeth Sands provided food and shelter for many months.

My journalistic mentors include Charlotte Alter, Alex Altman, Jon Caramanica, Jamie Ducharme, Jack Hamilton, Julia Jacobs, Sam Lansky, Michael Paulson, Simon Shuster, and Matt Stevens. My crypto gurus include Matt Dryhurst, Erich Dylus, Holly Herndon, Joseph Schweitzer, Evan Van Ness, and the Vitalik documentary team. I talked to well over 150 sources over the course of reporting this book; thanks to all of you for your time.

I'm raising a glass to Jeremy Judelson, my creative sparring partner; Jacob Sunshine, my pomodoro partner; and the rest of the Crew of 12. I also cannot thank my parents, Jane and John, and my sister, Liana, enough; they lent me a lifetime of support and encouragement, as well as a steady stream of snacks during the SBF trial. This book is dedicated to my grandparents Phoebe and Paul Bock, who are no longer with us.

Covering crypto and writing a book are both emotional roller coasters, and Laura Petty bore the brunt of these wild swings. When I rode too high, she served as a ruthlessly effective editor. When I sank into emotional abysses, she gently coaxed me back into myself. OMI said it best: She is always right there when I need her.

GLOSSARY

Alameda Research: A crypto trading firm started by Sam Bankman-Fried in 2017 that specialized in arbitrage.

arbitrage: The strategy of exploiting the price disparities of an asset in between different markets. Arbitrageurs buy low in one market and sell high in another, pocketing the difference.

bitcoin: The first, and most popular, cryptocurrency.

blockchain: A digital database of transactions. Blockchains are maintained and secured over a dispersed network of computers. Blockchains are designed to be tamper-proof, transparent, and decentralized.

collateral: An asset pledged to secure a loan. If the borrower fails to repay the loan, the lender can seize the collateral, which could be a house, cash, or cryptocurrency.

cryptocurrency: A digital form of currency that lives on a blockchain.

DAO (decentralized autonomous organization): A blockchain-based organization or community. DAOs are designed to operate without centralized or hierarchical leadership, and do so by relying on blockchain-based voting and transactions. Pronounced "dow."

degen: Short for "degenerate," a self-anointed label for crypto diehards who trade aggressively.

derivatives: Financial instruments whose value stems from an underlying asset. Traders use derivatives to bet on whether an asset will go up or down, without needing to own the asset directly. Trading derivatives often heightens both risks and rewards.

Discord: A social platform that serves as the central social hub for many crypto communities.

effective altruism: A philosophy that attempts to quantify how individuals might best impact the world.

Ethereum: A blockchain launched by Vitalik Buterin in 2015. Ethereum allows developers to write all types of programs and applications on top of it. Its native cryptocurrency, ether, is second only to bitcoin in value.

EV (expected value): The average result one can expect from a given situation, calculated by considering all possible outcomes and their likelihood of happening. Sam Bankman-Fried made most of his decisions based on expected value calculations.

fiat: A government-issued currency that is not backed by a commodity like gold or silver.

FTX: A cryptocurrency exchange started by Sam Bankman-Fried in 2019. FTX allowed users to buy and sell cryptocurrencies, and collapsed in late 2022.

FUD (fear, uncertainty, doubt): A derisive term on Crypto Twitter describing pessimism about crypto. Any criticisms or negative reports about crypto are often dismissed as "FUD."

futures: A type of derivative in which two parties bet on an asset's price on a specific future date. Futures can be used to protect against risk, or to increase risk in the hopes of winning big. FTX specialized in allowing its users to trade futures.

margin call: When an investor is forced to quickly come up with cash to cover losses from a failed margin trade. Failure to do so can result in the complete loss of the investor's collateral.

margin trading: Trading with borrowed funds. FTX allowed its users to trade crypto on margin, i.e., with funds they didn't actually own, borrowed from the exchange itself.

market cap: In traditional finance, market cap measures the total value of a company's shares of stock. In crypto, market cap measures a cryptocurrency's price multiplied by the total number of coins in circulation. Market caps are often misleading in crypto, as it would be impossible to sell all coins for a single, stable value.

metaverse: A vision of the internet in which users might enter a singular, immersive 3D world to play games, socialize, work, and buy and sell stuff.

NFT (non-fungible token): A digital asset on a blockchain. An NFT can contain a piece of artwork, a song, a video game character, a land deed. Each NFT comes with a certificate of ownership and authenticity that marks it as one of a kind.

OpenSea: The primary platform for buying and selling NFTs during the pandemic.

proof of work: A mechanism that powers and secures some blockchains, like Bitcoin. Proof of work requires "miners" to solve complex math problems in order to verify transactions; they are then rewarded with cryptocurrency for doing so. The process is incredibly energy-intensive.

proof of stake: A mechanism that powers and secures some blockchains, like Ethereum. Proof of stake requires "validators" to deposit a lot of money into the network in order to verify transactions; they are rewarded with cryptocurrency for doing so.

pump and dump: A scam in which fraudsters artificially boost the price of an asset, which causes other investors to purchase the asset in droves. The fraudsters then sell off their shares for a profit, causing the asset's price to fall.

risk neutrality: The idea that traders shouldn't mind any risk associated with an investment and make decisions solely based on expected value.

Solana: A blockchain launched in 2020, with a corresponding cryptocurrency called solana. Sam Bankman-Fried championed and heavily invested in the Solana ecosystem.

speculation: When an investor puts their money into an asset based on the hopes its price will increase, rather than a belief in the asset's intrinsic value.

stablecoin: A cryptocurrency that's supposed to hold the value of another currency. Most stablecoins are designed to exchange one unit for $1 U.S.

WAGMI (We're all gonna make it): A rallying cry on Crypto Twitter to convince people to buy crypto.

wash trading: When someone sells an asset to themselves at increasing prices, creating an illusion of market activity.

NOTES

PROLOGUE

1 *On November 15, 2022*: U.S. v. Bankman-Fried, government exhibit 3, presented October 16, 2022.

1 *twelve-thousand-square-foot penthouse*: Seaside Real Estate, "orchid bldg.– ph #6," accessed November 16, 2022, https://www.seasidebahamas.com/view /NassauNew+Providence/Orchid+Bldg.+-+PH+6/20046/buy/.

1 *His eyes were strained*: U.S. v. Bankman-Fried, government exhibit 406, presented October 11, 2022.

1 *But Sam liked and trusted*: Sam Bankman-Fried (@SBF_FTX), Twitter post, November 16, 2022, 5:55 p.m., https://twitter.com/SBF_FTX/status /1593014934207881218.

1 *The next day*: Kelsey Piper, "Sam Bankman-Fried Tries to Explain Himself," *Vox*, November 16, 2022, https://www.vox.com/future-perfect/23462333 /sam-bankman-fried-ftx-cryptocurrency-effective-altruism-crypto-bahamas -philanthropy.

1 *She claimed that they*: Kelsey Piper (@KelseyTuoc), Twitter post, November 16, 2022, 8:38 p.m., https://twitter.com/KelseyTuoc/status/159305600901 0176001.

1 *He had spent hundreds*: Leo Schwartz, "FTX Sends Confidential Letters to Politicians," *Fortune*, February 6, 2023, https://fortune.com/crypto /2023/02/06/ftx-and-sam-bankman-fried-93-million-political-donations/.

2 *"My childrens future"*: U.S. v. Bankman-Fried, Document 410-1, "Selected Twitter Messages Sent to Samuel Bankman-Fried's Account," filed March 15, 2024.

2 *All told, Sam had somehow*: U.S. v. Bankman-Fried, government exhibit 406, presented October 11, 2023.

2 *It wasn't so long ago*: Ryan Browne, "Cryptocurrency Exchange FTX Hits $32 Billion Valuation Despite Bear Market Fears," CNBC, January 31, 2022, https://www.cnbc.com/2022/01/31/crypto-exchange-ftx-valued-at-32 -billion-amid-bitcoin-price-plunge.html.

INTRODUCTION

3 *On March 11, 2021*: Jacob Kastrenakes, "Beeple Sold an NFT for $69 Million," *The Verge*, March 11, 2021, https://www.theverge.com/2021/3/11 /22325054/beeple-christies-nft-sale-cost-everydays-69-million.

3 *Exactly twenty months*: David Yaffe-Bellany, "Embattled Crypto Exchange FTX Files for Bankruptcy," *New York Times*, November 11, 2022, https: //www.nytimes.com/2022/11/11/business/ftx-bankruptcy.html.

3 *While crypto had made*: Tim Hakki, "Peter Singer and SBF Talk Crypto's Environmental Impact," *Decrypt*, March 12, 2022, https://decrypt.co/94921 /peter-singer-sbf-discuss-crypto-environmental-impact-russia-ukraine -helping-unbanked.

3 *leading to "financial inclusion"*: Robert Wiblin and Keiran Harris, "Sam Bankman-Fried on Taking a High-Risk Approach to Crypto and Doing Good," on *80,000 Hours*, podcast, April 14, 2022, 1:48:28, https://80000hours .org/podcast/episodes/sam-bankman-fried-high-risk-approach-to-crypto -and-doing-good/.

CHAPTER 1

9 *And on top of his current debt*: Etherscan, blockchain transaction, February 26, 2021, https://etherscan.io/tx/0xe46d96f080d6472004d4dddd7475ff4ffda 0b819ecb41759211dbefff8573a5a.

9 *"We might struggle"*: Owo Anietie, interview with Andrew R. Chow, February 28, 2023.

10 *His artwork, which depicted*: Owo Anietie, *Masked*, NFT, https://known origin.io/tokens/285726.

CHAPTER 2

15 *In March 2019*: Andrew R. Chow, "Lil Nas X Talks 'Old Town Road' and the Billboard Controversy," *Time*, March 30, 2019, https://time.com/5561466 /lil-nas-x-old-town-road-billboard/; Andrew R. Chow, "Musicians Are Using AI to Create Otherwise Impossible New Songs," *Time*, February 5, 2020, https://time.com/5774723/ai-music/.

15 *England had just*: Luke McGee, "England to Enter Second Lockdown in Days, Says Boris Johnson," CNN, October 31, 2020, https://www.cnn .com/2020/10/31/europe/uk-lockdown-coronavirus-europe-intl/index .html.

15 *The U.S. had just*: Rob Stein, "U.S. Confirmed Coronavirus Infections Hit 10 Million," NPR, November 9, 2020, https://www.npr.org/sections/corona virus-live-updates/2020/11/09/933023659/u-s-confirmed-coronavirus -infections-hit-10-million.

15 *and 250,000 deaths*: Laurel Wamsley, "As U.S. Reaches 250,000 Deaths from COVID-19, a Long Winter Is Coming," NPR, November 18, 2020, https://www.npr.org/sections/coronavirus-live-updates/2020/11/18/935930352/as-u-s-reaches-250-000-deaths-from-covid-19-a-long-winter-is-coming.

15 *In January 2021, Clubhouse's*: Tae Kim, "Forget TikTok. Clubhouse Is Social Media's Next Star," *Bloomberg*, January 24, 2021, https://www.bloomberg.com/opinion/articles/2021-01-25/forget-tiktok-clubhouse-is-social-media-s-next-star.

17 *"That period was"*: Nsikak Owo, interview with Andrew R. Chow, October 9, 2023.

17 *He had now achieved*: Mike Winklemann, *Beeple: Everydays, the First 5000 Days* (New York: Cernunnos, 2023).

17 *"People take their work"*: Debbie Millman, host, "Beeple," on *Design Matters with Debbie Millman*, podcast, May 17, 2021, 36:30, https://open.spotify.com/episode/4CP1e8a0hSNLFNUOGuABIH?si=7accfee48fec48f2.

18 *Beeple released a new*: Mickey Rapkin, "'Beeple Mania': How Mike Winkelmann Makes Millions Selling Pixels," *Esquire*, February 17, 2021, https://www.esquire.com/entertainment/a35500985/who-is-beeple-mike-winkelmann-nft-interview/.

18 *Beeple thought that NFTs*: Ibid.

18 *"This is exactly like"*: Mike Winklemann, interview with Andrew R. Chow, August 2, 2023.

18 *One of his first NFTs*: Beeple, CROSSROAD #1/1, *Nifty Gateway*, NFT, https://www.niftygateway.com/marketplace/item/0x12f28e2106ce8fd8464885b80ea865e98b465149/100010001.

18 *A few weeks later*: Cooper Turley, "A Record $3.5M in Crypto Art Was Sold Over the Weekend," *The Defiant*, December 15, 2020, https://thedefiant.io/a-record-3-5m-in-crypto-art-was-sold-over-the-weekend.

18 *Friends and family*: Beeple (@beeple), Twitter post, December 13, 2020, 7:21 p.m., https://twitter.com/beeple/status/1338277789645090822.

19 *In February 2021, Owo*: Samuel Haig, "Two Feet and FEWOCiOUS's NFT Auction Becomes the Third to Top $1m in Sales," *Cointelegraph*, February 16, 2021, https://cointelegraph.com/news/two-feet-and-fewocious-s-nft-auction-becomes-the-third-to-top-1m-in-sales.

19 *Social-service authorities*: Matt Medved, "Fewocious' New Frontier: How Teen Artist Is Leading an NFT Renaissance," *Gotham*, March 18, 2021, https://gothammag.com/fewocious-nft-artist-interview.

19 *In February, the monthly*: Elizabeth Howcroft and Ritvik Carvalho, "How a 10-Second Video Clip Sold for $6.6 Million," Reuters, March 1, 2021, https://www.reuters.com/business/media-telecom/how-10-second-video-clip-sold-66-million-2021-03-01/.

CHAPTER 3

22 *After the U.S. government bailed out*: David M. Herszenhorn, "Congress Approves $700 Billion Wall Street Bailout," *New York Times*, October 3, 2008, https://www.nytimes.com/2008/10/03/business/worldbusiness/03 iht-bailout.4.16679355.html.

22 *ECash's issuing corporation*: "Digicash Outta Cash," *Wired*, November 6, 1998, https://www.wired.com/1998/11/digicash-outta-cash/.

22 *Satoshi wrote in the paper*: Satoshi Nakamoto, "Bitcoin: A Peer-to-Peer Electronic Cash System," October 31, 2008, https://bitcoin.org/bitcoin.pdf.

23 *"Chancellor on brink"*: "An Abridged History of Bitcoin," *New York Times*, November 19, 2013, https://archive.nytimes.com/www.nytimes.com/inter active/technology/bitcoin-timeline.html#/#time284_8155.

24 *Bitcoin served as a lifeline*: Nermin Hajdarbegovic, "Assange: Bitcoin and WikiLeaks Helped Keep Each Other Alive," *CoinDesk*, September 16, 2014, https://www.coindesk.com/markets/2014/09/16/assange-bitcoin-and -wikileaks-helped-keep-each-other-alive/.

25 *By 2012, there were*: "Bitcoin Active Addresses historical chart," BitInfo-Charts, accessed January 9, 2024, https://bitinfocharts.com/comparison /bitcoin-activeaddresses.html#alltime.

25 *In Toronto, Vitalik Buterin*: Vitalik Buterin, "Overcoming Moral and Visceral Objections to Bitcoin," *Bitcoin Magazine,* July 28, 2013, https://bitcoin magazine.com/culture/overcoming-moral-and-visceral-objections-to -bitcoin-good-and-bad-responses-1375066915.

26 *She and Vitalik's father*: Dmitry Buterin, interview with Andrew R. Chow, February 17, 2022.

26 *To continue to test*: Camila Russo, *The Infinite Machine* (New York: Harper-Business, 2020), 55.

26 *In one tongue-in-cheek*: Vitalik Buterin, "Five Reasons You Should Not Use the Internet," *Bitcoin Magazine*, June 11, 2013, https://bitcoinmagazine .com/culture/five-reasons-you-should-not-use-the-internet-1370985264.

27 *He proudly stated*: Vitalik Buterin, "Ethereum White Paper," December 2013, https://ethereum.org/en/whitepaper/.

27 *Facebook's auditors warned*: Greg Bensinger, "Does Zuckerberg Understand How the Right to Free Speech Works?," *New York Times*, July 8, 2020, https: //www.nytimes.com/2020/07/08/opinion/facebook-civil-rights-audit .html.

27 *"We as cryptocurrency developers"*: Vitalik Buterin, *Proof of Stake: The Making of Ethereum and the Philosophy of Blockchains* (New York: Seven Stories Press, 2022).

28 *"I deeply believed in"*: Vitalik Buterin, interview with Andrew R. Chow, February 1, 2022.

28 *Developers loved Ethereum*: Alex Vitaki, "Ranking Ethereum Smart Con-

tracts," *Medium*, June 13, 2018, https://medium.com/@vikati/ranking
-ethereum-smart-contracts-a27e6f622ac6.

28 *Reed had navigated*: Harper Reed, interview with Andrew R. Chow, November 14, 2023.

29 *In June 2019, his trading firm*: FTX White Paper, June 2019, https://api-new
.whitepaper.io/documents/pdf?id=HJRMXAOeU.

29 *"How many unbanked"*: Vitalik Buterin (@VitalikButerin), Twitter post, December 12, 2017, 4:46 p.m., https://twitter.com/VitalikButerin/status
/940744820406013954.

CHAPTER 4

31 *But as governments sent*: Nathaniel Whittemore, host, "The Great Monetary Inflation: Paul Tudor Jones' Complete Case for Bitcoin," on *The Breakdown with NWL*, podcast, May 11, 2020, 1:20, https://www.coindesk.com
/markets/2020/05/11/the-great-monetary-inflation-paul-tudor-jones
-complete-case-for-bitcoin/.

31 *Jones himself said*: Thomas Franck, "Paul Tudor Jones Calls Bitcoin a 'Great Speculation,'" CNBC, May 11, 2021, https://www.cnbc.com/2020/05/11
/paul-tudor-jones-calls-bitcoin-a-great-speculation-says-he-has-almost-2
percent-of-his-assets-in-it.html.

32 *Speculation has long*: Edward Chancellor, *Devil Take the Hindmost* (New York: Penguin, 1999),119.

32 *In Washington, thousands of rioters*: "The Jan. 6 Insurrection," *Washington Post*, accessed October 23, 2023, https://www.washingtonpost.com/january
-6-capitol-riot/.

32 *That year, Federal Reserve data*: Robert Frank, "The Wealthiest 10% of Americans Own a Record 89% of All U.S. Stocks," CNBC, October 18, 2021, https:
//www.cnbc.com/2021/10/18/the-wealthiest-10percent-of-americans
-own-a-record-89percent-of-all-us-stocks.html.

32 *The Financial Stability Board*: "Global Monitoring Report on Non-Bank Financial Intermediation 2021," Financial Stability Board, December 16, 2021, https://www.fsb.org/2021/12/global-monitoring-report-on-non-bank
-financial-intermediation-2021/.

32 *People across the world felt*: Hyun-Jung Lee and Bom-Mi Park, "Feelings of Entrapment During the COVID-19 Pandemic Based on ACE Star Model: A Concept Analysis," *Healthcare (Basel)*, September 30, 2021, https://www
.ncbi.nlm.nih.gov/pmc/articles/PMC8544561/.

33 *"I thought working in finance"*: Christine Chew, interview with Andrew R. Chow, October 8, 2023.

33 *Popular EA blogs like*: Benjamin Todd, "Which Jobs Help People the Most?," on *80,000 Hours* podcast, October 2014, https:/80000hours.org/career
-guide/high-impact-jobs/.

34   *A CNBC study*: Victoria Rodriguez, "CNBC|Momentive Poll: 'Invest in You,' August 2021," Survey Monkey, August 26, 2021, https://www.survey monkey.com/curiosity/cnbc-invest-in-you-august-2021/.

34   *In the minutes before*: ONE37pm, "Becoming Beeple—a ONE37pm Documentary," November 5, 2021, YouTube video, 18:30, https://www.youtube .com/watch?v=S_8Q7irfOvQ.

34   *"The art is almost irrelevant"*: Anand Venkateswaran, interview with Andrew R. Chow, March 29, 2022.

35   *By the time the dust*: Debbie Millman, "Beeple," on *Design Matters with Debbie Millman*, podcast, May 17, 2021, 4:08.

35   *CNBC journalist Robert Frank*: ONE37pm, "Becoming Beeple," 0:45.

35   *Guillaume Cerutti*: Guillaume Cerutti, "Christie's CEO on the Record-Breaking Sale of Beeple's NFT Artwork," CNN, March 12, 2021, YouTube video, 2:20, https://www.youtube.com/watch?v=1wxrxxJQqFw.

35   *The underbidder*: Justin Sun, @justinsuntron, March 11, 2021, 11:12 p.m., https://twitter.com/justinsuntron/status/1370226049208836100?lang =en.

36   *"I do believe very strongly"*: Changpeng Zhao, "Clubhouse Conversation Between BEEPLE and CHRISTIES," cryptoJonny, February 25, 2021, YouTube video, 4:57, https://www.youtube.com/watch?v=JZt2J6r1ZG w&t=2060s.

CHAPTER 5

37   *"A lot of critics describe"*: Andrew Benson, interview with Andrew R. Chow, March 9, 2021.

37   *"You can figure out"*: ONE37pm, "Becoming Beeple."

38   *Thompson spent years*: Don Thompson, *The $12 Million Stuffed Shark: The Curious Economics of Contemporary Art* (New York: St. Martin's Griffin, 2010).

39   *So LeWitt started to sell*: Georgina Adam, "Conceptual: Only Worth the Paper It's Written On," *Financial Times*, June 8, 2012, https://www.ft.com /content/3e8ff348-a3f1-11e1-84b1-00144feabdc0.

40   *Four years earlier, Ethereum researchers*: Rachel-Rose O'Leary, "Ethereum's ERC-20 Token Standard Has Been Formalized," *CoinDesk*, September 11, 2017, https://www.coindesk.com/markets/2017/09/11/ethereums-erc-20 -token-standard-has-been-formalized/.

40   *Ether had increased fifteenfold*: Philip van Doorn, "These Are the Best Performing Nasdaq and S&P 500 Stocks of 2020," *Marketwatch*, January 2, 2021, https://www.marketwatch.com/story/these-are-the-best-performing -nasdaq-and-sp-500-stocks-of-2020-2020-12-29.

40   *It allowed Frances Haugen*: Ben Smith, "Inside the Big Facebook Leak,"

New York Times, October 24, 2021, https://www.nytimes.com/2021/10/24/business/media/facebook-leak-frances-haugen.html.

41 *Beeple himself was criticized*: Dan Kahan, "The Betrayal of Cashing Out," *The Defiant*, March 25, 2021, https://thedefiant.io/the-betrayal-of-cashing-out.

41 *"Instead of looking at candlestick"*: Daniel Maegaard, interview with Andrew R. Chow, March 10, 2021.

41 *A company called NBA Top Shot*: Tim Copeland, "NBA Top Shot Dipped in March, While CryptoPunks and Sorare Grew," *Decrypt*, April 1, 2021, https://decrypt.co/63644/nba-top-shot-dipped-in-march-while-cryptopunks-and-sorare-grew.

42 *In February 2021, Danny*: Shaurya Malwa, "Biggest Ever NFT Sale Made as 'Axie Land' Goes for $1.5 Million," *Decrypt*, February 9, 2021, https://decrypt.co/57092/biggest-ever-nft-sale-made-as-single-axie-land-goes-for-1-5-million.

42 *"In the beginning"*: Daniel Maegaard, interview, March 10, 2021.

42 *A 2021 study from*: 2021 TIAA Digital Engagement Survey, June 2021, https://www.tiaa.org/public/pdf/digital_engagement_survey.pdf.

42 *paid by financial projects*: Katherine J. Wu, "Radical Ideas Spread Through Social Media," March 28, 2019, PBS Nova, https://www.pbs.org/wgbh/nova/article/radical-ideas-social-media-algorithms/.

43 *while sometimes profiting directly*: Reethu Ravi, "The Saudis NFT Pump After Farokh's Blessing," *NFT Evening*, July 11, 2022, https://nftevening.com/the-saudis-nft-pump-after-farokhs-blessing/.

43 *Eleven days after Beeple's*: Jamie Crawley, "Jack Dorsey's First Tweet Sells for $2.9M," *CoinDesk*, March 22, 2021, https://www.coindesk.com/markets/2021/03/22/jack-dorseys-first-tweet-sells-for-29m/.

43 *A few days after that, Sam*: Douglas Hanks, "Miami Heat to Play in FTX Arena," *Miami Herald*, March 26, 2021, https://www.miamiherald.com/news/local/community/miami-dade/article250228430.html.

CHAPTER 6

45 *In 2019, the World Economic Forum*: George Lwanda, "Cryptocurrency Could Help Zimbabwe Overcome Its Economic Crisis," World Economic Forum, June 24, 2019, https://www.weforum.org/agenda/2019/06/zimbabwe-needs-its-own-cryptocurrency/.

46 *Sam wrote on Twitter*: Sam Bankman-Fried (@SBF_FTX), "This offensive content was produced and published by a competitor exchange of ours who maliciously gained access to someone else's Blockfolio News/Signal capabilities," Twitter post, February 9, 2021, 4:05 a.m., https://twitter.com/SBF_FTX/status/1359111189142200326?s=20.

47 *The country had banned financial*: MacDonald Dzirutwe, "Zimbabwe

Bans Banks from Processing Payments for Cryptocurrencies," Reuters, May 14, 2018, https://www.reuters.com/article/us-crypto-currencies -zimbabwe/zimbabwe-bans-banks-from-processing-payments-for-crypto -currencies-idUSKCN1IF0V4/.

47 *"Imagine you have three hundred people"*: Liam Vries, interview with Andrew R. Chow, April 21, 2023.

48 *"When it comes to crypto"*: Ameer Carter, interview with Andrew R. Chow, July 20, 2021.

49 *He told* Vox *in March*: Theodore Schleifer, "How a Crypto Billionaire Decided To Become One of Biden's Biggest Donors," *Vox*, March 20, 2021, https://www.vox.com/recode/2021/3/20/22335209/sam-bankman -fried-joe-biden-ftx-cryptocurrency-effective-altruism.

49 *He was particularly invested*: Anthony Olasele, "Crypto Round Up Africa," Twitter Spaces, October 26, 2021, https://podcasters.spotify.com/pod /show/cryptoroundupafrica/episodes/CryptoRoundUpAfrica---Sam -Bankman-Fried-CEO-FTX-e19bi48.

49 *On FTX's homepage, an animated*: U.S. vs. Bankman-Fried, government exhibit 1566, presented October 4, 2023.

49 *In March, Sam delivered a keynote*: Bitcoin Events, "Blockchain Africa Conference 2021—Sam Bankman-Fried," YouTube video, 20:55, https://www .youtube.com/watch?v=hagdQ-GIMEk&t=1247s.

50 *At a Zambian open market*: Vitalik Buterin, "My 40-liter backpack travel guide," blog, June 20, 2022, https://vitalik.ca/general/2022/06/20/back pack.html.

50 *Vitalik was surprised*: Vitalik Buterin (@vitalikbuterin), Twitter post, September 1, 2021, 9:07 p.m., https://twitter.com/VitalikButerin/status/1433 235034756972544.

50 *"It depends on active"*: Vitalik Buterin, "The Most Important Scarce Resource Is Legitimacy," blog, March 23, 2021, https://vitalik.ca/general/2021/03/23 /legitimacy.html.

50 *Africa's cryptocurrency market*: Chainalysis, *The 2021 Geography of Crypto-currency Report*, October 14, 2021, https://go.chainalysis.com/rs/503 -FAP-074/images/Geography-of-Cryptocurrency-2021.pdf.

50 *making the continent the*: "P2P Platforms, Remittances, and Savings Needs Power Africa's Grassroots Cryptocurrency Adoption," Chainalysis, October 14, 2021, https://www.chainalysis.com/blog/africas-grassroots-crypto currency-adoption/.

50 *Also in June 2021, El Salvador's*: Sam Jones and Bryan Avelar, "El Salvador Becomes First Country to Adopt Bitcoin as Legal Tender," *Guardian*, June 9, 2021, https://www.theguardian.com/world/2021/jun/09/el-salvador -bitcoin-legal-tender-congress.

CHAPTER 7

53   *Apes were held aloft*: Eminem & Snoop Dogg, "From the D 2 the LBC," June 24, 2022, YouTube video, https://www.youtube.com/watch?v=Rjr A-slMoZ4.

54   *Hollywood writers built stories*: Brittany Chang, "I ate at Bored and Hungry, the wildly hyped Bored Ape Yacht Club–themed fast food concept in California," *Business Insider*, May 8, 2022, https://www.businessinsider.com /photos-i-dined-at-a-bored-and-hungry-nft-themed-fast-food-restaurant -2022-5.

54   *But a friend advised them*: Kyle Forgeard et al., "Bored Ape Creators x Nelk Boys," *Full Send Podcast*, podcast, August 18, 2022,16:00, https://podcasts .apple.com/cl/podcast/bored-ape-yacht-club-creators-explain-how -steph-curry/id1582758729?i=1000576547766.

55   *A few months later*: Joon Ian Wong, "The Ethereum Network Is Getting Jammed Up Because People Are Rushing to Buy Cartoon Cats on Its Blockchain," *Quartz*, December 4, 2017, https://qz.com/1145833/cryptokitties -is-causing-ethereum-network-congestion.

55   *The Punks' creators*: Larva Labs, "Autoglyphs," accessed January 4, 2024, https://www.larvalabs.com/autoglyphs.

57   *Other owners were ecstatic*: Cathy Hackl, "CAA Signs Jenkins the Valet: Is This a Sign That Hollywood Is Embracing NFTs?" *Forbes*, September 25, 2021, https://www.forbes.com/sites/cathyhackl/2021/09/25/caa-signs-jenkins -the-valet-is-this-a-sign-that-hollywood-is-embracing-nfts.

58   *In July 2021, he referred*: Samuel Haig, "Ethereum Must Innovate Beyond Just DApps for DeFi Degens: Vitalik Buterin," *Cointelegraph*, July 22, 2021, https://cointelegraph.com/news/ethereum-must-innovate-beyond-just -dapps-for-defi-degens-vitalik-buterin.

58   *"It could lead, frankly"*: "Non-Fungible Tokens Are Going Mainstream 'Faster Than Anything I've Ever Seen,' Says Billionaire," CNBC *Street Signs Asia*, August 24, 2021, https://www.cnbc.com/video/2021/08/24/non-fungible -tokens-are-going-completely-mainstream-says-ftx-ceo.html.

CHAPTER 8

59   *GBV and FTX*: Protos Staff, "Genesis Block: FTX Had More Than Prostitutes in Thailand," *Protos*, October 20, 2023, https://protos.com/genesis -block-ftx-had-more-than-prostitutes-in-thailand/.

59   *Blockchain analysts would later*: "Blockchain Evidence Suggests Genesis Block Was a Front for Alameda Research," Dirty Bubble Media, December 9, 2022, https://www.dirtybubblemedia.com/p/blockchain-evidence-suggests -genesis.

60   *The prior month*: Nina Bambysheva, "10 Giant Crypto and Blockchain

Rounds Single-Handedly Raised $3.9 Billion This Year," *Forbes*, August 11, 2021, https://www.forbes.com/sites/ninabambysheva/2021/08/11/10-giant -crypto-and-blockchain-rounds-single-handedly-raised-39-billion-this-year.

60 *In pitches*: Adam Fisher, "Sam Bankman-Fried Has a Savior Complex—and Maybe You Should Too," Sequoia, September 22, 2022, https://archive.ph /qFJJN#selection-163.0-163.63.

60 *and bragged that acquiring*: Eva Szalay, "Crypto Exchange FTX Sets Sights on Blue-Chip Acquisitions," *Financial Times*, July 13, 2021, https://www .ft.com/content/c8ffb228-1dbe-4e8a-b30b-be7203d71e7d.

60 *FTX's investors included*: Erin Griffith and David Yaffe-Bellany, "Investors Who Put $2 Billion into FTX Face Scrutiny, Too," *New York Times*, November 11, 2022, https://www.nytimes.com/2022/11/11/technology/ftx-investors -venture-capital.html.

60 *Deven Parekh*: FTX Trading Ltd., "FTX Trading Ltd. Closes $900M Series B Round—Largest Raise in Crypto Exchange History," *PR Newswire*, July 20, 2021, https://www.prnewswire.com/news-releases/ftx-trading -ltd-closes-900m-series-b-round----largest-raise-in-crypto-exchange-history -301337709.html.

60 *FTX was still logging*: Win Win et al., "Quarterly Report: Q3 2021," September 24, 2021, *CoinGecko,* https://assets.coingecko.com/reports/2021-Q3-Report /CoinGecko-2021-Q3-Report.pdf.

CHAPTER 9

63 *At that time*: CryptoSlam!, Bored Ape Yacht Club historical sales volume, accessed October 14, 2023, https://www.cryptoslam.io/bored-ape-yacht -club?headerPeriod=all&tab=historical_sales_volume.

63 *The economist Edward Chancellor*: Chancellor, *Devil Take the Hindmost*, 26.

63 *The comedian Groucho Marx*: Groucho Marx, *Groucho & Me* [1959] (London: Da Capo Press, 1995), 147.

64 *"It was every adjective-animal"*: Michael Keen, interview with Andrew R. Chow, April 26, 2023.

64 *James Block, a psychiatry*: James Block, interview with Andrew R. Chow, June 27, 2023.

64 *Zeneca, a prominent NFT*: Zeneca, "Letter 24: Infinite Regret," *Letters from a Zeneca*, blog post, January 17, 2022, https://zeneca33.substack.com/p/letter -24-infinite-regret.

65 *The project listed its founders*: Lindsay Dodgson, "An 'All Female' NFT Project Was Exposed as Being Founded by 3 Men. Now, They're Trying to Give Back to Women," *Business Insider*, August 23, 2021, https://www.insider .com/nft-fame-lady-squad-all-female-women-created-fls-men-2021-8.

66 *"My penguin is"*: @icebergy_, Twitter video, August 18, 2021, 12:29 p.m., https://twitter.com/icebergy_/status/1428031398489862149.

67 *"When we go to sleep"*: Esther Eze, interview with Andrew R. Chow, April 21, 2023.

69 *It had scraped by*: Adaobi Tricia Nwaubani, "Dancing for Dreams, the Nigerian Street Kids Capturing the Stars," Thomson Reuters Foundation, April 13, 2018, https://news.trust.org/item/20180413010028-w3f62/.

69 *Inflation in Nigeria*: "Nigeria Inflation Rate 1960–2023," World Bank Data, https://www.macrotrends.net/countries/NGA/nigeria/inflation-rate-cpi.

69 *"I have even considered"*: Seyi Oluyole, @Seyioluyole, Tweet, June 13, 2021, 8:16 a.m., https://twitter.com/seyioluyole/status/14040500665082 42944.

70 *One minor influencer*: Chris Coffee, "What Are AfroDroids and Why Is Everyone Talking About Them?," YouTube video, 9:40, https://www.you tube.com/watch?v=ZS4coIYeUZg.

70 *Liam devoted himself*: Interview with Andrew R. Chow, May 12, 2023.

70 *"We are offering"*: CryptoNovo, "NFTs AfroDroids Created by Owo," Crypto Novo311, YouTube video, 21:37, 31:13, https://www.youtube.com /watch?v=bsZ8yo8VsI8.

71 *The sale made the AfroDroids*: Seyi Oluyole, interview with Andrew R. Chow, April 11, 2023.

71 *Oluyole recorded a video*: @0xcryptovert, September 5, 2021, 10:41 p.m., Twitter video, https://twitter.com/0xcryptovert/status/1434708322247118849.

71 *Oluyole withdrew $100,000*: Seyi Oluyole, interview with Andrew R. Chow, April 11, 2023.

71 *"For weeks I have panicked"*: Seyi Oluyole, text message to Esther Eze, September 5, 2021, 6:17 p.m.

72 *"I was just crying"*: Owo Anietie, interview with Andrew R. Chow, April 20, 2023.

CHAPTER 10

75 *This was double*: Tracy Wang, "Sotheby's Auction of 101 Bored Ape NFTs Fetches $24M, Smashing Estimates," *CoinDesk*, September 9, 2021, https: //www.coindesk.com/markets/2021/09/09/sothebys-auction-of-101 -bored-ape-nfts-fetches-24m-smashing-estimates/.

75 *Sotheby's head of contemporary art*: Wave, "The Traditional Collector," Surfing the Waves, May 2, 2023, https://waveninja.substack.com/p/the-traditional -collector.

75 *By this point*: Steven Ehrlich, "Meet the World's Richest 29-Year-Old: How Sam Bankman-Fried Made a Record Fortune in the Crypto Frenzy," *Forbes*, October 6, 2021, https://www.forbes.com/sites/stevenehrlich/2021/10/06 /the-richest-under-30-in-the-world-all-thanks-to-crypto/?sh=22ccb 8db3f4d.

75 *He had criticized them on CNBC*: CNBC *Street Signs Asia*, August 24,

2021, 2:32, https://www.cnbc.com/video/2021/08/24/non-fungible-tokens -are-going-completely-mainstream-says-ftx-ceo.html.

76 *The pair had taught there*: David Gura, "It's Not Just FTX's Sam Bankman -Fried. His Parents Also Face Legal Trouble," NPR, October 2, 2023, https://www.npr.org/2023/10/02/1200764160/sam-bankman-fried-sbf -parents-ftx-crypto-collapse-trial-stanford-law-school.

76 *regularly hosted Sunday dinners*: David Yaffe-Bellany, Lora Kelley, and Kenneth P. Vogel, "The Parents in the Middle of FTX's Collapse," *New York Times*, December 12, 2022, https://www.nytimes.com/2022/12/12/technology /sbf-parents-ftx-collapse.html.

76 *Gabe later told the author*: Michael Lewis, *Going Infinite* (New York: W.W. Norton & Company, 2023), 22.

76 *Sam made few friends*: Ibid., 24.

77 *His mother, Barbara*: Barbara Fried, U.S. v. Bankman-Fried, Letters in Support of Samuel Bankman-Fried's Sentencing Submission, Document 15, submitted February 27, 2024.

77 *George Lerner, who*: George Lerner, U.S. v. Bankman-Fried, Letters in Support of Samuel Bankman-Fried's Sentencing Submission, Document 17, submitted February 27, 2024.

77 *But he made friends*: Lewis, *Going Infinite*, 36.

77 *Some of his friends affectionately*: Sam Bankman-Fried, Facebook photo, September 12, 2008.

77 *to be ruthless in fighting*: Barbara Fried, *Facing Up to Scarcity: The Logic and Limits of Nonconsequentialist Thought* (New York: Oxford University Press, 2020), xv.

77 *"You can never be sure"*: Tyler Cowen, "Sam Bankman-Fried on Arbitrage and Altruism," on *Conversations with Tyler*, podcast, March 9, 2022, 5:35, https://conversationswithtyler.com/episodes/sam-bankman-fried/.

77 *Sam had become vegan*: Ibid.

78 *In 2012, Sam*: Sam Bankman-Fried, "Utilitarianism Part 2: Total, Average, and Linearity," *Measuring Shadows*, blog post comment, July 31, 2012, 6:25 p.m., https://measuringshadowsblog.blogspot.com/2012/07/utilitarianism -part-2-total-average-and.html.

78 *Sam devoted one blog*: Sam Bankman-Fried, "The Utilitarian Boogeymen," *Measuring Shadows*, blog post, July 20, 2012, https://measuringshadows blog.blogspot.com/2012/07/the-utilitarian-boogeymen.html.

78 *When Sam started college*: Tristan Yver, "Sam Bankman-Fried Discusses Altruism," on *The FTX Podcast*, June 4, 2022, 0:53, https://archive.org/details /youtube-OOf8S3SbmMs.

78 *Before the talk*: Wiblin and Harris, "Sam Bankman-Fried on Taking a High-Risk Approach."

78 *If a wealthy banker*: Zeke Faux, "A 30-Year-Old Crypto Billionaire Wants to

Give His Fortune Away," *Bloomberg*, April 3, 2022, https://www.bloomberg
.com/news/features/2022-04-03/sam-bankman-fried-ftx-s-crypto-billion
aire-who-wants-to-give-his-fortune-away.

78 *"Taking on risk"*: Milo Beckman, interview with Andrew R. Chow, November
9, 2023.

CHAPTER 11

81 *He confessed in 2019*: Tessa Dao and Ian Cox, "Sam Bankman-Fried—Leaving
Wall Street, Entering Crypto Chaos," on *Chat with Traders*, podcast, July 23,
2019, 9:00, https://www.youtube.com/watch?v=gSDk5PAJss4.

81 *"In U.S. stock markets"*: Ibid., 8:00.

82 *Much of Alameda's initial funding*: Reed Albergotti and Liz Hoffman,
"Charity-Linked Money Launched Sam Bankman-Fried's Empire," *Semafor*,
December 8, 2022, https://www.semafor.com/article/12/07/2022/charity
-money-launched-sam-bankman-frieds-empire.

82 *On Japanese exchanges*: Nicholas Pongratz, "Sam Bankman Fried Explains
His Arbitrage Techniques," *BeInCrypto*, April 9, 2021, https://finance.yahoo
.com/news/sam-bankman-fried-explains-arbitrage-132901181.html.

82 *Eventually, Sam put together*: Zeke Faux, *Number Go Up* (Toronto: Crown
Currency, 2023), 87.

83 *and another team waited for hours*: Benjamin Wallace, "The Mysterious
Cryptocurrency Magnate Who Became One of Biden's Biggest Donors,"
Intelligencer, February 2, 2021, https://nymag.com/intelligencer/2021/02
/sam-bankman-fried-biden-donor.html.

83 *"I felt guilty every time"*: Interview with anonymous source.

83 *"Sam was incredibly creative"*: Alex Pack, interview with Andrew R. Chow,
May 21, 2023.

83 *"This sleep schedule echoed that"*: Chancellor, *Devil Take the Hindmost*, 254.

83 *Sam had long battled insomnia*: Sam Bankman-Fried, Facebook photo, September 27, 2009, https://www.facebook.com/photo/?fbid=121664912986
9&set=ecnf.1038086748.

83 *In September 2019, he tweeted*: Sam Bankman-Fried (@SBF_FTX), September 15, 2019, 5:42 p.m., https://twitter.com/SBF_FTX/status/1173351344
159117312?lang=en.

83 *At work, Sam sat*: U.S. v. Bankman-Fried, testimony from Nishad Singh,
October 16, 2023.

83 *He shuffled cards so vociferously*: U.S. v. Bankman-Fried, testimony from Sam
Bankman-Fried, October 27, 2023.

84 *The solutions that Sam landed upon*: Sam Bankman-Fried, written testimony notes, December 12, 2022, https://ssets.bwbx.io/documents/users
/iqjWHBFdfxIU/rbgv1U_v6edA/v0.

84   *Emsam's primary substance*: Petra Heiden et al., "Pathological Gambling in Parkinson's Disease: What Are the Risk Factors and What Is the Role of Impulsivity?," *European Journal of Neuroscience* 45, no. 1 (January 2017): 67–72, https://www.ncbi.nlm.nih.gov/pmc/articles/PMC5215459/.

84   *Sam's poor trading*: Lewis, *Going Infinite*, 84.

84   *It didn't distinguish between*: Charlotte Alter, "Exclusive: Effective Altruist Leaders Were Repeatedly Warned About Sam Bankman-Fried Years Before FTX Collapsed," *Time*, March 15, 2023, https://time.com/6262810 /sam-bankman-fried-effective-altruism-alameda-ftx/.

84   *In February 2018, the company lost $4 million*: Lewis, *Going Infinite*, 94.

85   *But Sam refused*: Alter, "Exclusive: Effective Altrust Leaders Were Repeatedly Warned About Sam Bankman-Fried Years Before FTX Collapsed."

85   *Going forward, Sam*: Jacquelyn Melinek, "Alameda Had a $65B Line of Credit and 'Unlimited Withdrawals'," *TechCrunch*, October 5, 2023, https: //techcrunch.com/2023/10/05/sbf-trial-gary-wang/.

85   *Sam successfully raised*: Frank Chaparro, "Alameda Promised 'High Returns With No Risk' in 2018 Pitch," *The Block*, November 11, 2022, https: //www.theblock.co/post/.

86   *Caroline had wandered into*: Tristan Yver, "From a Jane Street Equities Quant to an Alameda Crypto Quant," on *The FTX Podcast*, July 3, 2020, 7:50, https://archive.org/details/youtube-1yjIq-_0kPs.

86   *In the summer of 2018*: U.S. v. Bankman-Fried, testimony from Caroline Ellison, October 10, 2023

86   *After several meetings*: Alex Pack, interview with Andrew R. Chow, November 24, 2023.

CHAPTER 12

89   *In 2014, hackers*: Robert McMillan, "The Inside Story of Mt. Gox, Bitcoin's $460 Million Disaster," March 3, 2014, *Wired*, https://www.wired .com/2014/03/bitcoin-exchange/.

89   *Many crypto idealists*: "Vitalik Buterin Speaks at TC Sessions: Blockchain," Facebook video, posted by *TechCrunch*, July 9, 2018, https://fb.watch /lL1qTc7Hbs/.

90   *They conceptualized and engineered*: U.S. v. Bankman-Fried, government exhibit 1083, "Signal Groups Samuel Bankman-Fried Participated in from 2020 to 2022," presented October 26, 2023.

90   *There, they fostered*: Natalie Tien, interview with Andrew R. Chow, October 23, 2023.

90   *"He was basically"*: Alex Pack, interview with Andrew R. Chow, November 24, 2023.

90   *A year later, Sam*: Sam Bankman-Fried (@SBF_FTX), "1) I've only been in crypto for 3 years, and out of college for 6, so feel free to ignore this 'built up

wisdom'. But I think it's hard to think well about the role VCs play. I know I've fucked it up before! . . ." Twitter post, August 6, 2020, 12:35 a.m., https://twitter.com/SBF_FTX/status/1291231303682027520.

91   *"As a trader the most"*: Tristan Yver, "FTX Podcast #36: Defi Summer Crypto Trading Strategy," on *The FTX Podcast*, January 22, 2021, 18:10, https://archive.org/details/youtube-zfcb9JAgWBs.

91   *Sam also forced trading firms*: Alex Pack, interview with Andrew R. Chow, November 24, 2023.

92   *Such a dynamic would*: Interview with anonymous source.

92   *Sam responded quickly*: Sam Bankman-Fried (@SBF_FTX), Twitter post, July 31, 2019, 6:40 p.m., https://twitter.com/SBF_FTX/status/1156696100729806849.

92   *The very same day*: U.S. v Bankman-Fried, testimony from Gary Wang, October 6, 2023.

92   *The funds of Alameda and FTX*: Andrew R. Chow, "Where Did FTX's Missing $8 Billion Go? Crypto Investigators Offer New Clues," *Time*, December 21, 2022, https://time.com/6243086/ftx-where-did-money-go/.

92   *Even those potentially interested*: Ash Bennington, "Building an Arbitrage Infrastructure for Traders," *Real Vision*, June 2, 2021, https://www.youtube.com/watch?v=YLCnGXawUj0.

92   *North Dimension was controlled*: U.S. v. Bankman-Fried, government exhibit 267, presented October 18, 2023.

93   *By the end of 2021*: FTX bankruptcy filings, Case No. 22-11068, filed June 23, 2023, Debtors, page 12.

93   *In 2019, FTX received*: Angus Berwick and Tom Wilson, "Exclusive: Behind FTX's Fall, Battling Billionaires and a Failed Bid to Save Crypto," Reuters, November 10, 2022, https://www.reuters.com/technology/exclusive-behind-ftxs-fall-battling-billionaires-failed-bid-save-crypto-2022-11-10/.

93   *Blockfolio's CEO, Edward*: Mitchell Moos, "Interview: Inside Look at FTX's $150M Blockfolio Acquisition," *Crypto Briefing*, August 26, 2020, https://cryptobriefing.com/inside-look-ftx-150m-blockfolio-acquisition/.

93   *Sam's exchange allowed people*: Martin Young, "FTX Reduces Max Leverage from 101x to 20x to Encourage 'Responsible Trading,'" *Cointelegraph*, July 26, 2021, https://cointelegraph.com/news/ftx-reduces-max-leverage-from-101x-to-20x-to-encourage-responsible-trading.

94   *"If you really want to make"*: Anthony Olasele, "African Art as NFTs w/ Tristan Yver of FTX and Anthony Azekwoh," on *Crypto Round Up Africa*, podcast, September 10, 2021, https://podcasters.spotify.com/pod/s how/cryptoroundupafrica/episodes/African-Art-as-NFTs-w-Tristan-Yver-of -FTX--Anthony-Azekwho-e176mgv.

94   *Sam replied evenhandedly*: Cowen, "Sam Bankman-Fried," 30:08.

94   *In 2021, this sort of approach*: Mario Gabriele, "FTX Trilogy, Part 1: The

Prince of Risk," *The Generalist*, August 1, 2021, https://www.generalist.com/briefing/ftx-1.

94 *"As real institutions get involved"*: Wiblin and Harris, "Sam Bankman-Fried on Taking a High Risk Approach."

94 *"It was embracing the mindset"* Tristan Yver, "FTX Podcast #36: Defi Summer Crypto Trading Strategy," on *The FTX Podcast*, January 22, 2021, 2:30, https://archive.org/details/youtube-zfcb9JAgWBs.

95 *But once the project*: @NTmoney, "I'm going to highlight one token that appears to be bought by Alameda, pumped by FTX, then offered to retail on FTX. ~1 yr later, the price and volume of the token fell by ~99% & the project seems abandoned. It's easy to find many more that follow the same pattern in '20 - '21," Twitter post, October 23, 2022, 8:10 a.m., https://twitter.com/NTmoney/status/1584155286343798784.

95 *"Every single time I saw"*: MacLane Wilkison, interview with Andrew R. Chow, May 20, 2023.

95 *By June 2019, Alameda*: FTX White Paper, 2019, https://api-new.whitepaper.io/documents/pdf?id=HJRMXAOeU.

96 *To take the first route*: Caroline Ellison (@CarolineCapital), Twitter post, March 7, 2021, 6:47 a.m., https://twitter.com/carolinecapital/status/1368528742889390088.

96 *In 2021, for instance*: Sam Trabucco (@AlamedaTrabucco), Twitter post, April 22, 2021, 6:37 a.m., https://twitter.com/AlamedaTrabucco/status/1385181048502329349.

CHAPTER 13

97 *But financial speculation and gambling*: Chancellor, *Devil Take the Hindmost*, xii.

97 *There are about twenty-three thousand cryptocurrencies*: "Today's Cryptocurrency Prices by Market Cap," CoinMarketCap, accessed September 14, 2023, https://coinmarketcap.com/.

98 *Their health was not tethered*: Aaron Mak, "Bitcoin and Dogecoin Are at Elon Musk's Mercy," *Slate*, May 13, 2021, https://slate.com/technology/2021/05/bitcoin-elon-musk-dogecoin-tesla-snl.html.

98 *"The individual incentive"*: Illia Polosukhin, interview with Andrew R. Chow, May 23, 2023.

98 *When he was gifted $6.7 billion*: Jamie Crawley, "Vitalik Buterin Burns $6B in SHIB Tokens," *CoinDesk*, May 17, 2021, https://www.coindesk.com/markets/2021/05/17/vitalik-buterin-burns-6b-in-shib-tokens-says-he-doesnt-want-the-power/.

98 *"There is no sense that"*: Cowen, "Sam Bankman-Fried on Arbitrage and Altruism," 42:38.

99   *Sam pledged*: Sam Bankman-Fried (@SBF_FTX), "Excited to announce that the first FTT buy and burn is about to start! Over the next three days we'll be buying and burning over 500,000 FTT, the first of many burns to come." Twitter post, July 29, 2019, 8:42 a.m., https://twitter.com/SBF_FTX /status/1155821008168935426?.

99   *First, Sam dictated*: Yong Li Khoo et al., "Blockchain Analysis: The Collapse of Alameda and FTX," Nansen, November 17, 2022, https://www.nansen .ai/research/blockchain-analysis-the-collapse-of-alameda-and-ftx.

100   *Caroline later testified*: U.S. v Bankman-Fried, testimony from Caroline Ellison, October 10, 2023.

100   *Because Sam controlled*: "Profile: Sam Bankman-Fried, December 20, 2023," *Forbes*, accessed December 3, 2023, https://www.forbes.com/profile /sam-bankman-fried/?sh=2312a89e4449.

101   *Sam directed Caroline*: U.S. v. Bankman-Fried, testimony from Caroline Ellison, October 10, 2023, transcript page 679.

101   *Sam responded that it was fine*: Affidavit, In the Matter of a request by The United States of America, Exhibit 1, page 4, May 8, 2023.

101   *That $200 million debt*: U.S. v. Bankman-Fried, government exhibit 1002, "Balance of Alameda Research Accounts on FTX.com with 'allow_negative' Enabled," created by Peter Easton, presented October 18, 2023.

101   *but Gary had coded in*: U.S. v. Bankman-Fried, government exhibit 5, presented October 16, 2023.

102   *"Maybe FTT should"*: FTX (@FTX_Official), Twitter post, January 18, 2021, 5:35 p.m., https://twitter.com/FTX_Official/status/13512971822 80765441.

102   *At the time, Ethereum*: Ethereum transactions per second chart, Blockchair, accessed January 4, 2024, https://blockchair.com/ethereum/charts/trans actions-per-second.

102   *Sam argued that if*: Andrew Fenton, "Sam Bankman-Fried: The Crypto Whale Who Wants to Give Billions Away," *Magazine by Cointelegraph*, February 24, 2021, https://cointelegraph.com/magazine/sam-bankman-fried -the-crypto-whale-who-wants-to-give-billions-away/.

102   *In December 2020, the two*: @VitalikButerin, Twitter post, December 28, 2020, 1:34 a.m., https://twitter.com/VitalikButerin/status/13434452276 09026563.

102   *Bankman-Fried, conversely, argued*: Brady Dale, *SBF: How The FTX Bankruptcy Unwound Crypto's Very Bad Good Guy* (New Jersey: Wiley, 2023).

102   *So in the summer*: Ian Allison, "Divisions in Sam Bankman-Fried's Crypto Empire Blur on His Trading Titan Alameda's Balance Sheet," *CoinDesk*, November 2, 2022, https://www.coindesk.com/business/2022/11/02/divisions -in-sam-bankman-frieds-crypto-empire-blur-on-his-trading-titan-alamedas -balance-sheet/.

103 *Alameda had served*: Andrew Asmakov, "Alameda Leads $50 Million Funding Round in Maps.me," *Decrypt*, January 17, 2021, https://decrypt.co/54326/alameda-leads-50-million-seed-funding-round-in-maps-me.

103 *Sam listed those coins*: "What Is FTX Crypto Token FTT Coin?," *PublishOx*, November 18, 2021, https://www.publish0x.com/stealthex/what-is-ftx-crypto-token-ftt-coin-xmmwkjn.

103 *As he'd done with FTT*: Matt Levine, "FTX's Balance Sheet Was Bad," *Bloomberg*, November 14. 2022, https://www.bloomberg.com/opinion/articles/2022-11-14/ftx-s-balance-sheet-was-bad.

103 *Then, he used some*: Emily Flitter and David Yaffe-Bellany, "FTX Founder Gamed Markets, Crypto Rivals Say," *New York Times*, January 18, 2023, https://www.nytimes.com/2023/01/18/business/ftx-sbf-crypto-markets.html.

103 *"Honestly, Solana did not"*: Ben Gilbert and David Rosenthal, "Race Capital, Crypto Investing, and FTX + Solana's Early Days," on *Acquired LP*, podcast, 41:12, https://www.acquired.fm/episodes/race-capital-crypto-investing-and-ftx-solanas-early-days.

104 *"I definitely hope centralized"*: "Vitalik Buterin speaks at TC Sessions: Blockchain," Facebook video, posted by *TechCrunch*, July 9, 2018, https://fb.watch/lL1qTc7Hbs/.

104 *"He was willing to have"*: Vitalik Buterin, interview with Andrew R. Chow, April 4, 2023.

104 *But according to Qureshi*: Haseeb Qureshi, interview with Andrew R. Chow, August 13, 2023.

CHAPTER 14

105 *OpenSea, the biggest platform*: Dune Analytics, OpenSea, @rchen8, accessed July 5, 2023, https://dune.com/rchen8/opensea.

105 *Sam didn't care a lick*: Axios on HBO, "FTX CEO Sam Bankman-Fried on the Appeal of NFTs," YouTube, 0:34, https://youtu.be/ti9QyT1ZyOI.

105 *(He was no fan)*: Lewis, *Going Infinite*, 29.

105 *Sam's first NFT*: @FTX_Official, "When asked about the inspiration behind his award winning installation 'test' Sam responded with: Sometimes it's not what you (MS) paint, it's what you don't," Twitter post, September 7, 2:30 a.m., https://twitter.com/FTX_Official/status/1435128332983554050.

105 *sold for $270,000*: @FTX_Official, "History being made. @SBF_FTX's 1/1 'test' NFT has been sold for $270,000 USD," Twitter post, September 7, 1:16 a.m., 2021, https://twitter.com/FTX_Official/status/1435124771394523137.

105 *The social media frenzy*: CoinMarketCap, FTT, accessed November 14, 2023, https://coinmarketcap.com/currencies/ftx-token/.

105 *Sam now proclaimed*: Joe Weisenthal, "Financial Innovation Summit," *Bloomberg Live*, November 5, 2021, https://twitter.com/BloombergLive/status/1456674665305411585.

106 *He excitedly auctioned*: Sam Bankman-Fried (@SBF_FTX), "Starting the auction for my NFT 4 inch tungsten cube #69 on @ftx_us! Cube #69 is considered by many to be the Holy Grail of @tungstencubenft collection," Twitter post, November 1, 2021, 7:24 p.m., https://twitter.com/SBF_FTX/status/1455314818076844034.

106 *Sam also retweeted*: Tristan Yver (@yver), Twitter post, October 25, 2021, 1:29 p.m., https://twitter.com/yver__/status/1452688721698963456.

106 *Yver appeared on the*: Olasele, *Crypto Round Up Africa*, "African Art as NFTs."

106 *Brett Harrison*: @FTX_Official, "Join us on Thursday for a FTX NFT Twitter Space with: @Brett_FTXUS, @zhusu, @baalazamon, @irvinxyz, @kyled116, and of course @jackshaftoes!," Twitter post, October 12, 2021, 12:13 a.m., https://twitter.com/FTX_Official/status/1447958700476583944.

106 *doling out billions*: Simon Hunt and Tom Maloney, "Ex-High School Classmates Are Among the World's Largest Crypto Holders," *Bloomberg*, May 25, 2021, https://www.bloomberg.com/news/articles/2021-05-25/ex-credit-suisse-traders-amass-billions-of-dollars-of-crypto.

106 *"He'd always post"*: Christine Chew, interview with Andrew R. Chow, October 13, 2023.

106 *"That was the height"*: Ibid.

107 *"You guys are the best"*: Anthony Boyd (@anthonyjboydii), Twitter post, September 1, 2021, 12:59 p.m., https://twitter.com/anthonyjboydii/status/1433112341902729218.

107 *A couple months later*: Anthony Boyd, interview with Andrew R. Chow, March 17, 2023.

107 *The exchange promised users*: Brett Harrison (@BrettHarrison88), Twitter post, July 20, 2021, 4:14 p.m., https://twitter.com/BrettHarrison88/status/1417578618243387392.

107 *And it also offered other*: "The FTX Podcast ft. SBF and Aravind Menon," on *Superteam Podcast*, April 3, 2023, 8:00, https://www.youtube.com/watch?v=0zUeuviJSoU.

107 *when someone bought*: Andrew Hayward, "Coachella NFTs Sold for $1.5M—Now They're Stuck on FTX," *Decrypt*, November 16, 2022, https://decrypt.co/114856/coachella-tomorrowland-solana-nfts-stuck-ftx.

107 *The same 101 Apes*: FTX Help Desk (@FTX_Helpdesk), "Holy…There's 101 @BoredApeYC's listed on FTXUS," Twitter post, December 2, 2021, 12:19 p.m., https://twitter.com/FTX_Helpdesk/status/1466456905665024003.

108 *Sure enough, the Apes*: "NFT Price Floor, Bored Ape Yacht Club," accessed December 9, 2023, https://nftpricefloor.com/bored-ape-yacht-club.

108   *Michael Bouhanna*: Michael Bouhanna (@michaelbouhanna), "Our Ape in! auction @sothebys just achieved an outstanding $26.2M - a great indicator of the level of confidence in this amazing NFT project. This is just the beginning," Twitter post, September 9, 2021, 10:19 a.m., https://twitter.com /michaelbouhanna/status/1435971090061332488.

108   *Analysts predicted*: Wang, "Sotheby's Auction."

108   *He even had an*: Alexander Osipovich, "This Vegan Billionaire Disrupted the Crypto Markets. Stocks May Be Next," *Wall Street Journal*, April 16, 2021, https://www.wsj.com/articles/this-vegan-billionaire-disrupted-the-crypto -markets-stocks-may-be-next-11618565408.

108   *Several months later, FTX Ventures*: U.S. vs. Bankman-Fried, government exhibit 14A, presented October 16, 2023.

108   *In September 2021, Jenkins*: Cathy Hackl, "CAA Signs Jenkins the Valet: Is This a Sign That Hollywood Is Embracing NFTs?" *Forbes*, September 25, 2021, https://www.forbes.com/sites/cathyhackl/2021/09/25/caa-signs-jenkins -the-valet-is-this-a-sign-that-hollywood-is-embracing-nfts/.

109   *Jenkins's production company*: Tom Farren, "Tally Labs strives to expand decentralized content ecosystem with $12M funding," *Cointelegraph*, May 18, 2022, https://.com/news/tally-labs-strive-to-expand-decentralized-content -ecosystem-with-12m-funding

109   *Jenkins's human owner*: Valet Jones, interview with Andrew R. Chow, October 31, 2022.

109   *On November 10, 2021*: @moonpay, Twitter video, November 11, 2021, 6:38 a.m., https://twitter.com/moonpay/status/1458761049075769351.

109   *In January 2022*: "@FallonTonight, "Jimmy & @ParisHilton compare #BoredApeYC NFTs," Twitter video, January 25, 2022, 12:15 a.m., https: //twitter.com/FallonTonight/status/1485843736345161737.

109   *(In a sign of how small)*: Faux, *Number Go Up*, 154.

109   *They had just surpassed the CryptoPunks*: Andrew Hayward, "Bored Ape Yacht Club NFTs Flip CryptoPunks Floor Price in Ethereum," *Decrypt*, December 22, 2021, https://decrypt.co/89060/bored-ape-yacht-club-nfts -flip-cryptopunks-floor-price-in-ethereum.

110   *From the stage*: Adlan Jackson, "How to Sneak into a Bored Ape Yacht Club Party," *The Verge*, December 13, 2021, https://www.theverge .com/22824387/bored-ape-yacht-club-nft-party-new-york.

110   *Blockchain evidence shows that Paltrow*: Elle Reeve and Samantha Guff, "A Twisted Tale of Celebrity Promotion, Opaque Transactions and Allegations of Racist Tropes," CNN, February 10, 2023, https://www.cnn .com/2023/02/10/business/crypto-nft-bored-ape-moonpay-lawsuits/index .html.

110   *Don Thompson wrote*: Thompson, *The $12 Million Stuffed Shark*, 16.

110   *In the first quarter*: *NonFungible*, "NFT Market Quarterly Report, Q1, 2022,"

April 28, 2022, https://nonfungible.com/reports/2022/en/q1-quarterly
-nft-market-report.

110   *"It was the greediest"*: Liam Vries, interview, with Andrew R. Chow, February
19, 2023.

111   *"It was a pretty boring"*: Christine Chew, interview with Andrew R. Chow,
April 24, 2023.

111   *"Nobody accounted for the moonboys"*: Michail Stangl, interview with Andrew
R. Chow, May 2, 2023.

CHAPTER 15

113   *Within two days*: CryptoNovo311, "Ethereans Afrodroids World of Women
Gauntlets Mutant Apes ETH," YouTube video, September 3, 2021, https:
//www.youtube.com/watch?v=GTkflYMkdZE&t=1505s.

113   *"We are very happy"*: @jhruth, Twitter post, September 14, 2021, 2:41 p.m.,
https://twitter.com/jhruth/status/1437848589322031113.

114   *One buyer, a teacher*: @wolf_warner, "I love to incorporate Arts into my
students Science lessons. #Afrodroids just opened up another avenue into
#Robotics and #Hereditary Traits," Twitter post, September 2, 2021, 2:18
p.m., https://twitter.com/wolf_warner/status/1433509737933545473.

114   *Another superfan, named Krystal*: CryptoNovo (@CryptoNovo311), Twitter
post, September 14, 2021, 10:11 a.m., https://twitter.com/CryptoNovo311
/status/1437780927237795844.

114   *Almost a quarter*: "24% of New Tokens Launched in 2022 Bear On-
Chain Characteristics of Pump and Dump Schemes," *Chainalysis*, February
16, 2023, https://www.chainalysis.com/blog/2022-crypto-pump-and-dump
-schemes/.

115   *"After everybody got"*: Owo Anietie, interview with Andrew R. Chow, April
20, 2023.

115   *"I think the art"*: Michael Keen, interview with Andrew R. Chow, April 26,
2023.

116   *September 2021 was the biggest*: Elizabeth Kerr, "NFT Art Sales Peak
at $881M in 2021 but Decline by 98% in April 2023," *Bankless Times*,
May 9, 2023, https://www.banklesstimes.com/news/2023/05/09/nft-art
-sales-peak-at-dollar881m-in-2021-but-decline-by-98percent-in
-april-2023/.

116   *"That was the time when"*: CryptoWizard, interview with Andrew R. Chow,
May 30, 2023.

116   *"This is a total rug"*: Ely Trader, Discord message, AfroDroids server, November 8, 2021, 1:31 p.m.

116   *"Charity was a"*: Scrooge McDuck, Discord message, AfroDroids server,
December 7, 2021, 2:16 p.m.

117   *"In general, they"*: daimondexe, Discord message, AfroDroids server, September 14, 2021, 7 p.m.

118   *"When you want to"*: Esther Eze, interview with Andrew R. Chow, April 25, 2023.

118   *"All hell broke"*: Ibid.

119   *"It was like I"*: Anietie, interview, April 20, 2023.

119   *"After I sold out"*: Ibid.

119   *"I don't understand"*: Owo Anietie, Discord message, AfroDroids server, November 25, 2021, 6:52 a.m.

119   *"I felt really disassociated"*: Anietie, interview, April 20, 2023.

120   *"Every day, you go"*: Ibid.

120   *"It's all an illusion"*: Protek, Discord message, AfroDroids server, November 3, 2021, 1:05 p.m.

120   *Like many crypto entrepreneurs*: Tage Kene-Okafor, "Nestcoin Raises $6.45M Pre-seed to Accelerate Crypto and Web3 Adoption in Africa and Frontier Markets," *TechCrunch*, February 1, 2022, https://techcrunch.com/2022/02/01/nestcoin-raises-6-45m-pre-seed-to-accelerate-crypto-and-web3-adoption-in-africa-and-frontier-markets/.

120   *Nestcoin's investors*: U.S. v. Bankman-Fried, government exhibit 14A, presented October 16, 2023.

121   *"FTX was positioned"*: Yele Bademosi, interview with Andrew R. Chow, August 19, 2023.

CHAPTER 16

123   *A Chainalysis study found Africa*: Chainalysis, "The 2021 Geography of Cryptocurrency Report," October 2021, https://go.chainalysis.com/rs/503-FAP-074/images/Geography-of-Cryptocurrency-2021.pdf.

123   *"Those are buzzwords"*: Bitcoin Events, "Blockchain Africa Conference 2021—Sam Bankman-Fried," YouTube video, 20:55, https://www.youtube.com/watch?v=hagdQ-GIMEk&t=1247s.

124   *"If I wanted a partnership"*: Harrison Obiefule, interview with Andrew R. Chow, June 12, 2023.

124   *Nigeria was the continent's*: Shola Lawal and Adenike Olanrewaju, "Nigerians Demand End to Police Squad Known for Brutalizing the Young," *New York Times*, October 12, 2020, https://www.nytimes.com/2020/10/12/world/africa/nigeria-protests-police-sars.html.

124   *and a 2022 CoinGecko study*: Julia Ng, "Top 15 Countries Most Curious about Cryptocurrency," *CoinGecko*, July 19, 2023, https://www.coingecko.com/research/publications/top-15-countries-most-curious-about-cryptocurrency.

124   *But they also offered cash*: Reeves Wiedeman, "How Did SBF Convince West

Africans Crypto Was Their Future?," *New York*, November 19, 2022, https://nymag.com/intelligencer/2022/11/sam-bankman-fried-ftx-africa-crypto-future.html.

124 *and received a 25–40 percent commission*: "FTX Exchange Opens Its Ambassador Program to Crypto Enthusiasts in Africa," *BitcoinKE*, June 10, 2021, https://bitcoinke.io/2021/06/ftx-ambassador-program-for-africa/.

124 *Ambassadors like Nduka*: Dilin Massand, "How African Students Became Victims of FTX's Collapse," *CoinDesk*, October 17, 2023, https://www.coindesk.com/consensus-magazine/2023/10/17/how-african-students-became-victims-of-ftxs-collapse/.

125 *"I saw how stressful"*: Anthony Nduka, interview with Andrew R. Chow, March 30, 2023.

125 *In 2012, Olasele was one*: Unesco, "Outbound Internationally Mobile Students by Host Region," data extracted December 1, 2023, http://data.uis.unesco.org/index.aspx?queryid=3807.

125 *TransferWise, another global*: Libby George, "TransferWise Says No Longer Sending Remittances to Nigeria Under New FX Rules," Reuters, December 17, 2020, https://www.reuters.com/article/nigeria-money-idAFL1N2IX1BM/.

125 *The World Bank found*: "An Analysis of Trends in Cost of Remittance Services," The World Bank, September 2022, https://remittanceprices.worldbank.org/sites/default/files/rpw_main_report_and_annex_q322_final.pdf.

126 *A decade later*: Exchange Rates, "US Dollar to Nigerian Naira Spot Exchange Rates for 2020," accessed July 15, 2023, https://www.exchangerates.org.uk/USD-NGN-spot-exchange-rates-history-2020.html.

126 *In 2016, the Central Bank*: Yomi Kazeem, "To Save Its Currency, Nigeria's Central Bank Wants People Jailed for Holding On to US Dollars," *Quartz*, November 16, 2016, https://qz.com/africa/837709/nigerias-central-bank-wants-to-jail-citizens-who-hold-on-to-forex-to-save-the-naira.

126 *"It became that my"*: Anthony Olasele, interview with Andrew R. Chow, November 9, 2023.

126 *In May 2021, Elon Musk*: Saturday Night Live, "Weekend Update: Financial Expert Lloyd Ostertag on Cryptocurrency," YouTube Video, May 9, 2021, https://www.youtube.com/watch?v=x5RCfQyTDFI.

127 *Unfortunately, the exact opposite*: Ethan Wolff-Mann, "Dogecoin Down Nearly 80% Since Elon Musk SNL Appearance," *Yahoo! Finance,* July 20, 2021, https://news.yahoo.com/dogecoin-down-nearly-80-since-elon-musk-snl-appearance-205625484.html.

127 *"There are a lot of poor"*: Anthony Olasele, interview with Andrew R. Chow, February 20, 2023.

127 *they operated in plain clothes*: "Nigeria: Horrific Reign of Impunity by SARS

Makes Mockery of Anti-Torture Law," Amnesty International, June 26, 2020, https://www.amnesty.org/en/latest/news/2020/06/nigeria-horrific-reign -of-impunity-by-sars-makes-mockery-of-anti-torture-law/.

127   *On October 20, 2020*: Mayeni Jones, "Nigeria's #EndSars Protests: What Happened Next," BBC, October 7, 2021, https://www.bbc.com/news/world -africa-58817690.

127   *They jailed many more*: Oladeinde Olawoyin, "#EndSARS: Nigerian Govt Moves Against Protesters, Freezes Bank Accounts," *Premium Times,* November 6, 2020, https://www.premiumtimesng.com/news/headlines/424932 -endsars-nigerian-govt-moves-against-protesters-freezes-bank-accounts .html.

127   *With no way to receive*: Yomi Kazeem, "How Bitcoin Powered the Largest Nigerian Protests in a Generation," *Quartz*, October 26, 2020, https: //qz.com/africa/1922466/how-bitcoin-powered-nigerias-endsars-protests.

128   *In the wake of the GameStop*: Tanzeel Akhtar, "FTX Follows Binance's Lead with Move into Tokenized Stocks, *CoinDesk,* June 24, 2021, https://www .coindesk.com/markets/2021/06/24/ftx-follows-binances-lead-with-move -into-tokenized-stocks.

129   *"That was how they"*: Alex Pack, interview with Andrew R. Chow, November 24, 2023.

129   *In October 2021,* Crypto Round Up: "Sam Bankman-Fried," *Crypto Round Up Africa*, October 26, 2021, https://podcasters.spotify.com/pod/show /cryptoroundupafrica/episodes/CryptoRoundUpAfrica---Sam-Bankman -Fried-CEO-FTX-e19bi48.

CHAPTER 17

131   *"It was a no-brainer"*: Yele Bademosi, interview with Andrew R. Chow, August 19, 2023.

131   *Anthony Olasele raved*: Anthony Olasele, *Crypto Round Up Africa*, September 10, 2021, 1:22:20, https://podcasters.spotify.com/pod/show/cryptoround upafrica/episodes/African-Art-as-NFTs-w-Tristan-Yver-of-FTX—Anthony -Azekwho-e176mgv/a-a6gjf3l.

131   *"[Axie] empowers gamers"*: @BloombergTV, "Blockchain gaming is a global phenomenon that'll create the next 'paradigm shift', and @alexisohanian doesn't use that word lightly," Twitter video, August 17, 2021, 7:58 p.m., https://twitter.com/BloombergTV/status/1427797029242216452.

132   *The "play-to-earn" model*: "U.S. Consumer Video Game Spending Totaled $60 billion in 2021," The Entertainment Software Association, January 18, 2022, https://www.theesa.com/news/u-s-consumer-video-game-spending-totaled -60-4-billion-in-2021/

133   *He played League of Legends*: Britney Nguyen, "Sam Bankman-Fried Was Once Caught Playing the Video Game 'League Of Legends' During a Pitch

Meeting for FTX," *Business Insider*, November 10, 2022, https://www
.businessinsider.com/ftx-sam-bankman-fried-league-of-legends-investor
-pitch-meeting-2022-11.

133 *FTX paid $210 million*: Kellen Browning, "A Pro E-Sports Team Is Getting
     $210 Million to Change Its Name," *New York Times*, June 4, 2021, https:
     //www.nytimes.com/2021/06/04/sports/esports-name-change-tsm-ftx
     .html

133 *Seven-year branding deal*: Protos Staff, "FTX Brands LoL League for 7 Years,
     Another Infinity Gem for Bankman-Fried," *Protos*, August 5, 2021, https:
     //protos.com/ftx-league-of-legends-lcs-crypto-exchange-infinity-gem
     -bankman-fried/.

133 *"We believe in a future"*: Axie Infinity FAQ, accessed November 16, 2020,
     https://web.archive.org/web/20201116092734/https://axieinfinity.com
     /faq.

133 *People left their call center jobs*: Faux, *Number Go Up*, 122.

133 *One Axie player*: Andrew R. Chow and Chad de Guzman, "A Crypto Game
     Promised to Lift Filipinos Out of Poverty. Here's What Happened In-
     stead," *Time*, July 25, 2022, https://time.com/6199385/axie-infinity-crypto
     -game-philippines-debt/.

134 *"Everything else was crashing"*: Khai Chun Thee, interview with Andrew R.
     Chow, September 7, 2023.

134 *The World Bank had found*: Amanina Abdur Rahman, Alyssa Farha Jasmin,
     and Achim Schmillen, "The Vulnerability of Jobs to COVID-19: The Case
     of Malaysia," ISEAS—Yusof Ishak Institute, November 2020, https://drive
     .google.com/file/d/1rxWt1-ewskKA5oZHY3ybIiSCRqJt5_Be/view.

135 *"If I can make money"*: Yele Bademosi, interview, August 19, 2023.

135 *By August 2021, Axie Infinity*: Andrew Hayward, "FTX Sponsors Play-to-
     Earn 'Scholars' in Ethereum Game Axie Infinity," *Decrypt,* August 5, 2021,
     https://decrypt.co/77708/ftx-sponsors-play-to-earn-scholars-ethereum
     -game-axie-infinity.

135 *Over a seven-day stretch*: CryptoSlam, NFT Collectible Rankings by Sales
     Volume, August 10, 2021, https://web.archive.org/web/20210810020601
     /https:/cryptoslam.io/.

136 *FTX announced its intention*: Tanzeel Akhtar, "FTX Strikes Deal with Yield
     Guild Games to Sponsor Axie Infinity Players," *CoinDesk*, August 5, 2021,
     https://www.coindesk.com/markets/2021/08/05/ftx-strikes-deal-with
     -yield-guild-games-to-sponsor-axie-infinity-players/.

136 *Two months later, FTX*: U.S. v. Bankman-Fried, government exhibit 14B,
     presented October 16, 2023.

136 *The company acknowledged*: Axie Infinity White Paper, updated November
     2021, accessed July 24, 2023, https://whitepaper.axieinfinity.com/gameplay
     /axie-population-and-long-term-sustainability.

136 *In August 2021, cofounder Jeff Zirlin*: Tristan Yver, "The Future of Blockchain

Games: Pay-to-Play vs Play-to-Earn," on *The FTX Podcast*, August 29, 2021, 35:10, https://archive.org/details/youtube-rHPhCOuEZgo.

137   *By the fall of 2021, Axie*: Andrew Hayward, "Ethereum Game Axie Infinity Daily Users Grow 10X Since June to Hit 1 Million," *Decrypt*, August 6, 2021, https://decrypt.co/77949/ethereum-game-axie-infinity-daily-users-10x -1-million.

137   *and average earnings for Axie scholars*: Jimmy Stone, Lars Doucet, Anthony Pecorella, Aaron Bush, and Abhimanyu Kumar, "Axie Infinity: Infinite Opportunity or Infinite Peril?," Naavik, November 12, 2021, https://naavik.co /deep-dives/axie-infinity/#axie-decon='.

137   *In November 2021, FTX partnered*: Eli Tan, "FTX, Lightspeed, Solana Ventures to Invest $100M in Web 3 Gaming," *CoinDesk*, November 5, 2021, https://www.coindesk.com/business/2021/11/05/ftx-lightspeed-solana -ventures-to-invest-100m-in-web3-gaming/.

138   *"Things like conferences"*: Ian Tan, interview with Andrew R. Chow, August 28, 2023.

138   *"So you've gotten SLPs"*: @GalaxieCup, Tweet, November 24, 2021, 9 p.m., https://twitter.com/GalaxieCup/status/1463688893903949825.

CHAPTER 18

139   *In Japan, he bought*: Ryan Browne, "Crypto Exchange FTX to Buy Japanese Rival Liquid for Asia Expansion," CNBC, February 2, 2022, https://www .cnbc.com/2022/02/02/crypto-exchange-ftx-to-buy-japanese-rival-liquid .html.

139   *In the Middle East, he created*: "FTX wins full approval to operate crypto exchange in Dubai," Reuters, July 29, 2022, https://www.reuters.com /business/finance/ftx-wins-full-approval-operate-crypto-exchange -dubai-2022-07-29/

139   *By October 2021, FTX accounted*: Steven Ehrlich, "Meet the World's Richest 29-Year-Old," *Forbes*.

139   *facilitating over $10 billion*: Alexander Osipovich, "This Vegan Billionaire Disrupted the Crypto Markets. Stocks May Be Next," *Wall Street Journal*, April 16, 2021, https://www.wsj.com/articles/this-vegan-billionaire-disrupted -the-crypto-markets-stocks-may-be-next-11618565408.

139   *Bitcoin hit a record*: @Bitcoin, "After the Strong Q3 Performance #Bitcoin Is Now Up +49.1% Year-to-Date," Twitter post, October 4, 2021, 6:34 p.m., https://twitter.com/Bitcoin/status/1445155518608142336.

139   *$420 million in capital*: Alexander Osipovich, "Crypto Exchange FTX Reaches $25 Billion Valuation," *Wall Street Journal*, October 21, 2021, https://www.wsj.com/articles/crypto-exchange-ftx-reaches-25-billion -valuation-11634817601.

140 *"The decision criteria"*: Christine Chew, interview with Andrew R. Chow, April 10, 2023.

140 *This was ironic*: Alex Pack, interview with Andrew R. Chow, May 21, 2023.

140 *Before 2021, FTX*: "End of Year 2021," FTX Blog, January 18, 2021, accessed November 9, 2022, https://web.archive.org/web/20220220093638/https:/blog.ftx.com/blog/end-of-year-2021.

140 *"If a crypto company"*: Zack Guzman, "FTX CEO: 'The biggest mistake I made' in crypto 'is not getting involved sooner,'" *Yahoo Finance*, November 9, 2021, https://news.yahoo.com/ftx-ceo-biggest-mistake-made-201555327.html.

141 *FTX embarked on*: Hanks, "Miami Heat to Play in FTX Arena."

141 *American Airlines had posted*: Leslie Josephs, "American and Southwest Report Stronger Bookings, Ramp Up Schedules Ahead of Summer," CNBC, April 22, 2021, https://www.cnbc.com/2021/04/22/southwest-airlines-luv-and-american-airlines-aal.html.

141 *At the Heat's season opener*: @FTX_Official, "Catching up with @SBF_FTX during the Miami HEAT Opening Night, courtside with @WillManso of @BallyHEAT," Twitter post, October 22, 2021, 12:34 p.m. https://twitter.com/FTX_Official/status/1451587835690197027.

141 *This was just the beginning*: Suzanne Vranica, "FTX's Unraveling Is Latest Blow to Softening Ad Market," *Wall Street Journal*, November 17, 2022, https://www.wsj.com/articles/ftxs-unraveling-is-latest-blow-to-softening-ad-market-11668681001.

141 *On the opening night of the NFL*: Amy Houston, "Ad of the Day: Tom Brady and Gisele Bundchen tease NFL rivalries in cryptocurrency ad," *The Drum*, September 9, 2021, https://www.thedrum.com/news/2021/09/09/ad-the-day-tom-brady-and-gisele-bundchen-tease-nfl-rivalries-cryptocurrency-ad.

141 *The Commodity Futures Trading Commission*: CFTC v. Sam Bankman-Fried et al., Case No. 1:22-cv-10503-PKC, filed December 21, 2022.

142 *FTX's relentless marketing campaign*: Erika Wheless, "Inside Crypto Exchange FTX's Push to Become a Household Name," *Ad Age*, December 13, 2021, https://web.archive.org/web/20220209185501/https://adage.com/article/special-report-marketers-year/ad-age-2021-best-marketers-ftx/2383226.

142 *"The normal human brain"*: Liam Vries, interview with Andrew R. Chow, December 6, 2022.

142 *"That's when he really"*: Natalie Tien, interview with Andrew R. Chow, October 23, 2023.

143 *Caroline Ellison similarly testified*: U.S. v. Bankman-Fried, testimony from Caroline Ellison, October 11, 2023.

143 *"The moral of the story"*: Sam Bankman-Fried (@SBF_FTX), Twitter post, October 15, 2021, 7:03 a.m., https://twitter.com/SBF_FTX/status/1448967781601484800.

143   *On November 4, he published*: Sam Bankman-Fried (@SBF_FTX), Twitter post, November 4, 2021, 2:26 p.m., https://twitter.com/SBF_FTX/status /1456327112592445440.

143   *he estimated his odds*: Wiblin and Harris, "Sam Bankman-Fried on Taking a High Risk Approach," 15:00.

144   *Sam himself secretly funded*: Btccasey, "Crypto News Outlet The Block Was Secretly Funded by Alameda Research," *Bitcoin Magazine*, December 9, 2022, https://bitcoinmagazine.com/business/the-block-secretly-funded-by-sbf -alameda.

144   *He was a "capitalist monk"*: Faux, "A 30-Year-Old Crypto Billionaire."

144   *His family foundation sent grants*: Shawn McCreesh, "Why Didn't More Reporters See This Coming? How SBF Sweet-Talked the Media," *New York*, November 19, 2022, https://nymag.com/intelligencer/2022/11/how-sbf -sweet-talked-the-media.html.

145   *While Sam was giving away*: Ehrlich, "Meet the World's Richest 29-Year -Old."

145   *Sam defended himself by claiming*: Guzman, "FTX CEO: 'The biggest mis- take I made.'"

145   *The rest of his billions*: Ehrlich, "Meet the World's Richest 29-Year-Old."

145   *So in August 2021, he stepped*: Sam Bankman-Fried (@SBF_FTX), "1) Long overdue, and bringing titles in line with what reality has been for a while: Congratulations to some of the most impressive people I know, @AlamedaTrabucco and @carolinecapital, the CEOs of @Alameda Research," Twitter post, August 3, 2021, 1:03 a.m., https://twitter.com /SBF_FTX/status/1422422964557942786.

145   *"SBF did try to tell"*: Interview with anonymous source.

145   *Sam instructed Alameda*: U.S. v. Bankman-Fried, testimony from Caroline Ellison, October 10, 2023.

146   *By late 2021, Alameda had borrowed*: Ibid.

146   *And he thought*: U.S. v. Bankman-Fried, testimony from Sam Bankman-Fried, October 27, 2023.

146   *When Caroline tallied up*: U.S. v. Bankman-Fried, government exhibit 36, "NAV Minus Sam Coins," presented October 10, 2023.

146   *"It was the only available"*: U.S. v. Bankman-Fried, testimony from Sam Bankman-Fried, October 27, 2023.

146   *He proceeded to*: Sheldon Reback and Brandy Betz, "Crypto Exchange FTX Establishes $2B Fund to Invest in Crypto Startups," *CoinDesk*, January 14, 2022, https://www.coindesk.com/business/2022/01/14/crypto-exchange -ftx-establishes-2b-fund-to-invest-in-crypto-startups-report/.

146   *Sam preferred that*: U.S. v. Bankman-Fried, testimony from Caroline Ellison, October 10, 2023.

CHAPTER 19

149   *Pro-democracy protests*: Amy Hawkins, "Hong Kong: Over-the-Top Punishment for 2019 Democracy Protesters, Report Finds," *Guardian*, October 31, 2023, https://www.theguardian.com/world/2023/nov/01/hong-kong-over-the-top-punishment-for-2019-democracy-protesters-report-finds.

149   *Western companies that had*: Allison Morrow, "Nearly Half of Foreign Businesses in Hong Kong Are Planning to Relocate," CNN, March 24, 2022, https://www.cnn.com/2022/03/24/business/hong-kong-expats-covid-restrictions/index.html.

149   *The Chinese government, in the process*: Alun John, Samuel Shen, and Tom Wilson, "China's Top Regulators Ban Crypto Trading and Mining, Sending Bitcoin Tumbling," Reuters, September 24, 2021, https://www.reuters.com/world/china/china-central-bank-vows-crackdown-cryptocurrency-trading-2021-09-24/.

149   *China had hosted around 75 percent*: Charlie Campbell, "Why China Is Cracking Down on Bitcoin Mining and What It Could Mean for Other Countries," *Time*, June 2, 2021, https://time.com/6051991/why-china-is-cracking-down-on-bitcoin-mining-and-what-it-could-mean-for-other-countries/.

150   *But in May 2021, China*: Arjun Kharpal, "China's Renewed Crypto Crackdown Wipes $400 Billion off the Market as Bitcoin Slides," CNBC, June 22, 2023, https://www.cnbc.com/2021/06/22/china-crypto-crackdown-wipes-nearly-300-billion-off-market-btc-slides.html.

150   *In August, in the face of pressure*: Scott Chipolina, "Binance Restricts Derivatives Products in Hong Kong 'With Immediate Effect,'" *Decrypt*, August 6, 2021, https://decrypt.co/77857/binance-restricts-derivatives-products-hong-kong-with-immediate-effect.

150   *(The U.S. Department of Justice would)*: U.S. Department of Justice, "Justice Department Announces Eight Indictments Against China-Based Chemical Manufacturing Companies and Employees," October 3, 2023, https://www.justice.gov/opa/pr/justice-department-announces-eight-indictments-against-china-based-chemical-manufacturing.

150   *Finally, an Alameda employee named*: U.S. v. Bankman-Fried, government exhibit 64, written by Caroline Ellison, November 2021.

151   *After the DARE Act passed*: Tim Craig, Drew Harwell, and Nitasha Tiku, "FTX's Bahamas Crypto Empire: Stimulants, Subterfuge and a Spectacular Collapse," *Washington Post*, November 24, 2022, https://www.washingtonpost.com/technology/2022/11/24/ftx-bahamas-albany-fried/.

151   *"That was really"*: Christine Chew, interview with Andrew R. Chow, April 24, 2023.

151   *His face mask sagged*: Office of the Prime Minister—The Bahamas, "FTX

Digital Markets Opening," October 8, 2021, video, https://www.facebook.com/watch/?v=842237263156293.

151   *Memes were created*: @MonkDoesnt, "I'm An Island Boy (ft. @SBF_FTX)," Twitter post, October 31, 2021, 6:20 p.m., https://twitter.com/Monk Doesnt/status/1454936438399700992.

151   *When Sam changed*: Tyler Gordon (@Rxnin), Twitter post, October 6, 2021, 11:43 p.m., Twitter post, https://twitter.com/Rxnin/status/1445957 840053669888.

151   *"Everyone was like"*: Michael Armogan, interview with Andrew R. Chow, February 27, 2023.

152   *"Couldn't sleep"*: Sam Bankman-Fried (@SBF_FTX), Twitter post, October 16, 2021, 6:44 a.m., https://twitter.com/SBF_FTX/status/14493253 27357026304?lang=en.

152   *Bitcoin hit its all-time high*: Lyllah Ledesma, "Crypto Market Cap Surges to Record $2.7T," *CoinDesk*, October 21, 2021, https://www.coindesk.com /markets/2021/10/21/crypto-market-cap-surges-to-new-record-27 -trillion/.

152   *Over the course of 2021, $44 billion*: Chainalysis Team, "Crime and NFTs: Chainalysis Detects Significant Wash Trading and Some NFT Money Laundering In this Emerging Asset Class," *Chainalysis*, February 2, 2022, https: //www.chainalysis.com/blog/2022-crypto-crime-report-preview-nft-wash -trading-money-laundering/.

152   *Collins Dictionary named*: Jack Guy, "'NFT' is Collins Dictionary's Word of the Year for 2021, Beating Out 'Crypto' and 'Cheugy,'" CNN, November 24, 2021, https://www.cnn.com/style/article/nft-word-of-the-year-collins -scli-intl-gbr/index.html.

153   *Within a week, about eighteen thousand*: Nilay Patel, "From a Meme to $47 Million: ConstitutionDAO, Crypto, and the Future of Crowdfunding," *The Verge*, December 7, 2021, https://www.theverge.com/22820563 /constitution-meme-47-million-crypto-crowdfunding-blockchain-ethereum -constitution.

153   *Sure enough, ConstitutionDAO lost*: Kelly Crow, "Ken Griffin on Why He Spent $43 Million to Buy the U.S. Constitution," *Wall Street Journal*, August 9, 2022, https://www.wsj.com/articles/ken-griffin-constitution-museum-1166 0068328.

153   *When the hedge fund Melvin Capital*: Theron Mohamed, "The Firms of Billionaire Investors Steve Cohen and Ken Griffin Pour $2.8 Billion into a GameStop Short-Seller That's Lost 30% This Year," *Business Insider*, January 26, 2021, https://markets.businessinsider.com/news/stocks/steve-cohen -ken-griffin-invest-3-billion-gamestop-short-seller-2021-1-1030003305.

153   *A December 2021 study by professors*: Paul Vigna, "Bitcoin's 'One Percent' Controls Lion's Share of the Cryptocurrency's Wealth," *Wall Street Journal*,

December 20, 2021, https://www.wsj.com/articles/bitcoins-one-percent
-controls-lions-share-of-the-cryptocurrencys-wealth-11639996204.

153 *"2021 is the story"*: Interview with anonymous source.

154 *"Fortune favors the brave"*: Matt Damon, "Fortune Favors the Brave," *The Hall of Advertising*, April 1, 2022, YouTube video, https://www.youtube.com /watch?v=dHv2FBMtlUc.

154 *"The craziest stuff"*: Harper Reed, interview with Andrew R. Chow, November 14, 2023.

154 *But by the fall*: Ibid.

155 *"Su Zhu and"*: Chew, interview, October 13, 2023.

156 *Beck, after the fall*: Anthony Bianco, *Rainmaker: The Saga of Jeff Beck, Wall Street's Mad Dog* (New York: Random House, 1991), 461.

156 *But pesky regulations*: Tanzeel Akhtar, "FTX.US Aiming to Offer Crypto Derivatives Trading in Less Than a Year: Report," *CoinDesk*, August 12, 2021, https://www.coindesk.com/markets/2021/08/12/ftxus-aiming-to-offer -crypto-derivatives-trading-in-less-than-a-year-report/.

156 *He had barely spent*: Scott Melker, "FTX Will Change Finance Forever," on *Wolf of All Streets*, podcast, March 1, 2022, 28:25, https://podcasts.apple .com/us/podcast/ftx-will-change-finance-forever-brett-harrison-president /id1500066831?i=1000552570210.

157 *"Crypto is the ultimate"*: Dana Sanchez, "FTX and the Crypto Industry Set Up Base in Bahamas: 5 Things We Know So Far," *Moguldum Nation*, April 8, 2022, https://moguldom.com/402597/ftx-and-the-crypto-industry-set-up -base-in-bahamas-5-things-we-know-so-far/.

157 *"Given the opportunity to make"*: Matthew Walsh and Nic Carter, "Crypto Market Structure with Brett Harrison," on *On the Brink with Castle Island*, podcast, March 17, 2022, 23:24, https://onthebrink-podcast.com/ftxus/.

157 *There were no senior executives*: FTX bankruptcy filings, document 1242, filed April 9, 2023, page 6.

158 *The exchange earned revenues*: U.S. v. Bankman-Fried, testimony from Sam Bankman-Fried, October 27, 2023.

158 *Sam then signed his name*: U.S. v. Bankman-Fried, government exhibit 323, "Rewards Agent Agreement," presented October 16, 2023.

158 *It was at this point*: U.S. v. Bankman-Fried, testimony from Nishad Singh, October 17, 2023.

159 *At the end of the year, Alameda's*: U.S. v. Bankman-Fried, government exhibit 1002, "Balance of Alameda Research Accounts on FTX.com with "allow _negative" Enabled," presented October 18, 2023.

CHAPTER 20

161   *Olufemi Akola, a Lagos-based*: FTX Africa (@FTXAfrica), Twitter post, December 15, 2021, 11:17 p.m., https://twitter.com/FTX_Africa /status/1471152386207064076

161   *"There is no better time"*: Olufemi Akola (@_JustFEMI), Twitter post, December 31, 2021, 5:18, https://twitter.com/_JustFEMI/status/1476860 232206848001.

161   *At another event*: FTX Africa (@FTX_Africa), "Vincent van Gogh Who? #FTXAfricaNFTParty," Twitter video, December 13, 2021, 4:12 a.m., https://twitter.com/FTX_Africa/status/1470320771788587008.

161   *"He's a force to be reckoned"*: Yoruba Demons (@YorubaDemonsNFT), Twitter post, December 28, 2021, 11:51 a.m., https://twitter.com/Yoruba DemonNFTs/status/1475872090758828038.

162   *"I think it's going to happen"*: Adaora Nwangwu, "Interview: Owo Anietie Talks Art, Creating AfroDroids and His NFT Journey," *Culture Custodian*, March 1, 2022, https://culturecustodian.com/interview-owo-anietie-talks -art-creating-afrodroids-and-his-nft-journey/.

162   *Before AfroDroids, founder*: @dreamcatchersda, Instagram caption, January 26, 2022, https://www.instagram.com/p/CZMkWlNKxNo/?hl=en.

162   *This was the first free*: Dream Catchers Academy, "Commissioning of Dream Catchers Academy," YouTube video, March 24, 2022, 14:00, https://www .youtube.com/watch?v=hEY60VNAOLc.

162   *Oluyole, in a tearful*: Patrick Okohue, "Excitement as Dream Catchers Academy Opens First Free Art School for Girls in Ikorodu," *New Telegraph Nigeria*, April 1, 2022, https://newtelegraphng.com/excitement-as-dream -catchers-academy-opens-first-free-art-school-for-girls-in-ikorodu/.

163   *"I've seen the girls"*: "Take a First Look at the First Formal and Arts Education School in West Africa," Dream Catchers Academy, YouTube Video, April 14, 2022, https://www.youtube.com/watch?v=C8KuawJsUo0&t=351s.

163   *"[Owo] did do the school"*: CLXRB, Discord message, AfroDroids server, January 19, 2023, 4:27 a.m.

163   *"At that time"*: CryptoWizard, interview with Andrew R. Chow, April 21, 2023.

164   *An estimated 60 million Nigerians*: "Nigeria: Ensuring Water, Sanitation and Hygiene for All," World Bank, May 26, 2021, https://www.worldbank.org /en/news/feature/2021/05/26/nigeria-ensuring-water-sanitation-and -hygiene-for-all.

164   *In 2021 UNICEF determined*: Maryanne Buechner, *Lack of Safe Water Far Deadlier Than Violence*, Unicef, June 28, 2021, https://www.unicefusa.org /stories/unicef-report-lack-safe-water-far-deadlier-violence.

164   *After Otu posted the photos*: Ruona Meyer, "Mayor Otu," on *Waterless*, produced by the Center for Collaborative Investigative Journalism, podcast, July

29, 2020, https://open.spotify.com/episode/6ir6Q5VQgLKCffDHnEx3Zc?si=ded4f0e642df4f8e.

165 *"Instead of begging"*: Mayor Otu, interview with Andrew R. Chow, May 25, 2023.

165 *The introductory paper*: Albert Polanco and Renato Munoz Osses, "The Meta Water Project—Using NFT's to Fund a Vital Public Good Litepaper," accessed June 18, 2023, https://web.archive.org/web/20220405180850/https://www.metawaterproject.io/litepaper.

165 *"It was tiring"*: Mayor Otu, interview with Andrew R. Chow, May 25, 2023.

166 *In early 2022, the NFT space*: Brian Quarmby, "Monthly NFT Buyers Dip Below 800K as Searches 'Fall Off a Cliff,'" *Cointelegraph*, March 3, 2022, https://cointelegraph.com/news/monthly-nft-buyers-dip-below-800k-as-searches-fall-off-a-cliff.

166 *the owner of the CryptoPunks*: @0x650d, Twitter post, February 23, 2022, 8:50 p.m., https://twitter.com/0x650d/status/1496663918927925253.

CHAPTER 21

169 *The price of Ethereum was double*: Ryan Browne, "Investors Fear 'Crypto Winter' Is Coming as Bitcoin Falls 50% from Record Highs," CNBC, January 25, 2022, https://www.cnbc.com/2022/01/25/crypto-winter-investors-fear-bitcoin-has-further-to-drop.html.

169 *FTX had just been*: Ryan Browne, "Cryptocurrency Exchange FTX Hits $32 Billion Valuation Despite Bear Market Fears," CNBC, January 31, 2022, https://www.cnbc.com/2022/01/31/crypto-exchange-ftx-valued-at-32-billion-amid-bitcoin-price-plunge.html.

169 *Sam had just testified confidently*: Sam Bankman-Fried, "Examining Digital Assets—Risks, Regulation, and Innovation," Hearing Before the U.S. Senate Committee on Agriculture, Nutrition and Forestry, February 9, 2022, https://www.agriculture.senate.gov/imo/media/doc/Testimony_Bankman-Fried_0209202211.pdf.

169 *"I'm offended you have"*: "Senate Hearing on Regulating Cryptocurrency Markets," February 9, 2022, https://www.c-span.org/video/?517737-1/senate-hearing-regulating-cryptocurrency-markets.

170 *a trillion-dollar ecosystem*: Josh Stark and Evan Van Ness, "The Year in Ethereum 2021," January 17, 2022, https://stark.mirror.xyz/q3OnsK7mvfGtTQ72nfoxLyEV5lfYOqUfJIoKBx7BG1I.

171 *"The good news"*: @VitalikButerin, Twitter post, September 1, 2021, 6:49 p.m., https://twitter.com/VitalikButerin/status/1433200468646252545.

172 *Vitalik compared Sam's*: Jose Antonio Lanz and Mat Di Salvo, "Vitalik Buterin Lays Into Sam Bankman-Fried and FTX," *Decrypt*, 11/11/22, https://decrypt.co/114244/vitalik-buterin-ftx-collapse-sam-bankman-fried.

172 *My interview with him*: Andrew R. Chow, "The Man Behind Ethereum

Is Worried About Crypto's Future," *Time*, March 18, 2022, https://time.com/6158182/vitalik-buterin-ethereum-profile/.

172 *In 2008, before he conceived*: Russo, *The Infinite Machine*, 34.

172 *His blog posts increasingly*: Vitalik Buterin and Glen Weyl, "Central Planning as Overfitting," blog post, November 25, 2018, https://vitalik.eth.limo/general/2018/11/25/central_planning.html.

174 *A 2022 study showed*: Chainalysis, "Dissecting the DAO: Web3 Ownership Is Surprisingly Concentrated," July 27, 2022, https://www.chainalysis.com/blog/web3-daos-2022/.

174 *But the rollout had been riddled*: Ciara Nugent, "El Salvador Is Betting on Bitcoin to Rebrand the Country—and Strengthen the President's Grip," *Time*, October 1, 2021, https://time.com/6103299/bitcoin-el-salvador-nayib-bukele/.

174 *But in reality, DeFi was*: "DeFi Statistics," Nansen, December 29, 2022, https://www.nansen.ai/guides/defi-statistics-in-202.

175 *Proof of Humanity had*: Andrew R. Chow, "How Blockchain Could Solve the Problem of Digital Identity," *Time*, January 27, 2023, https://time.com/6142810/proof-of-humanity/.

175 *"Why does legacy media"*: Jeff John Roberts (@jeffjohnroberts), Twitter post, March 18, 2022, 12:19 p.m., https://twitter.com/jeffjohnroberts/status/1504854958356713473.

176 *"How is it possible"*: Vitalik Buterin (@VitalikButerin), "The quote tweets on the new time article about me are truly amazing," Twitter post, March 18, 2022, 7:04 p.m., https://twitter.com/VitalikButerin/status/1504957024345501709.

176 *That month, Sam partnered with Stocktwits*: Paul Vigna, "Social-Media Platform Stocktwits Takes Cue from Brokerages, Adds Crypto Trading," *Wall Street Journal*, February 3, 2022, https://www.wsj.com/articles/social-media-platform-stocktwits-takes-cue-from-brokerages-adds-crypto-trading-11643889603?mod=e2tw.

176 *The ad, which netted David*: Lewis, *Going Infinite*, 16.

176 *He watched the Super Bowl*: David Yaffe-Bellany and Erin Griffith, "The Super Connector Who Built Sam Bankman-Fried's Celebrity World," *New York Times*, June 23, 2023, https://www.nytimes.com/2023/06/23/technology/sam-bankman-fried-celebrity-friends.html.

176 *Sam raved in a note*: U.S. v. Bankman-Fried, government exhibit 42, published October 16, 2023.

176 *"That crew was blatantly grifters"*: Interview with anonymous source.

177 *The day after Kives's dinner*: @katyperry, Instagram post, February 12, 2022, https://www.instagram.com/p/CZ5Qw2-vVoW/?hl=en.

177 *"All of the excitement"*: FTX advertisement, *Time*, print issue, March 28, 2022.

CHAPTER 22

179 *"FTX just wanted"*: Christine Chew, interview with Andrew R. Chow, April 24, 2023.

179 *There was Illia*: Amy Wu (@amytongwu), Twitter post, February 19, 2022, 2:58 a.m., https://twitter.com/amytongwu/status/1494944340304609284.

180 *But Sam was also directly*: U.S. v. Bankman-Fried, government exhibit 14B, presented October 16, 2023.

180 *"At the time, partnering"*: Illia Polosukhin, interview with Andrew R. Chow, May 23, 2023.

180 *"She was really sad"*: Chew, interview, April 24, 2023.

180 *Another FTX employee says that while Amy*: Interview with anonymous source.

CHAPTER 23

181 *The summer before, she*: Kevin Rose, "Gaming NFTs and DeFi vs CeFi with Amy Wu," on *Modern Finance*, podcast, August 3, 2021, 34:20, https://modern.finance/episode/the-origins-and-future-of-aave-the-decentralized-finance-protocol-to-lend-and-borrow-crypto-copy/.

181 *"After spending more time in"*: Amy Wu (@amytongwu), Twitter post, July 14, 2021, 1:44 a.m., https://twitter.com/amytongwu/status/1415185305196326918.

181 *In December 2021, Super Typhoon*: Stuti Mishra, "From Odette to Mawar: The Most Powerful Typhoons to Hit the Philippines," *Independent*, May 26, 2023, https://www.independent.co.uk/climate-change/news/typhoon-odette-vs-typhoon-mawar-philippines-b2346276.html.

181 *Several Axie guilds sprang into*: "#OdettePH Funds Allocation," YGG Pilipinas, spreadsheet, December 17, 2021, https://docs.google.com/spreadsheets/d/1XYOJ7fM19USgwvswqMabPsQqqoNhI5J5kHu3Nwo6kU0/edit?usp=sharing.

181 *"We think games can onboard"*: Ben Strack and Macauley Peterson, "FTX Launches $2B Venture Fund," *Blockworks*, January 14, 2022, https://blockworks.co/news/ftx-launches-2b-venture-fund.

181 *But a month after that, Axie*: CoinMarketCap, SLP, accessed July 25, 2023, https://coinmarketcap.com/currencies/smooth-love-potion/.

182 *"All scholars are just"*: Ian Tan, interview with Andrew R. Chow, August 17, 2023.

182 *"At first I was happy"*: Chow and de Guzman, "A Crypto Game."

182 *"I see a lot of sad"*: Khai Chun Thee, interview with Andrew R. Chow, December 5, 2023.

182 *"Many people would spend two"*: Jeremy Ng, interview with Andrew R. Chow, October 18, 2023.

183 *"Thee hoped a well-financed Cup would"*: Thee, interview, December 5, 2023.

183 *"We were having meetings"*: Ng, interview, October 18, 2023.

183 *"When Axie was up high"*: Sonia Amadi, interview with Andrew R. Chow, September 1, 2023.

184 *Pegaxy, Crabada, StepN*: U.S. v. Bankman-Fried, government exhibit 49A, presented October 10, 2023.

184 *"A lot of the games that"*: Thee, interview, December 5, 2023.

184 *The game was hacked for $624 million*: Adi Robertson and Corin Faife, "A Hacker Stole $625 Million from the Blockchain Behind NFT Game Axie Infinity," *The Verge*, March 29, 2022, https://www.theverge .com/2022/3/29/23001620/sky-mavis-axie-infinity-ronin-blockchain -validation-defi-hack-nft.

184 *While blockchains are supposed to*: Benjamin Pimentel, "Hackers Stole Nearly $650 Million from the Axie Infinity NFT Game," *Protocol*, March 29, 2022, https://www.protocol.com/bulletins/axie-infinity-ronin-hack.

184 *The U.S. Treasury Department accused*: U.S. Department of the Treasury, "Treasury Sanctions North Korean State-Sponsored Malicious Cyber Groups," September 13, 2019, https://home.treasury.gov/news/press-releases /sm774.

184 *"The world has yet"*: Amy Wu, "Inside the Crypto VC Boom," Crypto Bahamas, June 20, 2022, YouTube video, 3:30, https://www.youtube.com/watch? v=uuHACHCT0OI.

CHAPTER 24

185 New York *magazine*: Wallace, "The Mysterious Cryptocurrency Magnate."

185 *"I had a mini panic"*: Milo Beckman, interview with Andrew R. Chow, June 22, 2023.

186 *At this point, around $15 billion*: Sam Bankman-Fried, "Testimony of Sam Bankman-Fried, Digital Assets and the Future of Finance: Understanding the Challenges and Benefits of Financial Innovation in the United States," U.S. House of Representatives, Committee on Financial Services, December 8, 2021, 10 a.m., https://democrats-financialservices.house.gov/uploadedfiles /hhrg-117-ba00-wstate-bankman-frieds-20211208.pdf.

186 *"You saw a number of bilateral"*: "Crypto CEOs Testify Before House Financial Services Hearing Transcript," December 8, 2021, https://www.rev.com /blog/transcripts/crypto-ceos-testify-before-house-financial-services -hearing-transcript.

187 *FTX calculated its traders'*: Sam Bankman-Fried, "Changing Market Roles: The FTX Proposal and Trends in New Clearinghouse Models," Hearing Before the U.S. House Committee on Agriculture, May 12, 2022, https: //docs.house.gov/meetings/AG/AG00/20220512/114729/HHRG-117 -AG00-Wstate-Bankman-FriedS-20220512.pdf.

187 *He added that if too many*: Sam Bankman-Fried, "Examining Digital Assets—Risks, Regulation, and Innovation."

187 *"There were a lot of stars"*: Devina Khanna, interview with Andrew R. Chow, July 11, 2023.

188 *While the FTX website stated*: U.S. v. Bankman-Fried, testimony from Gary Wang, October 6, 2023.

188 *In 2011, the FBI explicitly*: U.S. Attorney's Office, Western District of North Carolina, "Defendant Convicted of Minting His Own Currency," March 18, 2011, https://archives.fbi.gov/archives/charlotte/press-releases/2011/defendant-convicted-of-minting-his-own-currency.

189 *"They know their shit"*: Sam Bankman-Fried (@SBF_FTX), Twitter post, May 25, 2022, 4:11 p.m., https://twitter.com/SBF_FTX/status/1529555721481818116.

189 *It had one-third of the budget*: Timi Iwayemi and Dylan Gyauch-Lewis, "Don't Fall for FTX's Final Con," Revolving Door Project, November 23, 2022, https://therevolvingdoorproject.org/dont-fall-for-ftxs-final-con/.

189 *SEC chair Gary Gensler had*: Tory Newmyer, "Gary Gensler Sharpens Criticism of Cryptocurrency in Senate Hearing," *Washington Post*, November 14, 2021, https://www.washingtonpost.com/business/2021/09/14/gensler-sec-crypto-crackdown/.

189 *"To put the CFTC"*: Timi Iwayemi, interview with Andrew R. Chow, May 24, 2023.

190 *Sam pushed the bill so*: Cheyenne Ligon, "The 'SBF Bill': What's in the Crypto Legislation Backed by FTX's Founder," *CoinDesk*, November 15, 2022, https://www.coindesk.com/policy/2022/11/15/the-sbf-bill-whats-in-the-crypto-legislation-backed-by-ftx-founder/.

190 *"In the land of the blind"*: Rohan Grey, interview with Andrew R. Chow, March 30, 2023.

191 *"Many of the policy groups"*: Khanna, interview, July 11, 2023.

191 *He described this policy*: Melker, "FTX Will Change Finance Forever," 5:05.

192 *Vitalik Buterin even suggested*: Vitalik Buterin, "Ethereum White Paper."

192 *In 2003, Warren Buffett*: Warren Buffett, "Berkshire's Corporate Performance vs. the S&P 500," February 21, 2003, https://www.berkshirehathaway.com/letters/2002pdf.pdf.

192 *In 2008, the downfall of Lehman*: Blinder, *After the Music Stopped*, 121.

192 *"Instruments that are originally"*: Ibid., 66.

193 *The FTX team was aggressively courting*: Gabe Kaminsky, "Sam Bankman-Fried Told Crypto Regulator FTX Was 'Natural Choice' to Be 'Umpires' of Industry, Emails Show," *Washington Examiner*, December 16, 2022, https://www.washingtonexaminer.com/news/disgraced-sam-bankman-fried-told-crypto-regulator-ftx-choice-to-be-umpires-of-industry.

193 *"I'm not sure why"*: Ibid.

193 *One skeptical futures brokerage*: Jesse Hamilton, "FTX's Bankman-Fried

Pitches CFTC on Directly Clearing Customers' Crypto Swaps," *Coin-Desk*, May 25, 2022, https://www.coindesk.com/policy/2022/05/25/ftxs -bankman-fried-pitches-cftc-on-directly-clearing-customers-crypto-swaps/.

193 *"Most of the traders"*: @aguye_, Twitter video, May 25, 2022, 3:37 p.m., https://twitter.com/aguye_/status/1529547230318718976.

193 *In 2021 and 2022, Sam met*: Dave Michaels, "Sam Bankman-Fried Met with Top CFTC Officials 10 Times, Agency Chairman Says," *Wall Street Journal*, December 1, 2022, https://www.wsj.com/livecoverage/stock-market-news -today-12-01-2022/card/sam-bankman-fried-met-with-top-cftc-officials -10-times-agency-chairman-says-Q9KqZUGcE8aI75wjeZ92.

193 *In March 2022, the SEC*: U.S. Securities and Exchange Commission, "SEC Division of Examinations Announces 2022 Examination Priorities," March 30, 2022, https://www.sec.gov/news/press-release/2022-57.

194 *In the coming months, five*: David Dayen, "Congressmembers Tried to Stop the SEC's Inquiry into FTX," *American Prospect*, November 23, 2022, https://prospect.org/power/congressmembers-tried-to-stop-secs-inquiry-into -ftx/.

194 *Budd alone received*: "American Dream Federal Action Independent Expenditures," Open Secrets, accessed November 15, 2023, https://www.open secrets.org/political-action-committees-pacs/american-dream-federal -action/C00809020/independent-expenditures/2022.

194 *"I indicated to them"*: Ankush Khardori, "Can Gary Gensler Survive Crypto Winter?," *New York*, February 23, 2023, https://nymag.com/intelligencer /2023/02/gary-gensler-on-meeting-with-sbf-and-his-crypto-crackdown .html.

CHAPTER 25

195 *Gabe had lived in Washington*: Theodore Schleifer, "The Brothers Bankman-Fried," *Puck*, January 31, 2023, https://puck.news/the-brothers-bankman -fried/.

195 *Sam quickly funneled $27 million*: Ben Terris, *The Big Break* (New York: Twelve, 2023), 116.

195 *"He thought it was very"*: U.S. v. Bankman-Fried, testimony from Caroline Ellison, October 10, 2023.

195 *Their mother, Barbara Fried*: Theodore Schleifer, "S.B.F. Mama Drama," *Puck*, January 24, 2023, https://puck.news/s-b-f-mama-drama/.

196 *"I'm assuming Nishad would"*: FTX bankruptcy filings, document 2642, filed September 18, 2023.

196 *Sam agreed to front the money*: Complaint, FTX debtors v. Allan Joseph Bankman and Barbara Fried, 34.

196 *Gabe also found a willing*: Terris, *The Big Break*, 2.

196 *Together, they held court*: Ibid., 157.

196   *"It was still a:"* Rohan Grey, interview with Andrew R. Chow, March 30, 2023.

196   *Sam rewarded him with a cool*: Ben Mathis-Lilley, "A Crypto Billion-aire Shattered the Primary Spending Record to Back a Candidate Who Is Getting Clobbered," *Slate*, May 18, 2022, https://slate.com/news-and-politics/2022/05/sam-bankman-fried-cryptocurrency-carrick-flynn-loss.html.

197   *"One, it was an announcement"*: Timi Iwayemi, interview with Andrew R. Chow, May 24, 2023.

197   *Allam declared that she would*: Nida Allam (@nidaallam), Twitter post, December 31, 2021, 11:58 a.m., https://twitter.com/NidaAllam/status/14769 60934493044740.

197   *By March, she had rallied*: Jeffrey Billman, "Buying a Blue Seat," *The Assembly*, May 10, 2022, https://www.theassemblync.com/politics/elections/buying-a-blue-seat-4th-district/.

198   *AIPAC's contributions*: Lena Geller, "Who Will Be the Successor in NC's Bluest Congressional District?" *Indy Week*, April 27, 2022, https://indy week.com/news/elections-news/nc-4th-congressional-district-democratic-primary-2022/.

198   *"If you really cared"*: Nida Allam, interview with Andrew R. Chow, May 30, 2023.

199   *The Foushee-Allam race*: Max Berger, "SBF and the Injustice Democrats," Substack, January 3, 2023, https://maxberger.substack.com/p/sbf-and-the-injustice-democrats.

199   *Sam ended the 2022 election*: "Who Are the Biggest Donors," Open Secrets, accessed December 28, 2023, https://www.opensecrets.org/elections-over view/biggest-donors?cycle=2022.

200   *At more local levels*: Daniel Strauss, "Inside Sam Bankman-Fried's Long, Long, Long Money Trail," *New Republic*, November 23, 2022, https://newrepublic.com/article/169104/sam-bankman-fried-ftx-political-donations-democrats-republicans-congress.

200   *Over the prior decade, prominent Democrats*: Jenna Wortham, "Obama Brought Silicon Valley to Washington," *New York Times*, October 25, 2016, https://www.nytimes.com/2016/10/30/magazine/barack-obama-brought-silicon-valley-to-washington-is-that-a-good-thing.html.

200   *He was the perfect poison*: Grey, interview, March 30, 2023.

200   *Leaders of Sam's*: Bryan Metzger, "A Crypto-Funded Super PAC Poured More Than $24 Million into This Year's Democratic Primaries and Became a Top Outside Spender. Now, It's Going Dark," *Business Insider*, August 30, 2022, https://www.businessinsider.com/bankman-fried-brothers-protect-our-future-pandemic-prevention-pac-crypto-2022-8.

200   *"Sam wants to donate to both"*: U.S. v. Bankman-Fried, government exhibit 505, November 2, 2021, presented September 8, 2023.

201   *"Reporters freak"*: Tiffany Fong, "SBF's First Interview After FTX's Collapse,"

YouTube video, November 29, 2022, 12:58, https://www.youtube.com /watch?v=6DezodR9hNI.

201   *Sam was on the chat*: U.S. v. Bankman-Fried, government exhibit 475, presented October 26, 2023.

201   *At one point, to expedite*: U.S. v. Bankman-Fried, testimony from Nishad Singh, October 16, 2023.

201   *He flowed more than $23 million*: Tory Newmyer, "Sam Bankman-Fried's Fraud Ran Through Washington, Prosecutors Say," *Washington Post*, October 2, 2023, https://www.washingtonpost.com/business/2023/10/02 /bankman-fried-fraud-ftx-trial/.

201   *(FTX also doled out $200,000)*: Corinne Ramey and James Fanelli, "Former FTX Executive Linked to Campaign-Finance Probe of New York GOP Race," *Wall Street Journal*, July 11, 2023, https://www.wsj.com/articles /former-ftx-executive-linked-to-campaign-finance-probe-of-new-york-gop -race-c2b50252.

201   *Financial forensics experts*: U.S. v. Bankman-Fried, testimony from Peter Easton, October 18, 2023.

202   *So Sam took meetings*: Theodore Schleifer, "Inside the Fall of S.B.F.'s Big Cool Buddy," *Puck*, September 12, 2023, https://puck.news/inside-the-fall-of-s-b -f-s-big-cool-buddy/.

202   *Ultimately, a majority of the candidates*: Mohammad Ismam Huda, "Protect Our Future's Crypto Politics," Effective Altruism Forum, January 29, 2023, https://forum.effectivealtruism.org/posts/45EMKCpPesvhGxwey/protect -our-future-s-crypto-politics.

202   *More than $26 million flowed*: Allyson Versprille and Bill Allison, "Crypto Bosses Flex Political Muscle With 5,200% Surge in US Giving," *Bloomberg*, June 2, 2022, https://www.bloomberg.com/news/articles/2022-06-02/crypto -industry-eclipses-defense-big-pharma-in-political-giving.

202   *All in all, an astounding*: Jesse Hamilton, Cheyenne Ligon, Elizabeth Napolitano, "Congress' FTX Problem: 1 in 3 Members Got Cash From Crypto Exchange's Bosses," *CoinDesk*, Jan 17, 2023, https://www.coindesk.com /policy/2023/01/17/congress-ftx-problem-1-in-3-members-got-cash-from -crypto-exchanges-bosses/.

202   *that he was aiming for a $1 billion "soft ceiling"*: Alex Seitz-Wald, "Crypto billionaire says he could spend a record $1 billion in 2024 election," *NBC News*, May 24, 2022, https://www.nbcnews.com/politics/2022-election /crypto-billionaire-says-spend-record-breaking-1-billion-2024-election -rcna30351.

CHAPTER 26

203   *But The Bahamas and the*: Adam Tooze, "The Hidden History of the World's Top Offshore Cryptocurrency Tax Haven," *Foreign Policy*, January 14, 2023,

https://foreignpolicy.com/2023/01/15/the-hidden-history-of-the-worlds
-top-offshore-cryptocurrency-tourist-trap/.

203   *The Bahamian government eagerly courted*: Adam Tooze and Cameron
      Abadi, "What FTX's Collapse Tells Us About The Bahamas," *Foreign Policy,
      Ones and Tooze*, YouTube video, January 6, 2023, 14:40, https://www.youtube
      .com/watch?v=N90-hNiuRzE.

204   *According to a 1979 Ford*: Jim Drinkhall, "CIA Helped Quash Major,
      Star-Studded Tax Evasion Case," *Wall Street Journal*, April 24, 1980, https:
      //www.washingtonpost.com/archive/politics/1980/04/24/cia-helped
      -quash-major-star-studded-tax-evasion-case/a55ddf06-2a3f-4e04-a687-a3
      dd87c32b82/.

204   *A 1991 study asserted*: Bruce Bullington, "A Smugglers Paradise: Cocaine
      Trafficking Through the Bahamas," *Crime, Law and Social Change* 16 (July
      1991): 59–83, https://link.springer.com/article/10.1007/BF00389738.

204   *In the nineties, the former*: Terence O'Hara and Kathleen Day, "Riggs Bank
      Hid Assets of Pinochet, Report Says," *Washington Post*, July 15, 2004, https:
      //www.washingtonpost.com/archive/politics/2004/07/15/riggs-bank
      -hid-assets-of-pinochet-report-says/8a3ad15d-39e0-4bf1-85cd-e63fde
      d63b7d/.

204   *In recent years, The Bahamas*: "EU adds Anguilla, Bahamas, Turks and Caicos
      to Tax Blacklist," Associated Press, October 4, 2022, https://apnews.com
      /article/business-bahamas-european-union-commission-cd8de45f6036d1
      70c860c05c3f99ab28.

204   *money laundering*: Chester Robards, "Bahamas Removed from EU List
      of AML/CFT Deficient Countries," *Nassau Guardian*, January 13, 2022,
      https://www.thenassauguardian.com/business/bahamas-removed-from
      -eu-list-of-aml-cft-deficient-countries/article_514e66d9-0309-5e6d
      -96bf-f73fd6c0fb71.html.

204   *By 2022, tourism and related*: "Bahamas—Country Commercial Guide,"
      International Trade Administration, October 19, 2022, https://www.trade
      .gov/country-commercial-guides/bahamas-market-overview.

204   *the country was $9 billion*: Lewis, *Going Infinite*, xv.

204   *The country's brand-new prime minister*: Ibid., 144.

204   *The Bahamian real estate mogul Mario Carey*: "Businessman Mario Carey
      Calls FTX's Landing in The Bahamas 'the Holy Grail of Financial Services';
      Compares FTX Impact to Sol Kerzner's," *Eyewitness News*, January 11, 2022,
      https://ewnews.com/businessman-mario-carey-calls-ftxs-landing-in-the
      -bahamas-the-holy-grail-of-financial-services-compares-ftx-impact-to
      -sol-kerzners.

204   *Sure enough, FTX spent*: Alexander Saeedy and Danny Dougherty, "Here's
      How FTX Executives Secretly Spent $8 Billion in Customer Money," *Wall
      Street Journal*, October 7, 2023, https://www.wsj.com/finance/regulation
      /sbf-trial-ftx-customer-money-missing-6ba13914.

204   *FTX ads popped up*: Ken Sweet, "'The Money Is Gone': Bahamas Tries to Turn Page After FTX," Associated Press, January 8, 2023, https://apnews.com /article/cryptocurrency-technology-bahamas-caribbean-nassau-7de9 ee0db46b532b3609a26572e31853.

205   *To ingratiate himself*: Serena Williams, "Donations Fueling a New Over-the-Hill Community Center," *Bahamas Weekly*, March 14, 2022, http://www .thebahamasweekly.com/publish/community/Donations_Fueling_a_New _Over-The-Hill_Community_Center69060.shtml.

205   *"This more than Emancipation"*: Pavel Bailey, "Praise the Lord—and FTX," *Tribune*, January 25, 2022, http://www.tribune242.com/news/2022/jan/25 /praise-lord-and-ftx/.

205   *"FTX became the gold mine"*: Travis Miller, interview with Andrew R. Chow, March 3, 2023.

205   *"FTX belongs in The Bahamas"*: Nahaja Black, "FTX Digital Markets VP of Communications—Valdez Russell Joins the Show," YouTube video, January 25, 2022, 12:15, https://www.youtube.com/live/S5zeWoq2_Hg?.

205   *"My impression was"*: Ann Sofie Cloots, interview with Andrew R. Chow, June 28, 2023.

206   *In the 1930s, a prominent*: Nicolette Bethel, "Navigations: The Fluidity of Identity in the Postcolonial Bahamas," PhD dissertation, University of Cambridge, March 2000, https://www.researchgate.net/publication/2795 23709_Navigations_The_fluidity_of_identity_in_the_post-colonial _Bahamas.

206   *On an effective altruism blog forum*: Caroline Ellison, comment on "FTX EA Fellowships," Effective Altruism Forum, October 26, 2021, https://forum .effectivealtruism.org/posts/sdjcH7KAxgB328RAb/ftx-ea-fellow ships?commentId=DdKShLmRzuXpmTT4E.

CHAPTER 27

207   *In December, after months*: U.S. v. Bankman-Fried, government exhibit 3012, presented October 18, 2023.

208   *FTX chartered planes*: U.S. v. Bankman-Fried, testimony from Sam Bankman-Fried, October 30, 2023.

208   *"The lavishness"*: Christine Chew, interview with Andrew R. Chow, July 4, 2023.

208   *Nishad Singh thought the penthouse*: U.S. v. Bankman-Fried, testimony from Nishad Singh, October 16, 2023.

208   *This belief stemmed from*: Tracy Wang, "Bankman-Fried's Cabal of Roommates in the Bahamas Ran His Crypto Empire—and Dated. Other Employees Have Lots of Questions," *CoinDesk*, November 10, 2022, https://www .coindesk.com/business/2022/11/10/bankman-frieds-cabal-of-roommates

-in-the-bahamas-ran-his-crypto-empire-and-dated-other-employees-have
-lots-of-questions/.

209   *"I've come to decide"*: Andrew Court, "Sam Bankman-Fried ex Caroline Ellison
      Made 'Foray' into 'Chinese Harem' Polyamory," *New York Post*, November 17,
      2022, https://nypost.com/2022/11/17/ftx-linked-caroline-ellison-was-into
      -chinese-harem-polyamory/.

209   *Polyamory was widely practiced*: Anonymous, "Polyamory and Dating in
      the EA Community," Effective Altruism Forum, February 13, 2023, https:
      //forum.effectivealtruism.org/posts/ajdhMQEe7e8nNagiM/polyamory
      -and-dating-in-the-ea-community.

209   *Other reports would claim that*: Hannah Miller, "Genie's Wish," on *Spellcaster:
      The Fall of Sam Bankman-Fried*, produced by Wondery, podcast, June 19,
      2023, 18:38, https://wondery.com/shows/spellcaster/episode/13284-genies
      -wish/.

209   *"Every time I hung out"*: Chew, interview, April 20, 2023.

209   *stuffed with video game monitors*: Lewis, *Going Infinite*, 186.

209   *"Sam always encouraged"*: Chew, interview, April 20, 2023.

209   *FTX employees like Sam*: U.S. v. Bankman-Fried, government exhibit 3,
      presented October 18, 2023.

210   *"He doesn't believe in"*: Natalie Tien, interview with Andrew R. Chow, Octo-
      ber 23, 2023.

210   *Sleeping at work*: Lewis, *Going Infinite*, 158.

210   *"Some people got"*: Gajesh Naik, interview with Andrew R. Chow, April 22,
      2023.

211   *"We would hire"*: Christine Chew, interview with Andrew R. Chow, May 29,
      2023.

211   *Gary Wang, FTX's cofounder*: U.S. v. Bankman-Fried, testimony from Adam
      Yedidia, October 5, 2023.

211   *"Gee Sam, I don't know"*: Complaint, FTX debtors v. Allan Joseph Bankman
      and Barbara Fried, 18.

211   *"It all boils down"*: Chew, interview, May 29, 2023.

212   *"It's sort of creating"*: Tien, interview, October 23, 2023.

212   *(Lerner told the* Journal*)*: Alexander Osipovich, Hannah Miao, and Caitlin
      Ostroff, "How Sam Bankman-Fried's Psychiatrist Became a Key Player at
      Crypto Exchange FTX," *Wall Street Journal*, February 5, 2023, https://www
      .wsj.com/articles/how-sam-bankman-frieds-psychiatrist-became-a-key
      -player-at-crypto-exchange-ftx-11675605200.

212   *"There were just so many"*: Tien, interview, October 23, 2023.

212   *As Lerner listened*: George Lerner, U.S. v. Bankman-Fried, Letters in Support
      of Samuel Bankman-Fried's Sentencing Submission, Document 17, submit-
      ted February 27, 2024.

213   *"I believe I'm not"*: Chew, interview, May 29, 2023.

CHAPTER 28

215 *Ryan Salame had asserted*: Natario McKenzie, "The Future Is Crypto? FTX to Invest $60M in HQ, Commercial Center and Boutique Hotel in The Bahamas," *EyeWitness News*, March 11, 2022, https://ewnews.com/the -future-is-crypto-ftx-to-invest-60-million-dollars-in-hq-commercial-center -and-boutique-hotel-in-the-bahamas.

215 *"Since moving to our shores"*: Philip Davis (@HonPhilipEDavis), Twitter post, April 25, 2022, 1:23 p.m., https://twitter.com/HonPhilipEDavis/status /1518641869110054914.

215 *He predicted that the new*: "FTX Breaks Ground on New Headquarters," *Our News Bahamas*, Facebook video, April 26, 2022, https://www.facebook .com/watch/?v=965936580785751.

215 *FTX surpassed Coinbase*: Catarina Moura, "FTX Surpassed Coinbase as Second-Biggest Centralized Crypto Exchange in May," *The Block*, June 1, 2022, https://www.theblock.co/linked/149654/ftx-surpassed-coinbase-as -second-biggest-centralized-crypto-exchange-in-may.

215 *She added: "Crypto has"*: Andrew Hayward, "FTX US Opens Chicago HQ, Will Sponsor Supplemental Income Pilot," *Decrypt*, May 10, 2022, https: //decrypt.co/99943/ftx-us-opens-chicago-hq-will-sponsor-supplemental -income-pilot.

215 *And in May, I myself*: Andrew R. Chow, "Time 100: Sam Bankman-Fried," *Time*, May 23, 2022, https://time.com/collection/100-most-influential -people-2022/6177770/sam-bankman-fried/.

216 *Later, Sam told the* New York Times: David Yaffe-Bellany, "Crypto Emperor's Vision: No Pants, His Rules," *New York Times*, May 14, 2022, https://www .nytimes.com/2022/05/14/business/sam-bankman-fried-ftx-crypto.html.

216 *(Brady and Bündchen)*: U.S. v. Bankman-Fried, government exhibit 343, pre-sented October 16, 2023.

216 *"You're breaking land speed"*: SALT, "Crypto State of the Union with Sam Bankman-Fried & Katie Haun," YouTube video, May 16, 2022, https: //youtu.be/ACgJFNAOdWo?si=sdl4OuRBphnjODAl.

217 *He said that FTX might*: Ibid., 129.

217 *Fidelity, the nation's largest*: Andrew R. Chow, "Bitcoin Is Coming to Your 401(k). But Your Employer Probably Won't Let You Invest in It," *Time*, May 4, 2022, https://time.com/6173458/bitcoin-401k-reitrement/.

217 *And the city of Buenos Aires announced*: Andrés Engler, "Buenos Aires City to Allow Residents to Make Tax Payments with Crypto," *CoinDesk*, April 26, 2022, https://www.coindesk.com/policy/2022/04/26/buenos-aires-city-to -allow-residents-to-make-tax-payments-with-crypto/.

217 *He urged his five hundred thousand followers*: Su Zhu (@zhusu), "This is not yet another cycle, this is the End of Cycles . . . ," Twitter post, February 20, 2021, 3 a.m., https://twitter.com/zhusu/status/1363035740507017216.

217   *Onstage at Crypto Bahamas, Zhu*: SALT, "Crypto Alpha: Investing in Mega trends," YouTube video, May 20, 2022, 10:10, https://www.youtube.com /watch?v=yY02AnbJiUk.

218   *"We're not on their radar"*: Tyler Gordon, interview with Andrew R. Chow, February 24, 2023.

218   *But what Sam might have lacked*: Melissa Alcena, interview with Andrew R. Chow, March 27, 2023.

219   *"He's a kind of"*: Zeke Faux, "A 30-Year-Old Crypto Billionaire Wants to Give His Fortune Away," *Bloomberg*, April 3, 2022, https://www.bloomberg.com /news/features/2022-04-03/sam-bankman-fried-ftx-s-crypto-billionaire -who-wants-to-give-his-fortune-away.

219   *"I was like, 'I need'"*: Alcena, interview, March 27, 2023.

219   *"It was a bunch"*: Ibid.

220   *"As you build"*: "SALT, "Art, Culture & Community in Web3," YouTube video, May 30, 2022, 17:14, https://www.youtube.com/watch?v=kiNJ4C MFZC0&t=1714s.

220   *"You had beach parties"*: Lamont Astwood, interview with Andrew R. Chow, March 18, 2023.

220   *(Naik would later admit)*: Gajesh Naik, interview with Andrew R. Chow, April 23, 2023.

221   *"That was insane"*: Illia Polosukhin, interview with Andrew R. Chow, May 23, 2023.

221   *"The biggest alpha"*: @TheKlineVenture, Tegan Kline, Instagram post, April 30, 2022, https://www.instagram.com/p/Cc_apAhLjVd/.

221   *"It felt like a rush"*: Alcena, interview, March 27, 2023.

CHAPTER 29

225   *"I'm followed by @katyperry"*: Su Zhu (@zhusu), Twitter post, April 29, 2022, 11:14 a.m., https://twitter.com/zhusu/status/1520059040352641024.

225   *Three Arrows' relentlessness*: Jen Wieczner, "The Crypto Geniuses Who Vaporized a Trillion Dollars," *New York*, August 15, 2022, https://nymag .com/intelligencer/article/three-arrows-capital-kyle-davies-su-zhu-crash .html.

226   *Also like Sam, Zhu*: MacKenzie Sigalos, "From $10 Billion to Zero: How a Crypto Hedge Fund Collapsed and Dragged Many Investors Down with It," CNBC, July 11, 2022, https://www.cnbc.com/2022/07/11/how-the-fall -of-three-arrows-or-3ac-dragged-down-crypto-investors.html.

226   *Axie Infinity, which Zhu called*: Joanna Ossinger, "Fund Manager Who Called End of Last Crypto Winter Remains Bullish," *Bloomberg*, April 7, 2022, https://www.bloomberg.com/news/articles/2022-04-07/three-arrows -capital-s-su-zhu-remains-bullish-on-crypto-investments.

226   *for its lack of transparency*: Sead Fadilpašić, "Ethereum's Buterin Says Tether

Is Bitcoin's 'Ticking Time Bomb Demon,'" *Crypto News*, March 10, 2021, https://cryptonews.com/news/ethereum-s-buterin-says-tether-is-bitcoin-s-ticking-time-bom-9494.htm.

226 *At its peak, Celsius*: Eliot Brown and Caitlin Ostroff, "Behind the Celsius Sales Pitch Was a Crypto Firm Built on Risk," *Wall Street Journal*, June 30, 2022, https://www.wsj.com/articles/behind-the-celsius-sales-pitch-was-a-crypto-firm-built-on-risk-11656498142.

226 *Mashinsky assuaged any doubts*: Joshua Oliver and Kadhim Shubber, "Alex Mashinsky, Celsius Founder Feeling the Heat," *Financial Times*, June 17, 2022, https://www.ft.com/content/18b6fb80-44dd-40ed-b5ea-3f3bf2814c7d.

226 *Three Arrows, for its part, often resisted*: Wieczner, "The Crypto Geniuses."

226 *As Caroline Ellison admitted*: Caroline Ellison: Alameda all-hands meeting, November 9, 2023, recording, 54:00, https://soundcloud.com/segray/caroline-ellison-alameda-research-all-hands.

227 *He then loaned it out to Sam*: Vicky Ge Huang, "Bankrupt Crypto Lender Celsius Network Says It Lent Alameda Research $13 Million," *Wall Street Journal*, November 11, 2022, https://www.wsj.com/livecoverage/stock-market-news-today-11-11-2022/card/bankrupt-crypto-lender-celsius-network-says-it-lent-alameda-research-13-million-jTnI38SvOBOB7JCy8DmJ.

227 *Zhu (at least $75 million)*: Tim Copeland, Yogita Khatri, and Ryan Weeks, "Crypto Lender Celsius Loaned $75 million to Three Arrows Capital," *The Block*, July 18, 2022, https://www.theblock.co/post/158164/crypto-lender-celsius-loaned-75-million-to-three-arrows-capital.

227 *("Ethereum has abandoned")*: @zhusu, "Yes I have abandoned Ethereum despite supporting it in the past. Yes Ethereum has abandoned its users despite supporting them in the past. The idea of sitting around jerking off watching the burn and concocting purity tests, while zero newcomers can afford the chain, is gross." Twitter post, November 20, 2021, 7:28 p.m., https://twitter.com/zhusu/status/1462216210116853762.

227 *He told critics to "have fun"*: Do Kwon (@stablekwon), Twitter post, January 29, 2022, 7:31 a.m., https://twitter.com/stablekwon/status/1355131416527335426.

227 *By April 2022, almost three-quarters*: Liam J. Kelly, "We Need to Talk About Terra's Anchor," *Decrypt*, April 23, 2022, https://decrypt.co/98482/we-need-to-talk-about-terras-anchor.

228 *In December 2021, Kwon told* CoinDesk: Daniel Kuhn, "Most Influential 2021: Do Kwon," *CoinDesk*, December 10, 2021, https://www.coindesk.com/policy/2021/12/10/most-influential-2021-do-kwon/.

228 *The comedian John Oliver*: John Oliver, "Cryptocurrencies II," *Last Week Tonight*, April 24, 2023, YouTube video, 8:15, https://www.youtube.com/watch?v=o7zazuy_UfI.

229 *"I don't debate the poor"*: Do Kwon (@Stablekwon), Twitter post, July 1, 2021,

2:51 a.m., https://twitter.com/stablekwon/status/1410491186196795398? lang=en.

229   *One prominent crypto executive*: Hannah Miller, "Crypto Investing and the Curse of the Luna Tattoo," *Bloomberg*, June 2, 2022, https://www.bloomberg .com/news/newsletters/2022-06-02/crypto-investing-mike-novogratz-and -the-curse-of-the-luna-tattoo.

229   *"There's this idea"*: James Block, interview with Andrew R. Chow, June 27, 2023.

229   *UST had hit a*: Liam J. Kelly, "Terra's Stablecoin UST Becomes Crypto's Third-Largest," *Decrypt*, April 18, 2022, https://decrypt.co/98069/terra -stablecoin-ust-crypto-third-largest.

229   *Kwon followed this up*: Sarah Guo and Christine Kim, "Terra, Stablecoins, and Programmable Money | Do Kwon," *Fungible Times*, March 23, 2022, YouTube video, 20:08, 27:58, https://web.archive.org/web/20220330064403 /https://www.youtube.com/watch?v=Tl-an5skBtA.

229   *"In that case"*: Ibid.

230   *In fact, Su Zhu likened*: @zhusu, "We're seeing some of the earliest and most ambitious ideas in crypto starting to unfold. Crosschain decentralized stable-coin backed entirely by digitally native assets was the holy grail in 2016. Bless $BTC $LUNA." Twitter post, March 28, 2022, 8:35 p.m., https://twitter .com/zhusu/status/1508603726143328256.

230   *invested $200 million*: Serena Ng, "Crypto Hedge Fund Three Arrows Capital Considers Asset Sales, Bailout," *Wall Street Journal*, June 17, 2022, https://www.wsj.com/articles/battered-crypto-hedge-fund-three-arrows -capital-considers-asset-sales-bailout-11655469932.

230   *"A financial system that is"*: Blinder, *After the Music Stopped*, 55.

231   *"In a world where"*: Guo and Kim, "Terra, Stablecoins, and Programmable Money," 24:40.

231   *crypto, once believed*: Steve Lohr, "Companies That Rode Pandemic Boom Get a Reality Check," *New York Times*, March 11, 2021, https://www .nytimes.com/2021/03/11/technology/pandemic-boom-stocks.html.

231   *On May 7, Caroline Ellison wrote*: U.S. v. Bankman-Fried, government exhibit 49A, "Alameda Updates 5/7/22," presented October 10, 2023.

231   *Alameda owed around $3 billion*: U.S. v Bankman-Fried, government exhibit 48A, presented October 10, 2023.

232   *UST had wobbled before*: Joe Hall, "LUNA meltdown sparks theories and told-you-sos from crypto community," *Coin Telegraph*, May 11, 2022, https://cointelegraph.com/news/luna-meltdown-sparks-theories-and-told -you-sos-from-crypto-community.

232   *"Deploying more capital"*: Do Kwon (@stablekwon), Twitter post, May 9, 2022, 2:36 p.m., https://twitter.com/stablekwon/status/15237335424920 16640.

232 *When the Luna Foundation Guard dumped*: Ryan Browne and MacKenzie Sigalos, "Bitcoin Investors Are Panicking as a Controversial Crypto Experiment Unravels," CNBC, May 10, 2022, https://www.cnbc.com/2022/05/10/bitcoin-btc-investors-panic-as-terrausd-ust-sinks-below-1-peg.html.

232 *Luna's $41 billion*: CoinGecko, Terra Luna Classic, accessed July 9, 2023, https://www.coingecko.com/en/coins/terra-luna-classic.

232 *The stablecoin UST hit*: Benjamin Pimentel, "Unstablecoin: Terra Halted Its Blockchain as UST Tumbles Toward $0," *Protocol*, May 12, 2022, https://www.protocol.com/bulletins/terra-ust-luna-stablecoin-crash.

232 *halted as exchanges like Binance*: Manish Singh, "Binance Halts Luna and UST Trading Following Meltdown," *TechCrunch*, May 12, 2022, https://techcrunch.com/2022/05/12/binance-halts-luna-and-ust-trading-across-most-of-its-spot-pairs-following-meltdown/.

232 *and OKX suspended*: Shaurya Malwa and Jamie Crawley, "OKX Delists Terra's LUNA and UST Citing User Protection," *CoinDesk*, May 13, 2022, https://www.coindesk.com/markets/2022/05/13/okx-delists-terras-luna-and-ust-citing-user-protection/.

233 *In 2023, the SEC alleged*: Alexander Osipovich, "Jump Trading Did Secret Deal to Prop Up TerraUSD Stablecoin, SEC Says," *Wall Street Journal*, May 15, 2023, https://www.wsj.com/articles/jump-trading-did-secret-deal-to-prop-up-terrausd-stablecoin-sec-says-11335951.

233 *"It definitely made me"*: Christine Chew, interview with Andrew R. Chow, October 13, 2023.

233 *A Korean family of three*: Michael Lee, "Bodies of Missing Schoolgirl, Parents Seem to Be Found," *Korean JoongAng Daily*, June 29, 2022, https://koreajoongangdaily.joins.com/2022/06/29/national/socialAffairs/Korea-crime-police/20220629183843752.html.

233 *"I'm going through some"*: Comment on the Reddit post, "My ex-colleague attempted suicide," @AdventurousAdagio830, May 15, 2022, https://www.reddit.com/r/terraluna/comments/un40h4/my_excolleague_attempted_suicide/.

233 *After that, the Horsemen*: Wieczner, "The Crypto Geniuses."

234 *In their efforts to pay*: Ibid.

234 *But in late June, Three Arrows*: MacKenzie Sigalos and Arjun Kharpal, "One of the Most Prominent Crypto Hedge Funds Just Defaulted on a $670 Million Loan," CNBC, June 27, 2022, https://www.cnbc.com/2022/06/27/three-arrows-capital-crypto-hedge-fund-defaults-on-voyager-loan.html.

234 *Voyager itself was insolvent*: MacKenzie Sigalos, "Voyager Customer Lost $1 Million Saved over 24 Years and Is One of Many Now Desperate to Recoup Funds," CNBC, August 15, 2022, https://www.cnbc.com/2022/08/15/voyager-customers-beg-new-york-judge-for-money-back-after-bankruptcy.html.

234 *In all, Three Arrows was*: David Yaffe-Bellany, "Their Crypto Company

Collapsed. They Went to Bali," *New York Times*, June 9, 2023, https://www
.nytimes.com/2023/06/09/technology/three-arrows-cryto-bali.html.

234 *They told* Bloomberg News: Joanna Ossinger, Muyao Shen, and Yueqi Yang,
"Three Arrows Founders Break Silence Over Collapse of Crypto Hedge
Fund," *Bloomberg*, July 22, 2022, https://www.bloomberg.com/news/articles
/2022-07-22/three-arrows-founders-en-route-to-dubai-describe-ltcm
-moment.

234 *While Mashinsky had bragged*: SEC v. Celsius Network Limited and Alex
Mashinsky, filed July 13, 2023, page 24, https://assets.bwbx.io/documents
/users/iqjWHBFdfxIU/rX4Q5pK6z_CI/v0.

234 *Celsius was leveraged about 19 to 1*: Brown and Ostroff, "Behind the Celsius
Sales Pitch."

234 *Celsius had lost some $350*: Arkham Intelligence, "Report on the Celsius Net-
work," July 7, 2022, https://www.arkhamintelligence.com/research/reports
/elsius-report.

234 *(The SEC had begun scrutinizing)*: Joe Light, Matt Robinson, and Zeke
Faux, "Crypto Lending Firms Celsius Network, Gemini Face SEC Scrutiny," *Bloomberg*, January 26, 2022, https://www.bloomberg.com/news
/articles/2022-01-26/crypto-lending-firms-celsius-network-gemini-face
-sec-scrutiny.

234 *Regulators contended that*: Jason Nelson, "Celsius Had Been Insolvent Since
2019: Vermont Regulator," *Decrypt*, September 7, 2022, https://decrypt
.co/109222/elsius-was-insolvent-since-2019-vermont-regulator.

234 *A shepherd in Ireland*: Faux, *Number Go Up*, 168.

235 *"One or two things"*: Alex Pack, interview with Andrew R. Chow, May 21, 2023.

235 *As many investors tried*: Jeff Benson, "Ethereum Gas Prices Soar as Traders Head for the Stablecoin Exits," *Decrypt*, May 12, 2022, https://decrypt
.co/100262/ethereum-gas-prices-soar-traders-head-stablecoin-exits.

235 *Coinbase, a major crypto*: "Coinbase Misses Revenue Estimates as Retail
Investors Head for the Door," Reuters, May 10, 2022, https://www.reuters
.com/business/crypto-exchange-coinbase-revenue-drops-35-retail-interest
-slows-2022-05-10/.

235 *Gemini, a crypto exchange*: Jacquelyn Melinek, "Crypto Exchange Gemini Ex-
ecutes Second Round of Layoffs Less Than Two Months After Axing 10%
of Staff," *TechCrunch*, July 18, 2022, https://techcrunch.com/2022/07/18
/crypto-exchange-gemini-executes-second-round-of-layoffs-less-than-two
-months-after-axing-10-of-staff/.

235 *From mid-May to mid-June*: CryptoSlam!, Global Indexes by Sales
Volume (30 days), accessed June 16, 2022, https://web.archive.org
/web/20220616131134/https://www.cryptoslam.io/.

235 *"Some of the gaming companies"*: Khai Chun Thee, interview with Andrew R.
Chow, September 7, 2023.

235 *A 2023 study from the gaming DAO*: George Isichos et al., "State of Web3

Gaming 2023," Research, Game7, November 13, 2023, https://research
.game7.io/state-of-web3-gaming-2023.

236 *"You're like, 'What the fuck'"*: Melissa Alcena, interview with Andrew R.
Chow, March 27, 2023.

CHAPTER 30

237 *On June 6, 2022, he posted*: Sam Bankman-Fried (@SBF_FTX), "1) Zig
Zag and hiring: why FTX is going to keep growing as others cut jobs," Twitter post, June 6, 2022, 6:59 p.m., https://twitter.com/SBF_FTX/status
/1533946713366568962.

237 *He scolded the public*: Sam Bankman-Fried (@SBF_FTX), "8) Luna was a case
of mass enthusiasm, excitement, and—frankly—marketing and memes—
driving people to believe in something which was going to falter according
to publicly available information. That marketing was probably bad. But it
wasn't the same type of bad as Theranos." Twitter post, May 14, 2022, 7:50
p.m., https://twitter.com/SBF_FTX/status/1525624605620281347.

237 *"The core driver of this"*: David Gura, "Crypto Billionaire Says Fed Is Driving Current Downturn," NPR, June 19, 2022, https://www.npr.org/2022
/06/19/1105853170/crypto-billionaire-says-fed-is-driving-current-down
turn.

237 *Alameda had invested directly*: U.S. v. Bankman-Fried, testimony from Caroline Ellison, October 12, 2023.

237 *For example, Alameda had*: U.S. v. Bankman-Fried, government exhibit 36,
"NAV Minus Sam Coins," presented October 10, 2023.

237 *On June 13, a Genesis representative*: U.S. v. Bankman-Fried, government exhibit 1647, presented October 11, 2023.

238 *Caroline was panicked*: Ibid., October 11, 2023.

238 *Alameda was already borrowing*: Ibid.

238 *Some of the money*: U.S. v. Bankman-Fried, testimony from Gary Wang and
Nishad Singh, October 6 and 16, 2023.

238 *Billions more had come through*: U.S. v. Bankman-Fried, testimony from Sam
Bankman-Fried, October 26, 2023.

238 *There was only one thing to do*: U.S. v. Bankman-Fried, testimony from Caroline
Ellison, October 11, 2023.

239 *In the next two weeks, Alameda*: Ibid.

239 *"You control the Digital Assets"*: Brady Dale and Felix Salmon, "FTX's Terms-
of-Service Forbid Trading with Customer Funds," *Axios*, November 13, 2022,
https://www.axios.com/2022/11/12/ftx-terms-service-trading-customer
-funds.

239 *Caroline was in a constant*: U.S. v. Bankman-Fried, testimony from Caroline
Ellison, October 11, 2023.

239 *So, on Sam's direction*: Ibid.

239 *"Just caught up with Sam"*: U.S. v. Bankman-Fried, government exhibit 1650, presented October 11, 2023.

240 *"We were bulletproof"*: U.S. v. Bankman-Fried, testimony from Adam Yedidia, October 4, 2023.

CHAPTER 31

241 *In late June, Sam announced*: Monika Ghosh, "Sam Bankman-Fried Steps In to Bail Out BlockFi," *Forkast*, June 22, 2022, https://finance.yahoo.com/news/sam-bankman-fried-steps-bail-050707164.html.

241 *Analysts called him*: "J.P. Morgan," Encyclopedia Britannica, last updated October 17, 2023, https://www.britannica.com/biography/J-P-Morgan.

241 *In August, Sam's smiling face*: Jeff John Roberts, "Exclusive: 30-Year-Old Billionaire Sam Bankman-Fried Has Been Called the Next Warren Buffett. His Counterintuitive Investment Strategy Will Either Build Him an Empire—Or End in Disaster," *Fortune*, August 1, 2022, https://fortune.com/2022/08/01/ftx-crypto-sam-bankman-fried-interview/.

241 *"We're willing to do"*: Steven Ehrlich, "Bankman-Fried Warns: Some Crypto Exchanges Already 'Secretly Insolvent,'" *Forbes*, June 28, 2022, https://www.forbes.com/sites/stevenehrlich/2022/06/28/bankman-fried-some-crypto-exchanges-already-secretly-insolvent/?sh=2012514647f7.

241 *"Backstopping customer assets"*: Sam Bankman-Fried, @SBF_FTX, Twitter post, June 27, 2022, 1:29 p.m., https://twitter.com/SBF_FTX/status/1541473744119631872.

241 *He told Caroline that*: U.S. v. Bankman-Fried, testimony from Caroline Ellison, October 11, 2023.

242 *Sure enough, BlockFi*: U.S v. Bankman-Fried, testimony from Zack Prince, October 13, 2023.

242 *At the time of Sam's*: Voyager Digital Holdings bankruptcy filing, document 15, July 6, 2022, https://cases.stretto.com/public/x193/11753/PLEADINGS/1175307062280000000036.pdf.

242 *"If you have the ability to move*: Changpeng Zhao (@cz_binance), Twitter post, July 7, 2022, 10:41 a.m., https://twitter.com/cz_binance/status/1545055439867428866.

242 *"Bailouts here don't make sense"*: Changpeng Zhao, "A Note on Bailouts and Crypto Leverage," *Binance Blog*, June 23, 2022, https://www.binance.com/en/blog/from-our-ceo/a-note-on-bailouts-and-crypto-leverage-421499824684904048.

242 *Ryan Salame, Christine's*: Ryan Salame (@rsalame7926), Twitter post, July 7, 2022, 10:06 a.m., https://twitter.com/rsalame7926/status/1545091789698306048.

242 *To twist the knife*: "FTX and SALT Announce Crypto Bahamas 2023," FTX press release, June 29, 2022, https://www.prnewswire.com/news-releases

/ftx-and-salt-announce-2023-crypto-bahamas-conference-301577653
.html.

243   *Sam was lauded for signing*: Sam Bankman-Fried (@SBF_FTX), "I'm excited
      and honored to sign the Giving Pledge," Twitter post, June 1, 2022, 11:50
      a.m., https://twitter.com/SBF_FTX/status/1532072177415372801.

243   *In July 2022, FTT DAO*: Morgan Eggah, "FTT DAO: A Humanity
      Centered Community-Led DAO," *Medium*, September 16, 2022, https:
      //morganeggah2017.medium.com/ftt-dao-a-humanity-centered-community
      -led-dao-a56981562c25.

243   *Organizers constructed a*: @SanGracee, Twitter video, August 10, 2022,
      2:55 a.m., https://twitter.com/SanGracee/status/1557304611853291520.

243   *"The participants of the event"*: Ibid.

243   *That summer, FTT DAO raised*: Oliver Knight, "FTX Token DAO
      Raises $7M from Community of Sam Bankman-Fried Fans," *CoinDesk*,
      June 27, 2022, https://www.coindesk.com/business/2022/06/27/ftx-token
      -dao-raises-7m-from-community-of-sam-bankman-fried-fans/.

243   *In May, he announced charges*: "Investment Adviser Allianz Global Inves-
      tors US Charged with $5 Billion Fraud," Associated Press, May 17, 2022,
      https://www.cnbc.com/2022/05/17/investment-adviser-allianz-global
      -investors-us-charged-with-5-billion-fraud.html.

243   *Within months, his office*: Ava Benny-Morrison, "Prosecutors Opened Probe
      of FTX Months Before Its Collapse," *Bloomberg*, November 21, 2022,
      https://www.bloomberg.com/news/articles/2022-11-21/us-prosecutors
      -opened-probe-of-ftx-months-before-its-collapse.

CHAPTER 32

245   *Its market cap had been slashed*: CoinMarketCap, Global Live Cryptocurrency
      Charts & Market Data, accessed January 10, 2024, https://coinmarketcap
      .com/charts/.

245   *"We believe in the power"*: Cyber Baat, The Cyber Baat Fundraiser, Mirror,
      February 1, 2022, https://cyberbaat.mirror.xyz/P6b9unXXdg-TiQ08EH
      KVTKNufNrH_IcVOK1d_spM8Xs.

245   *It made just $2,500*: African NFT Community DAO, Mirror, https:
      //mirror.xyz/0x24A760d440A7d74A02728b1a7877f6176C5861BD
      /crowdfunds/0xe9a217DcFd0ceca1ea5416D7EE0890e67FfD938E.

246   *"Africa is such a rough"*: Owo Anietie, interview with Andrew R. Chow, May
      12, 2023.

246   *"I've had a dry spell"*: Taslemat Yusuf (@hotgirltas), Twitter post, Septem-
      ber 6, 2022, 6:43 p.m., https://twitter.com/hotgirltas/status/156732757
      9811504129.

246   *Instead of investigating*: @africannftclub, Twitter post, September 3, 2022,
      https://twitter.com/ancurated/status/1566164281858686982.

246 *"You never expected social"*: Liam Vries, interview with Andrew R. Chow, April 21, 2023

247 *"Everything was childish"*: Taslemat Yusuf, interview with Andrew R. Chow, June 7, 2023.

247 *"If the spread of technology"*: Alex Tapscott, *Web3* (New York: HarperCollins, 2023), xi.

248 *"'WAGMI' is mostly BS"*: Michael Keen, interview with Andrew R. Chow, April 26, 2023.

248 *"To make these technologies usable"*: Moxie Marlinspike, "My First Impressions of Web3," blog post, January 7, 2022, https://moxie.org/2022/01/07/web3-first-impressions.html.

248 *artists from both countries*: Megan Janetsky, "Cuban Artists Blocked from Once-Promising NFT Trading Sites," Associated Press, December 20, 2022, https://www.seattletimes.com/business/cuban-artists-blocked-from-once-promising-nft-trading-sites/.

249 *A November 2021 study found*: Anders Petterson and James Cocksey, 2021 NFT Market Report, *ArtTactic*, November 2021.

249 *Another study showed that CryptoPunks*: Misyrlena Egkolfopoulou and Akayla Gardner, "Even in the Metaverse, Not All Identities Are Created Equal," *Bloomberg*, December 6, 2021, https://www.bloomberg.com/news/features/2021-12-06/cryptopunk-nft-prices-suggest-a-diversity-problem-in-the-metaverse.

249 *Stoner Cats*: Todd Spangler, "Producers of 'Stoner Cats' Series, with Cast Including Ashton Kutcher and Mila Kunis, Charged by SEC with Illegal Sale of $8 Million Worth of NFTs," *Variety*, September 13, 2023, https://variety.com/2023/digital/news/stoner-cats-nfts-sec-charges-ashton-kutcher-mila-kunis-1235722381/.

249 *Kim Kardashian was forced to pay*: U.S. Securities and Exchange Commission, "SEC Charges Kim Kardashian for Unlawfully Touting Crypto Security," October 3, 2022, https://www.sec.gov/news/press-release/2022-183.

249 *And Logan Paul*: Andrew R. Chow, "How Logan Paul's Crypto Empire Fell Apart," *Time*, February 2, 2023, https://time.com/6252093/logan-paul-cryptozoo-liquid-marketplace/.

249 *Two factions*: Isaiah Poritz, "'Caked Ape' NFT Artist Mostly Advances Suit Against Ex-Partners," *Bloomberg Law*, December 8, 2022, https://news.bloomberglaw.com/ip-law/caked-ape-nft-artist-mostly-advances-suit-against-ex-partners.

250 *And Vignesh Sundaresan*: Richard Whiddington, "Beeple Collector Metakovan Is Suing Twobadour, Claiming His Ex-Partner Is Falsely Taking Credit for Buying the $69 Million NFT," Artnet News, June 20, 2023, https://news.artnet.com/art-world/metakovan-suing-twobadour-beeple-nft-2324373.

250 *Wash trading is illegal in*: Chainalysis Team, "Crime and NFTs."

250 *One blockchain analysis found*: hildobby, "NFT Wash Trading on Ethereum,"

Dune, December 16, 2022, https://community.dune.com/blog/nft-wash
-trading-on-ethereum.

250   *A Chainalysis report found hundreds*: Chainalysis Team, "Crime and NFTs."

251   *The National Bureau of Economic Research*: Lin William Cong, Xi Li, Ke Tang, and Yang Yang, "Crypto Wash Trading," National Bureau of Economic Research, December 2022, https://www.nber.org/system/files/working_papers /w30783/w30783.pdf

251   *By the end of 2022, many*: Cam Thompson, "Retract Royalties, Reduce Revenue: NFT Creators Are Suffering and So Are Marketplaces," *CoinDesk,* November 4, 2022, https://www.coindesk.com/web3/2022/11/04/retract -royalties-reduce-revenue-nft-creators-are-suffering-and-so-are-market places/.

251   *Rettig told Congress*: Scott Chipolina, "IRS Commissioner Concerned NFTs May Be Used for Tax Evasion, *Decrypt*, April 15, 2021, https://decrypt .co/66589/irs-commissioner-concerned-nfts-may-be-used-for-tax-evasion.

251   *According to Chainalysis, there was*: "The 2023 Crypto Crime Report," Chainalysis, February 2023, https://go.chainalysis.com/rs/503-FAP-074/images /Crypto_Crime_Report_2023.pdf.

252   *As newcomers flocked*: Philip Martin, Chainalysis Links conference, April 4, 2023, New York City.

252   *Between May and July 2022*: "Analysis of Recent NFT Discord Hacks Shows Some Attacks Are Connected," TRM Insights, July 25, 2022, https://www .trmlabs.com/post/trms-analysis-of-recent-surge-in-discord-hacks-shows -some-attacks-are-connected.

252   *"So a lot of hackers"*: CryptoWizard, interview with Andrew R. Chow, May 30, 2023.

252   *Tether, the reporters contended*: Faux, *Number Go Up*, 175.

253   *In June 2022, an employee*: U.S. Attorney's Office, Southern District of New York, "Former Employee of NFT Marketplace Charged in First Ever Digital Asset Insider Trading Scheme," June 1, 2022, https://www.justice.gov/usao -sdny/pr/former-employee-nft-marketplace-charged-first-ever-digital -asset-insider-trading-scheme.

253   *Chastain was later convicted*: U.S. Attorney's Office, Southern District of New York, "Former Employee of NFT Marketplace Sentenced to Prison in First-Ever Digital Asset Insider Trading Scheme," August 22, 2023, https://www .justice.gov/usao-sdny/pr/former-employee-nft-marketplace-sentenced -prison-first-ever-digital-asset-insider.

CHAPTER 33

255 *"As an artist"*: Liam Vries, interview with Andrew R. Chow, December 6, 2022.

256 *"I told him to"*: CryptoWizard, interview with Andrew R. Chow, May 30, 2023.

256 *"Did like a bit of trying"*: U.S. v. Bankman-Fried, government exhibit 64, presented October 11, 2023.

256 *But the prices of the cheapest*: "Bored Ape Yacht Club Price Floor," accessed November 30, 2023, https://nftpricefloor.com/bored-ape-yacht-club.

256 *The actor Seth Green*: Sarah Emerson, "Someone Stole Seth Green's Bored Ape, Which Was Supposed to Star in His New Show," *BuzzFeed News*, May 24, 2022, https://www.buzzfeednews.com/article/sarahemerson/seth-green -bored-ape-stolen-tv-show.

256 *Green's show was supposed*: Will Stephenson, "Bored Ape Is Going Hollywood," *GQ*, June 2, 2022, https://www.gq.com/story/bored-ape -profile.

257 *Jenkins's owner, who went by*: Lucy Harley-McKeown, "How Bored Apes Became the Foundation for a Metaverse," *The Block*, June 22, 2022, https: //www.theblock.co/post/153349/how-bored-apes-became-the-foundation -for-a-metaverse.

257 *"If I was a deformed"*: Peter Van Valkenburgh (@valkenburgh), Twitter post, October 1, 2022, 4:25 p.m., https://twitter.com/valkenburgh/status /1576352658042269697.

257 *"Did you hire a blind"*: @professordilly, Twitter post, September 30, 2022, 1:31 p.m., https://twitter.com/professordilly/status/1575946553327599616.

257 *One community member on Discord*: Anti-Hiro, Discord message, Writers Room server, September 27, 2022, 4:33 p.m.

257 *"I began this phase"*: Neil Strauss, interview with Andrew R. Chow, June 20, 2023.

258 *In March 2022, the company had*: Tim Baysinger, "Andreesen Horowitz Leads Yuga Labs' $450M Funding Round," March 23, 2022, *Axios*, https: //www.axios.com/pro/media-deals/2022/03/23/yuga-450m-investment -andreesen-horowitz-metaverse.

258 *Because Yuga had bought out*: "NFT Statistics 2023: Sales, Trends, Market Cap and More," Nansen, September 30, 2022, https://www.nansen.ai/guides /nft-statistics-2022.

258 *FTX had already invested $50 million*: U.S. v. Bankman-Fried, government exhibit 14B, presented October 16, 2023.

258 *"We felt like with killer content"*: Interview with anonymous source.

258 *Greg Solano, the cofounder*: Greg Solano, interview with Andrew R. Chow, January 18, 2024.

CHAPTER 34

262   *In 2022, crypto miners burned*: "Fact Sheet: Climate and Energy Implications of Crypto-Assets in the United States," The White House, The Office of Science and Technology Policy, September 8, 2022, https://www.whitehouse.gov/ostp/news-updates/2022/09/08/fact-sheet-climate-and-energy-implications-of-crypto-assets-in-the-united-states.

262   *In the U.S., when power-thirsty*: Sarah Bowman, "A Crypto Mine Comes to Town and a Coal Plant Gets New Life," *Indianapolis Star*, December 5, 2023, https://www.indystar.com/story/news/environment/2023/12/05/crypto-mine-comes-to-indiana-and-major-polluting-coal-plant-stays-open/70992299007/.

262   *In Texas, crypto miners'*: Chris Tomlinson, "Bitcoin Miners Running Up Texans' Electricity Bills, Industry Fighting New Regulations," *Houston Chronicle*, October 13, 2023, https://www.houstonchronicle.com/business/columnists/tomlinson/article/texas-bictoin-eletric-grid-higher-bills-18420115.php.

262   *In one Texas town*: Andrew R. Chow, "A Texas Town's Misery Underscores the Impact of Bitcoin Mines Across the U.S.," *Time*, February 1, 2024, https://time.com/6590155/bitcoin-mining-noise-texas.

262   *One Twitter poster snarkily*: Simon Spichak, "How Crypto Is Failing Spectacularly to Greenwash Itself," *Daily Beast*, April 22, 2022, https://www.thedailybeast.com/how-cryptocurrencies-are-failing-spectacularly-to-greenwash-themselves.

262   *Vitalik called proof of work*: Vitalik Buterin, "On Silos," blog post, December 31, 2014, https://blog.ethereum.org/2014/12/31/silos.

262   *which consumed 99.9 percent*: Carl Beekhuizen, "Ethereum's Energy Usage Will Soon Decrease by ~99.95%," blog post, May 18, 2021, https://blog.ethereum.org/2021/05/18/country-power-no-more.

263   *But in September 2022, Ethereum researchers*: Andrew R. Chow, "Why the Ethereum Merge Matters," *Time*, September 7, 2022, https://time.com/6211294/ethereum-merge-preview/.

263   *Vitalik, joined by*: Vitalik Buterin, "Should There Be Demand-Based Recurring Fees on ENS Domains?," blog post, September 9, 2022, https://vitalik.eth.limo/general/2022/09/09/ens.html.

263   *Vitalik had actually met Russian*: Michael del Castillo, "Vladimir Putin and Vitalik Buterin Discuss Ethereum 'Opportunities,'" *CoinDesk*, June 5, 2017, https://www.coindesk.com/markets/2017/06/05/vladimir-putin-and-vitalik-buterin-discuss-ethereum-opportunities/.

263   *Nevertheless, he condemned Putin*: Jeff John Roberts, "Ethereum Founder Vitalik Buterin to Putin: Ukraine Invasion Will 'Harm Humanity,'" *Decrypt*, February 11, 2022, https://decrypt.co/92728/vitalik-putin-ethereum-ukraine.

263 *personally contributed millions*: Aid for Ukraine (@_AidForUkraine), ".@VitalikButerin donated almost $2.5M in $ETH to @_AidForUkraine 2 days ago, and didn't say a word! He's also donated $2.5M to @Unchain fund," Twitter post, April 6, 2022, 11:37 a.m., https://twitter.com/_AidFor Ukraine/status/1511775118736961544.

264 *"We saved the lives"*: Mykhailo Fedorov, documentary footage, Nicholas Kraus, cinematographer, September 9, 2022.

264 *In the first couple weeks of the invasion*: Illia Polosukhin, "How Crypto-currency Is Helping Ukraine," *Wall Street Journal*, March 23, 2022, https://www.wsj.com/articles/how-crypto-is-helping-ukraine-russia-currency -donations-transfer-infrastructure-11648065166.

264 *"Sending money via"*: Illia Polosukhin, interview with Andrew R. Chow, May 23, 2023.

265 *as the invasion stretched on*: Ben Schreckinger, "In Ukraine, War Crimes Go On-Chain," *Politico*, January 17, 2023, https://www.politico.com /newsletters/digital-future-daily/2023/01/17/ukraine-war-crimes-block chain-00078170.

265 *The latter body acknowledged*: United Nations General Assembly, "Report of the Special Rapporteur on the right to education, Farida Shaheed," June 27, 2023, https://www.ohchr.org/en/documents/thematic-reports /ahrc5327-securing-right-education-advances-and-critical-challenges.

265 *"For the blockchain community"*: Vitalik Buterin, documentary footage, Nicholas Kraus, cinematographer, September 9, 2022.

CHAPTER 35

267 *In September 2022, about*: U.S. v. Bankman-Fried, government exhibit 224, presented October 17, 2023.

267 *The number on Caroline's*: U.S. v. Bankman-Fried, testimony from Caroline Ellison, October 11, 2023.

267 *FTX also owed*: Ibid.

267 *he had already raised $400 million*: Jamie Crawley, "FTX Reaches $32B Val-uation with $400M Fundraise," *CoinDesk*, January 31, 2022, https://www .coindesk.com/business/2022/01/31/ftx-reaches-32b-valuation-with -400m-fundraise/.

267 *FTX had gained approval*: Niket Nishant, "FTX Wins Full Approval to Op-erate Crypto Exchange in Dubai," *Bloomberg*, July 29, 2022, https://www .reuters.com/business/finance/ftx-wins-full-approval-operate-crypto -exchange-dubai-2022-07-29/.

267 *and was scaling up its FTX MENA*: Yueqi Yang and Ben Bartenstein, "Crypto Exchange FTX Wins License, Plans Regional HQ in Dubai," Reuters, March 14, 2022, https://www.bloomberg.com/news/articles/2022-03-14/crypto -exchange-ftx-wins-license-and-plans-regional-hq-in-dubai.

267 *Anthony Scaramucci—Sam's co-organizer*: Reem Abdellatif, "Anthony Scaramucci Wants Presence in Saudi Arabia; 'Bullish' on Aramco IPO," *Al Arabiya English*, October 29, 2019, https://english.alarabiya.net/business /2019/10/29/Anthony-Scaramucci-wants-presence-in-Saudi-Arabia-bullish -on-Aramco-IPO.

267 *He offered to help Sam*: William D. Cohan, "S.B.F. and The Mooch's Arabian Nights," *Puck*, April 19, 2023, https://puck.news/s-b-f-and-the-moochs-arabian-nights/.

267 *and badmouthing rival Changpeng Zhao*: Anthony Scaramucci, "Sam Bankman-Fried & the Unravelling of FTX with Brady Dale," on *Open Book,* podcast, August 16, 2023, 31:50, https://www.youtube.com/watch?v=wOYR4NNCO68.

267 *While he didn't return with*: U.S. v. Bankman-Fried, testimony by Sam Bankman-Fried, October 30, 2023.

267 *In an interview in late September*: CNBC Television, "FTX Still Has $1 Billion to Deploy, Says CEO Sam Bankman-Fried," YouTube video, September 16, 2022, https://www.youtube.com/watch?v=uGZrZq6z-Ig.

268 *In August, Sam took his anger*: U.S. v. Bankman-Fried, testimony from Caroline Ellison, October 11, 2023.

268 *So they simply borrowed*: Ibid.

268 *"It was probably time"*: U.S. v. Bankman-Fried, government exhibit 18F, Sam Bankman-Fried, "We Came, We Saw, We Researched," presented October 16, 2023.

268 *He also blamed Alameda*: Jon Brodkin, "SBF Called Alameda "Unauditable," Joked About Losing Track of $50 Million," *Ars Technica*, April 11, 2023, https://arstechnica.com/tech-policy/2023/04/sbf-called-alameda-unaudit able-joked-about-losing-track-of-50-million.

268 *Nishad suggested over Signal*: U.S. v. Bankman-Fried, testimony from Nishad Singh, October 16, 2023.

268 *Modulo Capital, which just*: David Yaffe-Bellany, Matthew Goldstein, and Royston Jones Jr., "The Unknown Hedge Fund That Got $400 Million from Sam Bankman-Fried," *New York Times*, January 24, 2023, https://www .nytimes.com/2023/01/24/business/ftx-sbf-modulo-capital.html.

268 *Caroline hated this idea*: U.S. v. Bankman-Fried, testimony from Caroline Ellison, October 12, 2023.

269 *Gary, in the chat*: U.S. v. Bankman-Fried, testimony from Nishad Singh, October 16, 2023.

269 *Of the quartet*: Ibid.

269 *"Jesus fucking Christ"*: Ibid.

270 *And in August 2022,* CoinDesk: Danny Nelson and Tracy Wang, "Master of Anons: How a Crypto Developer Faked a DeFi Ecosystem," *CoinDesk*, August 4, 2022, https://www.coindesk.com/layer2/2022/08/05/the-fake -team-that-made-solana-defi-look-huge/.

270 *The brothers would later face*: Danny Nelson, "Justice Department Prob-
ing Saber Labs Founders Over Solana-Based Projects: Sources," *CoinDesk,*
January 11, 2023, https://www.coindesk.com/business/2023/01/11/doj
-said-to-probe-saber-labs-founders-over-solana-based-defi-stablecoin
-projects/.

270 *And Solana's price drop further*: U.S. v. Bankman-Fried, government exhibit
19, presented October 11, 2023.

270 *Nicolas Roos*: U.S. Attorney's Office, Southern District of New York, "Former Employee of NFT Marketplace Charged in First Ever Digital Asset Insider Trading Scheme," June 1, 2022, https://www.justice.gov/usao-sdny/pr
/former-employee-nft-marketplace-charged-first-ever-digital-asset-insider
-trading-scheme.

270 *Samuel Raymond*: U.S. Attorney's Office, Southern District of New York,
"Founders and Executives of Off-Shore Cryptocurrency Derivatives
Exchange Charged with Violation of the Bank Secrecy Act," October 1,
2020, https://www.justice.gov/usao-sdny/pr/founders-and-executives-shore
-cryptocurrency-derivatives-exchange-charged-violation.

CHAPTER 36

271 CoinDesk *had covered Sam's rise*: Jeff Wilser, "Sam Bankman-Fried: The
Man, the Hair, the Vision, *CoinDesk,* April 14, 2022, https://www.coindesk
.com/business/2022/04/14/sam-bankman-fried-the-man-the-hair-the
-vision/.

271 *But on November 2, the* CoinDesk *reporter*: Allison, "Divisions in Sam
Bankman-Fried's Crypto Empire."

272 *How could he have*: @myoder79, "Are we really suggesting that SBF is going
to go bankrupt? The guy that just bought Voyager, that did buy BlockFi,
the guy that was said to be worth $29B? How is this not FUD?," Twitter
post, November 2, 2022, 3:34 p.m., https://twitter.com/myoder79/status
/1587936251608412160.

272 *But in June, a rumor*: Katie Clinebell, "KuCoin Denies Rumors That It's Insolvent. What's Really Going On?" *The Ascent,* July 5, 2022, https://www.fool
.com/the-ascent/cryptocurrency/articles/kucoin-denies-rumors-that-its
-insolvent-whats-really-going-on/.

272 *Bankman-Fried himself had thrown fuel*: Ehrlich, "Bankman-Fried Warns."

272 *Caroline had created it*: U.S. v. Bankman-Fried, testimony from Caroline Ellison, October 11, 2023.

272 *Its widespread usership made*: Tom Maloney, Yueqi Yang, and Ben Bartenstein, "World's Biggest Crypto Fortune Began with a Friendly Poker
Game," *Bloomberg,* January 9, 2022, https://www.bloomberg.com/news
/features/2022-01-09/binance-ceo-cz-s-net-worth-billionaire-holds-world-s
-biggest-crypto-fortune.

273 *In November 2019, it acquired*: Berwick and Wilson, "Exclusive: Behind FTX's Fall."

273 *Sam later described*: Dale, *SBF*, 276.

273 *Caroline vehemently disagreed*: U.S. v. Bankman-Fried, testimony from Caroline Ellison, October 10, 2023.

273 *Caroline wrote in a*: U.S. v. Bankman-Fried, government exhibit 25B, presented October 11, 2023.

273 *"Various regulators"*: U.S. v. Bankman-Fried, testimony from Caroline Ellison, October 11, 2023.

273 *On Twitter, Sam thumbed his nose*: Steven Zeitchik, "This Enigmatic Billionaire Just Took Down a Crypto Rock Star," *Washington Post*, November 9, 2022, https://www.washingtonpost.com/business/2022/11/08/binance -ftx-crypto-zhao/.

274 *On November 6, Zhao publicly*: Changpeng Zhao (@cz_binance), "As part of Binance's exit from FTX equity last year, Binance received roughly $2.1 billion USD equivalent in cash (BUSD and FTT). Due to recent revelations that have came to light, we have decided to liquidate any remaining FTT on our books," Twitter post, November 6, 2022, 7:47 a.m., https://twitter.com /cz_binance/status/1589283421704290306.

274 *Zhao wrote that the decision*: Changpeng Zhao (@cz_binance), Twitter post, November 6, 2022, 1:49 p.m., https://twitter.com/cz_binance/status/1589 374530413215744?lang=en.

274 *But cautious traders decided*: U.S. v. Bankman-Fried, testimony by Caroline Ellison, October 11, 2023.

274 *In a Signal group chat*: U.S. v. Bankman-Fried, government exhibit 1621, presented October 11, 2023.

274 *Together, they workshopped a response*: Caroline Ellison (@carolinecapital), "@cz_binance if you're looking to minimize the market impact on your FTT sales, Alameda will happily buy it all from you today at $22!" Twitter post, November 6, 2022, 8:03 a.m., https://twitter.com/carolinecapital /status/1589287457975304193.

274 *They had blown tens of millions of dollars*: U.S. v. Bankman-Fried, testimony by Caroline Ellison, October 11, 2023.

275 *FTX's stablecoin reserves sunk*: Ki Young Ju (@ki_young_ju), "FTX's stablecoin reserve just reached a year-low. $51M as of now. -93% over the last two weeks." Twitter post, November 6, 2022, 3:17 p.m., https://twitter.com /ki_young_ju/status/1589396703421272064.

275 *As withdrawals cascaded*: Nathaniel Whittemore, "Sam Bankman Fraud: Inside the Collapse of FTX's Hollow Empire," YouTube video, November 14, 2022, 15:55, https://www.youtube.com/watch?v=jD9m5vB8fc4&t.

275 *"A competitor is trying"*: Andrew R. Chow, "What to Know About Binance Buying FTX," *Time*, November 8, 2022, https://time.com/6230648 /binance-buys-ftx/.

275 *Just a few hours later, he*: U.S. v. Bankman-Fried, government exhibit 406, presented October 11, 2023.

275 *"She was using"*: Aditya Baradwaj, interview with Andrew R. Chow, November 7, 2023.

275 *"I thought that we would be happy"*: Interview with anonymous source.

276 *"What we need is a few billion"*: U.S. v. Bankman-Fried, government exhibit 21, presented October 11, 2023.

276 *FTX International held just $900 million*: Antoine Gara, Kadhim Shubber, and Joshua Oliver, "FTX Held Less Than $1bn in Liquid Assets Against $9bn in Liabilities," *Financial Times*, November 12, 2022, https://www .ft.com/content/f05fe9f8-ca0a-48d5-8ef2-7a4d813af558.

276 *Only 3 percent of Serum*: Matt Levine, "FTX's Balance Sheet Was Bad," *Bloomberg*, November 14, 2022, https://www.bloomberg.com/opinion /articles/2022-11-14/ftx-s-balance-sheet-was-bad.

276 *On Tuesday, November 8, Zhao accepted*: Berwick and Wilson, "Exclusive: Behind FTX's Fall."

277 *"That's when I knew it"*: Interview with anonymous source.

277 *The only people who had known*: Caroline Ellison, Alameda all-hands meeting, November 9, 2023, recording, https://soundcloud.com/segray/caroline -ellison-alameda-research-all-hands.

277 *As the East Coast*: Jasper Williams-Ward and Remy Tumin, "Tropical Storm Nicole Strikes the Bahamas," *New York Times*, November 9, 2022, https: //www.nytimes.com/live/2022/11/09/us/hurricane-nicole-tropical-storm.

277 *That day, reports circulated*: Lydia Beyoud, Yueqi Yang, and Olga Kharif, "Sam Bankman-Fried's FTX Empire Faces US Probe into Client Funds, Lending," *Bloomberg*, November 9, 2022, https://www.bloomberg.com /news/articles/2022-11-09/us-probes-ftx-empire-over-handling-of-client -funds-and-lending.

278 *He announced the news on Twitter*: @binance, "As a result of corporate due diligence, as well as the latest news reports regarding mishandled customer funds and alleged US agency investigations, we have decided that we will not pursue the potential acquisition of http://FTX.com," Twitter post, November 9, 2022, 1 p.m., https://twitter.com/binance/status/1590449161069268992.

278 *Hours later, bitcoin sank*: Andrew Asmakov, "Crypto Chaos Continues as Market Drops Over $100 Billion Overnight," *Decrypt*, November 10, 2022, https://sports.yahoo.com/crypto-chaos-continues-market-drops-1129 17239.html.

278 *At 4:30 a.m. the following morning*: Sam Bankman-Fried, written testimony notes, December 12, 2022.

278 *"I fucked up"*: Sam Bankman-Fried (@SBF_FTX), Twitter post, November 10, 2022, 6:13 a.m., https://twitter.com/SBF_FTX/status/1590709 166515310593.

CHAPTER 37

279   *Just two years earlier, Sam*: Anatoly Yakovenko, "Sam Bankman-Fried—CEO of FTX, Co-founder of Serum," on *Validated*, podcast, August 3, 2020, https://solana.com/validated/episodes/sam-bankman-fried-ceo-of-ftx-co-founder-of-serum-ep-24-k6oebn6b.

279   *But Serum was losing value*: Serum chart, CoinMarketCap, accessed June 12, 2023, https://coinmarketcap.com/currencies/serum/.

280   *"The entire week"*: Christine Chew, interview with Andrew R. Chow, May 29, 2023.

280   *Natalie Tien, FTX's head*: Lucinda Shen, "Q&A with Sam Bankman-Fried's Former Assistant," *Axios*, November 6, 2023, https://www.axios.com/2023/11/06/sam-bankman-fried-ftx-assistant-natalie-tien-guilt-tells.

280   *He started receiving threats*: Harrison Obiefule (@Harri_obi), "I should start by saying that I'm currently in hiding," Twitter post, November 11, 2022, 7:59 a.m., https://twitter.com/Harri_obi/status/1591098297573203968.

280   *"It quickly went from"*: Natalie Tien, interview with Andrew R. Chow, July 10, 2023.

280   *Dozens of shoes and boxes*: Zeke Faux, "11 Hours with Sam Bankman-Fried: Inside the Bahamian Penthouse After FTX's Fall," *Bloomberg*, December 1, 2022, https://www.bloomberg.com/news/features/2022-12-02/inside-sam-bankman-fried-s-bahamian-penthouse-after-ftx-s-collapse.

281   *Bankruptcy filings indicated*: Steven Zeitchik, "FTX Says It Owes More Than $3 Billion to Creditors," *Washington Post*, November 20, 2022, https://www.washingtonpost.com/business/2022/11/20/ftx-crypto-bankruptcy-creditors/.

281   *"My family is asking"*: ForIranians, "How FTX has ruined my life," Reddit post, November 20, 2022, https://www.reddit.com/r/FTX_Official/comments/z0ial2/how_ftx_has_ruined_my_life/.

281   *"My life is over"*: Pangteddit, "My life is over. See you on the other side." Reddit post, November 9, 2022, https://www.reddit.com/r/FTX_Official/comments/yqgrr0/my_life_is_over_see_you_on_the_other_side/.

281   *Overall, NFTs had fallen 97 percent*: Sidhartha Shukla, "NFT Trading Volumes Collapse 97% from January Peak," *Bloomberg*, September 28, 2022, https://www.bloomberg.com/news/articles/2022-09-28/nft-volumes-tumble-97-from-2022-highs-as-frenzy-fades-chart.

281   *"Many were already"*: Liam Vries, interview with Andrew R. Chow, December 6, 2022.

282   *"I don't have the words"*: Izuchukwu Offia, interview with Andrew R. Chow, April 3, 2023.

282   *Nestcoin, the Nigerian crypto startup*: Tage Kene-Okafor, "African Web3 Startup Nestcoin Declares It Held Its Assets in FTX, Lays Off Employees,"

TechCrunch, November 14, 2022, https://techcrunch.com/2022/11/14 /african-web3-startup-nestcoin-declares-it-held-its-assests-in-ftx-lays-off -employees/.

282   *A year later, however, Nestcoin*: Tage Kene-Okafor, "Base Ecosystem Fund, Hashed Emergent Invest $1.9M in Nestcoin to Scale Its Onboard Product," *TechCrunch,* September 7, 2023, https://techcrunch.com/2023/09/07 /base-ecosystem-fund-hashed-emergent-invest-1-9m-in-nestcoin-to-scale -its-onboard-product/.

282   *"It's astonishing how many"*: Alpha01, Discord message, AfroDroids server, December 27, 2022, 11:20 p.m.

283   *"We believed it was"*: Seyi Oluyole, interview with Andrew R. Chow, April 11, 2023.

283   *The Ontario Teachers'*: Josephine Cumbo and Arash Massoudi, "Ontario Teachers Fund Steers Clear of Crypto After $95mn FTX Loss," *Financial Times,* April 21, 2023, https://www.ft.com/content/29c67711-377c-4435 -9c90-280852374e93.

283   *A promised grant of $600,000*: Manny Ramos, "FTX Collapse Leaves Program to Help Formerly Incarcerated Chicagoans in Jeopardy," *Chicago Sun-Times,* December 2, 2022, https://chicago.suntimes.com/politics /2022/12/2/23484859/ftx-cryptocurrency-equity-transformation -sam-bankman-fried-incarcerated-chicagoans.

283   *The Miami Heat*: "Miami Heat's Home Arena Will Get New Name Following FTX Collapse," *Guardian,* November 12, 2022, https://www.theguardian .com/sport/2022/nov/12/miami-heat-arena-ftx-bankruptcy.

284   *But adoption of the new technology*: Andrew Singer, "Central Bank Digital Currencies at a Crossroads," *Global Finance Magazine,* February 6, 2023, https://gfmag.com/features/central-bank-digital-currencies-crossroads/.

284   *"Reputationally, it has affected"*: Nicholas Rees, interview with Andrew R. Chow, March 12, 2023.

284   *At a Nassau church*: Ken Sweet, "'The Money Is Gone': Bahamas Tries to Turn Page After FTX," Associated Press, January 8, 2023, https://apnews.com /article/cryptocurrency-technology-bahamas-caribbean-nassau-7de9ee 0db46b532b3609a26572e31853.

284   *Crypto auditors*: Nate DiCamillo, "Crypto Auditors Are Disappearing Right When the Industry Needs Them," *Quartz,* December 20, 2022, https://finance.yahoo.com/news/crypto-auditors-disappearing-industry -needs-215400152.html.

284   *"The reputational harm"*: Alex Pack, interview with Andrew R. Chow, May 21, 2023.

285   *"No question it basically"*: Haseeb Qureshi, interview with Andrew R. Chow, August 13, 2023.

285   *By March 2023, one study found*: Elizabeth Kerr, "Crypto Project Financing Plummeted 80% YoY in March to Stand at $770M," *Crypto Monday,* April 5,

2023, https://cryptomonday.de/news/2023/04/05/crypto-project-financing-plummeted-80percent-yoy-in-march-to-stand-at-dollar770m/.

285 *And the data company PitchBook*: Brady Dale and Crystal Kim, "For Investors, SBF is the Biggest Loser," *Axios,* November 16, 2023, https://www.axios.com/2023/11/16/sbf-ftx-money-loss-trial-how-much.

285 *"When FTX happened"*: Harper Reed, interview with Andrew R. Chow, November 14, 2023.

285 *"Fuck regulators"*: Piper, "Sam Bankman-Fried Tries to Explain Himself."

286 *Representative Ritchie Torres*: Caitlin Reilly, "House GOP Tries Panel Collaboration on Crypto; Democrats Leery," *Roll Call*, May 2, 2023, https://rollcall.com/2023/05/02/house-gop-tries-panel-collaboration-on-crypto-democrats-leery/.

286 *FTX's new management declared*: Tory Newmyer, "Sam Bankman-Fried's Fraud Ran Through Washington, Prosecutors Say," *Washington Post*, October 2, 2023, https://www.washingtonpost.com/business/2023/10/02/bankman-fried-fraud-ftx-trial/.

286 *The SEC's crypto actions*: Jesse Coghlan, "SEC's Crypto Actions Surged 183% in 6 Months After FTX Collapse," *Cointelegraph,* June 08, 2023, https://cointelegraph.com/news/sec-crypto-lawsuit-increased-six-months-following-ftx-binance-coinbase.

286 *In June 2023, the agency tagged Binance*: U.S. Securities and Exchange Commission, "SEC Files 13 Charges Against Binance Entities and Founder Changpeng Zhao," June 5, 2023, https://www.sec.gov/news/press-release/2023-101.

286 *By this point, Binance had*: Tom Wilson, Angus Berwick, and Elizabeth Howcroft, "Binance's Books Are a Black Box, Filings Show, as It Tries to Rally Confidence," Reuters, December 19, 2022, https://www.reuters.com/technology/binances-books-are-black-box-filings-show-crypto-giant-tries-rally-confidence-2022-12-19/.

286 *All the members of*: Nick Beckstead et al., "The FTX Future Fund Team Has Resigned," Effective Altruism Forum, November 10, 2022, https://forum.effectivealtruism.org/posts/xafpj3on76uRDoBja/the-ftx-future-fund-team-has-resigned-1.

287 *"Many people have been saying"*: Dustin Moskovitz (@Moskov), Twitter post, November 13, 2022, 12:42 a.m., https://web.archive.org/web/20221117005134/https://twitter.com/moskov/status/1591592377692594178.

CHAPTER 38

289 *"You were my family"*: Tim Craig, Drew Harwell, and Nitasha Tiku, "FTX's Bahamas Crypto Empire: Stimulants, Subterfuge and a Spectacular Collapse," *Washington Post*, November 24, 2022, https://www.washingtonpost.com/technology/2022/11/24/ftx-bahamas-albany-fried/.

289 *"I wasn't spending any time"*: George Stephanopoulos, "FTX Founder Sam Bankman-Fried Denies 'Improper Use' of Customer Funds," *Good Morning America*, December 1, 2022, YouTube video, 9:12, https://www.youtube.com/watch?v=0Hxf4Vf54PI.

289 *"Go on Tucker Carlsen"*: Sam Bankman-Fried, U.S. v. Bankman-Fried, "Google Document from Samuel Bankman-Fried's Email Account," filed March 15, 2024.

289 *On December 12, Sam was*: Andrew R. Chow, "FTX Founder Sam Bankman-Fried Charged with Fraud by SEC After Arrest in the Bahamas," *Time*, December 12, 2022, https://time.com/6240579/ftx-sam-bankman-fried-arrested-bahamas/.

290 *Sam spent eight days in the medical*: Ava Benny-Morrison and Katanga Johnson, "Sam Bankman-Fried's Harsh Bahamas Jail Could Shift His Stance on Extradition," *Bloomberg*, December 14, 2022, https://www.bloomberg.com/news/articles/2022-12-14/bankman-fried-s-harsh-bahamas-jail-could-shift-extradition-stance.

290 *He didn't even want to hear*: U.S. v. Bankman-Fried, testimony from Nicholas Roos and Mark Cohen, October 3, 2023.

290 *On December 22, he was released*: Benjamin Weiser, Matthew Goldstein, and David Yaffe-Bellany, "Sam Bankman-Fried Released on $250 Million Bond with Restrictions," *New York Times*, December 22, 2022, https://www.nytimes.com/2022/12/22/business/sam-bankman-fried-ftx-bail.html.

290 *They sat for what*: David Yaffe-Bellany and Matthew Goldstein, "Emails, Chat Logs, Code and a Notebook: The Mountain of FTX Evidence," *New York Times*, May 23, 2023, https://www.nytimes.com/2023/05/23/technology/ftx-evidence-sam-bankman-fried.html.

291 *In July 2023, he leaked*: David Yaffe-Bellany and Matthew Goldstein, "Inside the Private Writings of Caroline Ellison, Star Witness in the FTX Case," *New York Times*, July 20, 2023, https://www.nytimes.com/2023/07/20/technology/ftx-caroline-ellison-bankman-fried.html.

291 *When Ghislaine Maxwell*: "Ghislaine Maxwell Subjected to Raw Sewage in New York Jail, Lawyer Says," *Guardian*, June 16, 2021, https://www.theguardian.com/us-news/2021/jun/16/ghislaine-maxwell-new-york-jail-sewage.

291 *Ray declared that*: John Ray, bankruptcy filings, November 17, 2022, page 2, https://www.documentcloud.org/documents/23310509-john-ray-declaration.

291 *Ray's first forty-eight hours*: Allison Morrow, "FTX to Politicians: Give Us Back Our Donations or We'll Sue You," CNN, February 6, 2023, https://www.cnn.com/2023/02/06/investing/ftx-political-funds-bankruptcy/index.html.

CHAPTER 39

293 *He told the content creator Tiffany Fong*: Tiffany Fong, "SBF Extorted in Jail," on *Tiffany Fong*, podcast, November 29, 2023, 25:20.

294 *it now seemed possible*: Hannah Miller, "AI Startup Anthropic's Burgeoning Value Has FTX Creditors Speculating About Being Made Whole," *Bloomberg*, October 4, 2023, https://www.bloomberg.com/news/articles/2023-10-04/ftx-creditors-speculate-over-fate-of-burgeoning-anthropic-ai-stake.

294 *"This is like saying"*: U.S. v. Bankman-Fried, Judge Lewis Kaplan, October 11, 2023.

294 *"I was blindsided"*: U.S. v. Bankman-Fried, testimony from Nishad Singh, October 16, 2023.

295 *"The money belonged to customers"*: U.S. v. Bankman-Fried, testimony from Gary Wang, October 6, 2023.

296 *"If I messed something up"*: U.S. v. Bankman-Fried, testimony from Caroline Ellison, October 11, 2023.

296 *When she recounted*: Ibid.

297 *"There were a lot of things"*: U.S. v. Bankman-Fried, testimony from Sam Bankman-Fried, October 26, 2023.

297 *In one exchange*: U.S. v. Bankman-Fried, testimony from Sam Bankman-Fried, October 30, 2023.

298 *"Did you tell Faux"*: Ibid.

298 *"There was something like a dinner"*: U.S. v. Bankman-Fried, testimony from Sam Bankman-Fried, October 31, 2023.

298 *Judge Kaplan later ruled that Bankman-Fried*: Andrew R. Chow, "Why Sam Bankman-Fried Received a 25-Year Prison Sentence," *Time*, March 28, 2024, https://time.com/6961068/sam-bankman-fried-prison-sentence/.

CHAPTER 40

301 *Gold rushes tend to*: Bill Gates, *The Road Ahead* (New York: Viking Penguin, 1995), 231.

301 *Bernie Madoff, too*: "A Liar, Not a Failure," *Madoff: The Monster of Wall Street*, Netflix, January 4, 2023, 41:55.

301 *(Amusingly, Enron commercials)*: Alex Gibney, director, *Enron: The Smartest Guys in the Room*, 2005.

301 *Like Lehman Brothers, FTX*: Blinder, *After the Music Stopped*, 121.

301 *And like the Bank of Credit*: Steven Mufson and Jim McGee, "BCCI Scandal: Behind the 'Bank of Crooks and Criminals,'" *Washington Post*, July 28, 1991, https://www.washingtonpost.com/archive/politics/1991/07/28/bcci-scandal-behind-the-bank-of-crooks-and-criminals/563f2216-1180-4094-a13d-fd4955d59435/.

301 *Michael J. Hsu*: Michael J. Hsu, "Trust and Global Banking: Lessons for

Crypto," IIB Annual Washington Conference, March 6, 2023, https://www
.occ.gov/news-issuances/speeches/2023/pub-speech-2023-23.pdf.

302 *In the 1980s, the financier George Soros*: George Soros, "General Theory of
Reflexivity," *Financial Times*, October 26, 2009, https://www.ft.com/content
/0ca06172-bfe9-11de-aed2-00144feab49a.

302 *"Human psychology:"* James Block, interview with Andrew R. Chow, June 27,
2023.

302 *An April 2023 study*: Joseph Pacelli, Kenneth J. Merkley, Brian Williams,
and Mark Piorkowski, "Crypto-Influencers," Working Paper, June 2023,
https://papers.ssrn.com/sol3/papers.cfm?abstract_id=4412017.

303 *A November 2022 study*: Agence France Presse, "Three Out of Four Bitcoin
Investors Have Lost Money: Study," *Barron's*, November 14, 2022, https:
//www.barrons.com/news/three-out-of-four-bitcoin-investors-have-lost
-money-study-01668454507.

303 *"The real business was selling crypto"*: Interview with anonymous source.

303 *By the start of 2022*: @DefiIgnas, "1/ How many DeFi users are there? A
simple question, with a surprisingly difficult answer. I did some digging, and
... there aren't that many," Twitter post, April 12, 2023, 4:52 a.m.

303 *"The promise of decentralization"*: Christine Chew, interview with Andrew R.
Chow, April 10, 2023.

304 *"Axie Infinity became a huge"*: Cordel Robbin-Coker, interview with Andrew
R. Chow, March 4, 2024.

304 *The Australian stock exchange*: Byron Kaye, "Insight: Australian Stock Exchange's Blockchain Failure Burns Market Trust," Reuters, December 19, 2022,
https://www.reuters.com/markets/australian-stock-exchanges-blockchain
-failure-burns-market-trust-2022-12-20/.

304 *so did IBM*: Jacob Gronholt-Pedersen, "Maersk, IBM Discontinue Shipping Blockchain Platform," Reuters, November 29, 2022, https://www
.reuters.com/technology/maersk-ibm-discontinue-shipping-block
chain-platform-2022-11-29/.

304 *The Universal Basic Income token*: CoinMarketCap, Universal Basic Income,
accessed January 13, 2024, https://coinmarketcap.com/currencies/universal
-basic-income/.

304 *One study found that blockchain*: Trading Strategy, "How Blockchain Developer Interest Has Evolved over the Last Decade," September 18, 2023,
https://tradingstrategy.ai/blog/how-blockchain-developer-interest-has
-evolved-last-decade.

305 *"After FTX went down"*: Anthony Olasele, interview with Andrew R. Chow,
November 9, 2023.

305 *One 2023 study found*: Miles Klee, "Your NFTs Are Actually—Finally—
Totally Worthless," *Rolling Stone*, September 20, 2023, https://www.rolling
stone.com/culture/culture-news/nfts-worthless-researchers-find
-1234828767/.

305 *"I was never an NFT"*: Zachary Small, "Beeple's Post-NFT Chapter," *Vulture*, July 21, 2022, https://www.vulture.com/article/beeple-mike-winkelmann-art-profile.html.

305 *In February 2023*: Andrew Hayward, "OpenSea: How Much Wash Trading Is Really Happening on Blur?," *Decrypt,* February 28, 2023, https://decrypt.co/122369/wash-trading-blur-ethereum-nfts.

305 *"Blur has shown what"*: Owo Anietie, interview with Andrew R. Chow, March 3, 2023.

305 *In the summer of 2023*: André Beganski, "Bored Ape Yacht Club Prices Crash to Two-Year Low, Down 88% from Peak," *Decrypt*, June 3, 2023, https://finance.yahoo.com/news/bored-ape-yacht-club-prices-212902099.html.

305 *And in August 2023*: Christy Choi, "'Bored Apes' Investors Sue Sotheby's, Paris Hilton and Others as NFT Prices Collapse," CNN, August 17, 2023, https://edition.cnn.com/style/article/bored-apes-sothebys-lawsuit/index.html.

EPILOGUE

307 *Perhaps fittingly, Do Kwon*: Sandali Handagama, "Do Kwon's Attorneys Propose $437K Bail, Deny Falsified Travel Documents Charges in Montenegro," *Coindesk*, May 11, 2023, https://www.coindesk.com/policy/2023/05/11/do-kwons-attorneys-propose-437k-bail-deny-falsified-travel-documents-charges-in-montenegro/.

308 *"Especially with everything"*: Vitalik Buterin, interview with Andrew R. Chow, May 9, 2023.

308 *"My biggest fear"*: Ibid.

308 *In March 2024, bitcoin*: Andrew R. Chow, "Why Bitcoin Just Hit Its All-Time High," *Time*, March 6, 2024, https://time.com/6846934/bitcoin-all-time-high-price-holdings/.

308 *Filipino gamers started harvesting*: Eli Tan, "What Meltdown? Crypto Comes Roaring Back in the Philippines," *New York Times*, March 18, 2024, https://www.nytimes.com/2024/03/18/technology/crypto-video-games-philippines.html.

308 *Enthusiasts declared*: Haseeb Qureshi, interview with Andrew R. Chow, March 5, 2024.

308 *People continued to use stablecoins*: Cristina Polizu, Anoop Garg, and Miguel de la Mata, "Stablecoins: A Deep Dive into Valuation and Depegging," S&P Global, September 7, 2023, https://www.spglobal.com/en/research-insights/featured/special-editorial/stablecoins-a-deep-dive-into-valuation-and-depegging.

309 *And some DAOs persevered*: Makoto Takahiro, "Gitcoin Unveils Grants 2.0: A More Modular and Decentralized Approach to Funding Public Goods," *DAO Times*, March 1, 2024, https://daotimes.com/gitcoin-unveils-grants

-2-0-a-more-modular-and-decentralized-approach-to-funding-public-goods.

309 *Seven years after that*: David Emery, "Did Paul Krugman Say the Internet's Effect on the World Economy Would Be 'No Greater Than the Fax Machine's'?," Snopes, June 7, 2018, https://www.snopes.com/fact-check/paul-krugman-internets-effect-economy/.

309 *Despite harboring many skepticisms*: Cam Thompson, "Beeple Goes Punk With $208K NFT Purchase," *Coindesk*, August 2, 2023, https://www.coindesk.com/web3/2023/08/02/beeple-goes-punk-with-208k-nft-purchase/.

309 *"We're coming off"*: Beeple, interview with Andrew R. Chow, August 2, 2023.

309 *"We are sharing"*: Liam Vries, interview with Andrew R. Chow, January 15, 2024.

310 *"There's a wall"*: Harper Reed, interview with Andrew R. Chow, November 14, 2023.

310 *"The idea that bitcoin"*: Qureshi, interview, March 5, 2024.

310 *Institutions like BlackRock*: Hannah Lang, Suzanne McGee and Manya Saini, "US Bitcoin ETFs See $4.6 Billion in Volume in First Day of Trading," Reuters, January 12, 2024, https://www.reuters.com/technology/spot-bitcoin-etfs-start-trading-big-boost-crypto-industry-2024-01-11/.

310 *"What we're going to be"*: Dennis Kelleher, interview with Andrew R. Chow, February 29, 2024.

INDEX

Page numbers in *italics* refer to illustrations.

ABOUT THE AUTHOR

A ndrew R. Chow is a correspondent for *Time* who covers technology, culture, and business. He has written five *Time* cover stories, including one about the impacts of the AI corporate arms race and a prescient profile of Vitalik Buterin months before the 2022 crypto crash. He has previously written for the *New York Times*, *Pitchfork*, and NBC News. *Cryptomania* is his first book.